Sublime Desire

History and Post-1960s Fiction

Amy J. Elias

The Johns Hopkins University Press
Baltimore and London

© 2001 The Johns Hopkins University Press
All rights reserved. Published 2001
Printed in the United States of America on acid-free paper
9 8 7 6 5 4 3 2 1

The Johns Hopkins University Press
2715 North Charles Street
Baltimore, Maryland 21218-4363
www.press.jhu.edu

Library of Congress Cataloging-in-Publication Data
Elias, Amy J., 1961–
   Sublime desire : history and post-1960s fiction /
   Amy J. Elias
     p.   cm. — (Parallax: re-visions of culture and
  society)
   Includes bibliographical references and index.
   ISBN 0-8018-6733-9 (acid-free paper)
   1. Historical fiction—History and criticism.   I. Title.
II. Parallax (Baltimore, Md.)
PN3441 .E44 2001
809.3'81—dc21   00-012493

A catalog record for this book is available from the
British Library.

An earlier version of chapter 4 appeared in *Contemporary
Literature* 37, no. 4 (1996) under the title "The Postmodern Turn on the Enlightenment." It is reprinted
here, with revisions, by permission of the University of
Wisconsin Press.

Space and Time are the names of the exterminating angels that expelled us from Eden. They must be watched with great cunning. Only they can indicate to us the return path to the desired Gates.

—Abel Posse, *The Dogs of Paradise*

Facts are but the Play-things of lawyers,—Tops and Hoops, for-ever a-spin. . . . Alas, the Historian may indulge no such idle Rotating. History is not Chronology, for that is left to lawyers,—nor is it Re-membrance, for Remembrance belongs to the People. History can as little pretend to the Veracity of the one, as claim the Power of the other,—her Practitioners, to survive, must soon learn the arts of the quidnunc, spy, and Taproom Wit,—that there may ever continue more than one life-line back into a Past we risk, each day, losing our forebears in forever,—not a Chain of single Links, for one broken Link could lose us All,—rather, a great disorderly Tangle of Lines, long and short, weak and strong, vanishing into the Mnemonick Deep, with only their Destination in common."

—Thomas Pynchon, *Mason & Dixon*

Kant begins his logic, his last book, by saying that "the source of all error is metaphor." Well, too bad. He is wrong. Metaphor is maybe the source of all error but it is also the source of all truth, too.

—Hayden White

Contents

Preface

The present volume examines late-twentieth-century examples of the historical novel in relation to recent postmodern cultural assumptions and the traditional historical novel form, which was (at least in Walter Scott's novels, the most famous case) predicated on epistemological and historiographical assumptions of the Age of Reason. By examining only novels published after 1960 in "First World" nations, I assume cultural and aesthetic definitions of postmodernism as a post-1945 social phenomenon and artistic sensibility. By examining these texts in relation to the historiography of their time, this study upholds the assumptions of cultural critics who claim that postmodernism is the zeitgeist of postindustrial, late-twentieth-century capitalism. Likewise, by almost exclusively examining novels by authors from the United States, Great Britain, Australia, and Canada, I highlight the difference between First World postmodernist literature and literary movements and developments outside of these nations, such as the development of postcolonial literature or the perpetuation of underground political arts movements throughout the world. Fredric Jameson was correct to identify postmodernism with late capitalism, and this study assumes, for example, that while it is possible to discuss Charlotte Brontë's feminist or politically oppositional sensibility, it is not accurate to discuss her "postmodernism." Perhaps contradictorily, however, my linking of these post-1960 novels to the historical novel tradition illustrates how these novels are also postmodern in an epistemological sense, for they almost always criticize, undermine, complicate, or try to position themselves against the precepts of Enlightenment modernity.

The novels I consider are primarily those originally written in English by authors who live in or identify themselves with so-called First World capitalist nations. While tempted to put the phrase *First World* and the term *Western* within inverted commas throughout this book to indicate my discomfort with these geopolitical terms, I have refrained for stylistic reasons from doing so. Nevertheless, there is a difference in political agenda, origin, and narrative effect between novels fitting these descriptors and novels that might be termed *postcolonial* or otherwise outside the Western tradition and originally not written in English. Thus, I do not treat works such as Carlos Fuentes's *Terra Nostra,* Chinua Achebe's *Things Fall Apart,* Gabriel Garcia Márquez's *One Hundred Years of Solitude,* Jack Davis's *Kullark/The Dreamers,* V. S. Naipaul's *The Middle Passage,* Ngugi wa Thiong'o's *Weep Not, Child,* Raja Rao's *Kanthapura,* Caryl Phillips's *Cambridge,* and many other texts that call for different or more extensive definitional parameters as postcolonial texts yet clearly share affinities with the metahistorical romance.

This is sticky critical territory, however, for a number of reasons. First, some literature, such as Native American fiction, stands in a problematic relation to postcolonial politics and theory. Second, there is a metahistorical continuity between the postmodernist and postcolonialist metahistorical imagination. I have tried in this book to respect cultural and political difference, yet certain texts I discuss—J. M. Coetzee's *Foe,* Ishmael Reed's *Mumbo Jumbo,* Leslie Marmon Silko's *Ceremony*—might easily be understood from one critical perspective as postcolonial novels that clearly fall outside the parameters of First World *metahistorical romance,* as I define that term. The editorial and political problem of naming—if not my solution to it—will, I hope, stimulate further discussion.

Chapter 1 ("Sorting Out Connections: The Historical Romance in Hyper-reality") defines the classic historical romance and argues its importance to what I call the "postmodernist metahistorical romance." The first part of the chapter focuses on Walter Scott: the historiographical influences on Scott's fiction, particularly those of the Scottish philosophical school, and then the paradoxical wedding of romance and history in Scott's work. A comparison between Leo Tolstoy's *War and Peace* and Jeanette Winterson's *Sexing the Cherry* leads me to define the implicit claims about history embedded in the classic historical romance that Scott's work to a large extent engendered. Thus, the discussion shows the relationship of Scott's fiction first to historiography and then to romance.

The second part of the chapter focuses on postmodernist fiction. Inverting the order of ideas of the first section, I examine postmodernist historical fiction in relation to romance and then historiography. Important to my argument that literary fiction and historiography are traversing similar historiographical territory is defining *the sublime* (the term has different meanings in different eras) and illustrating the correspondences between Jean-François Lyotard's theory of the postmodern sublime, postmodern theories of the historical sublime (most lucidly defined by Hayden White, F. R. Ankersmit, and Jean-Luc Nancy), and the presentation of the past as a sublime territory in metahistorical romance. My overall claim is thus twofold: that the metahistorical romance reverses the dominant focus of the classic historical romance genre from history to romance, and that it does so because, like the postmodernist historiography and postmodernist philosophy of its own time, it turns from belief in empirical history to a reconsideration of the historical sublime.

Chapter 2 ("The Metahistorical Romance and the Historical Sublime") specifically defines the characteristics of metahistorical romance as a literary genre. The chapter argues four propositions:

1. the postmodern historical imagination, as a post-traumatic imaginary, confronts rather than represses the historical sublime;

2. the metahistorical romance confronts the historical sublime as repetition and deferral;

3. the motivation for this confrontation is desire for and a concomitant distrust of the humanist value of *fabula;*

4. the metahistorical romance learns from the texts of the literary modernists to combine historicism with narrative form, but unlike the modernists, the postmodernists reverse the dominant of classic historical romance.

Each is discussed with reference to critical discussions of postmodern fiction, such as Toni Morrison's *Beloved*, Barry Unsworth's *Sacred Hunger*, Thomas Berger's *Little Big Man*, Charles Johnson's *Dreamer*, Simon Schama's *Dead Certainties (Unwarranted Speculations)*, and Eric Zencey's *Panama*. My argument is that the metahistorical consciousness models itself as post-traumatic consciousness, akin to the state of mind of war survivors, and that as such it finds traditional models for Western history inadequate to deal with the late-twentieth-century realities it faces. Caught between its post-traumatic turn toward the historical sublime and its obsessions with social realities, the metahistorical romance is led to a compulsive, repetitive turning toward the past that is a ceaselessly deferred resolution to the questions of historical agency that it poses.

If chapters 1 and 2 discuss *why* metahistorical romance has developed, chapter 3 ("Cracking the Mirror: Spatializing History in Metahistorical Romances") examines *how* it reconstructs historical models within the linear novel form. Metahistorical romances often use avant-gardist narrative strategies to redefine post-Enlightenment Western models for history. Specifically, the avant-gardist metahistorical romance subordinates time (or models of historical linearity) to space (or spatializing models of history). A similar operation takes place in historiography, such as in the work of Michel Foucault, who often replaces linear models of history with what have been considered "spatial" models. Recontextualizing Joseph Frank's theory of modernist spatial form in *The Widening Gyre: Crisis and Mastery in Modern Literature* (1963), I argue that modernist spatial form becomes postmodernist spatial history in many metahistorical romances. The first part of the chapter defines this shift and its specific relation to the metahistorical romance's recuperation of the historical sublime—what I see as a key feature of the genre. The two subsequent sections define how the metahistorical romance "spatializes history": by replacing linear history with "paratactic history" and by replacing linear history with "simultaneous history." I illustrate all of these points with examples from contemporary fiction, such as Peter Ackroyd's *Hawksmoor*, Ishmael Reed's *Flight to Canada*, Julian Barnes's

Flaubert's Parrot, N. Scott Momaday's *House Made of Dawn,* and T. Coraghessan Boyle's *World's End.*

Chapter 4 ("Metamodernity: The Postmodern Turn on the Enlightenment") examines a different kind of "metahistoricity": the interrogation by metahistorical romance of its own origin in Enlightenment rationalism. This chapter correlates the post-1960s proliferation of novels set in the eighteenth century to heated debates in postmodern theory concerning the character and value of Enlightenment modernity. These metahistorical romances rehearse debates in postmodern theory concerning the value of the Enlightenment as a foundational Western epistemology: some novels uphold a premodern anti-rationalism, some construct a Habermasian defense of modernity, and others align themselves with a Lyotardian postmodern figurality. The metahistorical romances I examine here place different values on romance, particularly when it is aligned with aesthetics as a sublime realm of art. However, they have in common a discomfort with their Enlightenment inheritance and a desire for an alternative to history in the form of the aesthetic or historical sublime. Some of the novels discussed include Francis Sherwood's *Vindication,* Allen Kurzweil's *A Case of Curiosities,* Lawrence Norfolk's *Lemprière's Dictionary,* J. M. Coetzee's *Foe,* Steve Erickson's *Arc d'X,* John Fowles's *A Maggot,* and Susan Sontag's *The Volcano Lover: A Romance.*

Chapter 5 ("Western Modernity versus Postcolonial Metahistory") contrasts the novels discussed in chapter 4 (which looked back to an Enlightenment "Father") to other postmodernist fictions that stand outside or attempt to escape from their Western inheritance. It illustrates a third kind of metahistorical focus in the metahistorical romance: the attempt to come to terms with the West's own colonial history and Others. The chapter first puzzles out the differences between postcolonial and postmodern metahistory. What has emerged forcefully since 1968, particularly in the 1980s and 1990s, are novels written by First World authors that look at their own Western androcentric history from the perspectives of women and of those peoples of different, non-Western ancestry and cultures. Both postmodernist historical fiction and postcolonial fiction share a metahistorical imagination, an imagination that returns to history and questions the grounds on which it has been epistemologically and politically established. Both postmodernist and postcolonial fiction attempt to counter the forces of modernization and are a reaction-formation to the trauma of history itself. Moreover, both question the relation between narrative and historical documentation, and both raise thorny and politically volatile questions about authorial presence and intentionality and about the politics of historical critique. However, while postcolonial metahistory clearly announces itself as a critique of the West from outside its political, epistemological, economic, or cultural borders, postmodernist metahistory is an inquiry from within the First World frame, an insider's reevaluation of Western history and cultural politics. The difference between postmodern and postcolonial metahistory therefore may be understood in terms of what Fredric Jameson calls "situational consciousness" and, in a different context, in terms of their respective approaches to what Hayden White has called the "figure-fulfillment" model of history.

Finally, in keeping with the book's goal of relating metahistorical romance to classic historical romance, the chapter shows how the former continues thematic concerns of the classic form. A focus on ethnicity and national identity is inscribed as romance in the traditional historical romances of Walter Scott (e.g., in *Ivanhoe* or *Rob Roy*), and the metahistorical romance swerves from but also partakes of this generic tradition. What was understated or romanticized in Scott's fiction is foregrounded as cultural politics in the postmodern metahistorical romance. Fiction discussed in this chapter includes Madison Smartt Bell's *All Souls' Rising*, William T. Vollmann's *The Rifles*, Leslie Marmon Silko's *Ceremony*, Günter Grass's *The Flounder*, and Salman Rushdie's *The Satanic Verses*.

Chapter 6 ("Coda: *The Sot-Weed Factor* and *Mason & Dixon*") compares John Barth's *The Sot-Weed Factor* and Thomas Pynchon's *Mason & Dixon* to illustrate how the four characteristics of metahistorical romance remain constant in this narrative form throughout the second half of the twentieth century but also to illustrate how the postmodern search for a new approach to Western history grows in force between 1967 and 1997, as the millennium approaches. Huge, baggy monsters of novels, *The Sot-Weed Factor* and *Mason & Dixon* are separated in time by thirty years. Yet like the novels discussed in chapter 4, both recuperate an eighteenth-century context that metafictionally rebounds to the cultural politics of the present; like the novels discussed in chapter 5, both are self-reflexive about the First World colonial gaze; and like almost all of the novels discussed in this book, both reenergize the historical romance genre by inverting its dominant, melding fantasy, anachronism, metafictionality, and other fabulatory techniques with the facts of history.

The Sot-Weed Factor illustrates how the late-modernist historical romance morphs into the postmodern form by reversing the dominant of the classic historical novel from history to romance, yet it also illustrates how difficult it is to unveil the situational consciousness of the First World or to offer an alternative logic to it. In contrast, in *Mason & Dixon* Pynchon returns to what he implies is the historical beginning of the multinational military-industrial complex and European imperialism and colonialism. As a definitive metahistorical romance, *Mason & Dixon* goes beyond academic joking and asks serious questions about what history is, what a sublime apprehension of time and space might lead us to do, and what really counts in the final reckoning of First World history. Taken together, these novels crystallize the issues raised by metahistorical romance and illustrate the range of narrative techniques available to this postmodern genre.

My thanks to the School of Arts and Humanities at the University of Alabama at Birmingham, which provided research support for this project in the form of a sabbatical leave in 1998, and also to the University of Alabama at Birmingham for a Faculty Research Grant in 1997, which helped me research this topic. I would also like to thank the seminar leaders and lecturers at the 1998 session of the School of Criticism and Theory at Cornell University for their scholarship and for helping me to rethink portions of this manuscript. My thanks go also to the UAB School of Arts and Humanities, for funding my attendance at the SCT and for providing support for the publication of this text, and to the UAB English department.

My own work is indebted to the work of Hayden White and the work of Linda Hutcheon at the University of Toronto, and I am particularly grateful for the encouragement and advice they have given in relation to this manuscript but also for their exemplary personal generosity and kindness. Thanks also to Marilyn Kurata and Leland Person, for their support of my research activities, and to Ewa Domanska, Rebecca Bach, Randa Graves, David Cowart, and Kathryn Hume, for astute readings of this project at its various stages. Deborah Akers did a marvelous job helping me to prepare this manuscript for publication; Juanita Sizemore and Eddie Luster cannot receive enough praise for their professionalism and good humor. To my family and to Deborah Gibson, Steven Epley, Teresa Laeger, Alison Schmied, Jerry Sims, Theresa Owens, Thyme Council, Ron Council, Ron Berry, Tim and Frankie Smith, thank you for your sustaining support. Foremost and lastly, I thank Jon Barnes, for everything.

Introduction

In contrast to the ahistorical postmodernism of the streets—"reality" TV, Disneyland, and the tribalist, consumerist, presentist mall culture of global capitalism—postmodernism in the arts is a cultural mindset characterized by an obsession with history and a desperate desire for the comforting self-awareness that is supposed to come from historical knowledge. But because of its philosophical and social underpinnings, postmodern art also projects skepticism and irony about the possibilities for true historical knowledge and suspicion of any social or historical narrative that purports to make sense of a chaotic world of seemingly endless and contradictory lifestyles, cultures, and political viewpoints. Postmodern literature, for example, seems hyperconsciously aware that the drive to write and know history may be a futile endeavor, at worst an imperialist drive to control the past, at most a Hollywood-inspired move to profit from history's revision and simulation. In part, this book argues that what is left to postmodernists in this between-state of belief is only "metahistory," the ability to theorize and ironically desire history rather than access it through discovery and reconstruction.

I make three claims: first, that in various fields, the postmodern attitude toward history is paradoxical, an attitude of supplication and desire as well as an attitude of skepticism; second, that there exists an interrelationship between post-1960s historical fiction and the antifoundationalist historiography of its own time; and third, that there are shared characteristics between the conventional historical romance (of the type created by Walter Scott in the nineteenth century) and certain kinds of post-1960s, "First World" fiction. A common thread linking theories of postmodernism, genre theory concerning the historical romance, and post-1950s historiography is the notion of the *historical sublime,* a phrase that combines the territories of Kantian aesthetics and post-*Annales* historiography. My thesis is that the late-twentieth-century, postmodernist consciousness models itself as a post-traumatic consciousness that redefines positivist or stadialist history as the historical sublime, a desired horizon that can never be reached but only approached in attempts to understand human origins and the meaning of lived existence. For the postmodern, post-traumatic, metahistorical imagination, history is not knowledge we learn and "own" once we learn it; rather, postmodern arts and sciences posit that history is something we know we can't learn, something we can only desire. Fulfilling Marx's prophecy that under capitalism, "all that is solid melts into air," history becomes a process rather than a stable block of knowledge. Once the postmodernist mind intuits or is taught by relativizing social forces that true history is unfathomable, "history" comes to be merely "desire" for solid ground beneath one's feet—a desire for a Blakean organized innocence, a desire for the Truth that is Out There. This is true for postmodern historiography as well as for postmodern fiction.

Moreover, this desire for History, for the "secular sacred" sublime—for awe, certainty, and belief in the absence of the Word—leads postmodern narrative fiction to new representations of the historical past. I claim that what used to be called historical romance novels are reshaped by this postmodern desire for history into "metahistorical romances." Specifically, situating late-twentieth-century, First World historical fiction in relation to literary and generic history reveals how the historical romance genre swings in pendulum motion from the "realism" of Scott's historical novel form, through the abstraction of modernist spatial form and postmodern fabulation, back toward the "realism" of postcolonial politics. Inheriting the dialectic between realism and romance inherent in Scott's novels, writers of metahistorical romances seem to hang suspended between these poles and captive to pendulum motion, unable to break free to a real access to History and caught between two literary genres they no longer associate with the Real.

This book also attempts an interdisciplinarity, a joining of two fields that often remain separated in contemporary criticism. It argues that just as the classic historical romance of Walter Scott reflected and influenced the historiography of that writer's time, today's metahistorical romances reflect and affect the historiography of their own time. I examine developments in post–World War II historiography in this context, illustrating how the shifts from political to social history and then to post-*Annales* historiography correlate to similar shifts in poststructuralist theories about history by Michel Foucault and Jean-François Lyotard and also to shifts in the historical romance genre.

My focus, however, is late-twentieth-century fiction. I discuss First World fiction published since 1960 by established writers such as Ishmael Reed, John Barth, Salman Rushdie, Thomas Pynchon, Peter Ackroyd, John Fowles, Leslie Marmon Silko, Günter Grass, Julian Barnes, Italo Calvino, N. Scott Momaday, Toni Morrison, J. M. Coetzee, D. M. Thomas, Nigel Williams, and Charles Johnson. I also introduce into the discussion fiction by writers newer to treatment by literary criticism: Jeanette Winterson, T. Coraghessan Boyle, Charles Frazier, Barry Unsworth, Steve Erikson, Simon Schama, Madison Smartt Bell, William T. Vollmann, Eric Zencey, Jane Smiley, John Steffler, Timothy Findley, Allen Kurzweil, and Lawrence Norfolk. This range of literary illustration will, I hope, not only clarify the discussion, bringing high theory into relation with real fiction, but also allow new and interesting novels into the fluid canon of contemporary fiction that is the subject of literary criticism and cultural studies.

 The present study differs from and extends the range of published scholarship on postmodernism and history in a number of ways. Linda Hutcheon's *Poetics of Postmodernism: History, Theory, Fiction* (1988) coined the term *historiographic metafiction* as a descriptor of late-twentieth-century avant-gardist literature and argued that postmodernists play with history and create a potentially subversive form of cultural critique; Fredric Jameson's *Postmodernism, or, the Cultural Logic of Late Capitalism* (1991) discussed postmodern history as "depthless pastiche," a collection of marketable, meaningless images that colludes with consumer capitalism and therefore has no potential for social critique. Much of the scholarship about postmodernism published between 1985 and 2000 falls within the range of these two positions: one that sees a postmodern turn on history as a challenge to the status quo and one that sees it *as* the status quo. Considering this critical focus on postmodern history in the past fifteen years, however, few scholars have dealt with postwar First World historical fiction in relation to actual debates in the discipline of history itself. This book emphasizes that what is now called the "postmodern crisis in history" is a crisis within literature or the literary imagination as well as within the discipline of history. It argues that the paroxysms experienced in post-1950s historiography have an important relation to changes in how history is recorded and represented in First World, post-1960s fiction; historiography and fiction are shown to be traversing similar terrain and exerting mutual influences. This cross-disciplinarity is particularly striking when we see historians writing metahistorical romances, as I illustrate in a discussion of Simon Schama's and Eric Zencey's novels.

The Question of Postmodernism

What postmodernism is—or whether it exists at all—is still a vital question for some critics, though many decry the "post-ness" of postmodernism and see it eclipsed by issues emerging in ethnic studies, queer and gender studies, postcolonial studies, and other critical arenas. Since the flurry of publications about postmodernism in the 1970s and 1980s, there has been an undercurrent of cynicism about defining this cultural and literary phenomenon. Now, however, a kind of general consensus among philosophers and cultural workers has emerged: that if one recognizes the existence of postmodernism, then one can categorize the kind of postmodernism one seeks.

Postmodernism may be usefully thought of as three interlocked, sometimes contradictory, discussions.[1] The first discussion defines postmodernism as *epistemological*. It occurs within the domains of Western philosophy, particularly within the Germanic philosophical tradition, and concerns the history of modernity, the modern *cogito,* and the evolution of the modern subject. The central questions structuring this debate concern the history of ideas and the history of Western thought itself. Writers attempting to define epistemological postmodernism often attempt to define (or redefine) modernity while positing definitions of the postmodern. This epistemological postmodernism is ensnared with modernity, a historical phenomenon birthed for Western Europe and the Americas in the Age of Reason. It concerns such questions as, When did modernity arise? What is the relationship between Descartes's separation of reason from history and later Western theories of knowledge acquisition? Should the eighteenth-century Enlightenment be understood as the birth time of modernity? Where do the various Enlightenment conceptions of reason stand in relation to developments in social and cognitive philosophy of the twentieth century? Is the project of modernity—including increased individual freedom and autonomy, democratization, and scientific pursuit of knowledge—dead, or is it entering a hitherto unimagined phase of development? Do the cultural politics of race, gender, or class newly expressed in the twentieth century in any way cancel or repudiate the project of modernity?[2]

This debate ranges through multiple disciplines: hermeneutics, historiography, sociology, psychology, and philosophy. Within this discussion one finds analyses of the "postmodernity" of Hegel and Nietzsche, the debate between Jürgen Habermas and Jean-François Lyotard, the assertions of poststructuralists in continental philosophy.[3] I call this debate "epistemological," because in many of its forms it deals mainly with questions about how late-twentieth-century peoples residing in First World nations cognitively apprehend their societies and their relation to the past and how they define the possibilities of future knowledge.

Defined as a way of knowing, postmodernism in this context can be seen as free-floating throughout modern history; it is defined as that which is outside of, or Other to, Cartesian definitions of self, world, and knowledge. Postmodernism becomes that which scientism ignores; that which reason represses; that which cannot be thought or spoken given the terms available to and the politics of representation governing Western discourse since the dawn of the European Enlightenment. One of the primary philosophers of this epistemological postmodernism is Jean-François Lyotard, whose text *The Postmodern Condition* is central to this discussion. Lyotard defines the postmodern as that which lurks within modernity. In a deconstructive sense, the postmodern is that which stands outside of or is repressed by language itself; in Derrida's terms, this postmodernism would be the aporia of Anglo-European discourse, or that which hovers on the margins of its representational modes. In these kinds of definitions, the postmodern is a way of knowing that is non-Western, or nondiscursive, or nonrepresentational. It stands outside the *cogito;* it undermines the tenets of modernity; it manifests itself in the "event" at the moment of paradigm shifts. As it is defined theoretically, this *post*modernism isn't really "post" or "after" the modern era; it is congruent with it. It is not what comes after the Enlightenment, but rather it is birthed at the same time yet can't be described or defined (or necessarily even perceived), because no terminology or conceptual frame is available to articulate it.

Since it's actually a modern phenomenon, the shadowy side of modernity, this epistemological postmodernism is really only "post"—or, really, only comes after—premodernity, which is generally defined for the European West as the time preceding the High Renaissance. Epistemological postmodernism does share with the premodern a mythic sense, a suspicion or rejection of rationality and positivism, and an antihumanist bias. But this epistemological postmodernism differs significantly from the premodern in that it tends to reject religion, state institutions, and social belief, what Lyotard would call "metanarrative." What is unique about epistemological postmodernism is that it is locatable but not limited in time, after the birth of the modern. (In recent criticism, this life span of the "postmodern" has been extended backward even further, into medieval history.) Consequently, epistemological postmodernism can be located in any post–eighteenth-century epoch: one can speak of "Lawrence Sterne's postmodernism" or of a "postmodernism across the ages."[4] This definition of postmodernism understandably infuriates materialist critics because of its ahistoricism and elicits condemnation from defenders of the Enlightenment project (such as Jürgen Habermas) for its antipositivist stance. Yet this definition of postmodernism has proven congenial to versions of postcolonial, feminist, and gender theories that position themselves against, or as Other to, Western patriarchal modernity.

The second predominant definition of postmodernism I would call *sociocultural,* and it too ranges widely among various disciplines. According to this definition, postmodernism is a post-1945 social and economic phenomenon of capitalist First World nations. Postmodern culture is defined as variously exhibiting the following characteristics: the diminished importance of the nation-state and of manufacturing industries; the increased importance of service and entertainment industries, communication technologies, and the military-industrial complex; ever more sophisticated war technologies; an increased disparity between rich and poor within and between nations and a concomitant rise in global exploitation of the poor; greater ethnic "tribalism"; more exploitation of diminishing natural resources; and a fracturing of markets to the advantage of capitalist production and ideology. Sociocultural postmodernism may also be understood as an increased aestheticization of everyday life. What this means is that reality becomes "reality"—increasingly influenced and controlled by media, advertising, and escapist entertainment technologies until it is impossible to distinguish what is a story from what is real, what is entertainment from what is political, what is a projection of human desires from what is material. The paradigmatic examples of this aestheticization of everyday life in the United States are Disneyland (where a certain class can now actually live in perfect, Disneylike planned communities) and the "infotainment" of the news broadcasting media. Rather than life influencing art, art *becomes* life but is stripped of its intellectual content and social critique. Art becomes "entertainment" linked to a consumerist lifestyle. Moreover, the media—including surveillance media and communication media—intrude into all aspects of private life, and there is an increased tendency to replace naturally existing phenomena with marketable simulations.[5]

Ranging from marxist condemnation to procapitalist triumphalism, prominent theories defining the *postmodern-ness* of post-1945 capitalist economics, cultures, and social institutions include those by Daniel Bell, Fredric Jameson, Mike Featherstone, David Harvey, Scott Lash, Philip Cooke, and Zygmunt Bauman, Edward Soja, Donna Haraway, and Francis Fukuyama, among others.[6] Other theorists have focused more on post-1945 capitalist culture industries, often citing them as indicators of new postmodern values and social tensions. Theorists in this second camp might include Jean Baudrillard, Fredric Jameson, Andrew Ross, or Andreas Huyssen. Questions raised by these discussions of sociocultural postmodernism include the following: Since 1945, what effects on society have been wrought by the seeming victory of multinational capitalism? What has happened to the concept of a nation-state since 1945? How has the emergence of the technological simulacrum, especially in the popular media and advertising, affected our conception of the Real, of History, and of social justice? Has spectacle replaced meaning in postmodern culture? What is the "postindustrial"? Since World War II, have First World nations developed a stage of capitalism unanticipated by earlier social theories, such as marxism? How does the concept of postmodernism affect or alter the aims and discourses of traditional social science disciplines? How has late-twentieth-century technology altered our conceptions of race, nationhood, gender roles and sexuality?

Because sociocultural postmodernism is defined as a twentieth-century phenomenon, it is generally understood as an historical epoch chronologically following the birth of the modern, though it may be discussed as a phase of late modernity. (Fredric Jameson, for instance, diagnoses sociocultural postmodernism as a "cultural logic of late capitalism.") Thus, unlike epistemological postmodernism, this sociocultural postmodernism is understood to be limited in history: it is a historical phenomenon specific to First World, capitalist nations in the late twentieth century. For those who define the postmodern this way, it would be absurd to speak of "Shakespeare's postmodernism." One might make comparisons between the social influences on Shakespeare's work and social influences on the work of contemporary U.S. writers, but these comparisons would be rooted in the historical (and economic) specifics of each respective historical period.

Moreover, this type of postmodernism is often compared to "modernity," but that modernity is, again, different from that assumed in the conversation about epistemological postmodernism. Sociocultural postmodernism tends to be defined against an economic modernity, one stemming from the nineteenth-century Industrial Revolution centered on the European continent and in the United States. Thus, sociocultural postmodernism tends to be opposed to or chronologically positioned after the nineteenth-century era of industrialization and colonial expansion and, later, twentieth-century assembly-line production; it is defined as a new network of relations between worker, work, space, technology, consumers, nation-states, and social values.

The third predominant discussion about postmodernism I would call *aesthetic,* a new, post-1945 artistic style or creative sensibility affecting virtually all late-twentieth-century art forms. This type of postmodernism is intimately tied to sociocultural postmodernism; many discussions of aesthetic postmodernism link late-twentieth-century philosophies of art with concurrent social movements.[7] Aesthetic postmodernism is not contrasted to modernity as much as it is to Modernism. Aesthetic postmodernism may be defined as a reaction to Realism as well as to High Modernism (understood as a movement in the arts reaching prominence between approximately 1895 and 1940). In painting, this postmodern aesthetic manifested itself as a reaction to abstract expressionism and was famously voiced by the work of Andy Warhol, the Pop artists, the photo realists and New Realists—Chuck Close, Robert Cottingham, Richard Estes, Duane Hanson, and Audrey Flack—and, later, in the photography of Cindy Sherman and the poster art of Barbara Kruger.[8] In architecture, this aesthetic postmodernism was a reaction against the modernist International Style and has been discussed in relation to the work of Robert Venturi, the European Neorationalists, Philip Johnson, James Stirling, and others, and has been critically discussed most famously by Charles Jencks and Robert Stern. In music, postmodernism began perhaps in rock-and-roll and political folk songs, but it has become more associated with the rise of punk rock, mosh pits, rave, rap, hip hop, and alternative rock and has been associated closely with the emergence of the MTV rock video and performance art, such as that by Laurie Anderson. In popular culture studies, writers discuss television as a postmodernist pop art form along with video and Web-based alternative media.

In literature, aesthetic postmodernism was a reaction against realism and a reaction against the High Modernism of European writers such as Franz Kafka, Virginia Woolf, James Joyce, and W. B. Yeats and American writers such as T. S. Eliot, Ezra Pound, Ernest Hemingway, and Gertrude Stein. The literary postmodernists emerged forcefully in the late 1960s and included poets and fiction writers; examples of artists might include Charles Olsen, John Ashbery, Amiri Baraka, John Barth, Thomas Pynchon, Ishmael Reed, William Gass, John Fowles, Kurt Vonnegut, Gilbert Sorrentino, Raymond Federman, Ronald Sukenick, Joseph Heller, and Italo Calvino. More recent writers might include Umberto Eco, Maxine Hong Kingston, Christa Wolf, Jeanette Winterson, Charles Johnson, Gerald Vizenor, Salman Rushdie, Peter Ackroyd, and Michael Joyce.

In literary studies, aesthetic postmodernism is characterized variously, but it is generally understood as having two stages of development: a late-modernist, metafictional phase predominating in the 1960s and 1970s, and an antimodernist phase of cultural critique predominating in the 1980s and 1990s, centering on politics of race, class, gender, and nationhood. Either phase may include a propensity toward theoretical self-reflexivity and irony; stylistic metafictionality that loosens traditional boundaries between the readers' and fictional worlds; a distrust of history or a felt need to revise it and, sometimes, to reduce it to a pastiche of styles; a blurring of traditionally separate literary genres; a reversal or destruction of traditional high art/low art hierarchies; experimentation with popular or "low" art genres, such as science fiction, romance, and detective fiction; unabashed participation in video and television culture; a fascination with profanity and pornography; politicization of narrative voice and an overt focus on the politics of the body; the construction of new metaphoric links between science and technology and literature; avant-gardism; an abdication of the modernist search for cosmological or cultural meaning via the literary medium or art itself.

These three categories of postmodernism overlap even when they seem to be mutually contradictory. Donna Haraway, for example, attempts to circumvent the central contradiction between essentialist feminism and antifoundationalist postmodernism by creating what she calls the "postmodern female cyborg."[9] This cyborg creation literally embodies different aspects of the postmodern: it is the product of technological society, yet it also resists patriarchal modernity. Consequently, Haraway's theory of the postmodern female body seems to assume definitions of the postmodern that are both epistemological and sociocultural. Equally crossing definitional boundaries, Fredric Jameson discusses postmodernism as a stage in the development of capitalism, yet as a marxist philosopher, Jameson dislikes much about postmodernism precisely because it undermines the materialist and "scientific" method on which marxist analysis depends. His is a marxist critique of both sociocultural and epistemological definitions of postmodernism. Moreover, many of the examples Jameson uses to support his assertions about postmodern culture are drawn from the arts, thereby including aesthetic postmodernism in his analyses as well. The most lucid and insightful discussions of postmodernism will acknowledge its tripartite character and incorporate the broadest, most inclusive definitions of this term.

Though definitions of postmodernism have been refined over time, after thirty years of scholarly conversation we are perhaps no nearer to a consensus about postmodernism—what it enacts, what it portends. One ariadnean thread, however, does run throughout even the most labyrinthine discussions, and that thread is history. The twentieth century has felt the aftershock of two world wars that sequentially threatened to obliterate human history and escalated the historical consequence of personal identity, social life, public and private discourse, and nationhood. The end of one age of empire, the globalization of political systems and market economies, the proliferating media technologies that mirror social life to itself in distorted reflections, and millennial hysteria of one form or another have all contributed to an increasing obsession about time and human events. It is not surprising, then, that for most of the twentieth century, various disciplines have to a greater or lesser degree been examining history's import. In fact, philosophy, historiography, and literature have reunited at the locus of history. More than anything else, this intersection at the point of history *is* postmodernism.

Sublime Desire

Theory

1 ▌ *Sorting Out Connections*

The Historical Romance in Hyper-reality

I had never felt this humiliation before—which is to say, the indignity of being terrorized by something you had trusted all your life.
——Timothy Findley, *Famous Last Words*

Postmodernism is debated as a social phenomenon, as an aesthetic, as an epistemology, and as a political philosophy, but a central tenet in all debates is that postmodernism embodies or attempts to project a new Western relation to history. Whether in a Jamesonian arena of late capitalism or a Lyotardian arena of cognitive figuralism, the specter of history haunts postmodern borderlands. Thus, William Spanos could write as early as 1979, "The traditional idea of the artist as a man speaking to men . . . becomes in the postmodern context, a historical man who speaks to historical men dialogically, with full awareness that what he says about being is ultimately 'grounded' in absence and thus is tentative, uncertain, discontinuous, and dispersed, always in need of interpretation, always in need of de-struction" ("De-struction and the Question of Postmodern Literature" 114).

The idea of historical men speaking dialogically to other historical men invokes certain aesthetic and political problematics in this postmodern debate. Linda Hutcheon's historiographic metafiction, Fredric Jameson's antihistorical postmodern pastiche, Charles Jencks's postmodern classicism, Brian McHale's literary postmodern ontologies, Leonard Orr's and David Cowart's schematic descriptors of history in fiction, Diane Elam's "ironic temporality," and Elisabeth Wes-

3

seling's "uchronian" fiction—these are just some of the more provocative attempts to deal with these problematics, specifically as they re-
late to the postmodern turn on history. Ethnic studies, New Historicism, and postcolonial studies are much indebted to the debates over
postmodernism, capitalism, and history that started in the early
1960s and raged through the two following decades. The discipline of
history itself has not remained unaffected by these debates and indeed has often been directly mired in them. What is now termed by
some *the crisis in history* is a crisis both within the discipline of history
itself and outside the discipline in the realm of philosophy, literary
criticism, and artistic production.[1]

Noticeably, however, most discussions of postmodern history
avoid or reject the historical novel genre as a valid starting point for
this kind of inquiry.[2] In the thorny definitional thickets of the postmodernism debates, the term *historical novel* tends to be absorbed
into discussions of sociocultural postmodernism's use and abuse of
historical facts; generic formalism is understood as an inheritance of
the western Enlightenment that postmodernism and poststructuralism vehemently and specifically reject. In the debates about postmodernism and history, the historical novel has largely gone by the
critical wayside even as literature's obsession with history and "gener-
icity" has overtaken critical discussion.

Contrary to popular trends, however, this study considers postmodernism within the context of the historical romance, thus both
acknowledging the historical romance as a subgenre with its own evolutionary literary history (contradicting critics such as Lukács, who
technically did not see the historical novel as a genre category in its
own right) and arguing for the importance of this evolutionary history to postmodernist fiction. In this book I define historical fiction
as a literary genre with a specific generic history. The historical novel
is presented as a subgenre of the novel that exhibits three primary
characteristics: (1) specific historical detail, featured prominently, is
crucial to plot or character development or some experimental representation of these narrative attributes; (2) a *sense* of history informs all

facets of the fictional construct (from authorial perspective to character development to selection of place); and (3) this sense of history emerges from and is constructed by the text itself and requires the text to participate in and differentiate itself from other discourses of various generic kinds that attempt to give a name to history.

Locating postmodernist fiction within the purview of historical romance makes it apparent that these two literary approaches to history share a surprising number of characteristics that link them through literary history. One example is easily cited: the fact that the historical romance tradition embodies many of the inherent contradictions of postmodernist fiction. Postmodern fiction (and postmodernism generally) has been defined by its split focus and contradictory character, specifically as it has attempted to address historical fact within narrative. The idea of postmodernism as a "border discourse"—relativistic yet political, nihilistic yet utopian—has become a critical cliché, but important scholarly work also specifically argues the historical/ahistorical paradox of postmodernism. Linda Hutcheon, for instance, repeatedly refers to postmodernism's "complicity with that which it critiques"; Fredric Jameson refers to postmodernism's "schizophrenic" sociohistorical consciousness; Zygmunt Bauman refers to postmodernism's "ambivalence." In a similar way, Avrom Fleishman has noted the characteristic hybridity of historical romance—its ahistorical humanist attempt to contemplate universal cultural processes while at the same time remaining firmly rooted in the factuality of history (8). Dekker observes that "calling a novel a 'historical romance' is therefore to direct attention to its extraordinarily rich, mixed, and even contradictory or oxymoronic character" (26). Indeed, as early as 1828, Alessandro Manzoni wrote *Del romanzo storico* (*On the Historical Novel*) during the twenty years after he published the historical novel *I promessi sposi* (*The Betrothed*); in this essay he pronounced dead the genre in which he had won his greatest fame, because in the historical novel, fact and fable were at odds. What is necessary to create a historical novel, wrote Manzoni, is precisely the impossible: historical reality must always be represented, yet the narrative must produce for readers a unified belief or theme, which history denies (72–73). In other words, the historical novel, like postmodernist historicism, was hopelessly self-contradictory.

The links between postmodernist fiction and the historical romance novel are explored in this study, as expressed in three deceptively simple questions. First, are there shared characteristics between the conventional historical romance and experimental post-1960s fiction, and what can we gain by looking at post-1960s fiction through the lens of the historical romance genre? Second, what is the relationship between post-1960s historical fiction and the historiography of its own time? Third, is there any thread linking these three post-1960 discourses—genre theory concerning the historical romance, historiography, and postmodern theory?

The Problem of History

Postmodern historical fiction stands in the refracted light of nineteenth-century historical novels, and much that has been claimed as groundbreaking postmodernist historical experimentation was nascent in these works. And yet certainly what I term *metahistorical romances* are different in scope and focus from their generic forebears in significant ways. To call novels such as Steve Erikson's *Arc d'X* or Alison Fell's *The Pillow Boy of the Lady Onogoro* historical novels without using inverted commas is to conflate these novels with *Waverley* or *War and Peace* in an absurd way. *Arc d'X* is not *Waverley,* though the former does bear an evolutionary relation to the latter. The problem becomes clear only when one tries to distinguish historiographical assumptions implied by texts themselves.

For instance, in *War and Peace,* a paradigmatic example of historical romance, Tolstoy waxes metafictional in the final pages, where an authorial voice comments directly upon the workings of history:

> We are forced to fall back on fatalism to explain the irrational events of history (that is to say, events the intelligence of which we do not see). The more we strive to account for such events in history rationally, the more irrational and incomprehensible do they

become to us. . . . Man lives consciously for himself but uncon-
sciously he serves as an instrument for the accomplishment of historical and social ends. . . . History, that is, the unconscious, universal, swarm-life of mankind, uses every moment of the life of
kings for its own purposes. . . . Every action of [great men], that
seems to them an act of their own freewill, is in the historical sense
not free at all but is bound up with the whole course of history
and preordained from all eternity. (717–19)

There is an implied Hegelianism to Tolstoy's statement; History is
the Mind of time, a teleological process that has its own logic and
momentum. Tolstoy critics, however, seem to accept Sir Isaiah
Berlin's summary of history in *War and Peace* as inexorable according
to nature. That is, history works according to natural law, in the manner of Newtonian physics.[3] In either interpretation, history is incomprehensible to the limited, mortal human intelligence. The life of the
individual is as nothing compared to the functioning of History, oblivious of and impervious to human overtures. Humankind can observe
the actions of History on both great and historically insignificant persons and reconcile itself to the logical necessity of the apparently illogical historical process through, ultimately, an abiding faith. Tolstoy's novel itself is such an observation, and his sympathy is directed
toward his fellow mortals, cut off from historical understanding and
set adrift in experiential, political life. *War and Peace* is a mimetic, fictional work of human sympathy and, ultimately, of faith in history as
a self-aware and universal (though not always congenial) plan.

In contrast, in Jeanette Winterson's novel *Sexing the Cherry*, the
narrator Jordon comments,

Until now religion has described it better than science, but now
physics and metaphysics appear to be saying the same thing. The
world is flat and round, is it not? We have dreams of moving back
and forward in time, though to use the words back and forward is
to make a nonsense of the dream, for it implies that time is linear,
and if that were so there could be no movement, only a forward
progression. But we do not move through time, time moves
through us. . . . The most prosaic of us betray a belief in the in-

ward life every time we talk about "my body" rather than "I". . . .
Language always betrays us, tells the truth when we want to lie,
and dissolves into formlessness when we would most like to be
precise. And so we cannot move back and forth in time, but we
can experience it in a different way. If all time is eternally present,
there is no reason why we should not step out of one present into
another. (99–100)

While attributed in this novel to a fictional character (unlike Tolstoy's
more direct address to the reader), this quote does illustrate how a
postmodernist sensibility re-envisions history as time and space de-
void of narrative "glue" that would stick the two together and focus
them on (and subordinate them to) heroic human endeavor. For Tolstoy, History is a machine, paradoxically outside of time, that can be
observed and perhaps defined, but not controlled, by human agency;
his history is defined by Newtonian physics and Enlightenment
metaphors for history such as the "great clock of time."[4] In contrast,
Winterson's Jordon seems to redefine History as time in a post-
Einsteinian universe. First, positivistic notions of progression (and
Progress) or linear time are discarded. Instead, the universe is represented in terms of relativity theory: space and time are not separate
entities but are interrelated and interchangeable. Their character is
dependent on the view of the observer, rather than on absolute and
inherent material or "spiritual" characteristics. If space and time are
therefore relative, History (even less materially grounded) has no
starting point and no definitional foundation. History can no longer
be understood as a linear process or stable narrative, and concepts
such as *forward* or *backward* in time become meaningless. Moreover,
to Jordon, science and metaphysics have merged the way they might
in a quantum world: both challenge notions of binary opposition
and syllogistic thinking as a means to revelation. A quantum universe
operates according to systems theories and mathematical probabili-
ties, and it leaves open the possibilities of mutually contradictory but
simultaneously existing states—an approach that the fictional Jordon
(and, one might add, many other real-world postmodernist writers
such as Thomas Pynchon) sees fraught with metaphysical overtones

and historical implications.[5] History is not ontological but has become redefined as something fluid, malleable, and (with the Heisenberg Uncertainty Principle as analogical reference) enmeshed with the human agent: "We do not move through time, time moves through us."

Furthermore, Jordan implies that history does not stand outside time, nor can it remove itself from the interpolation of human subjectivity through language. In this sense it is impossible to talk, as Tolstoy does, about the machine of history that orchestrates the movements of "great men." In a very poststructuralist gesture, Jordan states that only "the most prosaic of us" still believe in the separation of Self and world at all. Punning on "prosaic" as both "mundane" and "narrativistic," Winterson/Jordan implies that humankind is deluded by banal foundationalist narratives of self and history, though art and language theory can denature these constructs (which, Jordan nostalgically implies, is not necessarily a pleasant thing). It is lastly important to note that Jordan's monologue is completely anachronistic to the setting of the novel in which he appears. *Sexing the Cherry* is set in Restoration England, at the waning moment of the Renaissance and the dawning of the Enlightenment. The metaphysical view of history that Jordan espouses not only contradicts Enlightenment historiographical assumptions but also challenges the Western historical record outside the novel as it has been traditionally narrativized. In other words, setting Jordan's musings in this time frame enacts what it contemplates: the disruption of linear history and destruction of the old notion of history as outside of language, time, and human agency.

Thus, both the traditional historical romance and the postmodernist historical romance raise questions about how history can be narrated and what the relationship between historiography and fiction might be. I will argue that the relationship between these fictions (in relation to their representations of history) is evolutionary. But what does this really mean? What historiographical assumptions are encoded in both forms of this historical fiction?

The Historical Romance

While it is true that people were writing historical epics before Walter Scott took up the form, Scott's novels were central to the historical novel's influence as a literary genre. Moreover, studies of Scott's oeuvre, as well as general studies of the historical novel, assert that Scott reflected but also influenced nineteenth-century historians' work. George Dekker, for example, notes that Scott's novels provided an enlarged scope for the novel form and its historical consciousness *and* an example that inspired professional historians to reform their research methods and extend the range of topics considered in their accounts of historical causation (Dekker 29).

Scott wrote many of his novels just after the French Revolution and a half century before marxist dialectical materialism was formulated, when the premises of historical investigation were radically shifting. Scholars have argued that Scott's work influenced historians such as Augustin Thierry, whose *History of the Conquest of England by the Normans* (1871) turns to the particular and to the oral to fill in the gaps of official recorded history, and Thomas Babington Macaulay, who called for a redefinition of history that would include the specific and particular.[6] Scott's *Waverley* was published as the fury of the French Revolution ushered in the era of the great Romantic historiographers, including Bancroft and Michelet. Yet while Scott's work often seems a harbinger of the historiographical changes that swept through Europe after 1830, scholarship has convincingly argued that even though Scott would have been influenced by European Romanticism, he had stronger alliances with the eighteenth-century Scottish school of "philosophical historians." Scott, moreover, was open about his debt to John Bruce, Dugald Stewart, and Baron David Hume of the Scottish school. There is clear evidence from Scott's writings that the ideas of the philosophical historians greatly influenced him, though most studies acknowledge that he approached the ideas of the Scottish school in a pragmatic way.

There are many discussions of Scott and the Scottish philosophes to be found, and there is no need here to redo what has already been done well by others.[7] A few facts about Scott's views on history common to Scott studies are, however, important to my argument about the evolutionary ties between his historical fiction and that produced in the late twentieth century.

Implicit and explicit in the philosophy of the Scottish school was a fundamental uniformitarianism, a belief that a core of universal human nature is unalterable but can be channeled by social conditions. The philosophical historians affirmed the notion of progress (in terms of both technical innovation and social evolution), but they also affirmed the idea that all societies are equal insofar as they equally satisfy their constituents. Freedom, for example, was seen not as a natural right but as something society attained for its own utilitarian purposes (McMaster 54–63). Adam Smith construed human development as a four-stage process: hunting, pastoral, agricultural, and commercial; Dekker has summarized these as "savage," "barbarian," "civilized," and "over-civilized" stages of universal human cultural development (75). The Scottish philosophical historians granted a kind of respect for the accomplishments of each stage of social development, for each stage created unique mechanisms to adapt to its mode of production and social network, yet the earliest stage was construed as savage and the last civilized (McMaster 54–63). To say that this kind of schema could easily legitimate Western colonialist, racist, and sexist stereotypes is to repeat what has already been observed in Scott criticism. As Scott's contemporary critics argue effectively, this stadialist theory of social development also greatly influenced other writers after Scott, notably Fenimore Cooper and Margaret Mitchell in the United States.

Scott, then, clearly wrote with an idea in his mind about what history was, and this was encoded in his fictions as a set of historiographical assumptions aligned with prevailing historiographical views of his day. Some of these assumptions include the following: that historians could be social scientists in a true sense, observing cultures impartially and extrapolating through inductive logic the organizing patterns of societies, cultures, and history; that history was linear, a line of interlocked events developing from one point in historical time to another; that this linear time moved along a universal developmental continuum, based in a universal human nature, in which cultures progressed from lower to higher forms; that history was thus positivistic and progress was a realistically attainable goal; that cultures that were "low" on the civilization continuum nevertheless evinced admirable traits, and that "high" cultures paid for their advanced state with a loss of that admirable something; that the recording of such observations was an artistic science with political and social consequences.

From this set of ideas one can perhaps extrapolate four assumptions basic to the historical novel in its early forms:

1. it assumes the ontology of history;
2. it assumes that history, as the shaping force of culture, can be identified and assessed (particularly in economic structures) by an unmotivated, neutral human observer who can inductively extrapolate a developmental pattern in history itself;
3. it assumes and upholds notions of cultural and personal *value* derived largely from Western bourgeois economies;
4. it assumes the shape of history to be linear and the motivation of history to be Progress.

This list of attributes is, as it were, the genetic code of the historical novel, one that seems to be altered through evolutionary development through the nineteenth and twentieth centuries.

With such a list of assumptions common to the early historical romance in hand, it might be easy to thump Scott into a slot labeled *naive realist,* but this would do him a disservice.[8] What makes Scott interesting as a writer, and as an ancestor to postmodern historical novelists, is his complication of these empirical assumptions about history with the nostalgic romanticism for past cultural forms that runs throughout all of his novels. This nostalgia is built into the historiography of the Scottish school to some extent, but in Scott's fiction it forms a real tension between an Enlightenment and a Romantic conception of history and humankind.

Scott's twentieth-century critics have provided ample evidence, in other words, that Scott's predisposition toward a romantic nostalgia for past or fast-disappearing Scottish traditions also caused him to romanticize the Scottish Highlands and the Scottish past in a way that was antithetical to the value placed by Enlightenment philosophies on scientific observation.[9] Scott acknowledged in his own work this pull of opposing desires: on the one hand, a desire logically to observe and record social life in the interests of historical analysis, and on the other hand, a desire to eulogize the unique qualities of specific societies that (if they were at lower stages of historical development) were inevitably threatened and eventually superseded by higher forms of civilization with their own logic and social values, and that even in his day remained only as historical traces. Scott himself defines "romance" as "'a fictitious narrative in prose or verse; the interest of which turns upon marvelous and uncommon incidents'; being thus opposed to the kindred term *Novel* . . . a fictitious narrative, differing from the romance, because the events are accommodated to the ordinary train of human events and the modern state of society" ("Essay on Romance" 65). This is a modern definition of romance indeed, and provocative because it illustrates that for Scott, the romance was aligned with the false or with fable, while the novel was aligned with mimesis and modern, deductive observation of real life. The melding of the two produced a unique and self-contradictory form, the historical romance.[10]

I would like to claim this observation as uniquely my own, but virtually every study of Scott mentions this duality, or composite character, of his historical romances and argues that this is Scott's legacy to all subsequent contributors to the genre historical romance—in the United States, including Hawthorne, Emerson, and Hemingway. Even in the early nineteenth century, Scott's critics recognized that something new, growing out of existing literary traditions, was happening in his novels.[11] In the twentieth century, Richter and others contend that while Scott's novels were rooted in his culture's support of antiquarian history and Enlightenment rationalist historiography, his novels also bear a direct relationship to the Gothic romance tradition, which represented a specific mode of presenting history that focused on the primitive and picturesque. Dekker notes, "In historical romances the forces of progress (the future) are often invested with the oppressive characteristics associated with an expanding imperial state, while the retreating forces of reaction (the past) exhibit, along with some negative traits, such positive 'heroic' ones as 'nature,' 'freedom,' 'loyalty,' etc." (74).

In this light, Diane Elam has provided a brilliant poststructuralist discussion of the romance of Scott's history, remarking that "when history isn't itself, romance intervenes" (*Romancing the Postmodern* 53). Elam underscores how Scott himself recognized the elusiveness of the historical past and—because of historians' needs to aestheticize the past or render it more accessible—the inevitability of reconstructing that past as romance. In Elam's Lyotardian reading of Scott, the forces of modernity attempted to erase the Scottish Highland past but could be only partially successful, and that past remained as a postmodern trace, which Scott resuscitated as romance. Elam claims that this romance is self-aware; it embeds knowledge that the past is never fully recuperable and, more importantly, that any attempt to write history is also by definition anachronistic:

> We can no longer assume that modernist history "gets it right"; what it might mean to represent the past authentically is not certain. . . . Scott does not offer a mere escape from modernity; if anything Scott's romances confirm that modernity cannot be escaped because much of the work of modernity cannot be undone: we cannot bring back to life the obliterated Highlanders except in the pages of romance. . . . The past as past is untranslatable into another culture; the past is always a different culture, lost to the "now" of modernity. What Scott's postmodern romances can do is make the burden of the past felt as burden because it is lost, because it is irrecoverable in a way that we will never know (*Romancing the Postmodern* 63, 68).

Scott is constructed here as a writer consciously preserving the past while recognizing its inherent difference and unrepresentability. Elam contends that this is Scott's postmodern gesture, but one might ask why this is not Scott's Enlightenment scientism asserting itself, his underlying acceptance of a stadialism that constructed history as a series of paradigm shifts in which one entered new phases of historical development only at the expense of the loss of older, less developed phases. In Scott's historical romances, recognition of the loss of the past often seems nostalgic, and it bears many similarities to the modern historical construction of the Other as "vanished"—a subject to be mourned because it is extinct and hence unknowable except in its traces, which we can indeed look at, elegize, romanticize, and oppose to the present even if we can't know it. Elam claims that Scott's perspective on the past is not nostalgic, but if this trace Other were really contestatory, then it would provide a vehicle for resistance to modernity, an aporia within modernity that not only embodied representation's excess but also representation's felt counter. (One thinks, as an example, of the Other in the figure of the black man Friday in J. M. Coetzee's *Foe,* who is not vanished but whose presence irritates the acolyte of modernity, Susan Barton, precisely because she can neither cancel him out of her consciousness nor "understand" him and make him less threatening. He is, in effect, sublime.) In Scott's novels, the Other is unknowable but does not embody any kind of resistant knowledge to the forces of modernity. As in James Fenimore Cooper's novels, in Scott's historical romances the past is unknowable precisely because it is expired, vanished, and overridden by the forces of a new, modern paradigm.

However, the reason Scott can be understood as the ancestor to contemporary historical fiction is precisely because of the entanglement of romance and history in his work that Elam identifies. The entanglement happens when Scott links the material sublime to history and politics in the image of the Highlander or "vanishing" societies.

Before the eighteenth century, as Thurber notes, Longinus had defined the sublime as essentially rhetorical, as language that was attractive but potentially empty bombast, and as such it represented a lawlessness that needed to be governed in a political as well as a rhetorical sense. In the eighteenth century, theories of the sublime stemming from Longinus's work entered full force into British philosophical discourse. By 1704, John Dennis was suggesting that the natural universe could harbor the terror and ecstasy of the sublime as well. Dennis's relocation of the sublime from language to the material world apparently had enormous implications for writers such as Joseph Addison and Edmund Burke as well as Hugh Blair, David Hume, Adam Ferguson, Adam Smith, and Dugald Stewart, with whose work, as noted above, Scott was probably acquainted. Thurber notes, "The distinction [Blair] draws between the sublime and the beautiful, conventional enough even before Burke, occurs now in a way that makes it a potential *political* distinction, once Scotland is associated with the sublime; and Blair may even have given Scott a hint that the sublime could help him envision history, since in his lectures he speaks of the sublimity of objects removed in time as well as space" (94). Thurber's point is that the romance elements of Scott's work often are embodied in images of sublimity in the physical world, images (such as caves, terrifying waterfalls, mountain gorges scaled by troops) that link the sublime to the social world, to the political sphere, and to Scotland's history. For Walter Scott the Romantic gothicist, Scotland's history itself was marked by sublimity. It was terror-laden but also awe-inspiring, and it was also largely unknowable precisely because it incorporated all dead intellectual and economic paradigms. One can see why in many cases Scott's novels prefigured the Romantic sublime of the nineteenth century but at the same time disallowed the revolutionary potential of the sublime that would later be articulated so passionately by the British Romantic poets. Scott's historical romances are truly caught between radically different conceptions of history—supporting the Scottish philosophes' universalist theories of history while tying them to a nationalism symbolized in the material sublime.

The Metahistorical Novel and Romance

In late twentieth-century historical fiction of a literary kind (which excludes the bodice-rippers and Fabio-illustrated paperback thrillers of the kind sold in supermarkets), the relation between history and romance found in Scott's novels is often inverted: instead of being subordinated to "scientific" analysis of history, romance becomes the Luddite, jamming the machinery of Enlightenment historical theories and emphasizing the negative ramifications of modernity sometimes expressed or implied in Scott's historical fiction.

A novel such as Charles Frazier's *Cold Mountain* illustrates this shift. This is a late twentieth-century novel but it is firmly rooted in the historical romance tradition of Scott; indeed, Frazier's is a novel very near to *Ivanhoe* in its mixture of history and romance. Set in the Civil War South, the action focuses on Inman, a soldier fighting for the Confederacy. An ordinary man from the hills of North Carolina, Inman faces a personal turmoil that is a microcosm of the social and ideological foment around him: his personal journey from quiet farmer to brutal warrior, from natural to social man, from near-mystic to cynic to nihilist, are allegorically linked to violent upheavals in the national psyche as the war rips the nation's veil of Enlightenment progressivism and throws it into a bloody pool. When Inman realizes that as a mountain farmer he has become a pawn in the battle between two economic systems (the industrial economy of the North and the agrarian, slaveholding economy of the South), neither of which have anything to do with his life, he deserts. His act of desertion, and his subsequent journey back to his Cold Mountain farm and his lover Ada, is a rejection of both plantation agrarianism and industrial capitalism—shown in this novel to be two sides of the modern coin. What we see here, then, is a last attempt to reject modernity in favor of a premodern sociocultural value.

There seems to be a clear stadialist view of history at work in this novel: like Scott's *Rob Roy*, Frazier's novel posits a pure, natural, romantic—and Highland—culture under threat from the forces of modernity. Though this novel has been praised continuously for its "realistic" portrayal of Smoky Mountain life, the North Carolina mountain culture it portrays is highly romanticized: what we see here is a Rousseauian garden, where the land gives sustenance to simple, hardworking people who respect life and are one with nature. In this world, there is equality between the sexes (though men are men here, and women women), a practical approach to religion, utter generosity between neighbors, and little if any racism. This idyllic Highland culture of Cold Mountain (mirrored in the homosocial relationship of Inman and his Cherokee friend Swimmer) is doomed, and we see it in its first stages of change—threatened by a war that will lead someday to other changes such as the latter-day ills of land development, tourism, and suburbanization. The Highland way of life—like the (even more romanticized in this novel) Cherokee way of life that it itself supplanted—will die because the heroic male homosocial world upon which it depends cannot survive the forces of modernization. Aware that after the Civil War there is no escape from the industrial capitalism of the North, the novel posits only tragic romance as a solution to the problem of how to live in this postwar world. Inman will find his love, impregnate her, and die, but his progeny will live on, as will Ada, in a kind of New World Garden, secluded on Cold Mountain and living with Ruby and her family in new kind of matriarchal communal family.

This novel has significant ties to the historical romance of Scott, yet what Borges in "Pierre Menard, Author of the *Quixote*" and other postmodern writers have shown is that if *Waverley* were written today, even word for word by an author who had not read the original, the contemporary version would be different, infused with the sensibility of its time and thus utterly distinct from its (seemingly identical) precursor. *Cold Mountain* illustrates this precept: while reviewers have noted that the book is modeled on Homer's *Odyssey*, this American novel seems less about Homer or even the Civil War than it is about Vietnam. The war that Inman fights will teach the South precisely the lesson Vietnam will later teach the United States: the lesson of losing. Both wars will leave the nation divided, inexorably changed. Inman is in many ways less the Civil War deserter than the Vietnam vet, fighting in a war he doesn't believe in, fighting in a territory that is unfamiliar, manipulated by self-interested and jingoistic political and military leaders, harassed when he tries to return home. The vision at the heart of the book is stoical at best and seems to reflect a stadialist view of history. Actually, however, it reflects the post-Vietnam ennui of the United States: "For as was true of all human effort, there was never advancement. Everything added meant something lost, and about as often as not the thing lost was preferable to the thing gained, so that over time we'd be lucky if we just broke even. Any thought otherwise was empty pride" (Frazier 301).

As was true for the countercultures of the sixties, in this novel surviving in a world where Home Guard brutality, vigilantism, and corrupt wars are the norm requires one to reject the modern world and escape inward, to a secret garden. This is essentially the message given in the story of the Shining Rocks, a recurring motif in the novel. The story is a story of the Fall, told to Inman by a Cherokee woman who had escaped the Trail of Tears. She tells him of a city hidden in the mountain that can only be reached through the rock portal after days of fasting. In this place, a man from that city once told her, "Though we die as all men do and must struggle for our food, we need not think of danger. Our minds are not filled with fear. We do not endlessly contend with each other" (Frazier 197–98). His village is hidden inside the mountain; it is a womb, an interiorization, a desire for peace and oneness with Mother Earth.

The point of the story of the Shining Rocks, however, is that we can never get there. When the Cherokee try to fast and enter the abundant city in the belly of the earth, one man who has secretly broken the fast and betrayed their hopes becomes fearful and lets out a war cry, whereupon the golden city is sealed away from the Cherokee forever. The story, part of the strong romance element of the novel, seems to be an allegory about postmodern history. The place of ecstasy—figured in a material, physical image connoting the sublime—is always receding, always out of reach, and what is left in its place is our desire for it and our drive to come to terms with the material history—violent and warlike—that we create in its stead.

Thus Scott's romance was about specific cultures that had supposedly reached "higher," modern phases of culture, whereas postmodern romance is about history itself and expresses the loss not of culture but of certainty, precisely the certainty about history that Scott was able to experience. Both classic historical romances and postmodernist historical romances are about history—that is, they are

19

about the business of historical representation. However, they engage with history in different ways—mainly, I believe, because traditional historical novels tend to foreground different assumptions about historical representation. As the discussion of Scott's fiction illustrates, the historical novel foregrounded empirical historical reconstruction in the service of realism. In keeping with the historiographical thought of his time, Scott assumed that an observant investigator who trained his eye on the historical past and used a stadialist theory of cultural history as a guide could discern the strengths and weaknesses of a past culture.

But though Scott thus aimed at a picture of the past that was true in spirit to a universalist theory of cultural development, his novels often evince a romantic nostalgia for the heroic Highland past. Foregrounding realism contradictorily led Scott to assert the force of what he understood to be its literary opposite; setting his sights on realism/history, he stumbles over romance. What the above discussion of *Cold Mountain* illustrates is how, in contrast, postmodernist historical romances tend to foreground romance/fabulation but end up asserting the force of the politically real. Playing with romance, hoping to escape from or to history, they end up stumbling over the real, the political chaos (or their own society's political history) that prevents access to a clear notion or picture of how history works or what historical Truth may be.

In postmodernist historical romances, romance is linked to the romantic sublime as it was in Scott's fiction. Yet postmodern romance, as noted above, is a seeking toward history itself; it does not merely elegize a specific institution or culture from the past. Robert Scholes's *The Fabulators*—a small, colloquial discussion about early postmodernism, published in 1967—was enormously influential in early studies of literary postmodernism and still has importance to understanding this centrality of romance to postmodernist fiction. Scholes argues that the fictional, postmodernist narrative after 1950—exemplified in work by Durrell, Vonnegut, Hawkes, Murdoch, and Barth —was a new way of writing that harkened back to romance. His *fabulation* was characterized by an extraordinary delight in design, a pleasure in form combined with a simultaneous emphasis on the art of the designer that asserted his authority and control; an implicit didacticism that shaped the text into "ethically controlled fantasy"; a propensity to allegorize; a rejection of realism and empirical notions of characterization and reality upon which realism is based; more concern with ideas and ideals than with the representation of consensus reality; and, most important, elevation of the ethical and aesthetic values of romance (*Fabulation and Metafiction* 8–20).

What Scholes identifies in postmodernist fiction—and what I would argue characterizes metahistorical romance particularly of the 1960s through the 1980s—is its link to and continuation of the Romance/fabulatory tradition. The postmodernist revolt against realism and naturalism in favor of romance (fabulation), Scholes implied, was not a paradigm revolution; it was a return to the old opponent of realism that was always a part of the Western literary tradition. Elam in fact claims that "1) romance should be considered *as* a postmodern genre; 2) postmodernism *is* romance" (12). This was the initial point stated by the early postmodernists themselves, and increasingly in the novels of Robert Coover, Ishmael Reed, and Thomas Pynchon this focus on romance becomes aligned self-consciously with concerns about history. As Scholes noted, "The fabulative impulse has achieved its most impressive results when it has worked most closely with the raw material of history" (*Fabulation and Metafiction* 206). This fabulative impulse underlies musings such as Steve Erikson's narrator's in *Arc d'X:* "What if . . . time is relative not simply to the perspective of motion, not simply to what the eye sees from a passing train or a rocket hurtling at the speed of light, but to the heart as well, and the speed at which it travels? . . . Beyond three hearts in tandem was history" (207, 209). Like many of the bourgeois countercultures of the 1960s, postmodernist fiction desperately wants to get itself back to the Garden, the place where history is suspended and human history (as conflict, as separation, and as uncertainty) ends.

John Barth's 1967 essay "The Literature of Exhaustion" illustrates how strong was this influence of romance on the early postmodernist writers in the United States. Barth's work initiated discussions of literary postmodernism, and in novels and interviews he unabashedly acknowledged a fascination with romance. Barth repeatedly noted that a palimpsest for the many quest and labyrinth models in his novels and short stories was the Scheherazade story of the Arabian Nights tale cycles—tales that Barth perceived to be a model for the postmodern because of their combination of romance and self-reflexive artifice. Indeed, in "The Literature of Exhaustion," Barth remarks upon Jorge Luis Borges's "algebra and fire"—his artistic precision and self-reflexivity and his fabulatory passion, which, Borges had written, were the two vital components of literary art. Barth adopts this formula for contemporary fiction, claiming "neither the algebra nor the fire, metaphorically speaking, could achieve this result [obtruding itself into and eventually supplanting our prior reality] without the other" (32). To Barth the late modernist/early postmodernist, the writer and the narrative protagonist are both virtuosos and cultural heroes aided by very special gifts; the act of composing literature is a heroic act and by definition will produce romance, albeit one predicated on a new "algebra" of fiction. Barth picked a model for contemporary fiction that implicitly (if not directly) romanticized history: the Scheherazade tales construct in their form and celebrate in their content the intentional disruption of historical linearity and closure. This convergence of history and romance was recognized years later by the novelist Julian Barnes: "Our panic and our pain are only eased by soothing fabulation; we call it history" (*A History of the World in 10½ Chapters* 240).

Postmodernist historical fiction's turn toward fabulation may be understood as a tropological return, a swerving back, to the romance elements always embedded within classic historical romance.[12] Significantly, the postmodern historical romance (what I term the *metahistorical romance*) swerves back with a difference; it returns, but with different priorities and for specific reasons that can be located in the social and cultural fabric of First World nations. Romance infuses allegorical ethicism into the novel form after, and in reaction to what is sees as the triumph of, fin de siècle modernism.[13] But it also signals a longing for the past—not a longing for a past simpler time or a past simpler culture, but for *the past itself* as a situating, grounding foundation for knowledge and truth. Writers of metahistorical romance seem not to be able to take this longing seriously or even to acknowledge it without irony. The postmodernist historical romance is self-reflexive, even self-parodying in its most avant-gardist forms. As the narrating voice in the "historical romance" *The French Lieutenant's Woman* notes, "I live in the age of Alain Robbe-Grillet and Roland Barthes; if this is a novel, it cannot be a novel in the modern sense of the word" (80).

The Metahistorical Novel and Historiography

The postmodern metahistorical romance not only reembodies (escapist but also ethicist) romance; it is also enmeshed with contemporaneous cultural conversations about history, at least to the degree that Scott's historical fiction was shaped and influenced by contemporaneous eighteenth-and nineteenth-century historical models. To question the invocation of History (with a capital *H*) as an origin, as totalizing ground, as the location from which we have strayed and to which we need to return, as a fundamental mode of being, and as that which "is organized only by a certain closure, a 'shutting down,' of historicity" (Bennington and Young 9)—these are the circulating currents of thought in the works of the major twentieth-century poststructuralist thinkers about history. Two ideas are central to the postmodern turn on history: the dispersion of the *cogito* by the culturally located Subject, and the reevaluation of Western modernity. In particular, the historical philosophies—or philosophies of history—of Michel Foucault and Jean-François Lyotard construct a radical alterity to modernity's historical modeling and have erupted into disciplinary history as well as into the literary territory of metahistorical romance. Although these theorists' works are by now de rigueur, I will point out where their ideas seem to intersect with developments in contemporary historiography that, taken together, have significant overlaps with the approach to history in postmodern historical romance.

Nearly forty years after its initial publication, Foucault's archeological model is so well known that it can be found exposited and eviscerated in pop-culture books with titles like *Foucault for Beginners*. It has become the underlying philosophy of New Historicism, of much cultural studies work, and of much work in postcolonial theory. Foucault's "enunciative analysis" has percolated into all aspects of the late twentieth-century historical imagination, constructing a radical alternative to the mechanistic model implied by Leo Tolstoy in the passage from *War and Peace* cited earlier: "The analysis of statements operates therefore without reference to a cogito. . . . In fact, it is situated at the level of the 'it is said'—and we must not understand by this a sort of communal opinion, a collective representation that is imposed on every individual; we must not understand by it a great, anonymous voice that must, of necessity, speak through the discourse of everyone" (*Archeology* 122). For Tolstoy, history was motivated momentum, paradoxically outside of time, that encompassed human beings like a great oceanic Mind. Foucault redefines that Historical Mind as power, resituating the subject in language and thus, paradoxically, in history. As Thomas Docherty notes, "The question is not the simple phenomenological one of how to inhabit the space of the Subject; rather, that space is historically shifting, changing, mutating in and through time. It is a temporary or historical space which denies the possibility of the Subject coming to full self-presence."[14]

Historicism is redefined by Foucault as epistemic knowledge, knowledge of the possibilities of the "it is said" at any given moment. Instead of studying self-defining people at different historical "periods" (defined as conglomerates of specific economic, political, national, and epistemological characteristics), history thus becomes an analysis of what Hayden White calls "linguistic protocols"—what is sayable within the total set of relations within a specific slice of space/time. As early as 1971, Lecourt was suggesting that Foucault belonged in a group with Bachelard and Canguilhem as antipositivist and anti-evolutionary in the philosophy of science (Dews, "Foucault and the French Tradition" 348). Most distressing to disciplinary history was Foucault's transformation of historical "documents" into "monuments" in a process of historiographical transmogrification: "In the history of ideas, of thought and of the sciences, [transforming documents into monuments] . . . has broken up the long series formed by the progress of consciousness, or the teleology of reason, or the evolution of human thought; it has questioned the themes of convergence and culmination; it has doubted the possibility of creating totalities" (Foucault, *Archaeology,* 8).

The reciprocality between the social theory of Foucault and the postmodern philosophy of Lyotard is tenuous but clear. Both are concerned not with what is constructed (in/as history, in/as language) but with the possibilities of construction itself. Both argue that what is *not* possible to speak becomes the locus of meaning within history. Lyotard locates this "unspeakable" thing outside of representation and modernity's epistemological paradigms; he terms this unspeakable element the language of the *postmodern event.* Readings defines the *event* as an occurrence in space/time that "is the fact or case that something happens, after which nothing will ever be the same again. The event disrupts any pre-existing referential frame within which it might be represented or understood. The eventhood of the event is the radical *singularity* of happening, the 'it happens' as distinct from the sense of 'what is happening.' It leaves us without criteria and requires *indeterminate judgment*" (*Introducing Lyotard* xxxi).

The Lyotardian event is the eruption in history of that which cannot be articulated within history; it is the "not said" that silently explodes into the realm of representation, disrupting existing representational frames and leaving "nothing ever the same again." The "it happens" is a historical event without criteria, outside of judgment, outside of representational frames, outside of discourse. For Lyotard, the postmodern is always entwined with and inhabiting the modern as the event unspoken within discursive representation. The notion of historical periodization consequently becomes irrelevant in a way that it was and was not for Foucault. What matters is not when "periods" begin and end, but the interplay of the postmodern event and the (modern) discursive that form the tension and flux of historical time.

The Lyotardian event is that which is alluded to but deliberately untheorized in Foucault's epistemic theory. In *The Archeology of Knowledge,* for example, there is no definition of what causes the shift from one episteme to another or the character of what happens in the interruption between epistemes.[15] In light of Lyotard's theory, the shift occurs at the moment, or site, of the postmodern event. But as Lemert and Gillan note, for Foucault the event is the place of rupture in historical time. It cannot be said to be "caused," nor does it specifically "cause" something else; something so completely enmeshed in context paradoxically stands outside linear causality. Nonetheless, the event ruptures the epistemological, social, political, or linguistic norms in which it is enmeshed, and it thus opens a space for new knowledge. However, unlike Lyotard's postmodern event, the event for Foucault is not simply that which is unrepresentable in modern discourse, because to define the event this way can easily evade analysis of the real political, social, and physical consequences of the interplay between event and representation. In other words, from a Foucaultian perspective, Lyotard's "event" evades the question of power and its application on real bodies in real time. Foucault's definition of the "event" resituates it in the context of power, hatched in "moments of reversal in discourse, thought, and practice" (Lemert and Gillan 132). Lyotard centralizes the event, while Foucault to a large extent ignores it to focus instead on its consequences and reverberations; Lyotard attempts to enunciate this "unspeakable," while Foucault leaves it unsaid.

This reformulation of dialectic into unspeakable alterity has permeated the late twentieth-century historical imaginary and greatly influenced writers of metahistorical romance. Moreover, the Foucaultian and Lyotardian foregrounding of the historical event has led to a resurgence of the cult of the *sublime* unprecedented since the nineteenth-century Romantics redefined that aesthetic concept in their own century of social upheaval and uncertainty. If the Romantics materialized the sublime, relocating it from rhetorical and ethical discourse to the social and political environment, the postmoderns have historicized it.

The sublime has always been a fraught concept, primarily reworked for Europe during the eighteenth century out of the Longinian tradition. Philosophies of the sublime from the eighteenth century onward can be traced through at least two traditions, the Germanic (culminating in the eighteenth century in the philosophy of Immanuel Kant) and the English (most famously articulated by Edmund Burke) (Ashfield and de Bolla 12). Lyotard was deeply influenced by the former and published a full-length explication of Kant's discussion of the sublime and the beautiful in *Lessons on the Analytic of the Sublime* (1994). In *The Postmodern Condition,* Lyotard describes the Kantian sublime as a combination of pleasure and pain, taking place "when the imagination fails to present an object which might, if only in principle, come to match a concept" (78). In other words, the sublime exists when the imagination can conceive of an Idea but not of a presentation of that Idea, a way to make that Idea visible. The sublime is thus different from the beautiful, which is the realization of the embodiment of Idea in form. The significant feature of the sublime for Lyotard is not its inspiration of terror or ecstasy (the feature of the sublime, in contrast, seemingly most important to Edmund Burke and the British Romantic poets) but its unpresentability.

Likewise for Lyotard, the central defining characteristic of modern art is that its techniques are devoted not to presenting reality (as would be an aim of mimetic art) but to presenting "the fact that the unpresentable exists" (*The Postmodern Condition* 78), that is, to presenting the sublime: "It is in the aesthetic of the sublime that modern art (including literature) finds its impetus and the logic of avant-gardes finds its axioms" (77). Using the example of modernist painting (such as abstract expressionism, which attempts to present something negatively through its absence) Lyotard claims that the purpose of all modern art is to reveal the mechanisms and cultural sites at which the beautiful is surreptitiously substituted for the sublime, or where "derealized" reality (and, by implication, politically controlled or ideologically determined reality) replaces pure experiential reality: "Local tone, drawing, the mixing of colors, linear perspective, the nature of the support and that of the instrument, the treatment, the display, the museum: the avant-gardes are perpetually flushing out artifices of presentation which make it possible to subordinate thought to the gaze and to turn it away from the unpresentable" (79).

Even though it performs this operation, however, modern art is distinguishable from the postmodern in the degree of its commitment to "presenting the unpresentable." According to *The Postmodern Condition,* while modern aesthetics "is an aesthetic of the sublime," it is "a nostalgic one" because while it signifies that there are "missing contents" to the presentation, it contains that message within a form that still manages, in the manner of classic realism, to "give solace and pleasure" to the reader. In contrast, "The postmodern would be that which, in the modern, puts forward the unpresentable in presentation itself; that which denies itself the solace of good forms, the consensus of a taste which would make it possible to share collectively the nostalgia for the unattainable; that which searches for new presentations, not in order to enjoy them but in order to impart a stronger sense of the unpresentable" (81). The postmodern is thus the condition for articulating the sublime, for it is the modern aesthetic of the sublime unburdened of modernist nostalgia for meaning.

And it is in postmodernism then that the sublime, linked to avant-garde art as in the quote above, becomes the foundation for a liberatory politics. As commentators have noted, Lyotard thus revises the Kantian sublime in light of his own political activism and campaign against totalitarianisms, politicizing the sublime by moving it from the environment of cognition and imagination to the environment of culture.[16] Lyotard emphasizes repeatedly that this shift is figured in *narratives that resist narrative*—that is, in postmodern narrative that refuses empiricism and pursues the sublime in the interests of political and cultural resistance to totalization, to hegemony, to power. The sublime is that which stands outside of proof, empirical reason, the rule of truth, Knowledge, and narrative expression. "If early modern aesthetic innovation sought a new truth or a new way of telling the truth," Readings notes, "if late modernist innovation sought a new truth to the experience of telling, postmodern art does not seek a truth at all but seeks to testify to an event to which no truth can be assigned, that cannot be made the object of a conceptual representation [and hence co-opted]" (*Introducing Lyotard* 74).

Replacing historical sequence with a field of ruptures, the "event" transforms linear history into a plane perforated by unspeakable figures. To some extent, through the "event" Lyotard reconfigures the traditional spatial model of history—from a line to a plane, or even a set. The act of historical telling becomes refocused on the event that is unpresentable rather than on the minute study and empirical reconstruction of past actions; history becomes more about testifying to the unpresentable than about re-presenting the past.[17] This has implications for how a culture represents limit events such as the French Revolution or the Holocaust, for according to this theory, *representation itself* is what deforms history and is what must be resisted: "We have to write a history that will testify to the unrepresentable horror without representing it. . . . History, like literature, becomes the site of the recognition that there is something that cannot be said" (Readings, *Introducing Lyotard* 62). Any moral being who has viewed snapshots of the killing fields of Vietnam or the concentration camps of World War II (or the photos of carnage and violence perpetrated in Sierra Leone, printed in the October 2000 issue of *Vanity Fair,* directly following a life profile of Giorgio Armani) knows the uneasiness, even sickness, these "empirical" presentations provoke. Through the photograph, one feels dragged against one's will into participating in the humiliation of these bodies. Moreover, there is a desire to turn away from the obscenity, the photos too close to a pornographic exploitation in their attempts to "represent" these horrors.[18] What we need in these cases, writes Lyotard, is a performative history that remembers without appropriating, that stands between the space of remembering and the space of forgetting.

Of course, while this poststructuralist turn on history was seeping into and eventually irrevocably staining the late-twentieth-century historical imaginary, academic historians generally sniffed contemptuously at the poststructuralists' bad history and continued to do their work as usual. While world events of the 1960s and 1970s spawned a new poststructuralist concern about the historical past and the political present, history as an academic discipline remained notoriously conservative about its methods. Yet the attack on history had been mounted, and it has had irrevocable disciplinary consequences.

At first, the disciplinary dogfight was about the rise of U.S. and continental social history in the 1960s, a way of telling history that examined the lives of ethnic, racial, and gender groups in the Americas whose experiences complicated the U.S. work-ethic narrative of manifest destiny and upward mobility. Social historians revitalized the social context of political and intellectual figures and achievements, of disenfranchised populations such as slaves, women, and immigrants, and of specific national agendas. As a result, social historians tended to undermine methodological and philosophical assumptions entrenched in historical studies since the early nineteenth century, such as the Enlightenment-based belief that history was an empiricist study leading to a useful narrativization of archival facts about the past—namely, the kind of historical assumptions familiar to Walter Scott and the Scottish School.[19]

The social historians came to represent, and also to some extent grew out of, the "new history" in history studies. This "new history" was first associated in France with the first generation of *Annales* school historians—Henri Barr, Lucien Febvre, and Marc Bloch. The latter two men founded the journal *Annales* in 1929.[20] In the 1940s, Fernand Braudel (who directed the journal from 1956 to 1969) systematized the *Annales* objectives, and under his leadership in the 1960s the school developed a wide following in Europe and Latin America; by the 1970s the school had international influence. The *Annales* model was a "total history," an attempt to synthesize all the social sciences' topics and methods in the study of the historical past, particularly emphasizing economic and social history. Later generations of historians associated with the *Annales* school (such as Emmanuel Le Roy Ladurie, Jacques Le Goff, Pierre Nora, Roger

Chartier, and Jacques Revel) became advocates of *la nouvelle histoire,* a term used by Barr as early as 1890. *La nouvelle histoire* increasingly shifted scholarly emphasis to the study of shared mental practices or culture (*mentalités*) and raised questions about the goals and methods of historians. However, the term *new history* was most frequently associated with 1960s and 1970s revisions of history studies worldwide.

The new history, including but not limited to the *Annales* school writers, embodied a number of tenets for historical study, which have been aptly summarized by Peter Burke in *New Perspectives on Historical Writing:*

1. the old Rankean paradigm for history that had it concerned primarily with politics and the state was inadequate for the present time, and the new history would concern itself with virtually every kind of human activity. (This is the "total history" of the *Annales* historians.) This approach implicitly or explicitly asserts a cultural relativism in the sense that reality is assumed to be constructed;

2. the linear character of history was at least partially replaced by a view that understood history as interlocking structures;

3. the focus of traditional history on the actions of "great men" was replaced by a view of "history from below"—a perspective on and from the lives of ordinary people within society;

4. the traditional methodology of looking at official documents and records was expanded by a new definition of what constituted historical evidence that included visual, oral, and statistical evidence;

5. the Rankean notion of "objective history," history without bias, was replaced by a conception of history as culturally relative and heteroglossic.

From a contemporary perspective, these tenets of the new history embodied a number of assumptions that one might term *modern* or even *modernist.* For example, as Olábarri notes, all of the new histories (he sees a number of branches) share the conviction that the study of history is a social science (one thinks of T. S. Eliot's chemistry metaphor for criticism in "Tradition and the Individual Talent") and that collaboration with the other social sciences is essential; that the aim of achieving a "total history," particularly strong for marxists and *Annalistes,* is similar to the neopositivism of American "social scientific" history; that all of the new histories are more concerned with collective phenomena than with the creative role of the individual in history, and hence they evince both a kind of qualified social determinism and a predilection for structuralism; and that all of the new histories interpret the past according to the "ideology of emancipation" or the concept of progress characteristic of Enlightenment thought (9–11). (Again, one might note parallels with the emancipatory projects of the modernist avant-garde.) Even given this last characteristic, however, the new history approach was linked by traditionalist historians to a decline in the truth value of the discipline and an increasingly relativistic perspective on history that was undermining the effectiveness and social value of the field itself.

This new history led to the triumph of social history, which is now being challenged by a radical historiography informed by the writing of Foucault, Lyotard, and poststructuralist language theorists.[21] Practitioners of the so-called new history had incorporated many of the insights and methods of structuralism, often associated in the humanities with modernist approaches to cultural narratives. As such, the new history in its various forms is vulnerable to attack by a poststructuralist or post-*Annales* historiography that, like its counterpart in the humanities, questioned many of the very tenets of modernist thought.[22]

It is important, however, not to overstate this case. Different historical methods and priorities exist simultaneously in the modern disciplines—perhaps ironically testifying to Foucault's archeological claims. Though political history takes precedence from the Enlightenment onward, historical anthropology develops by its side throughout the late nineteenth century. Likewise, post-*Annales* historiography now sits uncomfortably alongside its two brethren approaches—political history and historical anthropology. Just as humanities theories in the past thirty years have been hard-pressed to articulate the actual break between modernism and postmodernism (largely failing to arrive at consensus on that point or even about whether postmodernism is distinct from modernism at all), so too it is difficult to articulate a clear distinction between the work of the new history associated with the *Annalistes* and what might be considered a poststructuralist historiography. One could cite many examples that show a continuum rather than a break between these approaches. After all, it is Jacques Le Goff, a figure prominently associated with the *Annales* school, who claims Michel Foucault as one of the greatest of the new historians (177) and who claims, "Historical facts are made and not given, and historical objectivity cannot be reduced to pure subservience to facts" (113).

Thus, many of the aims and approaches of the new history continue into a postmodern arena, amplified rather than transformed. Two general examples might suffice to illustrate this. The new history took as one of its objects the construction of a "total history" on a science model; paradoxically, however, this quest led these historians to fracture historical inquiry into numerous fields, often allied with the natural sciences, the life sciences, or the social sciences. Extended further, then, the same activity promoted by the *Annalistes* in the service of total history can become the idea that such a total history is impossible; once fragmented, the discipline of history may actually support the postmodern idea that only "histories," not "history," is possible. The *Annalistes* are not separated from the postmodernists in kind but in degree—that is, whether or not they see this fracturing as irreversible or ontological.

Another example may be the redefinition of the *event* by the new history, which relocated the focus of historical inquiry from political history to other locations such as the individual, the workplace, and the home. (This notion of *event,* one must remember, is conceived as an activity of note in the present that will be recorded as history in future accounts, and is different from the "event" conceptualized by Lyotardian poststructuralism.) While new history's relocation of the event has led to the expansion of historical fields and methodologies—creating what become known as the "history from below" approaches and increasing the influence, even authority, of the new history and the discipline—in a poststructuralist context the redefin-

ition of the historical event undermines the very integrity of historical reconstruction. Some, for instance, have argued that what constitutes an historical event in an age of CNN and infotainment has
become increasingly defined not by historians but by the media; if
the media decide what is an event worthy of documentation and
what isn't, then the event becomes increasingly aligned with partisan,
market-driven, and hence suspect forces. What will be left recorded
in the historical archives for future generations to consider as "history" will not be the real and important historical events of the time,
but rather a record of what news "sold" in our era. Redefining the
event in the context of the new history (leading to "history from below" approaches and broader definitions of what constitutes historically significant events) is only one step away from poststructuralist
historiography's questions about who controls the construction of the
historical present and to questions about the validity of historical
truth that could challenge the entire enterprise of historical inquiry
(Le Goff 212). Again, the redefinition of the event is crucial to both
la nouvelle histoire and to poststructuralist historiography, yet this act
can lead to very different perspectives on history in each.

As late as the 1990s, modern(ist) historians such as Gertrude Him-
melfarb have felt the need to decry the threat of poststructuralist philosophy to the civic function and cultural mission of historical studies. In the context of the *professional and academic discipline of history,*
however, it is still difficult to define precisely what is "poststructuralist historiography." One's answer would depend a great deal on how
one defined poststructuralism and how one understood various historians' work—and, perhaps, the emotional and professional investments one had in maintaining a certain definition of the historical
profession. Post-*Annales* historiography does seem distinguished from
previous perspectives primarily by its receptivity—in greater and lesser
degrees, depending on the theorist—to poststructuralism's focus on
language.[23] Its questions about history include questions about
whether history is knowable, how it is possible to speak the historical,
and what is the relation between rhetoric, the writing of history, and
the operations of language itself. Using this broad definitional param-

eter, it is possible to cast a wide net; such thinkers about history might include intellectual historians, literary theorists, and culture critics, among them Hayden White, F. R. Ankersmit, J. Rüsen, Michel de Certeau, and Robert Young;[24] historians and narrative theorists such as Joan Scott and Dominick LaCapra; in varying degrees, memory and trauma theorists such as Shoshana Felman and Cathy Caruth, who reframe an older psychoanalytic approach to history.

Very different in their approaches and politics, these writers have some things in common. First, all tend to some extent to question the epistemological and methodological premises of Enlightenment and Romantic historiography. Specifically, these historiographers tend to reject universalist theories of knowledge and history rooted in representational logic or an empiricism that terms history a social science akin to the pure sciences. The starting premise of post-*Annales* historiography may be rooted in Freudian psychology, Derridean language theory, Foucault's theories of history, or postmodern theories of representation; whatever the starting assumptions, the result tends to be an exposure of the scaffolding propping up Enlightenment theories of knowledge and identity and a reevaluation of Western assumptions about history that are born out of positivist, humanist, or eschatological theories. I say *reevaluation* rather than *rejection* here because to read work by de Certeau or White closely is to discover in that work a deep, sometimes existentialist commitment to social change and a desire to refrain from throwing the Enlightenment baby out with the positivistic bathwater. The commitment to social change in the work of post-*Annales* historiographers, however, tends to come not from a specific program for emancipation (such as Marxism) but through the alternative route of narrative theory and the evaluation of historical narratives as textual markers of social and disciplinary values.

Second, these historiographers tend to integrate poststructuralist theories about language and reality into their evaluation of historical process. The results are theories of history that question the difference between fiction and nonfiction; problematize the notion of objectivity by reintroducing, in a poststructuralist sense, the concept of narrative in or as history; and see the fragmentation of the object of study as a goal rather than a hindrance of historiographical inquiry.

Third, in light of globalization, the breakdown and redrawing of national boundaries, and philosophies of difference, these post-*Annales* historiographers tend to portray the possibility of a unifying, total history that is also an objective, "factual" history as an impossible empiricist dream. Totalizing views of historical process—even those of the new history—become untrustworthy in the face of increased disciplinary specialization, an impatience with political history, shifting postmodern politics and borders, and the undermining or reconceptualization of Western humanism as a defining standard of human action and thought. These theorists often assume a perspective stemming from a reformulation of the aims and methods of anthropological history and add to this the questions posed by philosophical poststructuralism.[25]

What, then, is the relationship between the postmodern historical romance and the historiography of its time? Walter Scott was influenced by the historiography of his time; likewise, historical fiction of the late twentieth century is influenced by the historiographical trends in the academic world, themselves part of the postmodern zeitgeist. In history, in philosophy, and in the arts—as well as in popular culture in debased forms—poststructuralist theories about language and history have permeated late-twentieth-century thought. Reared during the Cold War, today's novelists and intellectual historians tend to distrust institutionalized structures; writing after the cultural revolutions of the 1960s and 1970s, they tend to reject uniformitarianism in social or philosophical forms. And in numerous arenas—history, philosophy, literature—theorists reject the Real in favor of an ethicist romance, which is often figured in a return to the sublime.[26]

The Historical Sublime

Hayden White is best known for his claim that while history has been popularly and academically conceived as an objective pursuit of archival facts, history is in fact a collection of narratives by historians, and these narratives structure and are structured by specific ideological content manifested through the historians' choice of tropes, aesthetic modes, and narrative techniques. This claim was a direct response to the new history's claim—now hegemonic in history studies—that history could be pursued like a social science, and it gave rise in the 1980s and 1990s to heated discussion in *History and Theory, Clio,* and journals of literary criticism about the relation between historical inquiry and narrative emplotment.[27]

White also translated the Foucaultian event and the Lyotardian sublime into disciplinary history.[28] In "The Politics of Interpretation" (reprinted as a chapter in *The Content of the Form*), White asks what exactly transforms a field of study—in particular, the field of history—into a discipline.[29] Iterating that historians do not work from natural laws or empirical explanations that would explain historical phenomena but rather use narration to understand and interpret phenomena, White argues that this activity makes history a different kind of discipline than those in the empirical sciences. To "discipline" history, it was necessary to separate it from fiction, "especially from the kind of prose fiction represented by the romance and the novel" (*Content* 65). White further asserts that in the nineteenth century, the consolidation of history into a discipline divided what was considered a "properly disciplined historical consciousness" from "utopian thinking in all of its forms"; this historical consciousness was made synonymous with and custodian of realism in political and social thinking. Thus, in the disciplining of history, an opposition is set up between utopian thought (a precondition for a true revolutionary politics) and political thought (represented as realism and a precondition for professionalization); utopian thinking is repressed by those who wish to claim the authority of the discipline (61–63).

Putting these two disciplinary contexts for history—the political and the aesthetic—together, White argues that this disciplinizing of history "consisted in subordinating written history to the categories of the 'beautiful' and suppressing those of the 'sublime'" (*Content* 67). By excluding or proscribing certain ways of imagining historical reality—namely, those associated by Burke, Schiller, Hegel, and Kant with the sublime—history is disciplined. White emphasizes that it is Schiller who, early on, formulated a theory of the sublime imagination that correlated delight in the physical world to the attraction felt toward savagery, anarchy, and the confusion of the "spectacle" of history (68–69).[30] In contrast, Burke consistently linked historical process to the articulation and order of the beautiful (and thus could condemn the French Revolution as chaotic and monstrous). Burke's position won in the battle for history. This aesthetic supplantation of the sublime by the beautiful would later constitute a definition of the discipline of historical studies for *both* the political Left and Right.

That is, for marxists as well as for Leopold von Ranke, the writing of history depends on a historical perspective that effectively reduces the terrifying chaos of the sublime to the disciplined order of the beautiful, and thus, for White, eviscerates history's real utopian potential:

> Historical facts are politically domesticated precisely insofar as they are effectively removed from displaying any aspect of the sublime that Schiller attributed to them in his essay of 1801. By this I mean nothing more than the following: insofar as historical events and processes become understandable, as conservatives maintain, or explainable, as radicals believe them to be, they can never serve as a basis for a visionary politics more concerned to endow social life with meaning than with beauty. In my view, the theorists of the sublime had correctly divined that whatever dignity and freedom human beings could lay claim to could come only by way of what Freud called a "reaction-formation" to an apperception of history's meaninglessness. (72)

White asserts that a visionary politics intent on real social change can only convince people of its value if contrasted to the kind of history envisioned by Schiller—a sublime history manifested in spectacle and moral anarchy. The old religions knew this: their version of history contrasted a divine order to precisely this kind of vision of demonic confusion. They convinced people to change and adhere to their doctrines of change because they convincingly argued—

through persuasion, sometimes through force—that the alternative was chaos. But since the birth of modern secular societies, this religious approach to history has been revised. Secular theories of history claim that they have found the "pattern" to history and attempt to convert nonbelievers on the basis of reason, not ethics or religious devotion. The result, claims White, is that secular approaches to history lose the sense of sublime history that gave the older eschatological approaches their punch: "These ideologies deprive history of the kind of meaninglessness that alone can goad living human beings to make their lives different for themselves and their children, which is to say, to endow their lives with a meaning for which they alone are fully responsible" (*Content* 72). The existential condition resounds in this pronouncement. Since history as a discipline was birthed in the milieu of secular reason, practicing a Kantian "disinterested interest," it is removed from any kind of visionary politics and consigned to anti-utopianism (73).[31] White's metahistorical focus leads him to understand marxisms, disciplined history, and bourgeois positivist histories as all the same to the degree that they use reason to construct an analytic of history embedded in Burkean definitions of the beautiful and excluding Romantic definitions of the sublime. Romantic historians such as Michelet and Carlyle, who looked to history for sublime inspiration, were relegated to the status of "literary writers" under this analytic.

White acknowledges that the kind of sublime history he is advocating—opposed in many ways to bourgeois and Marxist histories—"is conventionally associated with the ideologies of fascist regimes" (*Content* 74). However, to White, historical approaches to the Holocaust illustrate the blindness of this accusation. These approaches fall into two categories: that which attempts to understand what happened "and simply purports to tell the truth about the past as an end in itself," and the approach that recognizes the meaninglessness of (sublime) history and prompts humans to aspire to freedom and dignity through an active response to this monstrous spectacle. The first approach is taken by disciplined historians and ironically allows for debate, based on the presentation of empirical evidence and argu-

ment, about whether the Holocaust occurred at all. That is, the first
approach is predicated on the operations of reason and its end is the
telling of the truth about an event. It thus allows for the presentation
of evidence (did the Holocaust happen? What evidence can you present
that explains why it did happen, and on what scale?) in the aim
of understanding the event.

The second approach, however, assumes that "understanding" is
impossible, that there can be no logical rationale for or cause-and-
effect logic to such unspeakable inhumanity. Constructing history as
sublime, the second approach would advocate not understanding but
action, a response of human self-preservation in the face of this horrifying and incomprehensible event.[32] Thus, the disciplining of history requires the erasure of the historical sublime, the privileging of
realism as a representation of history, and the construction of history
as narrative based on empirical evidence. Rejecting this disciplined
history, White queries that if it is possible

> to imagine a conception of history that would signal its resistance
> to the bourgeois ideology of realism by its refusal to attempt a nar-
> rativist mode for the representation of its truth, is it possible that
> this refusal itself signals a recovery of the historical sublime that
> bourgeois historiography repressed in the process of its disciplin-
> ization? And if this is or might be the case, is this recovery of the
> historical sublime a necessary precondition for the production of
> a historiography . . . "charged with avenging the people"? This
> seems plausible to me. (*Content* 81)

For White, opposition to domination means extricating oneself from
the limitations of a disciplined history. Liberation for subordinated or
emergent social groups might necessitate resisting the Enlightenment
value of "objectivity" called for by the historical profession, and the
writing of their histories may depend on the recovery or creation of
nonrealist narrative modes, as those modes have been defined in the
Western European literary tradition.

This is the point that links White to F. R. Ankersmit and Hans
Kellner, who predicate their work on his. For Ankersmit as well, history may be unrepresentable as such, understandable only as a do-

mesticated version of itself viewed through the lens of a professional-ized historiography. Ankersmit tends to use the opposition modern/postmodern to characterize the relation between a traditional, disciplinary view of history and post-1970s revisionary matrices. However, in arguing that two forms of philosophy of history are vying with one another, he notes, "One could speak simply of new philosophy of history versus traditional philosophy of history, of interpretative versus descriptivist philosophy of history, of synthetic versus analytic philosophy of history, of linguistic versus criterial philosophy of history, or, as does Hans Kellner, of postmodernist versus modernist philosophy of history. . . . I prefer the terms narrativist philosophy of history versus epistemological philosophy of history" ("The Dilemma of Contemporary Anglo-Saxon Philosophy of History" 1).

Significantly, Ankersmit links postmodernism to nostalgia as a more sophisticated and consistent form of historism. Nostalgia is related to an awareness of being displaced. It urges us to undo this displacement, though we know this to be impossible. It incorporates aesthetic desire as part of the quest for history and is a strange mixture of happiness and disappointment that does not attempt to relive the past but rather recognizes the difference between the present and the past. Nostalgia constructs a past that is static and silent and resistant to the patterning and clarifying tendencies of historism (*History and Tropology* 190–98). This has implications for the writing of history: if historical writing wants to be true to historical experience, "it will necessarily repeat at the level of historical representation the features of the fragmented, the contingent, and the isolated" (211).

White's formulation of the historical sublime also is a secularized version of Ricoeur's perception of history. In "The History of Philosophy and Historicity," Ricoeur writes, "It is necessary to say that history is history only to the extent that it has reached neither absolute discourse [i.e., metanarrative] nor absolute singularity [i.e., the unnarrativized fact]—to the extent that the meaning of it remains confused and entangled. . . . the historical is precisely that which cannot occur" (76, 77). Ricoeur (like White) attempts to salvage the activity of "making history" from relativist claims, in the face of infinitely proliferating details, that history can't be known and therefore doesn't matter *and* from disciplinary dogmatism that claims an empiricist path to truth. For Ricoeur, however, the "space between" these two approaches to history is overtly linked to Christian eschatology, for to Ricoeur this "space between" must be the space of hope, which for him can only exist in the religious realm of infinite becoming.

White vehemently rejects both of these ideas—the Christian paradigm for history as well as modern faith in social or historical progress. Yet his conception of the "historical sublime" does incorporate a wedding of the aesthetic and the ethical. The form of ideal Being he envisions results from humankind's confrontation with the historical sublime, as unsettling or disruptive as that confrontation may be. The *historical sublime* is the space of History beyond current human events, the space of the past. Like Tolstoy's History, this space is unknowable by human agents, but White's History is unnarrativized, alogical, unorganized, nonrational. History is sublime because it is both unknowable and unrepresentable in discourse; it is the space of the chaotic, and hence to rational beings, the terrifying, past.

As such, it can lead to contemplation and enactment of ethical action. This is a secularization rather than a rejection of Ricoeur's Christian history. Ricoeur argues that the

> meaning of history, however, remains an object of faith. . . . Faith in meaning, but in a meaning hidden from history, is thus both the *courage* to believe in a profound significance of the most tragic history (and therefore a feeling of confidence and resignation in the very heart of conflict) and a certain rejection of system and fanaticism, a sense of the *open.*
>
> But in return, it is essential that hope always remains in direct contact with the dramatic, disquieting aspect of history. It is precisely when hope is no longer the hidden meaning of an apparent nonsense, when it has freed itself from all ambiguity, that it comes back to rational and reassuring progress and heads toward stagnant abstractions. Thus it is necessary to remain attentive to this existential schema of historical ambiguity, situated between the rational schema of progress and the suprarational schema of hope. ("Christianity and the Meaning of History" 94, 96–97)

For Ricoeur, hope is true history; it is the space between one and zero, the Zone that stands between dead empiricism and religious fundamentalism. White's theory of the "historical sublime" is a similar faith in meaning that attempts to find the space between theology and empiricism, but it rejects the theological implications of this faith. Both theories posit that only through a recognition of the sublimity of History can hope exist in the face of political history.

The discourse of the sublime thus allows post-*Annales* historiography a way to reassert ethics, history, and value while maintaining a distance from religion. But the historical sublime is the "secular-sacred," the space of desire that is paradoxically located in the "space between"—or, as I argue in chapter 2, the space beyond—*both* the ambiguity and relativism of disciplinary history *and* the dogmatism of totalizing history in theological and empirical contexts. Freedom consists in reestablishing the relation between self and history through a radical interrogation of disciplinary scientism and a new understanding of the cultural power of *poesis*.[33]

We have come back to Lyotard and the discourse of the sublime, the point of intersection between a certain strain of contemporary historiography and a certain kind of poststructuralist theory. Lyotard's assertion that "it is our [the postmodern's] business not to supply reality but to invent allusions to the conceivable which cannot be presented" (*The Postmodern Condition* 81) is a direct correlative to White's injunction of the historical sublime. One hears echoes of White's advocacy in Lyotard's own rhetoric: "We have paid a high enough price for the nostalgia of the whole and the one, for the reconciliation of the concept and the sensible, of the transparent and the communicable experience. . . . Let us wage a war on totality; let us be witnesses to the unpresentable; let us activate the differences and save the honor of the name" (81–82). White and Lyotard both resuscitate the idea of a historical sublime as secular-sacred knowledge and Other to modernity. Both attempt to combine a social-justice agenda with an aesthetics of history through an investiture in desire, the desire actualized in the quest for the spectral sublime, which is also, oddly, the quest for freedom, for certainty, for belief.

To call up the sublime in relation to history is to dance in a field checkered with live political and theoretical mines. From the Left and the Right comes contempt for what is called aestheticism, "ivory tower" thinking, the apolitical, or a return to pre-Enlightenment religiosity.[34] Three typical objections are raised when the sublime or the aesthetic is linked to history. All of them are formidable. The first relates to ethics and raises the question of the ethical implications of a sublime conceived as "unspeakable" and the utilitarian value of such a concept in relation to real-life dilemmas and ethical quandaries. The second relates to the political, in particular to what has been termed *identity politics,* and raises the question of how the aesthetic and the notion of the sublime conceive of the possibility of freedom for disenfranchised and enslaved people. This second objection also raises the point, difficult to dispute, that positing the aesthetic as a sphere of value carves out spaces that are not (or not easily) analyzable in terms of power and its functioning in society. The third objection relates to the philosophical tradition itself and asks why the concept of the aesthetic is needed at all, given other methods of approaching art that seem more situated in medium specificity. One of the traditional problems of invoking the aesthetic is that it tends to reject the corporeal as absolute ground—be that corporeality figured in terms of the human body (allied for some analysts with human reason) or the materialist body politic. Moreover, this discourse tends to advocate a search for a noncorporeal space figured as language itself or as the imagination.

While one needs to be very much aware of the problematical philosophical history of this signifier in Plato through Shaftesbury and Kant and Burke to Adorno and Bataille, there is a need to recognize that in literary studies, whether or not such a historical sublime exists is less relevant than whether a literary text *posits* its existence. It is not necessary to answer the three kinds of objections to the historical sublime, objections that seem perfectly reasonable on many levels, in order to examine how post-1960s fiction is another arena where the historical sublime seems posited. It is important, however, to recognize how the historical sublime merges and contributes to the move toward "postsecularist" thinking at the end of the twentieth century.[35] Just as the dominant views about history influenced Scott and later writers of traditional historical romance, the historical romance that is written after 1960 is strongly influenced by the historiographical debates of its time. Moreover, one specific kind of historiography seems particularly influential in respect to First World, post-1960s literature and the historical novel genre: that which is exemplified in Lyotard's and White's philosophies of history. The place of intersection between Lyotard's postmodernism and White's post-*Annales* history is the territory of the metahistorical romance; after 1960, there is a conjoining of poststructuralist theory, post-*Annales* historiography, and postmodern fiction at the nexus of the historical sublime.

Postmodernist historical romances—what I hereafter call "metahistorical romances"—signal not only their own generic self-reflexivity but also their link to the "metahistory" of post-*Annales* historiography. In them, romance is linked to the sublime as it was in Scott's fiction. Like post-*Annales* historiography and Lyotard's postmodernism, metahistorical romances seem to move toward a desired, secular-sacred ontology that is History. They differ from Scott's historical romances in their presentation of romance and the sublime in that they tend not to elegize a specific institution or phase of culture from the past. Yet the metahistorical romance *does* continue to link the sublime and romance to the political in other ways.

2

The Metahistorical Romance and the Historical Sublime

> But it is Kali-Yuga; the children of the hour of darkness were born, I'm afraid, in the midst of the age of darkness; so that although we found it easy to be brilliant, we were always confused about being good.
> —Salman Rushdie, *Midnight's Children*

The postmodernist sensibility revels in linguistic play and raucous deconstruction of authoritative discourses. While postmodernist novels such as Robert Coover's "historical novel" *The Public Burning* can be carnivalesque, often in these kinds of novels the play is serious, an installation of irony *and* a search for an escape from irony into a genuine yet mature universe of belief. Throughout post-1960s art—even in Pop art and metafiction—there has been a serious strain of inquiry into the notion of origins, the character of history, and the place of the self within culture.

In metahistorical romance, techniques such as metafictionality, achronology, use of popular culture genres, and carnivalization are used consistently to defamiliarize history and the process of historical writing. Often, these novels' avant-gardist styles force readers to think about history in new ways. To some critics, these techniques signal postmodern fiction's transformation of history into depthless pastiche, the motivated play of late capitalist culture. In his famous formulation of "pastiche," Fredric Jameson has argued that instead of provoking analysis, these novels use irony to evacuate history of meaning and actually create an anti-intellectual, nihilistic disillusionment about historical knowledge that is the negative twin to the happy anti-intellectual ahistoricism of Disneyland and MTV. Both use history as "clip art" and thus collude with capitalism's reduction of history to surface image without cultural meaning or revolutionary potential. However, this seems hard to justify when examining texts such as T. Coraghessan Boyle's *The Road to Wellville* (1993), Robert Coover's *The Public Burning* (1976), Max Apple's *The Propheteers* (1987), or Richard Powers's *Gain* (1998), all texts that explicitly focus on and lambast the interrelation of capital, U.S. nationalist mythologies, and the creation of modern subjectivity. Apple's text, for instance, is a scathing indictment of Disneyland itself, showing through the depiction of Howard Johnson, Walt Disney, and Mrs. Margery Post Merriweather how capital constructs desire that is synonymous with *thanatos*. Like Apple's novel, *The Road to Wellville* plays with the idea of capitalist "consumption," as a synonym for sickness (a tubercular malignancy) that masks itself as health and can be purchased or consumed (as in spas). Even texts that have become *exempli* of postmodern narrative technique, such as Thomas Pynchon's *Gravity's Rainbow,* may be less pastiche than a search for "nongrounded" meaning. If the pursuit of knowledge in the twentieth century has led again and again to dogmatism and constriction of individual and collective freedoms—one could point, for instance, to the consequence of nineteenth- and twentieth-century race "science," to the atom bomb, to the real, material consequences to individual freedom in all societies that have subscribed to Marxist "science of history," to the selective freedom bestowed on some but not less fortunate others in theorized democracies—one can at least understand why the West is tired of trying to think its way to freedom.

Intellectuals and artists after 1960 in the United States and other "First World" nations seem desperate to find a "cognitive map" for history that is somewhere between science and myth, between pure empiricism and pure fantasy. They pursue meaning even after a century of documented corruption, war, genocide, and other evils have shown how such a pursuit of "meaning" and "order" can lead to hideous human actions and ingeniously repressive social institutions. In literature, the turn to history at the end of the twentieth century signals this desire to rediscover meaning, to make sense of the Void, in a way that potentially avoids the mistakes of the past.

The questions that need to be explored further are two. First, why does postmodern "historical" fiction attack history? That is, do these novels aim only to deconstruct Western Enlightenment models of history (and if so, how does this work, exactly, in the fiction?) or are the metahistorical impulses of this fiction also constructive of something, some meaningful way of viewing the historical past? Second, in what relation does avant-gardist historical fiction primarily from the 1960s and 1970s stand to later, often more realist, "historical" fiction of the century such as Toni Morrison's *Beloved*, Leslie Marmon Silko's *Almanac of the Dead*, Jane Smiley's *The All-True Travels and Adventures of Lidie Newton*, Anthony Burgess's *A Dead Man in Deptford*, or Charles Johnson's *Dreamer?*

I am claiming that in the metahistorical romance, as in post-*Annales* historiography and postmodern theory, serious poststructuralist play is linked to the invocation of the historical sublime as both a gesture of interrogation and a gesture of assertion. The metahistorical romance tries to resuscitate the sublime (in the form of the *historical sublime*) precisely in the context that the Kantian sublime and aesthetics traditionally have avoided, subsumed, or repressed—that is, in the context of the political. The relation between the metahistorical romance and the historical novel tradition can be stated in four related propositions:

Proposition 1: The postmodern historical imagination, as a post-traumatic imaginary, confronts rather than represses the historical sublime.

Proposition 2: The metahistorical romance confronts the historical sublime as repetition and deferral.

Proposition 3: The motivation for this movement and unceasing deferral of a historical ground in the metahistorical romance is a simultaneous distrust and assertion of *fabula* as a humanist value.

Proposition 4: The metahistorical romance learns from the texts of the literary modernists to combine metahistoricity with narrative form, but for the postmodernists this metahistoricity is situated differently as a tropological reversal of the historical romance genre.

Proposition 1
The postmodern historical imagination, as a post-traumatic imaginary, confronts rather than represses the historical sublime.

The twentieth century was not only one of the most violent in human history; in the twentieth century the West also saw its traditional humanist values inverted, displaced, and, more importantly, documented as the horrors of Stalinism, the Nazi political machine, atomic war, the gulags. As the century draws to a close, a spirit of millennial self-examination has gripped segments of the academic and literary First World, and this is combined with a felt urgency to record the testimonies of the now expiring generations who experienced the century's atrocities and who can for a brief time longer tell of them in testimony that can warn and instruct future generations. For the Anglo-European West, this is particularly true in relation to Holocaust survivors. Jane Bellamy, Michael André Bernstein, Cathy Caruth, Saul Friedlander, Marianne Hirsch, Dominick LaCapra, and numerous other literary theorists and intellectual historians are attempting to understand the Holocaust in terms of its cultural, social, moral, ethical, and psychological implications as well as its relation to other historical acts of genocide.[1] Recent studies have attempted not only to come to terms with the implications and consequences of the Shoah but also to theorize social trauma itself in relation to history. These studies ask questions such as, What is a limit event in sociocultural terms? What is the relationship between history and memory? What are the consequences of the limit event on historical reconstruction of the past or on definitions of history itself? Can we, and if so how can we, theorize trauma, or traumatic history, or the traumatized self in history? How can a traumatic limit event be narrativized as history?

This focus on trauma and history is a symptomatic reading of history in the First World, and it may open new approaches to metahistorical fiction published since 1960. While Michael André Bernstein makes a good point by warning that it can be dangerous to situate historical events in a progressive narrative that allows us to see some events "foreshadowed" and others "backshadowed" in history, nonetheless it seems that postmodernist historical fiction grew out of turmoil of post-1945 world events and might be thought of as participating in a post-traumatic imaginary. To say this is not to imply that other historical periods didn't experience trauma. To say this is to imply that genre matters historically, that certain forms of art can be understood at one level to be expressions of as well as resistances to the events and ideologies of their historical time and place. The postmodern historical imagination has a time and place in post–World War II First World history. In the United States, this kind of fiction emerges in the aftermath of World War II and the shattering unsettlements for Anglo-European and Anglo-American political and cultural mythologies not only of the war itself, the bombing of Japan, and the atrocities associated with Nazi and other fascist regimes, but also of the rise of communism and the Cold War, the wars in Korea and Vietnam, the violent sociocultural upheaval of the international student movements throughout the 1960s and 1970s, the U.S. civil rights movement, fights for women's liberation, AIDS, and the surreality of First World politics following Watergate, Thatcherism, the Reagan administration, political spin, and the increased visibility of religious and political fundamentalisms. The form emerges as the United States assumes its role as a world power and as capitalism tentacles outward to become global and hegemonic. The metahistorical romance also arises after Freud, at a time when the idea of trauma as a social and as a psychic process has become part of the cultural consciousness and vocabulary, and when in particular literary artists and critics in the United States and Great Britain are becoming increasingly self-reflexive about their own countries' histories as colonial, Anglo, androcentric, and protocapitalist nations.

The First World, particularly the United States in this context, constructs itself within an imagined community that is "under fire," exposed, and damaged, even as its economic power and cultural influence become world paradigms. The metahistorical romance tends to focus on very politicized issues of identity—specifically race, class, and gender identity as well as the problem of subjectivity itself—in relation to culture and historical contexts. Linda Hutcheon and other critics see this as the political content of the metahistorical romance, and constructing this content in this way often leads to a conclusion that postmodern historical fiction is compromised by internal political contradictions. This is correct; however, in addition to understanding the metahistorical romance as a compromised politics, we might need to recognize it as an interpellation of a shifting ideology, one that represents itself in the image of a traumatized consciousness. What is shifting and is imaged as traumatized, generally speaking, is the post-Enlightenment, Anglo, androcentric consciousness of the West. More specifically, what the First World seems to be approaching in the aftermath of two world wars, the Cold War, and the real as well as metaphysical devastation of Hiroshima and the Holocaust is the need to address its own history as a psychic, social, and ideological problem.

What this implies is a shift, one that reveals part of the ideology structuring social life at precisely the historical moment that democracy and capital gain globalizing force. In the late twentieth-century's narrative art as well as in its theoretical musings, what we see is an attempt to resist ideology but also acknowledge the impossibility of this resistance, to construct a narrative about Being in the world that is an alternative to *both* the modern cultural narrative of First World progress and liberation *and* the modernist First World antinarrative of meaninglessness, socially disengaged psychic alienation, or presentist anti-history. Faced with the failures of its own modern project—internally, for example, in the Nazi machine of World War II, and externally in the revelations of colonialism's contradictions and antiliberatory horrors—a segment of the West acknowledges the possibility of traumatic history and struggles to articulate it through the vehicle of metahistorical romance.

This is not to assert, as the political Right does in the United States, that cultural politics is turning everybody into a victim and that victimhood has become the marker of identity for the political Left and culture critics. The metahistorical romance tends not to portray individuals as unproblematically victimized, and I do not want to anthropomorphize the narrative form by implying that it itself is "a victim."[2] Seeing the metahistorical romance as a narrative form that uniquely attempts to articulate a post-traumatic imaginary, however, does open up a new critical approach to this fiction that can potentially integrate a historicist with a formalist analysis. As Efraim Sicher notes, "The shadow of the Holocaust, together with the mushroom cloud over Hiroshima, has thus fallen on our understanding of history, language, and literature. It informs the reading of previous texts and the writing of new texts in all the arts" ("The Holocaust in the Postmodernist Era" 304).

How does the metahistorical romance, a narrative form that participates in a Western post-traumatic "imagined community," present history? The historical fiction written after 1960, the fiction that I call *metahistorical romance,* is narrative that bears striking similarities to those produced by traumatized consciousness: it is fragmented; it problematizes memory; it is suspicious of empiricism as a nonethical resistance to "working through"; it presents competing versions of past events; it is resistant to closure; and it reveals a repetition compulsion in relation to the historical past. One thinks easily of examples: of the narrative fragmentation of metahistorical romances such as D. M. Thomas's *The White Hotel;* the problematization of personal memory in Graham Swift's *Waterland* or cultural memory in Robert Coover's *The Public Burning;* the suspicion of empiricism in Peter Ackroyd's *Hawksmoor;* the resistance to closure in Thomas Pynchon's *Gravity's Rainbow;* the repetition compulsion of memory in Art Spiegelman's *Maus: A Survivor's Tale* or Toni Morrison's *Beloved.*

I believe that the metahistorical romance is paradoxically a post-traumatic narrative that resists a narrativist mode of history (and the "bourgeois ideology of realism" bespoken by Hayden White). Writers of metahistorical romance, like writers of its predecessor the historical romance, look to the past to provide meaning for the present and to ask questions about what history in itself is. However, unlike writers of the classic historical romance, they tend not to turn to empiricist history in order to answer those questions because it is precisely this Enlightenment-based model that is under attack. The *postmodernist* gesture of metahistorical romance is to turn to the critique of realism that is always inherent in romance, which is the critique provided by fabulation. Its *metahistorical* gesture is to recuperate the sublime as an aestheticization of History. It posits the sublime not as metaphysical or divine sublimity but rather as the *historical sublime*. The metahistorical romance turns to the historical space paradoxically beyond history—beyond representation, beyond the present, beyond the mind. History must be felt as a state of "the mind without the mind" that Lyotard, speaking of art and music, writes is the territory of "the Sublime," a territory fraught with desire, anxiety, and a sense of loss: "This presence [of the Sublime] in the absence of an active mind is never anything but timbre, tone, nuance . . . the event of a passion, of a suffering for which the mind won't have been prepared, which will have left it at a loss, and for which it only retains the feeling—anxiety and jubilation—of an obscure debt" ("After the Sublime" 302).

The metahistorical romance does not articulate the historical sublime (articulation of sublimity is by definition impossible) or witness as a convert on its behalf but instead "feels it as an obscure debt." It gestures toward the sublime and attempts to enunciate the boundary or limit where lived human existence meets the past. What we live is the present; what we remember is the past; what is beyond that is History, and for all the efforts of scholars and researchers and novelists, History is untouchable, ultimately unknowable, and excruciatingly tantalizing as well as terrifying, for there resides Truth. *Truth* in this idealist sense is opposed to, or other to, the materiality of lived history.[3]

What writers of metahistorical romance attempt is the "acting out" as well as the "working through" of historical trauma, defined in idealist terms. Historical trauma for the metahistorical imagination is the West's awareness of its own history and its confrontation with what seem to be failures of the Enlightenment/modern project. The metahistorical romances examined in this book imply that this "working through" must be perpetual, for it can only be built on the Kantian idea that freedom is a regulative idea, a goal to be perpetually attempted rather than concretized in rule, state, or ideology. The metahistorical romance looks at Western history with a critical eye. It seems to assert the historical sublime (of a piece with that defined by Hayden White) as an alternative to both Western progressivism and Western nihilism, as a "secular sacred" conception of history opposed to a disciplinized history that attempts to make sense of the past. To the post-traumatic First World cultural consciousness, the acknowledgment of history's sublime nonsensibility and unknowability may be one of only a very few secular beliefs possible after the monstrous spectacle of history in the twentieth century. It may be a beleaguered return to the gods after Nietzsche; it indubitably is symptomatic of the Anglo-European West's exhaustion with and distrust of empiricism after two centuries of documented genocidal wars throughout and between Westernized nations.[4]

In *Representing the Holocaust,* Dominick LaCapra speaks specifically about testimony by trauma survivors and how victims of trauma may "work through" their experiences in historical time. LaCapra rightly seems to have little patience for "massive generalizations about modernity" and the construction of all of history as trauma with "no alternative to symptomatic acting-out and the repetition compulsion other than an imaginary, illusory hope for totalization, full closure, and redemptive meaning" (*Representing the Holocaust* 197, 193). Yet ironically, LaCapra's statement defining what a narrative that depicts a "working through" of trauma might *be* is as close to a description of metahistorical romance as any I've seen:

> The nonfetishistic narrative that resists ideology would involve an active acknowledgment and to some extent an acting out of trauma with the irredeemable losses it brings, and it would indicate its own implication in repetitive processes it cannot entirely transcend. But it would also attempt to conjoin trauma with the

possibility of retrieval of desirable aspects of the past that might be of some use in counteracting trauma's extreme effects and in rebuilding individual and social life. This effort would be deeply problematic and, particularly for nonvictims, easily subject to ideological abuse. But it should not simply be foreclosed through an overly restricted conception of possibilities. (199–200)[5]

Rather than asserting a modernist alienation from history-as-trauma *or* maintaining the fiction of disciplinized history as a knowable space accessible to the rational subject through empirical study, the metahistorical romance accepts and projects a conception of upper-case *H* History, History as the receded, never-to-be-accessed sublime realm of Truth that can be yearned for and glimpsed beyond politicized, biased, incomplete attempts to capture it. Different from Hegel's History in that it has no motivation or dialectical movement, this postmodern, "postsecular" History nonetheless partakes of the spiritual. It is the realm of terror, of chaos, but also the realm of potential revelation. But it also refuses the modernist flight from history; it is highly politicized art. Its secular-sacred conception of History is indeed deeply problematic and easily subject to ideological abuse even as it offers the West a new (or old) possible relation to the past.

Proposition 2
The metahistorical romance confronts the historical sublime as repetition and deferral.

The metahistorical romance certainly inherits a modernist tradition in its turn toward the secular sacred. Modernist artists also often saw Western aesthetics and values as compromised or even shattered, and they also consequently moved toward pre-Western or non-Western cultures and returned to myth. In literature, for example, this is most notably seen in T. S. Eliot's "mythical method" as a kind of imagist technique and an assertion of a secular/spiritual a priori that the mind could reach through art. Postmodernists also turn back to myth in a way, but they turn back to a mythic apprehension of history and time itself. They tend to do so not literally, as the modernists did by invoking cultural myths and mythic time as it would be manifested in mythic allusions (as in Joyce's *Ulysses*), a religious experience or spiritual quest (as in Eliot's *Four Quartets*) or the experience of art (as in, for instance, Yeats's "Sailing to Byzantium"). In its search for the *mythos* in and meaning of history, the metahistorical romance seems actually to reverse the trajectory and goal of the modernist search. The postmodern historical sublime is not the place of modernist stability and centered meaning, the sublime Presence; the historical sublime is not invoked in order to construct a stable center outside of political history. For the postmodernists, the historical sublime (at least as articulated by Lyotard, White, and others) seems to be the opposite of the modernists' still, stable point: it is the place where history cannot be fathomed at all, or is perceived as a sublime and decentered Absence, in all of its terrifying, chaotic, and humbling incomprehensibility.[6]

If this is so, the postmodernists predicate their history on Absence in a manner congenial to the post-Einsteinian physical universe in which they live. Metahistorical texts such as Italo Calvino's short story "All at One Point" or Jeanette Winterson's novel *Sexing the Cherry*, for example, overtly develop connections between time in a post-Einsteinian, quantum universe and a pre-Newtonian, mythic sense of history. In Calvino's comic short story, readers find human characters occupying one point in space, before the Big Bang has occurred. Since all of the universe is concentrated at one point, time stands still: "neither before nor after existed" (44). Yet Calvino plays with the similarities between this time and our own, populating this space with late-twentieth-century immigrants, lovers, cleaning women, and household appliances. In this time and our own, the story implies, time/history is constituted similarly: as human "matter" located in specific space rather than abstract linear, and often teleological, time. But in this story the humanity within the still single "point" does not have height, width, or dimension; it is Presence as Absence, there but *not* there as well. More important, the Presence at the heart of the Point can only have real meaning when it can escape from that Point, when the Point is blown apart in the Big Bang.

At the heart of this story seems to be an allegory about modernist presence and its inability to have real effects in real time as well as an allegory about how there can be only a "point" to history when history does not lie "all at one point" outside of time. When meaning lies "all at one point," it is latent meaning, kinetic potential. Only when history escapes from the unknowable past into the present as narrated, human history can it have political and ethical meaning, yet it is then no longer History, but secular myth. In a very different style, *Sexing the Cherry* presents two epigraphs that alert readers to a similar dual focus on non-Western concepts of time and post-Einsteinian science:

> The Hopi, an Indian tribe, have a language as sophisticated as ours, but no tenses for past, present and future. The division does not exist. What does this say about time?

> Matter, that thing the most solid and the well-known, which you are holding in your hands and which makes up your body, is now known to be mostly empty space. Empty space and points of light. What does this say about the reality of the world?

Winterson's epigraphs indicate a preoccupation with time and space, conceptualizations specifically linking non-Western epistemologies to post-Einsteinian physics. The novel itself, set in a fantasized seventeenth-century England, situates this preoccupation within the arena of narrativized historiography. What the epigraphs assert most forcibly is that Absence can have both mythic and rational/scientific meaning.

Both of these works illustrate how the metahistorical romance forms a double-pronged critique of Western teleological or progressivist history *and* of the West's more disciplinized historical studies. On the one hand, that is, like the modernists, the metahistorical romancers recuperate a sense of mythic, spatialized time that preceded Western scientific, linear time. The sense of myth recuperated in metahistorical romances differs, of course, from true explanatory myths such as creation or origin stories or religion-born cosmologies, at the least because it is based on secular philosophies. The term *secular-sacred* thus is a better descriptor than *mythic* to define metahistorical history. Metahistorical romances construct a conception of time that shares much in common with "mythic time," but they also reject or challenge notions of millennialism, teleology, and ontological value that living religious myths tend to construct. This is an activity they share with postmodern historiography, and this is, I believe, their recuperation of the historical sublime as a kind of "secular sacred."[7]

At the same time, however, the metahistorical romance correlates a sense of mythic time to Einsteinian quantum time/space, which (like myth) also dismantles Newtonian categories of time, space, and history. Again and again, as in these works by Calvino and Winterson (or in Winterson's later novel *Gut Symmetries,* Thomas Pynchon's *The Crying of Lot 49,* or any *Star Trek* episode), quantum space/time can become a metaphoric referent for historiographic inquiry.[8] The upshot, then, is that the metahistorical romance launches a double-pronged attack on Enlightenment history by quoting that which preceded it (myth) and that which followed and may redefine it (quantum science). Enlightenment history is flanked by postmodernism in a classic war maneuver.

Why the need for this two-sided and perhaps self-contradictory attack? The answer may lie in postmodernist art's constant search for methods of interrogation that avoid the trap of representation, that attempt to posit bounded meaning in the face of Absence. In an important and often overlooked article published in 1977, David Carroll noted that the structuralism of Sartre, Lévi-Strauss, and Barthes originated in opposition to a historicist sense of evolutionary history, but that most theorists misunderstand how "linearity and closed space are interdependent concepts rather than absolute and uncommunicating opposites." This is significant because the synchronic/diachronic historical opposition masks the reality that "the simultaneity attributed to space and the linearity attributed to time are both effects of *presence,* means of reappropriating the present in its integrity and imposing a final sense on temporal and spatial configurations" (800–801). To simply oppose linear models with spatial ones is not only impossible for the novel, predicated as it is on linear reading patterns (as, for instance, painting is not). To do so is also to continue to participate in exactly the system of representation one is attempting to deconstruct. For example, when Henry Ford famously intoned, "History is bunk," he did not repudiate representational history; the capitalist denial of history is simply the mirror image of the Marxist insistence on history as foundational. In contrast, a deconstructive approach to history would reverse hierarchies but also contaminate them, revealing the binary oppositions upon which they are predicated to be provisional, arbitrary, and motivated by the constraints of language or power rather than by a natural and ontological a priori. At best, what one gets as a result is History *sous rature.* This may account for why the metahistorical novel often references both pre-Newtonian and post-Newtonian categories in its challenge to Enlightenment history. Self-contradictory as this activity is (you can't have it both ways—Ptolemy wasn't Einstein), it effectively disrupts the tendency of representation to construct new paradigms or clean binary oppositions.

The distinction is a fine but important one. Metahistorical romances do not recuperate the modernist "still point" of history, the place of static Presence, but rather gesture toward the fluid Absence that is the historical sublime, a place at the borders of time that is *History itself.*[9] Because the historical sublime is spoken of as antithetical to, or outside of, representation, and because it is precisely a sense of the past that eludes capture within definitional parameters, one cannot speak of it as a territory beyond or at the center of representation. To indicate a beyond or a center is to indicate a border, a place of exchange between the knowable present and the unknowable past. But the past is not a place, it is a concept; the only border to traverse is the border of language itself. How then can fiction represent this space that is not a space, the conceptual space History? If the metahistorical romance jettisons the assumptions of disciplined, rationalist history (e.g., the assumption that we can reconstruct the past or at least a clear sense of it from the accumulation and interpretation of objective facts), then what does it assert as the relation between the present and this preceding but silent past?

Writers of metahistorical romance seem to intuit this dilemma and solve it by rejecting the notion of border and replacing it with the action of deferral. A nondialectical relation is established in this place of deferral, a boundary between a static and unspeakable historical past (History) and a dynamic historical present. The relation between sublime and political history is a mime of the movement of the aesthetic toward the sublime. The past as past may be sublime History, unspeakable or outside representation, but it also presents *différance,* its identity or essence both unremittingly different and ceaselessly deferred from the present. As they approach their own imaginative limit at the border of the historical sublime, writers of metahistorical romance narrate history only to glimpse the limits of history's narrativity, in a process similar to the approach of the aesthetic to the sublime: "At the limit, there is no longer either figure or figuration or form. . . . At the limit, one does not *pass* on. But it is there that *everything* comes to pass, it is there that the totality of the unlimited plays itself out, as *that which throws into mutual relief the two borders, external and internal, of all figures,* adjoining them and separating them, *delimiting and unlimiting the limit thus in a single gesture*" (Nancy, "The Sublime Offering" 41).[10] This is why Lyotard writes that "allusion . . . is perhaps a form of expression indispensable to the works which belong to an aesthetic of the sublime" (*The Postmodern Condition* 80). Allusion is the presenting of the unpresentable without presentation—another way of saying that allusion is reference that defers reference. Through its operation of deferral, the metahistorical romance can invert the notion of margin and center: the margin of history, the border, is what defines the center, History itself. In the context of metahistorical postmodernism, History is the marginalized center, always deferred in the operation at the hermeneutical border.

In other words, the postmodernism of the metahistorical romance thus is located in its resuscitation of the notion of the sublime (in the form of the historical sublime) precisely in the political and ethical contexts that the sublime and the discourse about the aesthetic traditionally have avoided, subsumed, or repressed—i.e., in the context of the political. That is, in the face of traumatic twentieth-century history, secular postmodernists turn to the historical sublime to attempt reconnection with ethical meaning and creative Being in the absence of the Word (after Nietzsche, after twentieth-century political history, after the supposed disappearance of God). Recognizing Fredric Jameson's famous pronouncement in *The Political Unconscious* that "history is what hurts," postmodern metahistory and marxisms move in different directions to stop that hurt from hurting. That is, both marxism and the discourse of the postmodern historical sublime have as their goals the attainment of a position outside or beyond history, defined as *that which hurts*. For metahistory of the kind described by Hayden White, action in the present is the operation of confronting the fluid border of knowable history; confrontation with the historical sublime in the face of history that hurts leads to ethical action.[11]

One could claim that because the metahistorical romance refuses to allow myth to escape from politics, it gets caught in an endless deferral of meaning, an endless search for History that always turns back on itself and back on the seeker. For instance, in Charles Johnson's novel *Dreamer*, myths from various traditions are melded with the politics of race through the figure of Martin Luther King Jr., the focus of the book. Johnson sets the novel's action in the worst phase of King's career, his Chicago campaigns, and at the time period directly before his assassination. This allows Johnson to present (and implicitly comment upon) different political factions involved in the 1960s race conflict, from CORE to Black Power, and also fictionally to expose the worst of the hatred on both sides of the racial divide. In addition, because King and his doppelgänger, Chaym Smith, are from different classes and life experiences, their juxtaposition allows Johnson numerous opportunities to comment on the relationship between class and race politics. In addition, however, King and Smith represent a gnostic bifurcation of the Judeo-Christian deity or, as the text makes explicit, the figures of Cain and Abel from the Book of Genesis. Smith is well trained in half a dozen world religions and is particularly well versed in Eastern philosophy; King has the same religious range, a brilliant if book-learned student of theology and intellectual history. Both characters yearn for meaning, justice, and peace; both grapple throughout the book with their own desire to escape politics and commitment to human community and spend the rest of their lives pursuing enlightenment. Neither character can, or ultimately chooses, to do this. Both enter the political fray, sacrificing the personal to the political while feeling themselves torn apart by longing for, and intimations of, the sublime.

The two characters give Johnson ample opportunity to explore the desire for transcendence characterizing a traumatized American consciousness. If Johnson wanted to write a political satire or a historical novel about the civil rights era, he could do so without invoking the mythic structure that he does; similarly, he could have written a novel about religious belief without invoking King. In the figure of Martin Luther King Jr., however, Johnson finds exactly the juxtaposition of the political and the transcendent that can form a crucial tension at the heart of his novel. The novel is pulled in two directions at once: toward the political and toward the historical sublime. In *Dreamer,* the divide between the political world and the transcendent realm is clear, but determining who is associated with which becomes complicated, because King and Smith each feel the yearning to enter—or escape to—both worlds. (For King, entering the political at the expense of the transcendent would be an escape; for Smith, the reverse is true.) Yet Johnson's construction of the doppelgänger figure does allow him to throw the iconic King into high relief. Smith is an uncanny duplication of the real that reverses its image but also highlights it in the manner of a shadow to a light.

Similarly, in Jim Crace's novel *Quarantine*, the sublime is starkly juxtaposed to the politics of history and material culture. The novel tells the story of Christ's forty-day fast in the desert wilderness, where, according to biblical account, he was tempted by Satan before beginning his earthly ministry. The novel explores Jesus' journey to enlightenment: he appears as human actor, a pilgrim, in the story and readers see his struggle to purify himself through starvation and prayer. Ironically, Jesus is both a success and a failure in this, for at the end of the novel he dies from starvation and exposure to the elements (he is thrashed by a great windstorm) *but also* (after his burial) appears and heals pilgrims as he makes his way out of the desert and toward Jerusalem. The novel implies not only that Jesus experienced two resurrections (one at the beginning of his ministry, and one after being crucified at the end of it) but also that Jesus experienced true enlightenment on the scale of transmutation, somehow replaced by a self-aware, supernatural, godlike spirit who was Jesus Purified. It is a provocative and disturbing story, managing to be both blasphemous and completely respectful of the Gospels' story of Jesus Christ.

Yet while one might expect that a novel about Jesus would give him center stage, in Crace's novel, what happens to Jesus happens almost in the story's background. In the foreground is Musa, a swift-tongued, unscrupulous, violent desert trader who has been abandoned for dead by his fellow traders and left in the care of his wife, Miri. The novel opens with Musa on the brink of death and the pregnant Miri rejoicing that she may finally be free from his beatings and brutality. Yet it is Jesus, entering their tent while Miri is out digging Musa's grave, who touches Musa and inadvertently brings him back to health. (Jesus is not aware that he performs this miracle.) As a result, Musa is alive and ready to resume his thievery with the band of pilgrims who arrived at the same time as Jesus, having come to these desert caves to pray, fast, and beseech God for earthly guidance. Musa manages to extort the pilgrims and profit from their weaknesses but is increasingly obsessed with luring Jesus from his cave to find out the (potentially profitable) secret of his healing powers.

Musa's story is one of materialism and earthly power. He not only is Satan in this novel, tempting Jesus with promises of relief from his suffering and with earthly profit; he also is an earthly dictator, powerfully overcoming everyone who stands in the way of his absolute authority. He delights in material vice (gluttony, sexual perversion), uses everyone for his profit and amusement (not hesitating to go as far as brutality, rape, and murder), and controls others through an uncanny ability to spin lies. His wife, Miri, suffers a miserable life as his sexual and domestic slave. At the novel's end, Miri escapes with a pilgrim named Marta, who has been raped and beaten by Musa, and the two women leave him to die in the hills. However, he is rescued by travelers, and the last words in this novel are not Jesus', but Musa's: "He'd trade the word." He plans to sell and profit by the story of Jesus' healing and resurrection, even as he watches "the Gally" come down from the distant hills and make his way toward the village. The novel ends with an unspoken question: Who will win in this battle for the world?

If Charles Johnson's *Dreamer* begins in the historical arena of politics (King and civil rights) and increasingly moves in the direction of the sublime, *Quarantine* starts in the realm of the sublime and increasingly moves in the direction of the political. For one thing, Crace's novel is feminist in outlook, showing the horrifying effects on Miri and Marta (the Mary and Martha figures of the story) of unchecked patriarchal power. The novel also dissects Musa's Machiavellian philosophy and, at times, seems an allegory about economic hegemony and spin culture. Musa is the capitalist titan, always on the make, ready to sacrifice anything to profit. The novel seems unable to deal with biblical myth without dealing with material politics, and vice versa. Like *Dreamer*, this novel is pulled in two directions at once.

This linkage of the uncanny to the sublime is actually quite common in metahistorical romance. Portraying the past as sublimely different and deferred, the metahistorical romance often constructs the border between the past and the present not as the archival fact but as the uncanny, a place revisited. Arguing that there is a material affinity between postmodernist history and the uncanny, and intuiting, I think, that the uncanny represents an alternative to the binary opposition of past/present, the postmodernist historiographer F. R. Ankersmit writes, "The uncanny independence of the objects discussed in the history of mentalities . . . suggests the mysterious existence of a realm lying *between* ourselves and the reified past of the historist and the positivist" (*History and Tropology* 233). Thomas

Pynchon baldly states the negative formulation of this idea in *The Crying of Lot 49*. Speaking of Oedipa Maas, the narrator notes, "She had heard all about excluded middles; they were bad shit, to be avoided; and how had it ever happened . . . with the chances once so good for diversity?" (181). At the deferred border of sublime history (the excluded middle on the border, located between empiricism and theology) is the historical uncanny. Ernst Van Alphen, speaking of Holocaust trauma, observes, "If the sublime is the master category, then, the uncanny is a subversive subgenre of the sublime. . . . Schelling sees the uncanny as a necessary precondition for the sublime, a force to be *overcome*. The overcoming of the uncanny results in the sublime (199).[12] In the context of the present discussion about the historical sublime, the uncanny is indeed the force to be overcome and a precondition for the sublime: it is the border of History itself, the place revisited. This is to differentiate it from the sublime.[13] The struggle to cross this border is the struggle toward and desire for History—for belief, Truth, annihilation—in the late twentieth century.

In the most self-reflexive or avant-gardist metahistorical romances, such as Jeanette Winterson's *Sexing the Cherry* or Peter Ackroyd's *Chatterton* or *Hawksmoor*, the border of history is figured as the uncanny in characters who return from the past to the present; the centuries echo one another, without any explanation, until they merge in the last sections of the novels in an uncanny meeting between twentieth-century characters and characters from the past. In *Sexing the Cherry*, the merging of Dog Woman and the ecofeminist and the meeting of a twentieth-century Jordan and his seventeenth-century counterpart; in *Chatterton*, the meeting of Chatterton and Charles Wychwood; in *Hawksmoor*, the co-presence of twentieth-century detective Nicholas Hawksmoor, the eighteenth-century architect Nicholas Dyer, and a third party who might be Ackroyd himself; in *Time and Again*, the overnight transportation of Si Morley from the twentieth to the nineteenth century; in *Milton in America*, the weird construction of John Milton as a tourist in Puritan America; in Robert Coover's *The Public Burning*, the co-presence of figures from differing historic decades and levels of being (such as Betty Crocker,

Richard Nixon, Uncle Sam, and Ethel and Julius Rosenberg)—these are examples of the uncanny history of the metahistorical romance. The novels construct the moments when the deferred border between past and present asserts itself, or the place where (as Brian McHale has noted) ontological boundaries meet, and at the place where present history meets its unspeakable past, at the ineffable border of the historical sublime.

But the representation of the historical sublime's uncanny border can take other forms as well. In Steve Erikson's *Arc d'X,* for example, numerous historical times ranging from the late eighteenth century to 1999 and beyond interpenetrate in a kind of simultaneous history. *Arc d'X* breaks down borders between narrative genres (incorporating elements of historical fiction, science fiction, alternative history, romance, and detective story) as well as between the real and the unreal, the mythic and the political, the logical and the fantastic. The novel fixates on and actually *locates its narrative at* the uncanny border not only between the present and the historical past but also between the present and the historical future. The novel seems to attempt to show readers what a "sublime history"—a history that cannot be disciplined—would look like. Lee Spinks has correctly noted that time in Erikson's novels "is *both* cyclical and linear, since it represents a continual return to an origin that is always being refigured through time" (218). The jostling time and space zones in the novel, the a-logical, associative links between 'historical' times, the blurring of the historically real, the historically possible and the historically imagined—all of these techniques serve this end.

In vivid contrast, Toni Morrison's *Beloved* constructs a very different kind of historical uncanniness that illustrates Jean-Luc Nancy's idea that "at the limit, one does not *pass* on. But it is there that *every-thing* comes to pass." Beloved, the child killed by her mother Sethe to keep her out of slavery's grasp, is known only by the adjective on her tombstone; her name confounds the distinction between the proper and improper name as the historical signifier. Beloved also cannot "pass on": she is a restless ghost. But of course she is also a figure for history, a specific kind of traumatic history that lingers outside the political histories attempting to explain the U.S. national experience. Neither in this world or the next, Beloved lives in the fluid space of the border. She embodies deferral: she embodies "history that hurts," but she also embodies the unspeakable. The ghost-child Beloved is the figure embodying relation, the relation between the unspeakable historical past (a traumatic History that cannot be empirically rationalized or understood and can only be faced with terror), and a dynamic historical present in which human beings can choose action and can strive for freedom in the face of what hurts.[14]

In sum, the metahistorical postmodern consciousness may be understood as enacting the repetition and deferral of resolution that characterizes the traumatized consciousness. At the border of experience, on the edge of History, the imagination confronts not its products (i.e., history as the known past) but its own operation, the construction of history itself. At the sublime border, "The imagination attains . . . to its maximum, and in the effort to go beyond this limit it sinks back into itself, and in so doing is displaced into a moving satisfaction."[15] A less elegant way of saying this is that the metahistorical romance ping-pongs between its knowledge of history as the historical sublime (the silent and unknowable past) and experiential history (the history that hurts). This opposition leads not to a synthesis but to a compulsive repetition of itself, a ceaselessly deferred resolution that is often identified as the compromised politics of postmodernism. Yet another way to state this is to say that for the postmodernist imagination, history is desire, the desire for the space of History that it finds is always deferred. Thus we return to the discussion of chapter 1, to fabulation as the integral component of the metahistorical romance and another of its links to the historical novel tradition. Fredric Jameson is very much correct when he calls postmodernism "libidinal history." The desire for history *is* the fabulatory, romance element of the metahistorical romance, the desire for the always receding, always beckoning Other.

D. M. Thomas's novel *The White Hotel*, the subject of considerable analysis in the past decade, directly addresses how traumatic history might be reconceptualized, and posits one way in which the unrepresentable historical sublime might be represented as gesture rather than construct.[16] In the novel, the future and the past simultaneously appear within the traumatized consciousness of Frau Anna G./Elisabeth (Lisa) Erdman, forming a kind of heterotopic history, a Foucaultian counter-memory. In this novel, the future, present, and past all appear simultaneously in Lisa's consciousness—an impossibility according to Freud, who appears as a character in the novel as a representative of Western science and historical models. In *The White Hotel,* as in *Gravity's Rainbow,* the parapsychological undermines the control of a rationalist and controlling system, that of psychoanalysis, but also that of androcentric and positivistic history.[17] This metahistorical romance does not merely imply that the official historical record may be a fabrication, or that the historical record is an emplotted story. By linking Lisa's psychoanalysis to historical event, Thomas posits that the historical record is an "open work," defined by Umberto Eco and others as a narrative engaged with readers in a process of movement and becoming. Eco and Pousseur describe an "open" musical composition as one in which the listener must place herself deliberately in the midst of an inexhaustible network of relationships and choose for herself her own modes of approach, her reference points and scales, simultaneously using as many dimensions as possible to multiply and extend her perceptual faculties. The statement applies equally well both to Lisa's project of subject formation and to history itself as it appears in this novel: a culture must approach its own lapses, its own atrocities, deliberately, and see them among an inexhaustible network of relationships to dynamize the event in cultural consciousness. When this is not done, horrors like that at Babi Yar are too easily explained away and repressed, become dead history that is, perhaps, doomed to repetition. Lisa's memories defy temporal order and logic, as does the Nazi massacre, "that afternoon . . . that was no conceivable part of time" (289). Both Lisa and the historical event are coopted and rewritten—Lisa by Freud and his psychoanalytic system, and Babi Yar by a capitalism that is always hostile to history:

When the war was over, the effort to annihilate the dead went on, in other hands. After a while Dina Pronicheva stopped admitting she had escaped from Babi Yar. Engineers constructed a dam across the mouth of the ravine, and pumped water and mud in from neighbouring quarries. . . . No one, however, saw fit to placate the ravine with a memorial. It was filled in with concrete, and above it were built a main road, a television center, and a high-rise block of flats. The corpses had been buried, burned, drowned, and reburied under concrete and steel. (297–98)

What is the difference between capitalism's denial of history and abuse of historical memory, and the turn toward the unspeakable historical sublime in the metahistorical romance? The former denies history and establishes an ahistorical perpetual market present; the latter is *obsessed* with history, even to the point of denying defensible interpretations of past events in favor of perpetual reinterpretation and re-presentation in the interest of ethical action. Lisa is like history because both she and it have been coopted by totalizing systems (capitalism, Freudianism), systems that themselves provide the semblance of progression, order, and development that is then said to stem from a human model. The remedy to this exploitation, White implies, is an assertion of History's essential *unknowability*, and the awe and humility that comes from facing the limits of one's own imagination as well as the depths of one's responsibility to act in the face of this sublimity.

Proposition 3
The motivation for this movement and unceasing deferral of a historical ground in the metahistorical romance is a simultaneous distrust and assertion of *fabula* as a humanist value.

For Jean-François Lyotard, modern narrative was separated from postmodern narrative via *form*. Postmodern narrative retained the modern aesthetic of the sublime but avoided modernist nostalgic form and was avant-garde in presentation, confrontational, and un-consoling. This position is modified in the metahistorical romance. It is true that in the most avant-gardist of metahistorical romances, such as Robert Coover's *The Public Burning* (1976) or Ishmael Reed's *Mumbo Jumbo* (1972), a realist narrativization of history is resisted by a radical form. It is fairly easy for one to posit how and even why Reed's *Mumbo Jumbo,* for example, inscribes a distrust of old humanist definitions of *poeta,* the poet/maker and poetic object, particularly in relation to historical narrative. As an African American writer intent on revealing the ethnocentrism embedded in those Anglo-European terms for creative production, Reed deconstructs them both through the form and the content of his novel. While it is, I believe, unwise to return to old form/content distinctions in literary analysis or historiographical analysis unless (as in the work of Jameson and White in different contexts) this is done to critical purpose, it is fair to say that the two most frequently analyzed aspects of *Mumbo Jumbo* are its experimental, disjunctive, multivoiced form and the alternative version of Anglo-European history it offers, a version of Western history that emplots events from the time of the Egyptian civilization very differently from history textbooks' emplotment of those events. The text's formal experimentation and reemplotment of Western history together defamiliarize the Anglo-Christian bias of Western narrative history and posit its racist origins by offering a different way of telling history and a different history itself, both of which Reed links to African mythology, Haitian religion, and African American historical experience. Reed attacks the humanist narrative *and* the historical method it supports.

While certainly other metahistorical romances such as Julian Barnes's *Flaubert's Parrot* or Thomas Pynchon's *Gravity's Rainbow* are also formally avant-gardist in their critique of history (and in chapter 3 I talk specifically of these kinds of avant-gardist novels), what the metahistorical romance seems to add to Lyotard's formulation is the possibility of a novel combining traditional realist form and radical historiographical content. That is, the metahistorical romance interrogates history and gestures toward the historical sublime, but not *necessarily* because it tells a historical tale in a weird and avant-garde way. Its critical, and postmodern, historiographical position stems as well from what the text itself says about history or implies about it through the story it tells. Metahistorical romances that look very conventional "on the surface" may, in fact, say fairly radical things about history and refuse the separation of form and content inherent in Lyotard's thesis. These metahistorical romances inscribe a distrust of the humanist value attached to disciplinized, narrative history, even when they seem conventional in form.

Barry Unsworth's *Sacred Hunger,* for example, seems to return to classical realist narration and form. However, this novel also raises serious questions about the political nature of historical narrative emplotment. There are numerous metafictional commentaries on historical narrative embedded in this novel that undercut a classical realist faith in *fabula* as a disinterested aesthetic activity or value. For example, this novel is told as a frame tale; the moving story of Matthew Paris, the Africans enslaved on the *Liverpool Merchant,* and the rise and fall of the egalitarian commune they establish on the Florida coast is framed within two or three levels of narrative and thus becomes nebulous, uncertain, and indirect. More important, Unsworth's novel also relies heavily in its early sections on the device of parallel chapters that depict two contrasting settings: life for white English sailors and captured black Africans onboard the *Liverpool Merchant,* a slaver running the triangle trade, and the leisured English life led by well-heeled daughters and sons of eighteenth-century English capitalists socializing at their fathers' mansion homes financed from this slave trade. Significantly, the activity shown at the latter setting is a rehearsal of Shakespeare's play *The Tempest.* Unsworth wrote this novel well after postcolonial studies had entered the academy and had identified *The Tempest* (and Caliban in particular) as an iconic marker of colonial and postcolonial discourses. There seems to be a clear metafictional reference in the selection of this particular play; it stands as a synecdoche of postcolonial issues and colonial blindnesses, a recognizable foil to the tragedy unfolding in the other, parallel chapters concerning the slave ship and its mutiny. The reference to

The Tempest is thus, in this context, a kind of shorthand recuperation of postcolonial theory's claims about how colonial power and ideology can be inscribed in narrative itself. In other words, a *mise en abyme* appears: characters blind to their own colonial privilege and racism perform a play that may be blind to its own discourse about colonialism and racism and appear in a framing narrative that also be blind to its own colonial discourse and racist assumptions read by an reading audience. . . . In a move typical of postmodern metafiction, the text sets up echoes and mirrors of this possibility at each level of reality in and outside the text.

The most forceful example of metahistorical deconstruction in the novel, however, is the presentation of the main, traumatic, revolutionary event of the novel as a lacuna, an Absence in historical time. This event is the mutiny aboard the *Liverpool Merchant,* owned by the enterprising Englishman William Kemp. Detailed scenes describe the events preceding the voyage and the ship's construction and the early part of the voyage itself; likewise, the story of how William's son, Erasmus, eventually tracks down the mutineers off the Florida coast and brings them to "justice" as revenge for his father's suicide and bankruptcy is well chronicled. The mutiny itself has drastic consequences: it financially ruins and eventually leads to the death of the ship's owner; it leads the mutineers to establish a multicultural commune on the coast of Florida where white Englishmen and former black African slaves live together peacefully, polyandry is practiced and children are raised communally, a new language is created, institutionalized religion is abolished, and law is tribally administered in accordance with democratic principles; and it leads to the demise of that community and the capture and death of Matthew Paris and many of the Africans. Significantly, however, the mutiny itself *is never shown.* This cinematic and historically catalytic event enters the text only as a gap in the chronology of the narrative, an absent and silent signified. In other words, *Sacred Hunger* "presents" the mutiny as a Lyotardian event, unspeakable and outside of representation as history; it locates the event in the realm of the historical sublime.

The mutiny *is* represented, however, as recollection or retold story at two points in the novel. First, the mutiny is recounted years later in the Florida commune, after it has passed from recent memory and has become legend. The commune's children reenact the mutiny in a pantomime game based on tales of the mutiny created by the commune's storyteller, Jimmy. The boy Fongo plays the role of Thurso the evil white ship captain, Kenka plays his father's (Paris's) role. Matthew Paris watches the performance, a history lesson staged by the children, and is bothered by its performance:

> It was the orderliness of the performance, mysterious in its effect, that marked it off from the confused reality. This, to the touch of his memory, was glutinous with blood, thick with discordant sound, grotesque. . . . Jimmy was a good teacher. He was one of those who had stumbled on a vocation here. He was gifted alike at pointing a moral or adorning a tale. And this was history now: heroic protest, concerted rebellion, execution of the tyrant, a new social order. It ran like a clear stream—useless to require it to resemble the viscous substance of truth. (*Sacred Hunger* 585)

It ran like a clear stream: the reference is not only to how the bloody (viscous) story has been "cleaned up" in its reconstruction as legend, but also to how it has been linearly arranged and emplotted as heroic comedy. Seeing how the event has become emplotted as history disturbs Paris, who was an actor in the original event and can see the difference between the "it happened" and its historical reconstruction, which serves clear social, political, and disciplinary ends. Once the Lyotardian event becomes "told," represented as part of the plot of history, it is inevitably distorted and inevitably serves political and social interests. This is not necessarily a bad thing in the sense that Jimmy's story will allow the community to form itself around shared values derived from what they perceive as a common historical experience. The novel's ambivalence about the value of historical emplotment is signaled by its implicit recognition of this and its realist depiction of the history of every other action surrounding the mutiny—the before and after, told in the realist, narrativist mode. On the one hand, in other words, the text seems to recognize the community-building potential of disciplined historical narrative.

On the other hand, as a metahistorical romance *Sacred Hunger* also seems to point to the dangers inherent in this activity and asks, with Hayden White, "if, by contrast, it is possible to imagine a conception of history that would signal its resistance to the bourgeois ideology of realism by its refusal to attempt a narrativist mode for the representation of its truth" (*Content* 81). The novel sides with *this* sentiment by depicting the mutiny itself as an event outside realism and the narrativist mode of representation, but also by illustrating the dangers of narrativist history in another scene where the mutiny is recalled. The second time the mutiny is recalled is when Barton, the smarmy, self-interested mate of the murdered captain, retells the story to Erasmus Kemp after the latter has found and dispersed the commune and retaken the Africans there as his property (*Sacred Hunger* 605–11). In this scene, we see Barton revising the story of the mutiny as is needed to further his own profit. His seems to be, metaphorically, the other side of the coin: the kind of historical emplotment that Jimmy employs to create community is used by Barton for vicious, egocentric ends.

The mode of narrativist realism preferred by bourgeois historiography seems an ambiguous blessing. In both emplotments of the mutiny as historical event—Jimmy's emplotment of it as romance, and Barton's emplotment of it as documentary realism—narrative is shown to be politically situated and entwined with the demands of power and the psychosexual desires of the historically situated Subject.[18] Both romance and realism are suspect here, both understood as only politicized forms of the history that actually transpired. It is in this sense that metahistorical romance is in line with Jameson's formulation of history: "We would therefore propose the following revised formulation: that history is *not* a text, not a narrative, master or otherwise, but that, as an absent cause, it is inaccessible to us except in textual form, and that our approach to it and to the Real itself necessarily passes through its prior textualization, its narrativization in the political unconscious" (*The Political Unconscious*, 35).

As this example illustrates, as the metahistorical romance develops from the 1960s through the 1980s and 1990s, history continues to be interrogated and new historical models explored. However, the need to wed experimental narrative form with narrative content becomes less imperative after 1980, seen in a shift from avant-gardist metahistorical romances such as Ishmael Reed's *Flight to Canada* to more conventionally realist narratives such as Barry Unsworth's *Sacred Hunger*. One explanation for this shift may be simply that different writers write differently or that the metahistorical romance of the United States reflects the political conservatism in the United States that gains public force from the 1980s onward. Another and very different explanation, however, is that as poststructuralist theories about language become increasingly mainstreamed in literary culture, writers' faith in the ability of narrative *form* singlehandedly to rescue narrative from historical nostalgia or totalitarian politics is lessened, and therefore the need to produce avant-gardist form is lessened as well.[19]

Little Big Man (1964), for example, tells the story of Jack Crabb, a 111-year-old white man who was brought up by the Cheyenne on the Midwest plains and spent his life traveling back and forth between his adopted Indian culture and the Anglo-American culture into which he was born. *Little Big Man* is divided into alternating sections: sections dealing with Crabb's life with the Cheyenne, and sections dealing with his various sojourns back into urban (Anglo) city life. Because Crabb has no home base and is equally out of place in both cultures, neither section is subordinate to the other. Crabb tells his own story to an interviewer, so readers supposedly get a first-person account not only of Native American life, but of battles such as that at Little Big Horn and of events such as the building of the American railroad. Historical figures from the Old West, such as Wild Bill Hickok, General George Armstrong Custer, and Calamity Jane, appear in Crabb's tale. In view of these historical settings, *Little Big Man* raises particularly postmodern questions, questions concerning pluralism, cultural marginalization, and Otherization; sexual repression; the effects of religion and gender roles upon human development. Moreover, the novel focuses intently on language and the social and linguistic construction of identity. Shuttling as he does between two warring cultures, Crabb finds he has no identity apart from language contexts: in Cheyenne culture he is Little Big Man, and his identity is formed by that name; in Anglo-American society he is Jack Crabb the businessman, drunk, and muleskinner. Jack's identities are completely circumscribed by culture and language. History is part of this shifting subjectivity, told as it is in a first-person account by a man who may or may not be senile or lying. Because Jack jumps between Cheyenne and Anglo cultures so frequently, a kind of parataxis begins to emerge as the two cultures are repeatedly juxtaposed.

Little Big Man illustrates how the metahistorical romance comments upon the emplotted nature of history; the novel, as Brooks Landon has noted, deals with the nature of mythmaking that is transformed over time into history itself (introduction to *Little Big Man* xiii). Form plays some role in interrogating history in this novel, yet equally important is the commentary on history provided by largely realist narration. This metahistorical romance raises the question of history's meaning and location because its author has learned the lessons of poststructuralist language theories, that narrative is both complicitous with and subversive of power and is never disinterested, and because modernist faith in the revolutionary force of avant-garde form has been eroded in the face of late capitalist, postmodern economies that can absorb any avant-gardist form into their own ideological programs. Poetics alone, it implies, will not rescue a meaning for history.

The simultaneous distrust and assertion of *fabula* as a humanist value in the metahistorical romance parallels the heated debates in contemporary historiography about the interrelation of narrative and history—debates that in turn were generated primarily by debates about narrative and language in poststructuralist theory. Until very recently, historians rabidly resisted identification of their mode of inquiry with that of narrative territories—that is, with narrative theory, theories of narrative history, or literary criticism. They did so because to identify history with narrative is to identify history as the articulation of desire rather than the outcome of empirical investigation. Yet because history—at least what has been accepted as history since the

eighteenth century in the Anglo-European West—can only be recalled in language, both the metahistorical romance and postmodern
historiography now raise questions about the relation between aesthetics and *fabula* and history itself.

These questions can be (and have been) easily banalized into
claims that "history is only fiction." The historians' debate has in
contrast led to real attempts to hash out the complex affiliation of
history and narrative and the implications of a strong alliance between them. The two poles of the debate are fairly easy to identify,
and though much is often made of them in literary criticism, few historians believe the ideas at either pole: that is, the idea at one pole
that history is only self-referential language and there is no such thing
as a referential or historical "fact" as that is commonly understood, or
the idea at the other pole that history is only an unbiased accumulation of facts systematically linked through an empiricist methodology
analogous to that used by the natural sciences (the famous Covering
Law Model).[20] These two positions are the straw men of the debate
about narrative and history, for both are limit positions, ultimately
unprovable and doomed to flounder on their own internal logical
contradictions.[21] However, the two ideas highlight the difficulty of a
real analysis of the narrative-history nexus, an analysis long delayed
in the discipline of history. For example, Robert Anchor has argued
that understanding history as a *form* of narrative akin to fiction but
adjudicating different cultural expectations does not lead to relativism but to an appreciation of history as another way a culture
makes sense of experiential and recorded events; history and fiction
both can present the truth of experience, but as narrative they serve
different cultural functions and expectations. Likewise, both realists
and anti-realist historiographers argue for the importance of narrative
to historical understanding. Paul Ricoeur recognizes many of the
poststructuralists' claims about language and language use but makes
a strong case for the referentiality of historical narrative, while T. Carlos Jacques argues that narrative inheres in reality itself as it appears
to the historian. Important to this debate about history and narrative
is a related debate, associated with the work of Hayden White, Hans

Kellner, and F. R. Ankersmit, about the role of metaphor in the interpretation of historical data and the construction of historical accounts.[22] Is a historical account dependent on metaphor for its construction? If a historical account is dependent upon metaphor, does it follow that the account is thus false? Can a metaphorical interpretation or description still be true?[23]

It is probably not productive here to rehearse all of the debates by historians over narrative and history; the case could be made, as Richard T. Vann implies, that the story of this debate is actually the story of the development of philosophy of history in the twentieth century.[24] As Vann notes, in the discipline of history from 1980 on, "historians' language, not explanation or causality, would be *the* topic around which most reflections on history would centre" (69). These debates revolved around competing claims made by Arthur Danto, J. H. Hexter, A. R. Louch, Louis O. Mink, Hayden White, and others about the constitution of historical explanation as statistical report or/and as narrative. In part, these theorists responded to arguments such as David Carr's Ricoeurian idea that historical reality consists of people's plans, actions and experiences and has an intrinsically narrative character from the start, making historical narrative a kind of mimesis, "a continuation by other means of the very reality it portrays" (Carr, 119). Mink responds with a theory of history, stated in *Historical Understanding* and elsewhere, that argues that narrative is central to human cognition, and thus in order to perceive history we must narrativize it.

In contrast, Hayden White consistently finds untenable the idea that reality is in and of itself structured as narrative. Most important to the debates about history and narrative/as narrative is White's notion of "emplotment" (the shaping of any chronicle into narrative history that involves the historian's conscious or unconscious use of literary tropes in the creation of the historical account) and his claims that professional historians have a political and psychological stake in the venerable Western value of *mimesis*. He implies that history as it is written as narrative is in fact a complex interweaving of many kinds of truth: the truth of facts and events (the "it happened"), the truth of narrative forms, the truths of ideology that are embedded in realist modes, the truths about the political and psychological drives of the historian, the truths about the desire for history as history is defined in Anglo-Western cultures. If White's supposition is heeded, the historiographer's task of explaining historical models grows exponentially:[25]

> Myths and the ideologies based on them presuppose the adequacy of stories to the representation of the reality whose meaning they purport to reveal. When belief in this adequacy begins to wane, the entire cultural edifice of a society enters into crisis, because not only is a specific system of beliefs undermined but the very condition of possibility of socially significant belief is eroded. This is why, I think, we have witnessed across the whole spectrum of the human sciences over the course of the last two decades a pervasive interest in the nature of narrative, its epistemic authority, its cultural function, and its general social significance. (*Content* x)

What White points to here is one source of tension for the post-traumatic postmodern imaginary. These debates about history and narrative blur the boundaries between art and science, fiction and history, and they emphasize how the simultaneous love and distrust of *fabula* crosses disciplinary boundaries in the aftermath of poststructuralism and the aftermath of twentieth-century political events.

This point is made with particular force when a practicing historian writes a metahistorical romance that centralizes questions about history and/as narrative. Simon Schama's *Dead Certainties (Unwarranted Speculations)* is such a novel. The book tells two stories. In "The Many Deaths of General Wolfe," readers are shown three versions of the death of General James Wolfe, killed at the battle of Quebec in 1759: one by a soldier on the field of battle, one telling the story of Benjamin West's idealization of the event in painting, and one telling the story of Francis Parkman's idealization of the event in historical narrative. The second, "Death of a Harvard Man," is a more traditionally plotted mystery story concerning the murder of George Parkman, the uncle of the historian Francis, whose death is finally blamed on a fellow Harvard professor of chemistry even though at least three different, all equally believable, versions of the event are heard by the court. In the first section Schama emphasizes the forceful disjunction between the messiness of real landscapes, real war, and real life and the idealized, epic portrayals of those events by painters and writers. In the second section he emphasizes how historical "evidence" is often incomplete, inconclusive, and arbitrary, more akin to conjecture and self-interested gossip than to scientific inquiry.

The title *Dead Certainties (Unwarranted Speculations)* indicates the book's torn loyalties: on the one hand, the empiricist study of the past on the natural sciences model (history as dead certainty); on the other hand (and notably stated in parentheses, as if the idea were too upsetting even to say out loud), history as narrative speculation, conjecture, gossip, even motivated lies (i.e., history as the opposite of certainty, which is dead). Set up fairly clearly for the reader (in title, epigraphs, and even the book jacket) is the central conflict of the text, which is not between characters, but between history and literature as ways of dealing with the past.

This is clearly the focus in a provocative chapter in the first section of the book dealing with the life and work of Francis Parkman. Schama calls Parkman a Boston Brahmin and includes him as the luminary of a group of historians for whom "history if not wholly on their side was at least firmly in their custody" (41). Parkman is famous for writing elegant narrative histories. In the novel he is explicitly aligned with the aristocratic intellectual class, Western science, and patriarchy ("a gentleman scholar, rose-grower and anti-feminist"), but in spite of this privilege and social power, the physical man is frail, a life-long invalid. Schama's Parkman eschews secondary source material and works only with primary materials to create his history of colonial North America; however, nearly blind, he has these materials read to him over and over "until from their scraps and shreds he had sewn together in his mind the splendid fabric of his history" (47). The picture of Parkman that Schama draws is that of a tortured literary artist: balking against his family's career plans for him, he attends Harvard and conceives of writing a great American history. But he also follows in the footsteps of his Romantic contemporaries Whitman and Longfellow and falls in love with the American landscape, a landscape that finally repels him in its stark physical actuality but entices his literary imagination. After the loss of his wife and a child, a mental and physical breakdown, and time spent in the field of horticulture, he writes his great history: "He had become a stitcher of tapestry, albeit with slowness. . . . As in such a tapestry, there were brilliantly fabricated moments, flights of pure fanciful embroidery, stitched into the epic. But when he and others could stand back and look at the thing, unfolding before them, the marvel of it all was unmistakable" (63). Clearly, what Parkman creates is a romantic emplotment of the American landscape that had in real life repelled him with its brutishness and disorder. History becomes epic here, the retelling of the past in a literary mode, and it is richly embroidered with the desire of the narrating subject.

In addition, Schama includes an afterword to the novel that spells out his *own* narrative concerns and implies his surprising ambivalence toward historical narrative. While Schama clearly identifies the dilemma inherent in narrativizing history in the chapter on Parkman, in the afterword Schama the writer/novelist seems oblivious that his "factual" narration of the Parkman family's history reenacts the emplotment he points out in Francis Parkman's work. My point is that Schama's split loyalties are clear: he cannot keep history out of the novel (he both writes a historical novel and writes an afterword that critically explains his intentions and the "point of the story" to readers) and he cannot keep novelization (or at least narrative emplotment) out of his "historical" account, for whenever he describes the "real" events in the afterword he ends up emplotting them as well.

Schama's ambivalence toward narrative, however, becomes more clear in other sections of the afterword, and his comments bear extensive quoting here:

> Both the stories offered here play with the teasing gap separating a lived event and its subsequent narration. Although both follow the documented record with some closeness, they are works of the imagination, not scholarship. Both dissolve the certainties of

events into the multiple possibilities of alternative narrations. . . . These are stories then, of broken bodies, uncertain ends, indeterminate consequences. And in keeping with the self-disrupting nature of the narratives, I have deliberately dislocated the conventions by which histories establish coherence and persuasiveness. Avoiding the framing of time-sequences supplied by historical chronologies, the stories begin with abrupt interventions—like windows suddenly opened—and end with many things unconcluded. . . . Both stories end with accounts at odds with each other as to what has happened, as to the significance of the deaths and the character of the protagonists. . . . Though these stories may at times appear to observe the discursive conventions of history, they are in fact historical novellas, since some passages . . . are pure inventions, based, however, on what documents suggest. That is not to say, I should emphasise, that I scorn the boundary between fact and fiction. It is merely to imply that even in the most austere scholarly report from the archives, the inventive faculty—selecting, pruning, editing, commenting, interpreting, delivering judgements—is in full play. This is not a naïvely relativist position that insists that the lived past is *nothing* more than an artificially designed text. (Despite the criticism of dug-in positivists, I know of no thoughtful commentator on historical narrative who seriously advances this view.) But it does accept the rather banal axiom that claims for historical knowledge must always be fatally circumscribed by the character and prejudices of its narrator. (320–22)

Schama's afterword asserts that his novel addresses all four of the propositions I am setting out here for the metahistorical romance. First, words and phrases common to discourse about postmodernism (e.g., dissolution, multiple possibilities, alternative narrations, uncertainty, indeterminacy, dislocation, self-disruption) pepper this description of intent. Schama's position is perfectly in keeping with the postmodern turn on history in his own and in other fields, and it illustrates none of the self-confident surety of the Rankean paradigm for historical study. In fact, Schama's language consistently undercuts this surety, replacing it with contingency and self-referentiality. Second, Schama invokes the historical novel to describe his text. Clearly, his text is meant to be an evolutionary development of that genre.

Third, the novel addresses a "teasing gap"—the gap between the "it happened" and the historical narration of that event. In this novel, as in Barry Unsworth's *Sacred Hunger,* the "it happened" is what is missing: there is no solution to the murder mystery, no privileged authorial view of the murder event put forward. Yet Schama implies that this lacuna does not show his distrust of history but rather his reverence for it. What Schama argues here is that his novel, like all historical accounts, can approach this gap but never delineate it, never infuse it with Presence. The novel itself illustrates the premise that history can approach, in an unceasingly movement toward, History, but the gap, the aporia, remains.

And finally, as a practicing historian Schama is still reluctant fully to part with the distinction between "a work of the imagination" and "a work of scholarship" even though every other statement in the afterword implies that this distinction is a false one. One wonders whether what we see here is the last grasp on disciplinary history, the reluctance of the academic historian who has won significant institutional rewards to undermine the prestige of academic work, rather than an actual belief in this distinction between fiction and historical "scholarship."[26] For all other statements in the afterword conflate the imaginative work of historical storytelling and the "scholarly" work of historical reconstruction. That word *fatally* is in fact quite emphatic and ominous: "Historical knowledge must always be *fatally* circumscribed by the character and prejudices of its narrator." The slip is telling: to be circumscribed is to be bounded, bordered, encircled; but it is also to restrict the action of, to restrain. If the character and prejudices of its narrator circumscribe historical knowledge, then while *H*istory may exist as an "it happened," for all practical purposes it stands encircled by consciousness, an activity of the desiring, and the writing (circum-scribing), Subject. To write *h*istory is also to circumscribe *H*istory. Moreover, according to Schama's statement, this circumscription is not just castrating (circum-cising), it is *fatal.* It restrains and confines to the point of killing the thing that it attempts to enunciate/annunciate (Heisenberg's uncertainty principle redux). To "fatally circumscribe" would be to restrain and suffocate, to border and strangle, to bind and kill. To "fatally circumscribe" History is to kill History by encircling it with narrative—the mind drawing a figure (a closed circle) around another figure (the Lyotardian figure of the event) "so as to touch it at as many points as possible," to become one with it, to merge with it, to supplant the absence of History with presence of Mind. Schama is caught between his distrust of *fabula* and his need for it, his longing for History after the narrative Fall. In his desire to find the excluded middle, the middle ground, he finds the border of the historical sublime, and commits historicide.[27]

In contrast, Eric Zencey, another practicing historian turned historical novelist, does all he can to save history from this fate. Zencey's *Panama* (1995), like part of Schama's novel, is a novel by a historian about a historian who writes novels: it tells a story in the life of the historian, diplomat, and essayist Henry Adams. Zencey's portrayal of Adams is provocative because his overt subject, like that of Schama's novel, is the contest between the world-making mythology of the premodern, the "civilizing" secular values of the modern, and depthless postmodernism grounded only in technology and speed. As in the real Henry Adams's nonfiction work *Mont-Saint-Michel and Chartres* (1904) and fictionalized memoir *The Education of Henry Adams* (1907), the central opposition of the text is between modernization and religion, each representing a different kind of Force. This theoretical approach to force is in Zencey's novel attributed to "Adams" in multiple political contexts, but specifically in the colonial and economic contexts of the Panama Canal project.

At first, *Panama* seems to question the possibility of historical knowledge in the face of political simulations and cover-ups and to question the tenets of modern empiricism upon which historical knowledge is based. Again and again, "Adams" remarks sorrowfully or angrily upon the supplantation of Old World values, particularly those associated with historical knowledge and religious faith. For example, at one point he notes, "Science, it was now, not faith; science cold, hard, lifeless. There could be no stained glass in the house of science, nothing to lend its color to the flat, clear glare of enlightenment. He wondered what would become of a culture that worshipped such a sterile god; would it become a kind of necropolis? Would it then school its young in its morgues?" (*Panama* 123).

One might remember, however, that Paul Ricoeur offers the rejoinder that "nothing is more misleading than to oppose progress and hope or progress and mystery" (*History and Truth* 81). Zencey's novel actually goes to great lengths to save the history from the clutches of unbelievers. For one thing, in contrast to the unsettling nonresolution offered by detection in Schama's novel, Zencey's Adams becomes an amateur detective and not only solves a murder mystery but also unravels a political intrigue using the tools of deductive logic. Reality is presented, finally, as understandable to a personality completely comfortable with, and to some extent championing, Enlightenment political and epistemological values. Moreover, as a Green historian who believes that "it's possible to derive regulatory moral value from nature historically understood" (*Virgin Forest* xi), Zencey rejects that which will inevitably negate history: the possibility of immanent History (i.e., the Historical Sublime outside the reach of empiricist deduction) as well as the possibility of singularity of events within known history (i.e., the existence only of unrelated phenomenological events, variation without coalescence). What he substitutes for both is deduction and the modern project, a constant search for meaning undergirded by a belief that totalization (the end product of deduction) is possible even if never attained. "What will ground us?" he asks. "What will guide us? The answer I've come to is 'history'" (*Virgin Forest* x).

History (with a lowercase *h*) exists for Zencey because it is phenomenal (a process of nature). Just as Henry Adams's theory of force based on the dynamo provided him with a vehicle to rescue history by making it subject once again to empiricist scrutiny and natural law, Zencey's theory of force based on a law of thermodynamics provides him with a like vehicle. In *Virgin Forest,* Zencey includes an essay on entropy that reminds us that his Ph.D. dissertation was about the social history of the second law of thermodynamics. Like Adams a century earlier, Zencey has turned to a theory of dynamic force for his own time that rescues history and modernity while seemingly undermining the possibility of either's continuance. For entropy is a law about the dissolution of laws; as Zencey himself informs us, it is the one constant law of the universe and operates at all levels of experience from the phenomenal to the experiential to the metaphorical. It is thus clarity in chaos, a constant about the impossibility of constants. What Zencey brilliantly mimics in this novel is Adams's own Hegelian maneuver in *The Education of Henry Adams,* for he sets up in *Panama* a negative portrait of modernity (and a despair about the possibilities for history) that by the end of the book has metamorphosed into merely one side of a dialect that eventually is overcome in a larger vision. History is possible because it can be observed in and through phenomenal reality and is subject to a constant of natural law, the law of entropy. What looks like the dissolution of culture and the end of the possibility of history is actually part of a natural entropic process, subject to natural law and therefore to some extent predictable. Surprisingly, history as entropy becomes something of a comforting thought.

Zencey's novel is thus firmly in the Waverley tradition, while Schama's book is metahistorical romance. Zencey's novel is about the loss of a particular cultural value (e.g., Force as theological or ontological meaning), a particular political value (e.g., statesmanship), and a particular way of life (e.g., the humane, non-technologized pace of the nineteenth century). While Zencey/"Adams" can decry the loss of something specific in the past, the implication is that this something belongs to an expiring paradigm; the role of the historian (as detective) is nonetheless secure, if changing with the times. In contrast, Schama's novel is about the loss of history itself as well as the loss of the possibility of successful detection. His novel raises disquieting questions about what the role of the historian should be in the face of a "crisis of history." Ironically, in this light one might read Simon Schama's final comment on the purpose of historical inquiry in the postmodern age as one of the best statements of how the metahistorical romance's confrontation with the uncanny border of the historical sublime can be a meaningful one for societies and individuals: "And so the asking of questions and the relating of narratives need not, I think, be mutually exclusive forms of historical representation. And if in the end we must be satisfied with nothing more than broken lines of communication to the past; if . . . we stumble only on 'unimaginable accidents,' and our flickering glimpses of dead worlds fall far short of ghostly immersion, that perhaps is still enough to be going on with" (325–26). The postmodern metahistorical romance unceasingly confronts History in its compulsion to make sense of a traumatic history, a history that hurts. Whether it struggles to save history or to find an alternative to it in secular-sacred faith, it struggles to the border of the enunciable and searches for the presence of meaning in the silent, haunted houses of the past. What it encounters at this ever-deferred border may be only the uncanny and partial reappearance of History, but even that may be "still enough to be going on with."

Proposition 4
Writers of metahistorical romance learn from the texts of the literary modernists to combine metahistoricity with narrative form, but this postmodern metahistoricity is situated differently as a tropological reversal of the historical romance genre.

If the historical romance is defined traditionally, using Scott's historical romances as paradigmatic examples, then a certain set of criteria for the genre emerges. While Harry E. Shaw in *The Forms of Historical Fiction* argues that historical novels don't make up a genre at all but are in fact realist novels with unresolvable problems of character development, George Dekker in *The American Historical Romance* does see the historical novel as a new genre birthed in the *Waverley* tradition. Dekker suggests that a historical novel is one whose action is set in the past and "often turns on the failure of a character or class to understand that attitudes and behavior recently appropriate and tenable are so no longer"; that demonstrates the shaping power of the forces of historical causality over character, attitude, and event; that often includes known historical events and persons as part of its plot; and that combines the contradictory impulses of history and romance (14–26). Using a different approach, Avrom Fleishman constructs a formalist definition that lists seven criteria for a historical novel: it is set approximately forty to sixty years in the past; it has a plot that includes a number of real historical events, particularly those in the public sphere; it has at least one real historical character; it has a realistic background for the action; it has a value and a meaning that stands in some relation to the reader's "habitual demand for truth"; it provokes or conveys, by "imaginative sympathy," the *sentiment de l'existence,* the feeling of how it was to be alive in another age; it uses the universals of literature (e.g., the modes of romance, satire, tragedy, and comedy) to interpret the course of historical man's career.

A very different kind of definition for the historical novel emerges if the genre is seen not formally but socially and historically, for example, from a marxist point of view. Georg Lukács's *The Historical Novel,* originally published in 1936 and still a central Marxist discussion of the form, starts with Scott to argue that "the historical novel in its origin, development, rise and decline follows inevitably upon the great social transformations of modern times; to demonstrate that its different problems of form are but artistic reflections of these social-historical transformations" (17). According to Lukács, the historical novel on Scott's model brings historical extremes into contact with one another through its portrayals of minor or fictional historical figures. As for Fleishman in his formalist analysis, for Lukács the historical novel strikes a balance between the personal and the collective experience: it centers on "the typical man of an age" whose life is shaped by world-historical figures and other influences in a way that epitomizes the processes of change going forward in the society as a whole (30–41).[28]

Linda Hutcheon has argued that there is a strong break between postmodernism and the historical novel tradition. Postmodernist fiction is, according to her thesis of "historiographic metafiction," fiction that is both intent upon posing questions about history and society *and* metafictional and self-reflexive about itself as a formal language structure. These are the contradictory impulses of postmodernism which lead it to a compromised, split politics: it challenges *doxa* but asserts nothing to replace that which it deconstructs. In contrast, Brian McHale sees more of an evolutionary relation between the classical historical romance and postmodern fiction about history: using strategies of displacement (rewriting of history) or supplementation (replacing what has been lost or suppressed), the postmodernist historical novel revises the official version of history "by violating the constraints on 'classic' historical fiction: by visibly contradicting the public record of 'official' history; by flaunting anachronisms; and by integrating history and the fantastic"(90).[29] In a very different vein, Fredric Jameson, both following and revising the analysis of Lukács and using Doctorow's *Ragtime* as his example, believes the postmodern historical novel to be a decadent form of the historical novel genre, a form of postmodern pastiche that is historically depthless ("Postmodernism and Consumer Society" 111–20). In all of these cases, how one defines the postmodern in relation to the classic historical novel radically affects one's reaction to postmodernist historical fiction.

I mention these studies and different approaches to the historical novel genre to underscore how any definition of the relation between post-1945 historical fiction and the historical novel tradition depends on what one considers "historical fiction" to be both before and after 1900. I believe that it is most useful to resituate postmodern historical fiction in literary history as an evolutionary form of the classic historical romance and suggest that the treatment of history in this fiction is also linked to a classical tradition in Western aesthetics, namely, the discourse of the sublime. While situating postmodernist historical fiction one way or another in relation to the classic historical novel is of primary importance, however, it is also important to note that the metahistorical romance, as an evolutionary form of the historical novel, also learned much from modernist experimentation with historical fiction and has clear alliances with modernist approaches to history. Modernist novels such as John Dos Passos's U.S.A. trilogy (*1919* [1932], *The 42nd Parallel* [1930], and *The Big Money* [1933]) challenged the formal conventions governing historical representation and exhibit many of the characteristics of postmodern historiographic metafiction, as defined by Linda Hutcheon. Preoccupied with the processes, effects, or construction of history, many modernist novels such as William Faulkner's *Absalom, Absalom!* are also formally metafictional and self-reflexive. Modernist historical fiction revamped the traditional form of the historical novel and added its own strain of social critique to the tradition started by Scott in the Waverley novels. The "realist romance" of Scott's and Tolstoy's nineteenth-century historical novels is replaced in Dos Passos's work, for example, by (metafictional) modernist experimentation (the disruption of linear narrative by cutting, repetition, devices such as "The Camera Eye" and "Newsreel") and the narrating consciousness of an omniscient nineteenth-century narrator is shattered into newspaper headlines, newsreel slogans, street slang, and stream-of-consciousness narrative. This formal experimentation aims to reawaken readers to reality and underscores how that reality has become increasingly fragmented and textualized by media, by human withdrawal in the face of mushrooming technologies, and by an emerging corporate point of view that replaces that of the individual subject in capitalist societies.

All of these ideas, as well as the interest in formal experimentation, are carried over into the postmodern metahistorical romance. What is not always carried over is the modernist focus on psyche rather than history. The modernists tended to place human consciousness at the center of history, to focus on how the mind perceives history. In contrast, postmodernists tend to focus on the question of what history itself might be. Gerald Graff made this point in 1973: "Postmodernism signifies that the nightmare of history . . . has overtaken modernism itself. For if history is seen as an unintelligible flux of phenomena, lacking in inherent significance and structure, then no exertions of the shaping, ordering imagination can be anything but a dishonest refuge from truth" (403). Unlike Barry Unsworth's presentation of the historical event as Absence and problematization of the idea of historical truth, Dos Passos's treatment of history focuses on the subject's response to it and the media representation, or simulacrum, of it. Clearly, the difference between these treatments of history is one of degree rather than of kind. In the modernist psychologizing of history in novels such as Faulkner's *The Sound and the Fury* or *Absalom, Absalom!,* James Joyce's *Ulysses,* or William Styron's *The Confessions of Nat Turner, how* we see is a question more important to these projects than is *what* it is that is seen by us. Barbara Foley remarks, "Faulkner's Quentin Compson in *Absalom, Absalom!* can be seen as a prototype of the Collingwoodian historian, for he boldly constructs a 'web of imaginative construction' in his '*a priori* imagination' and evaluates the explanatory power of facts on the basis of discursive coherence rather than referential correspondence" (*Telling the Truth,* 220–21).

I do not find it particularly useful to debate whether a text should be labeled modernist or postmodernist; the labels are less important than the point that the approaches to history in these texts are different but not unrelated. There are too many texts that straddle the lines, texts that, to use Lance Olsen's phrase, might be called *postmodernist Janus texts.* These are novels that stand in a transitional position between modernist and postmodernist, or realist and postmodernist, modes. Where would one put a text like Virginia Woolf's *Orlando,* for example, or Graham Swift's *Waterland,* or Don DeLillo's *Libra?* Novels such as these are "about" what history is, but they are also "about" problematizing how the subject imagines Self in history.

A novel that is often discussed as postmodernist historical fiction is Nigel Williams's novel *Star Turn,* and yet this book illustrates perfectly the ties between the modernist and postmodernist forms of metahistorical fiction. In it, the narrator Amos Barking recounts his personal history with his Jewish friend Isaac Rabinowitz and his friend/wife, Tessa Oldroyd. While the account is written by Amos during the course of twenty-four hours in 1945, its narrative focus concerns the period between roughly 1910 and 1945. Amos writes for self-revelation, and this account is partially a therapeutic "writing cure" for his disorientation and loneliness. The events of Amos's life—his infatuation with Tessa, his idolatry of Isaac (Zak), his disillusionment with himself and with politics as he contributes to England's war effort as a propaganda expert at the Ministry of Information—all contribute to Amos's increasingly cynical and detached adult world view. This world view is exploded, however, when he becomes an eyewitness to the Dresden fire bombings. His superior at the ministry, Alan, requires Amos to see these bombings because Alan is a German Jew who suffered the horror of World War II: "That's what it's like, my poor little Englishman! That is what people do to each other out there while you're having your bloody little cup of tea and telling yourself you have the finest democracy in the world! . . . Why? Because your nose has never been rubbed in the facts! All history evoked in you is a snigger! A defeated giggle!" (*Star Turn* 305). Amos's last words, the last words in the novel, are, "Make it all go away, somebody, can't you?"

This is the cry of bourgeois society, the desire of the middle class to blind itself to the ugliness, inequality, and injustice of a reality outside its own comfortable, regulated lifestyle. On the one hand, this novel is about the confrontation between propagandized, traumatic history and sublime history, a history that has been disciplined and that terrifies and defies rational boundaries. On the other hand, *Star Turn* stops short of asking what kind of history might *not* contribute to the horror it documents. The text's central concern seems not history *per se* but rather the struggle through which one defines and upholds Self under the constraints of Self-negating institutions. The image and plight of the Jew in diaspora is fundamental to and becomes symbolic of this concern, which is developed within the framework of (a failed) *bildungsroman*. Yet certainly this novel is informed by and reflects the anxieties of postmodern, post–World War II, First World societies about history, like Kurt Vonnegut's *Slaughterhouse Five*, which also concerns the Dresden bombings. Historical events are horrifying and dislocating and the notion of what history *is*, is complicated as a social question, as is the question of how the Subject is constructed in history.

Nonetheless, many critics intuit that a different degree of critique informs novels such as Günter Grass's *The Flounder* or Thomas Pynchon's *Gravity's Rainbow*. While both novels play with the idea of perception and subjectivity in a postmodern society, neither constructs

History as a product of psyche in quite the same way as does *Star Turn* or a novel such as William Faulkner's *Absalom, Absalom!* In fact, *The Flounder* and *Gravity's Rainbow* are probably less about the construction of subjectivity and more about the impact of rationalism and positivism on history itself. *The Flounder* is pure postmodern fabulation: millennial history is flattened into one continuous plane through the device of an immortal historical agent, a talking turbot out of the Grimm Brothers' fairy tale "The Fisherman and His Wife." The novel's action spans 4,000 years, beginning on May 3, 2211 B.C. and ending in September 1974. The narrator and his wife Ilsebill have lived thousands of years through various time phases; the story begins "before history" in Neolithic, matriarchal culture and moves through Western European history chronologically. The first event narrated is the narrator's discovery of the flounder, who jumps out of the sea and teaches the neolithic man about patriarchy. The story is told in retrospect, from Germany in 1974 (the construction of the Berlin Wall and the birth of the women's liberation movement are thematically significant), and the reason it is told is that the flounder is on trial. He has been caught again, this time by two women who help put him on trial before a feminist woman's tribunal for crimes committed against matriarchy throughout the centuries. The book is divided into nine sections, each corresponding to a month in Ilsebill's current pregnancy, and each section tells the story of a "cook" (a woman) with whom the narrator interacted in various time phases. At one point in the novel, the flounder

> listed his achievements—patriarchy, the state, culture, civilization, dated history, and technological progress—and went on to deplore the sudden turn from grandiose to monstrous action. . . . "Your era is ending on a sour note. In short: you men are finished. . . . In capitalism and Communism alike, everywhere I find madness impersonating reason. . . .
>
> . . . You can blame me for Alexander and Caesar, the Hohenstaufens and Teutonic Knights, even for Napoleon and Wilhelm II, but not for Hitler and Stalin. There I disclaim responsibility. Their crimes were none of my doing. The present is not mine. My book is closed; my history is done. (447)

While the flounder claims credit for Western European (specifically German) civilization, he conveniently disclaims responsibility for history's twentieth-century atrocities and apparently shifts loyalties to matriarchy in the face of them. His speech can be read in light of postwar German history as post-traumatic response to the genocidal atrocities of this century, which makes his claim that "the present is not mine" and that "history is done" less a pronouncement about the end of history itself than a manifestation of personal and national historical denial. This novel is not about the flounder's psychology but about historical responsibility.

The fabulation of Thomas Pynchon's *Gravity's Rainbow* is also metahistorical. Classic historical novels such as Tolstoy's *War and Peace* often situate their action at wartime, a time of intense change in which worn ideology is often exposed. In *War and Peace* we see the views of the dying aristocracy (in the acts of the Rostov family and Prince Nikolai Andreyevich Bolkonsky) contrasted to the nouveau-riche aspirations of Prince Vasili Kuragin and his children. The wartime reality that Prince Andrei understands is contrasted to Nikolai Rostov's fantasy of war that is gradually replaced by reality's cold lessons; Pierre Bezukhov's innocent and naïve world view is undercut and contrasted to that of the Kuragins. Similarly, a historical romance such as Giuseppe di Lampedusa's *The Leopard* contrasts the aristocratic world of Prince Fabrizio to the new social pragmatism of Tancredi and the middle-class upward mobility of Don Calogero Sedara and Angelica; Margaret Mitchell's *Gone with the Wind* depends on the clash between aristocratic southern values and those of the modern marketplace; Walter Scott's *Rob Roy* juxtaposes the ideological values informing the Highland clans and the English and Scottish nobility. *Gravity's Rainbow*'s wartime setting allows it to critique worn ideologies in similar ways. Most prominently, while characters and ideas are opposed in *Gravity's Rainbow*—that is, Leni and Franz Pökler, Roger Mexico and Pointsman, or the parapsychological world of The White Visitation and the rationalism of scientific communities—critical studies of this novel repeatedly note how Pynchon attacks oppositional, binary thinking characterizing Western rationalism. In *Gravity's Rainbow,* simultaneity, the fusion of opposites, constructs a middle ground both in and outside of history that offers an alternative to the binary oppositions created by ideology and exposed in wartime.[30] As it also does in Pynchon's *Mason & Dixon,* here this Zone, the place of the excluded middle in positivistic history, is the space of the historical sublime, where the "it happened" is undecidable and absent but can be usefully and humanly incorporated into a conception of history that "helps us to go on." In *Gravity's Rainbow,* the uncanny Zone where Slothrop dances with a ghost girl is the borderland of the historical sublime, the deferred border of History out of real time. Upholding the space of sublime History has theological overtones to Pynchon, as it does for Rushdie. Recognizing the space of the excluded middle might give one the opportunity to stop time and avoid the apocalyptic ending of millennial history without resorting to pre-Enlightenment religiosity.[31]

These postmodernist novels create an inverted historical romance often privileging romance over historical telling. Critics have argued that the postmodernist novel has incorporated (and inverted) forms of the detective story (Holquist, Spanos 1987, Tani), parody (Badley, Hutcheon 1985), satire, the grotesque and the carnivalesque (Hoffman 1982, Hutcheon 1983), fantasy (Hoffman 1982, Olsen 1987), and science fiction (Ebert et al.). As it did with these other pop genres, postmodernism has turned to the once popular genre of the historical novel and brought to it its program of inversion and resistance. Tropological turnings have characterized the historical novel genre for the past two hundred years. As Dekker notes, for Scott and his contemporaries, the historical romance was considered a modern version of the epic, "hence a heroic and masculine genre preoccupied with the fate of entire societies and but little concerned with individualistic introspection or, reversing the mirror, cosmic questionings." Later, Melville and Hawthorne would need to change the historical novel to accommodate psychological realism or metaphysical speculation (Dekker 28). While Dekker's conclusion in the face of this evidence is that the historical romance was thus a genre resistant to change, I would argue the opposite: that what these swervings in the genre illustrate is the genre's propensity to reformulation and reversal. The important questions that arise from a comparison between a novel by Leo Tolstoy and a text by Jeanette Winterson or those by Scott and the postmodernists are central to what I see as an evolutionary relation between classic historical romances and metahistorical romances. Both kinds of novels are "about history," that is, they concern history or take it as their subject. Yet they *go about history* from different angles of vision stemming from their respective historical positions, reflecting different historiographical and political values. To put this another way, each participates in a different historical imaginary. Moreover, if tropes are, literally, swervings, turnings away from one perspective to another, Harold Bloom in *The Map of Misprision* reminded us that they are also psychic defense mechanisms. It may be that the historical romance has tropologically turned ironic through a reaction-formation to the trauma of twentieth-century history. In the Waverley novels, Scott incorporated specific historiographical perspectives in the creation of his characters, plots, and settings; the postmodernists, saturated (rather than schooled) in the historiographical problematics of *their* time, tend toward a poststructuralist and antifoundationalist gesture toward the historical sublime.

Second, it is important to emphasize that the metahistorical romance learns from its modernist precursors that memory, desire, and history are not separable. Modernism taught the West about the secular subconscious; modernist historical fiction challenged positivistic history by psychologizing history, by contaminating empirically derived history with the detritus of desire. The postmodern metahistorical romance remembers modernist historical remembering—in *Beloved*'s terms, it "rememories" modernist history. It remembers memory as the human narrativization of History, as the only way possible for human beings to articulate the unrepresentable, absent past. Metahistorical romances such as Graham Swift's *Waterland* or John Fowles's *The French Lieutenant's Woman* are indebted to modernist experimentation with historical narration; one can see this in their self-reflexivity, incorporation of modernist anxieties about history, recognition of the narrative (un)grounding of historical representation, and willingness to recognize memory as one of the excluded middles of empiricist history.

A Summary Too Long Delayed

Postmodernist metahistorical romance hearkens to the Western historical romance but inverts the relationship between "history" and "romance" of that traditional genre. Going back to the "genetic code" of the historical novel, we can see an evolution in the form of metahistorical romance:

Historical Romance

1. assumes the ontology of history;

2. assumes that history, as the shaping force of culture, can be identified and assessed (particularly in economic structures) by an unmotivated, neutral human observer who, using inductive scientific method, can extrapolate a developmental pattern in history itself;

3. assumes and upholds notions of cultural and personal *value* derived largely from Western bourgeois economies;

4. assumes the shape of history to be linear and the motivation of history to be Progress.

Metahistorical Romance

1. assumes the cultural construction of history;

2. allows that the past may shape the present, but asserts that all we can know are its traces, and that all attempts to construct historical narrative are culturally contaminated. History is sublime, impossible to articulate, outside of representation, and as such leads to ethical action in the present;

3. radically questions the notion of cultural and personal value in any form, particularly those derived from Western capitalist economies;

4. conceptualizes History as planar, and replaces the notion of historical progress with the operation of deferral.

The following chapters illustrate that not only does metahistorical romance stand as an evolution of the historical novel but it also seems to move in a kind of pendulum motion from the "realism" of Scott's historical novel form, through the abstraction of modernist spatial form and postmodern fabulation, back toward a "realism" transformed by the politics of its time. Inheriting the opposition between realism and romance inherent in Scott's novels, writers of metahistorical novels seem to hang suspended between these poles and captive to pendulum motion (which is also the move toward the border of History and back again), unable to break free to a real access to History and confined within two literary genres—realism and romance—that they no longer associate with the Real. To the postmodernist imagination, preoccupied by history and bombarded by whizzing shards of exploded cultural and epistemological metanarratives, there is something smelling of lavender and Victorian parlors about the way traditional historical novels approach history. Therefore, while Walter Scott's novels often attempt to mute their romantic elements and foreground their historicity or grounding in a realist representation of life, postmodernist metahistorical fiction often foregrounds or conspicuously incorporates fabulation/romance.

What is the significance of this revisionary historical view in literary productions? Does the historical moment of these fictions ironically add to the importance of their interrogation of historiographical assumptions? The metahistorical romance surfaces precisely when modern history is under attack on many social and academic fronts. The metahistorical romance seems to reflect a postmodern reevaluation and reconstitution of history in the wake of poststructuralist theories of language and history, aligned in particular to the concept of the historical sublime as articulated by Jean-François Lyotard in postmodern theory and by Hayden White in historiography.

It is predictable that social scientists today like to claim that while the postmodern challenge to history in their disciplines is serious and threatening, in literature that same challenge produces "playful fantasy [that] adds interest, arouses the imagination, challenges the creative intellect. But in the humanities hardly anyone takes these transgressions of normal time and space seriously" (Rosenau 70). If the debates about postmodernism and history are studied carefully, it is clear that their full force issued precisely from the humanities (philosophy, after all, being one of us). Indeed, given the resistance to poststructuralism in the social science disciplines, one could argue that these disciplines (including that of history itself) are only now coming to terms with postmodern theory and its challenges, ideas which have been integral to literary debates since the mid-twentieth century. Significantly, historians such as Simon Schama have chosen literature as a vehicle for their deconstructive claims about history not only because literature has the power to challenge cultural assumptions and reach a broad-based audience, but also precisely because the postmodern challenge to history integrally involves the *narrative* issues of plot construction, point of view, political subtext, and readership. The humanities not only take seriously the challenge to history in fantasies and novels; they have forcefully asserted that history is fantasy and fiction allied with power, and have thrown down a gauntlet to the social sciences to prove otherwise.

TWO

Analysis

3 Cracking the Mirror

Spatializing History in
Metahistorical Romances

When you have once seen the chaos, you must make
some thing to set between yourself and that terrible
sight; and so you make a mirror, thinking that in it
shall be reflected the reality of the world; but then
you understand that the mirror reflects only appear-
ances, and that reality is somewhere else, off behind
the mirror; and then you remember that behind the
mirror there is only chaos.
—John Banville, *Doctor Copernicus*

Some of the most avant-gardist of metahistorical romances, many written in the 1960s and 1970s, go beyond declarations that history is a textual construct and attempt to reveal *how* history is textualized. By doing so, these metahistorical romances explore the literary problem of how to represent time and space. In particular, these novels explore ways of representing history that take into account culturally specific definitions of time and space and exploit the fact that how a culture represents time and space may reveal much about that society's values, priorities, and politics. Writers of these avant-gardist metahistorical romances use representation as a weapon and a political shield; they directly correlate their own cultural politics to how time and space, as history, are represented or configured. They also imply that to defamiliarize Western history (i.e., to expose its biases, crimes, absences, and silences) it is necessary to see this history multidimensionally, in terms of its spatial modeling. The consequence is often, in more ways than one, a new angle of historical vision. In this way, the metahistorical romance shares with other postmodern phenomena a new metaphor for representation: that of space or spatiality. The significance of this for the metahistorical romance is twofold. First, metahistorical romance can redefine linear models of history using other spatial models and metaphors. Second, the assertion of spatiality allows the metahistorical romance to recover the historical sublime often repressed in history's linear model.

Spatiality and Postmodernism

While Jean-François Lyotard was indebted to the Latin and Germanic philosophical traditions when formulating theories of the postmodern, even Lyotard was very much influenced by activities in the streets of Paris in 1968. In many ways, a critical focus on postmodern spaces initially spurred the philosophical debate about postmodernity and its relation to modernism and premodernism. Late twentieth-century developments in architecture, the plastic arts, and media technologies encouraged postmodernism to enter the critical conversation via spaces and multi-dimensional forms. The most influential for some time was the language of architecture and city planning. Well documented and discussed by now are the challenges posed to modernist painting and the International Style in architecture by the creation of postmodern space and the writing about it by Robert Venturi and Denise Scott Brown, Jane Jacobs, Robert Stern, Steven Izenour, Peter Blake, Charles Jencks, Leon Krier, Kenneth Frampton, Philip Johnson, Michael Graves, and others.[1] After postmodern architecture introduced the scale of hyperspace, the World Wide Web mechanized it and made it available to everyone, everywhere as a conceptual field, an interactive community space in real time, and a global market.

I am interested in this chapter in a different kind of postmodern spatiality, one on the level of the symbolic and related primarily to conceptual metaphors for historical process. Such a concept is evident in, for instance, Andreas Huyssen's famous essay, "Mapping the

Postmodern," where the history of postmodernism is figured in spatial terms—mapping—rather than linear historical ones. (This trend has continued in criticism. If the key verb for 1980s criticism was *critique,* the key verbs for 1990s criticism were *map* and *unpack,* two spatial images applied to thought and speech processes.) The primary characteristic of the postmodern has come to be its rejection of linear models (of time, history, positivism, progress) for other spatial models such as flatness, roundness, circularity, or pendulum motion.

Postmodern exploration into the topography of spatialized history takes many forms. For example, much of the discussion about postmodernist architecture concerns its playful historicity, a blending of space with history through use of architectural quotations. In geography studies, Edward Soja has called for a recombinant historicism that engages with spatial modes of thought. Soja argues that the nineteenth-century privileged historicism and sociality over spatiality and that postmodernism reasserts spatiality in critical thought and practice. By distinguishing different "paths" of spatialization—posthistoricism, postfordism, and postmodernism—Soja makes distinctions between types of postmodern sensibilities. His posthistoricism is a struggle between history, geography, and society in which "the reassertion of space arises against the grain of an ontological historicism" (*Postmodern Geographies* 61).[2]

Like Soja, Fredric Jameson correlates geographical spaces with sociohistorical (i.e., late capitalist) values. In one of his classic essays on postmodern space, for example, Jameson refers to the spatial disorientation created by urban spaces such as the Bonaventura Hotel and argues that this postmodern aesthetic annihilates the ability of subjects to locate themselves in their surroundings or in history. Formulating postmodernism as a period concept, Jameson's most well-known essays explore the shift from temporality to spatiality in postwar, late capitalist economies: "A model of political culture appropriate to our own situation will necessarily have to raise spatial issues as its fundamental organizing concern" ("Postmodernism" 89). Fragmentation is a visual metaphor; to fragment history, or to dig within its depths, is a metaphorically "spatializing"activity. For Jameson, postmodern "surface and fragmentation" of the temporal (as in video art) leads to the spatialization of time: "Time has become a perpetual present and thus spatial. Our relationship to the past is now a spatial one" (Stephanson 6). His analysis tends to equate "spatial" with "static" or the perpetually present. Jameson specifically links modernity to depth models and postmodernity to depthlessness; postmodern aesthetics is predicated upon "flatness and depthlessness," and this depthlessness is linked to the fragmentation of the subject and to what Jameson calls the "waning of affect" (a depersonalizing desensitization of ethical sensibilities and loss of a historical sense) within postmodern culture (*Postmodernism* 6–17). When perspective or depth disappears in the art object, he argues, the result is an inevitable loss of historicity, a loss of the Bergsonian concept of "deep time" and a thrusting into a perpetual spatial present. And by extension, losing our senses of time, space and history means that we run the risk of becoming stupid consumerist animals, living only for the next entertainment treat and unconcerned about whom we exploit to get it. Because postmodernist literature is of its time and place and partakes of the postmodern condition as much as it critiques that condition, Jameson sees it as a seriously compromised art form.

The irony of this, however, is that while Jameson's marxist orientation leads him to view history as a (dialectical but also linear) narrative of economic struggle, his notion of "cognitive mapping" is directly indebted to postmodernism's spatial logic and to some extent aligns Jameson with it. The concept of "cognitive mapping" provides Jameson with a spatial concept that offers an alternative to traditional Marxist teleology but also to the ahistorical postmodernism of Lyotard or Baudrillard. Jameson identifies cognitive mapping as an alternative to postmodernist fragmentation; the activity refers to the building of contingent perspectival starting points, sociocultural orientations, and political alliances that form a kind of hermeneutical landscape where the subject can relocate herself within a new, postmodern physical and political geography. Jameson advocates cognitive mapping as an alternative to postmodernist fragmentation and depthlessness. It is a way of approaching history that allows for new and politically efficacious historicism and a reintegrated (if contingent) subjectivity. However, rather than being an alternative to postmodernism, this idea is at least partially embedded in it. In postmodern historical fiction, for example, the desire for history combined with a fear of totalitarianism (metanarrative) results in a tug of war: a move toward the secular-sacred sublime (History), and a pull away from it, away from Presence and back to the arena of the mundane and the political. This opposite attraction within metahistorical romance leaves it in fact with only one approach to the problem of history: building sometimes poorly articulated or contradictory cultural alliances that at least form a contingent hermeneutics where the subject can locate him or herself in time and space.

This distinction between social theory and aesthetic theory and the pull between them is theorized by Steve Harvey in *The Condition of Postmodernity: An Enquiry into the Origins of Cultural Change* (1989) in a way that nicely complements Jameson's analysis. Harvey aligns Western social theories with a preoccupation with time and aesthetic theories with a preoccupation with space. He then shows how what he calls postmodern "time-space compression" has evolved since feudal times in Western Europe by illustrating how progressive monetization of relations in social life has transformed the qualities of time and space. In the first surge of late modern thinking occurring during the Enlightenment, he argues, dominating nature was linked philosophically to human emancipation, and so space and time were organized to aid the liberation of "Man" as a free individual endowed with consciousness and will. The growth of science as a way of commanding nature, social engineering and rational planning, regulation and control over systems, including the development of chronometers and maps, would help organize the world in order to promote human freedom and realize human potential. These ideas, however, were revamped by the modernists after 1847 when they made explicit the inherent tensions within Enlightenment conceptions of space, for example, the potential for Enlightenment emancipatory time/space to turn to surveillance and control through a desire for increased social order. Particularly between 1910 and 1914, ideas about the nature of space and meaning of money changed; Harvey argues that both shifted from certainty of absolute space to insecurities about relative space. Time and space are "pulverized by capital," shattered and rethought through the growth of a new internationalism in worker's movements, new ideas of money as credit ("floating" money not tied to place or metal standards), and new long-term investments in space by capital in the search for new global markets. Modernism in the arts reflects these changes by approaching space as the means to reinvigorate projects of emancipation in two ways: either as an opportunity for reinvigorating the Enlightenment project of emancipation by celebrating the newly constructed global community or as an anti-Enlightenment celebration of the *fragments* left over from capital's pulverization of space through globalization.

For Harvey, postmodern conceptions of time and space thus inherit much from the modernists. For the postmoderns, time and space have become even more interrelated and fragmented as a result of capital's globalization and creation of a culture predicated on images and desire. Importantly, for the postmodernists, space is increasingly pulverized by time: space becomes smaller and smaller, to the point of nonexistence, as globalized technologies (air travel, the Web) decrease the time needed to traverse global (and interglobal) space. In other words, all we have left at some point is time, but it is time without a referent, time without events. It is "delta T." It is speed.

The metahistorical romance certainly reflects these changes in culture. In the most avant-gardist of these novels—for example, Robert Coover's *The Public Burning* or Ishmael Reed's *Flight to Canada* or Steve Erikson's *Arc d'X*—all there is is time. Spaces become disorienting, different levels of "reality" are flattened out onto one plane, settings are surreal. What one gets is a view from above, a critical view akin to the perspective of aerial photography, flattening out time, space, and history in order to map them. What is left is often the spatialized time of metahistory.

This debate in postmodern theory has not left the discipline of historiography unaffected. Some contemporary historiographers are themselves calling for a new historiography that intersects with abstract models of space. For example, in his book *History and Tropology: The Rise and Fall of Metaphor,* F. R. Ankersmit explores implications of postmodern historicism and asserts the connection between new spatial metaphors and the writing of history: "One might say . . . that postmodernist historical consciousness 'spatializes' time: what was temporally different is transformed into spatial dispersion" (225 n. 90). In agreement with G. W. Stocking, Ankersmit notes that historical consciousness at the end of the eighteenth century was transformed "from a horizontal [or spatial] to the vertical [or temporal] mode of cognition"(225, n. 90).[3] This displacement from the vertical to the horizontal axis may be understood in different terms as the displacement of *langue* by *parole,* or as the displacement of diachrony by synchrony. In common is the idea that postmodernist conceptions of history move from the general to the particular, from the linear to the planar, from "depth" to "depthlessness," and from metanarrative to fragments.

The specific linking of postmodern spatiality to history is thus found in different disciplinary discussions but appears with the most force in the work of Michel Foucault, upon which the work of Soja and Ankersmit is partially built. Specifically, Foucault's definition of "heterotopias" as spaces uniquely located in historical time and his interest in Structuralism as a critical reorientation of time and space could be understood, as Soja notes, as "the spatialization of history, the making of history entwined with the social production of space, the structuring of a historical geography" (*Postmodern Geographies* 18). Foucault's vocabulary is rife with spatial metaphors and attempts to contaminate linear with spatial concepts. Examples abound: Foucault writes on the first page of *The Archeology of Knowledge* (1972) that "linear successions, which for so long had been the object of research, have given way to discoveries in depth" (3). Foucault's "archeological method" was a radical departure for the European and North American "West" from progressivist or positivist historiography. His alternative to Enlightenment-birthed Western history on a linear model is the identification of discursive formations and epistemic shifts: both have the effect of disrupting history as a narrative of un-interrupted flow. He challenges the progressivism of traditional his-tory by pitting against it an "effective history" which centers on the sites of rupture within culture and which looks to the body (rather than philosophy and metaphysics) for the inscription of social change. This effective history is built upon the premise that tradi-tional attempts to construct a comprehensive and developmental view of history must be discarded. The new history that should re-place this old view would "not permit itself to be transported by a voiceless obstinacy toward a millennial ending" ("Nietzsche, Geneal-ogy, History" 154). Foucault's methodology offers a planar alternative to linear history.[4]

But what does this really mean? To consider more deeply the no-tion of spatial history is to understand that Foucault not only dis-rupts the traditional linear conceptualization of historical time—time as a line—but also to understand that in doing so, he disrupts the univocal and homogeneous character of historical action and narra-tion. In other words, Foucaultian respatialized history allows for mul-tiple times to exist together at any moment through the actions of in-dividuals, institutions, and practices. Transforming documents into monuments "has led to the individualization of different series, which are juxtaposed to one another, follow one another, overlap and intersect, without one being able to reduce them to a linear schema" (Foucault, *Archaeology*, 8). In direct contrast to a traditional historical chronology that attempts to construct unified and univocal historical "periods," respatialized history allows for multiple historical voices (and contradictory historical voices) to exist simultaneously.[5] In Fou-cault's work, knowledge exists in independent layers, strata within so-ciety and within time. A major thinker such as Marx, for instance, might literally embody different times: his economic theory might be situated in the nineteenth century, his social theory or philosophy of mind might reflect eighteenth-century thought. In effect, Foucault poses that history itself is rather like an ocean current, with different depths or levels of water running at different speeds. History is lay-ered because it is made up of many different kinds of history: social history, material history, economic history, philosophical history, etc. Each of these histories exist simultaneously, yet each runs at its own speed. To read history, one needs to drop a plumb line, not construct a linear chronology. One needs to sound the depths of history at any given moment.

Foucault's metaphor of archeology is particularly apt for this kind of historical analysis, since the earth is geologically stratified, and these strata layers are both asymmetrical (running at different speeds) and directly reflective of material history (the earth's conditions at any given moment in geological time). Foucault further complicates this idea, however, by factoring in the human element in history and in historical analysis. Not only is history layered in this way; because they are the output of human activity, these historical layers also backtrack, intersect, and repeat themselves. In other words, to imagine history as an ocean current does not replace the chronologies of history but multiplies them; in a way, it increases rather than decreases linearity. Thus Foucault's radical complication of historical chronology is not only in the stratification of history, but in its anti-chronological path. Levels of history can backtrack, repeat, be interrupted, and intersect with other levels. Constructing history this way allows for history paradoxically to repeat itself as difference. To put it crudely, one layer of history may backtrack while another moves forward, thus allowing repetition of history to occur, but as a trace, or as difference, because it is highly improbable that the exact conjunction of all layers will be repeated at any two historical moments. It also allows one to posit the seemingly counterintuitive notion of discontinuous history, in which chronology seems radically disrupted or paradigms seem to shift.

This conception of history has immense importance to the metahistorical romance. On the one hand, understanding knowledge as existing within independent historical strata helps to explain the seeming paradoxes within the historical novel in its original form. In other words, understanding history this way helps to explain the paradoxical wedding of science and romance in Walter Scott's historical romances. Written in a time when material forces were intersecting with social thought in new and radical ways, the novels of Walter Scott illustrate the pull of paradoxical world views. While the scientism of the eighteenth-century Scottish philosophes clearly influences his work, nineteenth-century social and material forces seem to structure other, conflicting perspectives on history and cultural value in his historical novels. The tension between Enlightenment and Romantic historiographical assumptions in Scott's fiction may be a clear indicator of shifting epistemes in his own time.

Foucault's archeological theory of history, however, has even more relevance to the narrative techniques and historiographical assumptions of the metahistorical romance. The idea that history is not only *not* chronological but also "allows all the many layers of social formation to have their own times" seems a most useful way to understand the overt anachronism that appears in some avant-gardist metahistorical romances. For example, in Jeanette Winterson's *Sexing the Cherry,* historical periods seem blurred: while the novel is set in the seventeenth century, the characters espouse philosophies of history and time that seem characteristic of the late twentieth century. Even more overtly anachronistic is Ishmael Reed's novel *Flight to Canada,* where slaves on antebellum Deep South cotton plantations can hop jumbo jets and fly to Canada for asylum, where Lincoln cakewalks on a coffee table, and where Niagara Falls is a postmodern tourist attraction. How is it possible to see this as something other than bad writing, debilitating postmodern pastiche, or silly postmodern play?

This anachronism appears to be trivial, even dangerous, postmodern play unless it is understood as narratively enacting precisely the stratified, shifting, and discontinuous history present theoretically in Foucault's work. That is, reading Reed through Foucault, an analysis of historical strata would reveal that *all* historical periods are inherently "anachronistic" in certain respects, for all incorporate thought that is carried over from the past as well as thought that ruptures the past. In any given moment in history, old knowledge both exists as a living paradigm and *simultaneously* is replaced with new paradigmatic knowledge, depending on what kind of knowledge one is assessing, on what layer of knowledge-time one is analyzing.

The pre-and postcolonial history of African Americans actually appears in Reed's novel in much the same way that history is schematized in Foucault's work. *Flight to Canada* has a subtext: that while the 1960s saw improvements in African American life in terms of civil rights legislation and new opportunities for collective action, material conditions for many African American people changed little from the late nineteenth century. Industrial and then "post-industrial" economic growth often allowed slavery to mutate into labor servitude; de facto racism was often translated into equally repressive de jure racism as economics allowed segregation and discrimination to go underground and take new forms. African Americans did not suddenly move into a "new era" of equal opportunity in the 1960s. While civil rights legislation may have broken with the racist past and "moved forward," real economic opportunities and de facto civil rights for African Americans may have enacted a differential return.

From this perspective, one might argue that *Flight to Canada* narratologically enacts a Foucaultian archeological analysis and that *Flight to Canada* isn't about the antebellum South at all. Rather, its setting is actually the twentieth century. Rather than being set in the nineteenth century and being fraught with twentieth-century anachronisms, the novel may actually be set in the late twentieth century, and the anachronism may occur in the antebellum features of the text—and in the traces of past histories that remain in the present. Seen this way, the novel reveals that the twentieth century is fraught with historical anachronism—that while the 1960s and early 1970s civil rights movements in the United States may have been a postmodern event in both Foucault's and Lyotard's senses, the 1970s is not a new progressive era for African American people, but is constructed of multiple and often conflicting kinds of knowledge and discourses, some of which go back a long, long time. Rather than understanding the 1970s as a new era of emancipation for black folk, a break with the oppressive past and benefactor of enlightened 1960s civil rights radicalism, Reed presents the 1970s literally as discontinuous with the 1960s. Discourse by and about and affecting African American people is not homogeneous; different kinds of discourses

exist simultaneously to form a complexly layered, potentially contradictory discursive site. In *Flight to Canada,* Reed shows *through the
story itself* that the 1970s incorporates repetition and return to past
oppression in various social spheres. The time of slavery, in many
ways, is now.

Postmodernism—as a discourse, as a politics, and as a historiography—is tied to concepts of spatialization and new ways of cognitively
merging time and space. One might think of the postmodern as a
time of spatialized consciousness, exhibited in social phenomena as
different as billboard advertising and the disruption of linear logic
represented by the World Wide Web. Much has been made of hyper-
text as a new form of linear logic, one that incorporates planar
metaphors and encourages participants to think paratactically rather
than linearly. This correlation between space, discourse, history, and
power has generated a renewed interest in cartography itself, for maps
also are about lines that intersect and are not "progressive" in any
sense of the term, are about physical space, and are about (in the
sense that they both construct and are constructed by) discourses of
power. There is currently an immense critical interest in the intersections between mapping (i.e., cartography) and the construction of
history, in particular imperial history and the discourse of colonialism.[6] This postmodern fascination with space and spatiality as concepts or subsets of time is surely linked to the post-Einsteinian frame
within which postmodernism operates: the interrelation of time and
space is a central assumption of a quantum world. Postmodernism
embodies a quantum sensibility that refuses to separate time and
space into Newtonian mechanical entities. This linkage of time with
space, and both to history, permeates all areas of postmodern thought
and reconfigures physical as well as metaphysical categories. In historiography in particular, the conversation about alternate spatial models has gained significant force. Late-twentieth-century historiography now considers as viable alternatives to linear history other
models of history such as chaos and constancy, cyclical, dualistic, and
fractal models.[7]

Spatiality and Metahistorical Romance

While the correlation of spatiality to the debate about postmodernism and history is relatively recent, the linking of narrative form with concepts of spatiality has been featured in critical discourse about fiction for more than half a century. Literary critics transfer a focus on literal space to their own medium; some, for instance, have explored how space is constituted and evoked in literary texts. Of this group of researchers, some differentiate the kinds of space that a text constructs or to which it refers, the spatial aspects of the text's reconstructed reality or place.[8] These critics primarily are interested in spatial theory as it can be applied to literary techniques, and they tend to work with structuralism or the more recent field of cultural poetics. Many theorists linking postmodernism to spatiality have focused on poetry and contrasted the modernists' senses of "space outside of time" as a spatialization of time that is deconstructed by postmodernist art.[9] In literary studies, the recent explosion of interest in the academy with cartography and literature and the many studies defining postcolonial, gendered, racialized, or classed space in narrative are developments of a different course of inquiry, one that explores how literary texts narratologically or politically construct landscape or place.

But there is another type of spatiality in literary narrative, one with a rather long history. In 1927, Windham Lewis and E. M. Forster independently suggested this new term, *spatiality*, in relation to narrative art, and the phrase was repeated in 1928 by Edmund Muir. The kind of spatial theory that they all suggested implied that a literary text could have more affinities to spatial forms (such as geometric shapes or three-dimensional figures) than with temporal forms (artworks that depend on time to unfold their meanings, such as music). Critics note that the essential attribute of spatial art is simultaneity and of temporal art, succession. In literature, a spatial form would be one that broke up linear reading patterns, upset readers' expectations of sequentiality, and disrupted progressive story development.[10]

This at least was the contention of Joseph Frank in his 1945 essay "Spatial Form in Modern Literature," later expanded and reprinted in his book *The Widening Gyre: Crisis and Mastery in Modern Literature*. Referencing work by earlier critics such as Lessing, Frank examined the works of major modernist writers such as Eliot, Pound, Proust, and Joyce, and he concluded that their works could be considered spatial forms rather than temporal narratives because these works disrupted the linear reading flow, juxtaposed sections of text, suspended time progression, and repeated image patterns. Frank maintained that modern literature was "moving in the direction of spatial form" and that "all these writers ideally intend the reader to apprehend their work spatially, in a moment of time, rather than as a sequence."[11] Frank's argument thus allied spatialization in literature with a specific literary movement (modernism) and implied that spatial forms were static and stood outside time (vs. temporal forms, which depended upon movement within time). He also maintained that certain techniques of modernist fiction promoted readers' spatial apprehension of texts. One of these techniques was *reflexive reference*. Reflexive reference described a reader's process of coming to terms with a modernist text by cross-referencing and juxtaposing word groups, attending to puns and metaphors, and letting the sections of the work reverberate in mental suspension until finally grasping the work's significant form in a simultaneous, spatial "fitting together" of the work's components.[12]

The critical debate generated by Frank's theory raged in the pages of *Critical Inquiry* for nearly two years and still surfaces there and elsewhere.[13] Supporters of Frank's theory have worked both to clarify Frank's original concept and apply it to new contexts, such as to contemporary literature. Opponents of the theory maintain that it sets up false distinctions between time and space in narratives and distorts analyses concerning how readers read texts.[14] While all of these discussions must be noted, what is important for the present discussion about Frank's theory is that it identified a specific characteristic of modernist narrative in relation to time, one that, I would argue, is quoted but also redefined in the postmodern metahistorical romance.

As noted earlier, many of the most avant-gardist of metahistorical romances also reassign spatiality from the thematic or conceptual level to the level of narrative form in Frank's sense. It is important that this distinction between modernist and postmodernist *spatiality* be understood, for it illustrates both postmodernism's link to and break from modernist forms. Postmodern metahistorical romance novels tend to reject notions of a knowable a priori History; they claim that our knowledge of History is rooted in indeterminacy and cultural bias, doomed to inaccuracy and false closure. Like much of postmodern theory, these novels imply that the most we can know about history is that it hurts: it is political, it is violent, it is material. It is also not satisfactory; we long for more of the past, more meaning than political history, empirically derived, can give. To express this idea, metahistorical romances challenge traditional conceptual frameworks for historical representation. Attempting a critique of history and historical representation, these novels often strive to break through the limitations of their medium in order to "cognitively map" History itself, understood as the dislocating and disorienting space of the past. Metahistorical romance sometimes uses specific *narrative techniques* to break up linear reading patterns and also break up the narration of historical events through time. That is, they assert a "spatiality of history." In metahistorical romances such as *World's End* or *Almanac of the Dead,* modernist spatial *form* (of the kind outlined by Frank) becomes postmodernist spatial *history.*

In the metahistorical romances discussed in this chapter, history itself becomes spatialized in a nonlinear metaphor, in a manner akin to modernists' spatialization of narrative. Joseph Frank's notion of "reflexive reference" illustrated how reading patterns could be altered in a spatially (vs. temporally) organized narrative; in a similar manner but with a different focus, these metahistorical romances require us to read *history* differently, because history itself is the thing that is spatially altered, momentarily frozen and layered. History becomes narratologically terraced. Historical levels emerge in these novels, levels comprising elements of myth, legend, historical fact, and fiction that layer into one historically and ahistorically true moment in time. It is a geological method of historical perception which allows no "layer" to be more true than any other. As W. J. T. Mitchell notes,

Frank argued that the literary works produced by Eliot, Pound, and Joyce were "spatial" because "they replaced history and narrative sequence with a sense of mythic simultaneity" (541). As did modernist aesthetics, metahistorical romances that spatialize time harken back to mythic time. That is, this postmodern alternative to linear history looks much like premodern, non-Western conceptions of layered time that incorporates, rather than rejects as nonscientific, myth and fantasy as legitimate historical 'layers.'

While avant-gardist metahistorical romances thus can extend the modernist technique of spatialization into the realm of history, they also can carry forward the modernist interrogation of Western epistemology and redefinition of Western narrative forms. Comparing a work such as John Dos Passos's *U.S.A. Trilogy* to one such as Timothy Findley's *Famous Last Words* illustrates how the metahistorical romance extends modernist formal spatiality into the realm of conceptual history. In *U.S.A.,* Dos Passos uses techniques that he labels "The Camera Eye" and "Newsreel." The former is meant to represent what an observer of everyday events would actually see; "The Camera Eye" sections are written in an unpunctuated stream-of-consciousness style that mimics in prose the "eye" of a camera as it would pan a city scene. Usually these sections are written from a specific point of view, such as that of a child at one specific place and time. The effect of this angle of vision, combined with personalized voice, is similar to that in the opening scene of Joyce's *Portrait of the Artist as a Young Man.* "Newsreel" sections are a kind of collective media voice: in these sections, snippets from headlines, quotes from interviews, newsreel "footage," and radio blurbs are stacked without transitions or explanations. Quick cutting, montage, and juxtaposition of these voices work to produce in the reader a distinctive narrative effect and, according to Dos Passos, a more "honest" picture of political and social reality as a cacophony of voices and subjectivities pureed into the media hum of twentieth-century urban life.[15]

In contrast, metahistorical romances do not necessarily manipulate or experiment with narrative form in this way. Metahistorical romances don't necessarily spatialize history in the manner of Dos Passos's typographical spatialization. Instead, they spatialize history itself as that is recalled during the unfolding of the narrative. They cross-cut historical periods, juxtapose historical frames, anachronistically join historical characters and ideas from different epochs in one scene frame, mash together historical periods, or present actual metaphors for or commentaries on history as part of the work's narrative structure. They create "linear space" and "spatial time." In fact, the most avant-gardist of these metahistorical romances answer Lyotard's call for a narrative whose form is performative, disrupting representation and moving toward the historical sublime. They break up the linear form of the novel through typographical experimentation and other reflexive reference techniques, but the action of the stories also breaks up linear time sequence on a grand, historical scale. The difference between the modernist and postmodernist forms is one of focus and purpose as well as of narrative technique. Dos Passos spatialized narrative to slow down the reading process and defamiliarize the novel form. This had a thematic effect as well, for he also could represent spatially (as different typeset "voices") the idea that modern American life was a cacophony of voices, influences, experiences; that media had saturated American life; and that there seemed no authorial consciousness governing and ordering life in the modern age. Writers of metahistorical romances that spatialize history uncover equally unsettling ideas about history itself. *Historical periods themselves* are subject to quick cutting, montage, and juxtaposition in a postmodernist attempt to signal the layered indeterminacy of History and its lack of order and comprehensibility.

Findley's *Famous Last Words* illustrates how history can be both narratively and conceptually spatialized in this way. *Famous Last Words* at first presents itself to a reader as a conventional narrative; there are no typesetting effects, no columned type or pictures or font alterations or academic apparatus as there are in Dos Passos's work. However, on beginning the novel, readers are immediately made aware that something odd is happening at the conceptual level to the ontological boundaries between historical and fictional realities. History is spatialized conceptually in the interaction of the three "levels" of historical time—1945, when Mauberley scratches his writing narrative on the walls of a hotel in which he is imprisoned; the 1936 to 1945 time of the narrative he scribbles; and the "real time" in which the reader reads the novel. This last actually enters the narrative experience, for the reader's time should be the same *kind* of time in which Ezra Pound lived at the beginning of the twentieth century. But Ezra Pound isn't the narrator of this novel; his fictional character Mauberley is. Because Pound's Mauberley has become the central character in a historical narrative, "real time" also becomes fictive. The reader is somehow drawn into a blurring of ontological boundaries; his own time is no longer the "real" referent against which other, fictional, times can be measured. These levels of conceptual history seem to intermingle rather than build upon one another. History is not linear in this novel; rather, it zigzags between personal and national focuses, between conversations of persons in different times and places, between the fictive and the "real."[16]

Moreover, history is literally spatialized; Mauberley writes his account of the events occurring between 1936 and 1945 on sixteen walls of the Grand Elysium Hotel, where he is imprisoned for political reasons by German troops. Significantly, while Dos Passos described his narrative method using the names of modern technologies (e.g., "The Camera Eye" and "Newsreel"), the history Mauberley scribbles on the walls recalls a premodern world. His history becomes a hieroglyph, resembling some weird European version of Anasazi cave art, scribbled on the walls of a European aristocrat's abandoned boudoir. This history is far from impersonally "scientific"; it is a record of an imprisoned man's personal apprehension of his world, scrawled on a wall in a desperate and futile effort to order and make sense of an elusive, chaotic, and hostile present and past reality. Mauberley has formally spatialized history by writing it on the bedroom walls of a hotel—probably one of the best images of postmodern approaches to history in any contemporary novel. Encased in a room linked to desire as well as impermanence, history becomes a box, the intersection of planes. How one reads Mauberley's history depends on where one stands in the room or if one ever enters the hotel at all.

Some time ago William Spanos dismissed Frank's theory of spatial form because he believed that the latter attempted to escape history and responsible being in the world. Spanos usefully correlates modernist spatial form and New Criticism with a post-traumatic desire to escape history, to "escape the destructive impact of time and change, of which a disintegrating cosmic order has made it acutely and painfully conscious, by way of achieving the timeless eternity of the aesthetic moment or, rather, of 'spatial form'" ("Modern Literary Criticism 91). In other words, spatial forms are linked to a desire to escape history and enter sublime time, the Time-out-of-time that constitutes the other world of the platonic or religious Real. Postmodernist art to some extent recognizes that this anti-Romantic, post-traumatic modernist maneuver simply failed, and that denying history and retreating into art does not make history (or the present) simply go away. But the postmodernists also inherit the modernist metaphysics of transcendence (linked to geometric art) that Spanos identifies. They redefine rather than discard the "dehumanized, geometric art form [that] is predominant in cultures capable of expressing religious fear in the face of the contingencies of the concrete time-space world" (93). Avant-gardist, late modernist metahistorical romances of the 1960s and 1970s (e.g., Barth's *The Sot-Weed Factor,* Coover's *The Public Burning,* Pynchon's *Gravity's Rainbow,* Heller's *Catch–22,* Reed's *Mumbo Jumbo*) often seem to retain the modernist metaphysics of transcendence linked to spatialization while simultaneously, and paradoxically, reopening their eyes to history.

Comprehending that "freedom is thus radically dialogic," a recognition of the Other through time (Spanos, "Modern Literary Criticism" 102), the metahistorical romance attempts to re-enter history. However, it can't do so unproblematically. For one thing, it butts up against an entrenched modernist inheritance and bias that has relegated history to a space outside the province of art. (How many times, for example, was early postmodernist fiction lambasted for its disintegration of high art/low art distinctions? And while some of these critiques justifiably saw this eradication of boundaries as part of postmodernism's collusion with capital, others simply blasted postmodernism for being low.) Second, postmodernism reenters history at its own expense, for reentering history will force the Western consciousness to confront its own participation in (rather than mere victimization by) traumatic historical events. And third, the postmoderns seem to insist that re-entering history must be more than simply returning to modernist existentialism. The postmodern imagination seems to search for a new way to engage with history that reflects is own time and cultural zeitgeist, a search for history *and* meaning. As David Carroll has noted, the problem is not simply an opposition between synchrony and diachrony but rather "how to think space in terms of time and time in terms of space" (799). The return to history combined with a longing for Truth (or at least grounding) leads the metahistorical romance to spatialize not form but history itself. Turning back to history, but simultaneously unable to face its own reflection there and wanting something beyond the expressible event of disciplinary history, the metahistorical romance turns to the historical sublime. It spatializes History.

Understanding this metahistorical spatialization of history is crucial to understanding the avant-gardism of the mid-twentieth-century metahistorical romance. These novels relied heavily on two narrative techniques to spatialize time and interrogate disciplinary models for history: parataxis and simultaneity.

Paratactic versus Positivistic History

As noted, certain avant-gardist metahistorical romances construct nonlinear, "spatial" models for plot and for conceptual history and offer alternative models to linear, progressive history. Some types of metahistorical romances have plots that deviate from straight-line development; since, however, their plots concern the workings of history itself, they end up constructing different spatial historical models as well. Other metahistorical romances spatialize history by juxtaposing the past and present in a manner similar to parataxis, a rhetorical strategy. They thus create what can be called a *paratactic history.*

Simply defined, parataxis is a rhetorical term denoting a coordinate arrangement of words, clauses, phrases, or sentences with or without connectives ("I left. She cried."). It contrasts to hypotaxis, in which words, clauses, phrases, or sentences appear in subordinate constructions ("When I left, she cried."). Parataxis juxtaposes, while hypotaxis draws connections between semantic units. Some time ago an early analyst of the postmodern, Ihab Hassan, specifically linked parataxis to postmodernist and poststructural modes of thought. Hassan differentiated modernism from postmodernism on the ground that "modernism appears hieratic, hypotactical, and formalist, while postmodernism strikes us by contrast as playful, paratactical, and deconstructionist" (*The Postmodern Turn* 91). Similarly, in "The Culture of Criticism," Hayden White equates parataxis with political strategies of avant-garde art, claiming that parataxis threatens the humanist tradition of artistic realism perhaps more than any other avant-garde activity.[17] Hassan has claimed that indeterminacy favors paratactical styles and tends to valorize play over presence (*The Postmodern Turn* 74–75). Parataxis in narrative (employing juxtaposition, linear disjunction, deperspectivized space) thus has deeply embedded political implications that precisely identify the postmodern agenda of destabilization. It is significant as well, I would argue, that parataxis as a narrative style is consistently linked to spatialization as a quest for a Platonic Absolute, conceived in secular or religious terms. As noted above, this quest for the modernists led to the secular-sacred realm of Art, while Erich Auerbach has illustrated how this quest in a Christian context also leads to nonlinear, spatialized conceptions of history.[18]

In a work such as John Fowles's *The French Lieutenant's Woman* (1969), however, parataxis also serves to critique stable notions of *historical* causality. At the end of the novel, the narrator self-reflexively tells readers that he is opting for parataxis as a narrative strategy. He will do so because he is wary of conforming, or appearing to conform, to the conventions of Victorian fiction. Very conscious of himself as a textual persona, implicated in his narrative while distancing himself through authorial commentary about the conventions of realist fiction (317), the narrator has led Charles Smithson and Sarah Woodruff to an impasse, a point in their story where they inevitably act in a way that will lead to a happy or unhappy ending. At this point in literary history, both kinds of endings have become conventionalized, and, as the narrator recognizes, both endings imply a political stance on the part of the author. The narrator opts for the solution of presenting both endings paratactically, because "the only way I can take no part in the fight is to show two versions of it. That leaves me with only one problem: I cannot give both versions at once, yet whichever is the second will seem, so strong is the tyranny of the last chapter, the final, the 'real' version" (318). The narrator solves the problem by tossing a coin, by letting chance rule and implying that this is the only way to avoid authorial imposition and control.

The assumptions of teleological or linear history are defamiliarized and undermined at at least four different junctures here. First, the story that is being told is a historical romance; since its ending has now become multiple and arbitrary, the implication is that history itself is likewise. Second, the self-reflexive narrator has revealed the very Derridean insight that order itself implies hierarchy—and the reverse, that hierarchy may be accidental rather than ontological. This runs counter to many central historiographical assumptions about the nature and value of narrated history and the hierarchical ordering of events based on historical value. Third, by tossing a coin to determine the ending, the narrator implies that it simply doesn't matter which ending is chosen; both endings are equally important, equally true. No empirical method can determine either significance or just order, and no appeal to historical necessity seems necessary to make the story work. The implications for historical narrative itself are clear: history may be equally arbitrary, equally fictitious, equally estranged from the real, and finally the choices we make for telling history may be based more on rhetorical than scientific priorities.[19] Finally, the narrator's decision to flip a coin and thus avoid authorial control of narrative is suspect; he is no less in control because he does this. He has written the story, chosen the details, determined the number of possible endings; like a historian who claims objectivity because he is only reporting facts, Fowles's narrator abdicates responsibility for or implication in the politics of his narrative framing. What the novel reveals, perhaps inadvertently, is the absurdity, and futility, of this gesture, and so implies a futility to empiricist history as well.

Parataxis thus can be appropriated by the metahistorical romance in its attempt to deconstruct empiricist history. By applying the grammatical function of parataxis to history itself, the metahistorical romance finds (1) a way to disrupt and defamiliarize linear historical construction and (2) a model of narrative spatialization already proven effective by modernist and avant-garde precursors.

In addition, metahistorical romances are particularly well suited to explore parataxis not only at a formal, narrative level, but also at a thematic, conceptual level. Just as the postmodernist novel redefines modernist *formal* spatialization as *conceptual* spatialization of history, the metahistorical romances can redefine modernist (or avant-garde) formal parataxis as conceptual historical parataxis. Rather than juxtaposing narrative or plot segments, paratactic metahistorical romances juxtapose past and present. No longer is history upheld as a progressive linear movement; the past and the present seesaw on a precipice that overlooks sublime chaos.

Julian Barnes's *Flaubert's Parrot* illustrates how parataxis in metahistorical romance can be both formal and conceptual in this way. The chapter entitled "Chronology," for example, is open, and indeterminate, structured as a series of three chronologies of Flaubert's life, juxtaposed without connectives, or interpretive commentary. The reader is presented with multiple, spatialized histories in the form of the chronologies themselves. The chapter begins immediately with the first chronology, which presents Flaubert as a gifted writer born under a "lucky star." He is born into an "enlightened and encouraging" background, is easily befriended, is considered affectionate, and enjoys an "active and colourful erotic career." Ironically, epilepsy propitiously shifts the career goals of the pupating writer from law to literature, and the adult Flaubert emerges as a brilliant and acclaimed writer of artistic and commercial literary successes. No intrusive authorial commentary is needed to supplement the portrait of Flaubert that emerges from this chronology; the principle of selection of biographical details and the chronological method of their presentation has its own *ethos* and is constructed using the trope of comedy: Flaubert's biographical history is a comedic one here.

However, a very different Flaubert emerges from the details presented in chronology number two, appearing directly after the first chronology. Like its predecessor, the second chronology appears uncolored by authorial interpretation. But through the selection of biographical details in this chronology, Flaubert emerges as a miserable and bitter man doomed to a life of dark disappointment and fractured desires: born into a family where death overshadows youth, victim of unrequited or destructive love relationships, stricken with epilepsy that shatters his outlook and chains him to suffocating maternal care, he contracts syphilis, watches his friends expire, and dies impoverished, as a writer either detested or unknown. In this chronology, Flaubert's life is emplotted as tragedy.

Thus, the first two chronologies perform in narrative the claims about historical emplotment made by Hayden White in *Metahistory:* that rhetorical tropes structure all historical accounts, and thus all history is also a philosophy of history. The third and last chronology presented in Barnes's novel, however, emphasizes how *readers'* desires for coherent narrative affect the presentation of the past. Cognitively hardwired, perhaps, to read the world narratively, and culturally trained to expect authorial control and order in narrative, readers find order and narrative structure in a chronicle even when facts from the historical archive are presented seemingly without editorial bias. In the third chronology, Flaubert's own words are paratactically juxtaposed, though ordered by date. Interpretation is seemingly absent; no fact is subordinated to a controlling idea. The reader's immediate response to the chronology is to search for a unifying, interpretative key: to look for connectives between the quotes and to ask why these quotes appear instead of others. Ironically, because this chronology lacks the components of story such as plot or theme, the reader becomes aware that such story elements permeate the actual historical record. Because this chronology lacks connectives, it prods the reader to reexamine what connectives *are* in the context of a historical record. Hayden White asks, in *The Content of the Form,* "Could we ever narrativize without moralizing?" (25); in *Flaubert's Parrot,* the answer seems to be "no." The juxtaposition of these three chronologies leads readers to the conclusion Braithwaite, the protagonist, himself draws in a later chapter: "How can we know such trivial, crucial details? We can study files for decades, but every so often we are tempted to throw up our hands and declare that history is merely another literary genre: the past is autobiographical fiction pretending to be a parliamentary report" (*Flaubert's Parrot* 93–94). Here, parataxis, as a spatializing technique, makes us rethink historical narrative.[20] In his quest for knowledge about (his own, his wife, Ellen's, and Flaubert's) character and the working of history, Braithwaite finally writes not only an autobiography but also an inquiry into history beginning with the questions "Does the world progress? Or does it merely shuttle back and forth like a ferry?" (112). "Shuttling back and forth" is a paratactic gesture; lacking a sense of external guidance or the reassurance of *telos,* Braithwaite has only parataxis as a hermeneutic for understanding his world.

Through its support of syntagmatic over paradigmatic modes, avant-gardist metahistorical romance rejects a dialectical conception of history in favor of heteroglossia. Characters, time periods, ideologies may be juxtaposed or may even combat one another, but synthesis is by definition impossible. In Boyle's novel *World's End,* for instance, dialectic or evolutionary synthesis is undermined by paratactic history. Characters from the present (1968–69) echo (indeed, nearly reincarnate) characters from the recent past (1949) and characters from the more distant past (1664–92). In alternating chapters, three parallel stories of deceit and treachery are told and juxtaposed: the seventeenth-century story of Wouter Van Brunt, Jeremy Mohonk, and Cadwaller Crane; the 1949 story of Truman Van Brunt, Hesh Solovay, Jeremy Mohonk (the last of the Kitchawanks), and

Depeyster Van Wart; and the 1968 story of Walter Truman Van Brunt, his wife Jessica, Depeyster Van Wart, his daughter Mardi, and Tom Crane. In an author's note to the novel, Boyle calls *World's End* a "historical fugue." The paratactic form of the novel makes this term particularly apt: *World's End* is analogous to a fugue in both the musical and psychiatric senses. In music, a fugue is a strictly controlled form in which a musical subject is announced in one voice and then is echoed, varied, and developed in other voices; the composition leads to a resolution of these voices. *World's End* begins in the present (in 1968) and aborts chronological sequence in order to juxtapose time frames in alternate chapters, the different and modulating voices of history. The novel is also a "fugue" in a psychiatric sense: an amnesiatic forgetting, in which a person appears to act normally and rationally though she or he will forget those actions when returned to normal consciousness. In *World's End,* the relationship between the present and the past is essentially one of traumatic forgetting, and the novel centers on how the present becomes aware of itself only dimly as a reflection, product, or inheritor of the past.

Notably, however, the novel never explains the phenomena that start the plot moving: the appearance of the ghosts of his father and grandmother, which precede Walter's accidents—accidents that weirdly identify him physically with his ancestors. Walter has some "trouble with his eyes that made the past come alive in the present" (*World's End* 130). After seeing these ghosts, he becomes "sick with history, the past coming at him like a succession of screaming fire trucks" (10). But why these ghosts appear to him, why the coincidences between Walter's and his ancestors' lives occur, and why all of Walter's actions seem predetermined, is unexplained. The past seems motivated to reassert itself in the lives of the living: Walter "felt odd all of a sudden, felt the grip of history like a noose around his neck and he didn't know why" (169). Only two explanations are given for the uncanny intrusions of the past upon the present. The first is by Walter's father, who shrieks "Fate! . . . Doom! History! Don't you see?" and sneers that treachery is Walter's birthright: "It's in the blood, Walter. It's in the bones" (423, 424). The second explanation is his grandmother's: she sees "the world for what it was—a haunted place, where anything could happen and nothing was as it seemed, where shadows had fangs and doom festered in the blood" (78). As a metahistorical romance, *World's End* presents History not as a logical narrative or even a realist one but rather as the uncanny intrusion of the past into the present. Like other metahistorical romances, this novel moves toward and withdraws from History (the realm of the past that is forever inaccessible and lost to us) and gestures toward the uncanny border of the historical sublime. Rendering history as paratactic forces the reader to bounce between time and eternity.

Additionally, the strategy of parataxis seems to link the metahistorical romance yet again to post-*Annales* historiography. F. R. Ankersmit, for instance, noted that "with the collapse of [F. O.] Mink's metaphor of the vantage point, from which the flow of the river of time can be surveyed, and with the emergence of the postmodernist oxymoron of 'the point of view of the absence of points of view,' the elements of the past regain their autonomy and become independent of one another. And the result is the fragmentation of the past so characteristic of the postmodernist picture of the past" (*History and Tropology* 224). One way that this fragmentation of the past posited by a postmodern historiography is accomplished in the metahistorical romance is through the strategy of parataxis. Elements of historical narrative including events, characters, typical period language and costume and ideology are precipitated out of their seamless historical narrative and, paradoxically, gain identity as fragments of history. This is both the rationale and strategy of the paratactic metahistorical romance. While a novel such as *Little Big Man* (1964) uses parataxis as a formal narrative strategy (a way of telling the story), paratactic metahistorical romances use parataxis to comment about history itself. The result is that the present seesaws between an engulfing past and a sometimes terror-laden, sometimes hopeful future.

Sexing the Cherry employs parataxis to construct historiographical commentary in this way. The novel is set between 1630 and 1665, at a revolutionary time in English history (England's Civil War of 1642–46 and the rise and fall of Cromwell). The central character of the novel is Dog Woman, a monstrous and fantastic woman who adopts an abandoned child (Jordon) and raises fighting dogs to make money. During the course of the novel, Dog Woman experiences the horror of the 1640 plague; the outbreak of civil war, the closing of the theaters, and the rise of Puritan influence; the execution of Charles I and the consequent Interregnum; the death of Cromwell and end of the Protectorate. After the restoration of Charles II to the throne, she enjoys seeing Cromwell's associates half hanged, disemboweled, and quartered alive. Dog Woman becomes a synecdoche for the age; like the times, she is huge, contradictory, and violent.

Viewed from the perspective of metahistorical inquiry and postmodernist politics, the novel seems to construct a paratactic narrative structure in at least three significant ways. First, the novel itself is predicated on paratactical structure in an obvious and successful attempt to disrupt linear reading patterns and politicize the narrative. During the course of the novel, chapters alternate between Dog Woman's and Jordon's first-person points of view. This strategy allows Winterson to bring gender roles and stereotypes and sexual mores seen through both characters' eyes into the debate circle, for the speaking characters as well as secondary characters (such as the Roundheads and the Puritan Preacher Scroggs) challenge these by their physical appearances, their love interests, and their social behavior. (At one point, for instance, Jordon lodges with a convent of nuns. The nuns slip out at night to whore, and Jordon finds he likes dressing as a woman. Preacher Scroggs also frequents the ladies' brothel to participate in sadomasochistic sex. The episode allows Winterson simultaneously to stab at patriarchal gender politics within the religious establishment and to interrogate social definitions of masculinity.)

Second, parataxis also blurs the boundaries between reality and fantasy within these alternating chapters. The narrative juxtaposes historical material with retold fairy tales (e.g., "The Twelve Dancing Princesses"), fantasy (i.e., the stories of fantastic cities reminiscent of those in Italo Calvino's *Invisible Cities*), and editorializations inserted into the narrative by a unidentified narrator that seems to be Winterson herself.[21]

Third, parataxis also appears in *Sexing the Cherry* at a metahistorical level. At the end of the novel, Dog Woman seems reborn in a female eco-activist camping by a river in the 1990s in order to investigate rising mercury levels. The woman has visions of herself as a giantess, stuffing corrupt politicians and businessmen into a sack as Dog Woman was wont to do; the eco-activist is most comfortable in the company of dogs. The activist fantasizes that she has a huge woman inside of her—whom the reader knows to be, spiritually, Dog Woman, alive three centuries before. She leaves her parents' home and finds inside herself "an *alter ego* who was huge and powerful, a woman whose only morality was her own and whose loyalties were fierce and few. She was my patron saint, the one I called on" (142). In addition, at the end of the novel, Jordon sees a twentieth-century character named Nicholas Jordon (who looks exactly like the seventeenth-century Jordon) facing him in the Thames River fog (166). Readers of Winterson's novel are likely to question why characters in the present have somehow become reincarnations of seventeenth-century characters; no editorial voice intervenes with a comforting rationale for these dizzying, and somehow sinister, transports between historical periods. There is also no narrative justification (in terms of plot or character development) for the historical leaps. One explanation that does make sense is that the text has exploited another level of parataxis in order to question yet another ideological given in Western cultures, that of historical linearity and positivism.

Winterson's novel self-consciously fuses a Western perspective on history with Western gender politics and attempts to undermine both at once. The novel consistently links Western history to constructions of male and female subjectivity. Throughout, the characters Jordon and Dog Woman challenge Western assumptions about gender, but they also simultaneously challenge Western assumptions about time and space. Jordon can travel to fantastic places, such as the land of the Twelve Dancing Princesses or the home of Fortunata, "a woman who doesn't exist" (*Sexing the Cherry* 149), whereas Dog Woman seems reincarnated in the twentieth century. This fusion of gender politics with metahistorical inquiry is particularly obvious in the characterization of the female eco-activist. She is a freak, a feminist, and a loner who is frustrated with men and observes their weaknesses; likewise, as an ecoactivist she is accustomed to defamiliarizing and challenging Western ideas about consumption and about natural space. She is an apt figure to embody a similar critique of Western time and patriarchal history. "I don't know if other worlds exist in space or time," she says. "Perhaps this is the only one and the rest is rich imaginings. Either way it doesn't matter. We have to protect both possibilities. They seem to be interdependent"(145–46).

The concept of interdependency directly opposes Western patriarchy, individualism, and laissez faire capitalism; it is central to many non-Western cultures, particularly that of the Hopi, which Winterson specifically references a number of times in the novel. (As noted in chapter 2, one of the novel's epigraphs emphasizes the Hopi's non-Western conception of time.) The eco-activist perceives her ties to others in the past and future in a feminist vision of freedom and communion that bears striking resemblance to non-Western notions of cyclic time: "If I have a spirit, a soul, any name will do, then it won't be single, it will be multiple. Its dimension will not be one of confinement but one of space. It may inhabit numerous changing decaying bodies in the future and in the past" (*Sexing the Cherry* 144). The eco-activist's self-reflections on her politicized, spatialized body poses a challenge to Western patriarchy; her perspective on being-in-time harkens back to a non-Western conception of communal being and cyclic time that directly challenge Western notions of positivistic history. Parataxis at both levels of the narrative mount an attack on Western assumptions about history and its import.

One more observation might be made here about the metahistorical romance's attack on positivism through paratactic history. Many metahistorical romances address notions of Western logic and detection by including detectives as actual characters in their plots. But in metahistorical romance, these detectives must sort out not the workings of a criminal mind but the message of history. In other words, metahistorical detectives initially work within a hermeneutics that assumes meaning can exist and that causal relations can be established between events. However, these detectives are stuck in history, just as human beings are stuck in Jameson's prisonhouse of language; in these metahistorical romances the detectives cannot step outside the historical system they inhabit. They cannot effectively subordinate the past to the present and establish causality as could the detective of literary convention. The burden of detection is then thrust on readers, but with the consequence that readers also realize their implication in history. The dilemma of the fictional "detective of history" is the dilemma of humankind: to attempt the task of reconstructing, thwarting, or stepping outside the codes of historical representation that provide the only avenue of historical knowledge but that also enclose and blind us so that this knowledge is by definition incomplete, partial, or biased.[22]

In Peter Ackroyd's paratactic metahistorical romance *Hawksmoor,* for instance, the reader does not always learn why seesawing between historical periods occurs. The novel's protagonist, Nicholas Dyer, becomes the vehicle for an attack on Western positivism, while the novel's paratactic structure attacks linear structure in Western history. *Hawksmoor* shuttles the action between the eighteenth and twentieth centuries in alternating chapters. The novel begins in 1712: architect Nicholas Dyer writes his life story to an unnamed 'you,' referred to only once (24). In this account, Dyer describes his birth (in the manner of Dickens's *David Copperfield*) and his childhood that ends with the plague deaths of his mother and father. After watching his parents buried in an open pit with other plague victims, young Nicholas becomes a street urchin and eventually comes under the influence of Mirabilis, head of a satanic cult. As an adult and an architect working with the Enlightenment philosopher Christopher Wren, Dyer literally concretizes his demonic religion in the churches he builds, hiding in them the Mysteries he studies, and he commits sacrificial murders to consecrate each of his six churches.

The central conflict in this novel between rationalism and mysterious faith is directly related to its presentations of time and paratactic history. Dyer asserts a philosophy of mystical terror and social Contagion against the philosophy of his social superior and rival, Christopher Wren, who articulates the empiricism characterizing the Age of Reason. Even though he was actually an eighteenth-century personage, in this novel Nicholas Dyer is the mouthpiece of a Lyotardian postmodernism and the voice of its most disruptive and destructive tendencies—the voice of what Graff has called the apocalyptic strain of postmodernism. Within the novel Dyer arrives at a terrifying definition of non-linear time that is literally revolutionary: "Truly Time is a vast Denful of Horrour, round about which a Serpent winds and in the winding bites itself by the Tail. Now, now is the Hour, every Hour, every part of an Hour, every Moment, which in its end does begin again and never ceases to end: a beginning continuing, always ending" (*Hawksmoor* 82). Dyer, on the side of faith (albeit a satanic one), attempts to perform what all religion promises: to negate time by evoking eternity. (Again, we see an example of the metahistorical romance turning back to a mythic sense of time in order to interrogate the assumptions of Enlightenment historiography.) Dyer builds churches and attempts to impose on history a monument that refuses or denies evolutionary change and to inscribe himself as a human element into malevolent Time.

Structural parataxis appears in the novel in alternating chapters that flash from this eighteenth-century setting to the present (twentieth century), where murders are once again taking place at each of Dyer's churches. Detective Chief Superintendent Nicholas Hawksmoor must solve these crimes that leave behind no trace of the perpetrator. Hawksmoor himself, his activities, the murders—all facets of this twentieth-century scene—rehearses the scene of the eighteenth-century murders. The centuries echo one another, without any explanation, until they merge in a union between Hawksmoor, Dyer, and a third party (unidentified) in the last lines of the book.[23] Dyer alters Time's posture within the story by making his "own History . . . a Pattern which others may follow in the far Side of Time"

(*Hawksmoor* 274). Dyer wills the past to interact unnaturally with the present/future.

When Nicholas Hawksmoor in the twentieth century tries to investigate the six murders at Dyer's churches, he repeatedly encounters a drawing of "the figure of a man who had put a circular object up to his right eye and was peering through it as if it were a spy glass, although it might equally have been a piece of plastic or a communion wafer" (*Hawksmoor* 215). In Lee's reading of this novel, this figure represents Sherlock Holmes, "detective fiction's transcendental signifier."[24] However, this drawn figure might as easily represent the novel's central concern with time: the picture shows a man trying to see or understand external reality using the tools of the three modern ages of man: science (spy glass), technology (plastic), and religion (communion wafer). Significantly, these symbols are out of chronological sequence. Historical linearity as well as empirical detection are the victims of Dyer's (and postmodernism's) cross-temporal attack. Historical evolution is here linked to positivistic approaches to reality, and is countered by disruptive, de-centering mysticism, chance, and terror. The novel's paratactic structure is the antisystem that negates the detective's raison d'être. The two effects of Ackroyd's novel are a recovery of primordial terror and a dismantling of positivistic time as a function of artificialized Nature.[25]

As these examples illustrate, metahistorical romances that spatialize history as paratactic do not claim that history is "only a text." Much more significantly, they repudiate the notion that one can step outside the systems of power, language, politics, or ideology and view one's own cultural system from a privileged and impartial observatorial distance. We never leave the past in the past, these novels imply, just as we never leave our own life experience behind us. Just as our past life experience forms who we are now, and always flashes upon us in the present in the form of memories, the historical past too is alive and informing our present in myriad ways. After all, what paratactic history resembles most of all is *déjà vu,* the uncanny haunting of the present by the past. Seen this way, these novels illustrate how a post-traumatic, late-twentieth-century literature (the product of so-cieties that deify scientific rationalism) incorporates a culture's des-perate desire to come to terms with the past, its recognition that this is impossible, and its frenzied denial of that final limit to knowledge. "And," David Harvey astutely notes, "if it is true that time is always memorialized not as flow, but as memories of experienced places and spaces, then history must indeed give way to poetry, time to space, as the fundamental material of social expression. The spatial image . . . then asserts an important power over history" (218). These narratives not only compulsively return to the past in their subject matter and commentary on history; they also *perform* this compulsive repetition through specific plot structures and narrative techniques. Chronol-ogy in these novels takes the form of the chronology of memory, which is not chronology at all but parataxis, a 'shuttling back and forth' between the interwined times of past and present.

Eric Rabkin has noted that unlike hypotaxis (where plot relations are made clear), parataxis demands that writers and reader share value contexts. Metahistorical novels that depend upon a paratactic con-struction of history imply that when history is understood in psy-chological terms (akin to the ever-present and potentially interruptive state of memory), the deadness of disciplinary history may come alive again, even if in uncanny ways. "The paratactical style," notes Hay-den White, "is an intrinsically *communal* style, rather than a *societal* one; it is inherently democratic and egalitarian rather than aristo-cratic and elitist, and it is possible that the rebirth of parataxis in art and thought in this century does not represent the fall back into myth or the advent of a new totalitarianism so much as the demand for a change of consciousness that will finally make a unified human-ity possible" ("The Culture of Criticism" 69). Viewed this way, para-tactic history in metahistorical romance seems less an avant-gardism addressed to elite coterie audiences (as some critics have alleged) than an odd attempt to create a communal style, one that reflects the his-torical consciousness of its time.

Simultaneous History in Flatland

In 1884, Edwin A. Abbott published a science fantasy novel, *Flatland,* in which the first-person narrator A. Square tells of a two-dimensional world populated by living beings who take the form of geometric shapes. Flatland, with all its inhabitants and social structures, is entirely planar, constructed as a two-dimensional plane with length and width but not height as that is defined in a three-dimensional universe. Two momentous events have happened to A. Square, a middle-class male in the shape of a two-dimensional rectangle. First, he has dreamed of a world that is one dimensional, Lineland, inhabited by a king, men, and women who reside along a line in space; their world is a Straight Line. A. Square attempts to question the king about his world and also tell him about life in Flatland, but finds that it is impossible to translate his two-dimensional world into one-dimensional terms. The second event that changes A. Square's life is his contact, in his own two-dimensional world, with a Sphere—a being from a *three*-dimensional world. This being appears at the end of every millennium to the inhabitants of Flatland to reveal to them the mysteries of three-dimensionality; however, these mysteries have been suppressed by the ruling government. When A. Square finally conceptualizes three-dimensionality with Sphere's help, he is thrown into jail for preaching heresy or lunacy. Sphere has appeared in 1999.

While Abbott's book was originally meant to be both a social satire and metaphysical allegory, one can see it in our contexts as an historiographical allegory as well. Historiography since the Enlightenment has configured the passage of historical time as a line; as it did for Lineland, this kind of structure limits a line of sight to a (logical) Point and encourages single events to take up place along the line. In other words, on a true line, made up of points without length, width, or height, there is 'room' for only one point at a time in succession. By analogy, a time line for history may allow only limited numbers of events to be known: the ones that fall along the line of time. This analogy of course enormously oversimplifies what historians do, but it does not oversimplify how history is taught. Ordinary people in the West tend to learn history this way: as a series of interlocking, singular events along a time line that form a pattern and meaningful past.

The advantage of this linear model of historical time is that it allows for historical narrativization and duplicates the way time conceptually unfolds for most people: one event after another through the years and marked in memory by major social and personal events. The disadvantage of this linear model is that it tends to limit a line of historical sight, cutting off multiple views in favor of one focused on a Point, often that of the king—political or major social events recorded for political purposes at the expense of more ordinary, or less approved, points of view. The postmodernist novel has been accusing history of this kind of political partisanship for some time. A novel such as Ishmael Reed's *Mumbo Jumbo,* for example, which links Enlightenment historiography to racism and social control, makes precisely the argument that historiographical Lineland is a very small and politically dangerous world indeed.

What other insight might Abbott's book give about historical reconstruction? First, it implies that Lineland is more limited than Flatland, and the Flatland is more limited than Spaceland (the land of the Sphere), because options open for perception as dimensionality increases. Spaceland is not necessarily *better* than Lineland; it just offers more perspectives for vision. The Sphere can see more than can the king or A. Square. Moreover, Sphere is somehow a more complex and richer being (if not a better being) than is A. Square, because a sphere is comprised of infinite circles; Sphere can know Square, but not vice-versa. Certain kinds of metahistorical romance pursue this kind of logic and link it to Foucaultian insights about historical archeology. These novels implicitly claim that options open as dimensionality increases. They apply this insight to history itself to create a kind of spatial history very much related to paratactic history: that is, simultaneous history.

In the past, some literary critics, examining the work of Joyce, Proust, or Woolf, have equated simultaneity with spatial form according to Frank's definition. These critics understand simultaneity as a time sense implying stasis or the freezing of action at the level of sentence or plot structure. Most critics identifying simultaneity in certain fiction thus equate simultaneity with Frank's theory of spatiality: simultaneous equals spatial form. However, simultaneity in metahistorical romances may appear not only as a formal narrative technique, but also as spatial *history.* Like parataxis, simultaneity becomes both a model and a narrative technique for presenting history in certain metahistorical romances. Some of these novels erase the distinction between historical and fictional characters and thereby dissolve the boundaries between historical fact and fiction. Other simultaneous histories create a new fictional universe in which historical epochs, characters, or events appear together on the same historical plane.

Simultaneous history replaces the historical time line with multiple, coexisting historical planes. It creates a new fictional universe in which historical epochs, characters, or events appear together, thus challenging the entire notion of linear historical reconstruction. A metahistorical romance that constructs history as simultaneous, rather than successive, time periods offers a model for history that in many ways recalls pre-Enlightenment modes of mythic time and memory. Such a construction calls for multidimensional history, in the interest of escaping the limiting vision of Flatland and the Point of the King.

Metahistorical romances that reject linear models of history in this way challenge the notion of linear historical reconstruction and illustrate the close link between paratactic and simultaneous historical models. Peter Ackroyd's novel *Chatterton* (1987), for example, illustrates this linkage of parataxis and simultaneity in metahistorical romance. The first two sections of the novel are set in the twentieth century, where a poet Charles Wychwood finds a picture seemingly of Thomas Chatterton in his fifties, an impossible representation if the historical accounts of Chatterton's death were accurate. Committed himself to a Romantic vision of poetry, Charles becomes obsessed with the painting and with what appears to be a collection of Chatterton's papers, pursued by other characters who want control of these for profit or the promise of scholarly accolades. The novel's third section switches to the eighteenth century, and is an account of Chatterton's last days. The story of Thomas Chatterton's death is re-told, replacing the historical account of his suicide with a tragic story of youthful naïveté and death by unintentional drug overdose. In a postmodern updating of *Dorian Gray,* Ackroyd puns on the post-structuralist redefinition of "self" as "subject" (in this case, self as the subject of art) and the old poststructuralist claim about the "death of the author." Here the author literally dies but lives on in the art ob-ject. Chatterton the poet literally becomes a text (a picture and a story) in this novel.

But the novel offers an alternative even to its own emplotted ver-sion of this event by providing two kinds of evidence that Chatter-ton, or at least his spirit, never died at all. The first involves the por-trait itself. Chatterton's portrait is revealed finally to be a bad forgery, merely disguising another picture beneath it. At least, this is the con-sensus of art critics who appraise the painting. However, when one painter tries to remove the forged topcoat to reveal the original, the novel flips rapidly between sections relating the paint removal process and sections relating the death of the poet Chatterton three hundred years before. As the narrative switches between time periods, we see the twentieth-century painting bubbling and boiling as Chatterton's body boils from the effects of opium-arsenic overdose. The implica-tion is that this indeed was a picture of Chatterton, or that it pos-sessed his spirit in some way—a spirit that aged even though the cor-poreal Chatterton died in 1770. The novel asserts Chatterton's viability in the present in a second way by showing how Chatterton possesses Charles's spirit and eventually kills him. Chatterton's spirit lives in the twentieth-century: Charles and Harriet Scrope both see it (though the one is sick and the other drunk when the apparitions ap-pear) and Charles's son Edward senses it in a Wordsworthian, child-like kind of way. When Charles dies, he joins Chatterton and a third, unnamed figure.

Chatterton rewrites history as an uncanny ghost story, but it implies also that what historians label the dead past is terrifyingly vital, shaping the present constantly without our conscious knowledge.[26] While the novel depends on formal parataxis to construct its narrative (alternating sections of narrative dealing with different plot lines) and upon metahistorical parataxis to defamiliarize history and/or historical models (alternating a focus on different historical periods and showing their interaction), this parataxis ends up as simultaneity, the joining together of different historical times on one plane of reality. The same kind of merging of parataxis with simultaneity happens in Ackroyd's *Hawksmoor* but also in other novels, such as *Sexing the Cherry* and William T. Vollmann's *The Rifles*. The reality that these novels construct is outside the parameters established for history by disciplinary rules; it may be an attempt to represent the historical sublime. Parataxis and simultaneity are kindred metahistorical strategies of defamiliarization that imply that history is weird, uncanny, and dimensionally complex.

Narratologically working out the different ways that texts present history as simultaneous dimensionality would require a more extensive treatment than is possible here, but I will suggest that there seems to be a kind of continuum of possibilities available to the metahistorical imagination when working with simultaneous history. The continuum ranges from nihilistic deconstruction on the one hand to reconstructed cultural or secular-sacred belief on the other.

What is the difference in metahistorical perspective, that is, between the simultaneous history constructed in *Chatterton* and that constructed in N. Scott Momaday's *House Made of Dawn?* Ackroyd's novel leaves one with a sense of immobility, a sense that we humans set in motion some course of action a very long time ago, and the present is, if not determined by, then at least significantly shaped by that course. The protagonist Charles in the novel only chances on the portrait of Chatterton, but once he does, in an almost classically tragical sense, his fate is sealed. As it is in *World's End,* in *Chatterton* the past is a haint, a succubus; it interacts with us to our doom or redemptive death. There is an ironic quality to the observation of history here, a kind of fatalism in the face of the mystery of historical movement. Asserting that History is unknowable, illogical, and un-representable, the novel recuperates the uncanniness and the terror of the historical sublime.

In contrast, in Momaday's text, simultaneous history is the bedrock of historical understanding and the formation of a positive, if problematized, subjectivity. In *House Made of Dawn,* Momaday writes his life story not as traditional autobiography but as a het-eroglossic, spatialized text. The text cuts up the linear narrative story line and spatializes form in Frank's sense. But also it spatializes *history,* a subject equal in importance in this text to the narrator's personal story. For example, a frame story encompasses the narrative at the start and end of the work, telling how Momaday visits his family homestead to attend a funeral and there is reminded of, and feels the need to come to terms with, his personal and cultural past. Inside this frame, there are short narratives that tell the stories of Kiowa mythol-ogy since the creation of the universe; narratives that tell the story of Kiowa history as that story has been written by anthropologists and ethnographers in modern times; narratives that tell the story of Moma-day's own life experience in the world; and, in some editions, pen-and-ink drawings illustrating many of the mythological stories. The text is divided into units comprised of facing pages that are them-selves divided into three paragraph-length sections. In each unit, the order of sections is the same: first a section telling a story from Kiowa Apache mythology or legend, then an ethnographical story about Kiowa history, then a brief paragraph or two of personal memory re-counted from Momaday's own life.

The implications of this style as a *way of writing history* are multi-ple. First, the presentation implies that historical writing is not dif-ferent in kind from other kinds of narrative such as myth or fiction or memory, and second, it implies that historical narrative based in disciplinary methods and models should not be elevated or valued above any other kinds of historical narratives. The ethnographical ac-count is just one of many ways to approach the past. Third, through-out the narrative, especially in the frame sections, Momaday implies that parataxis-leading-to-simultaneity is the only alternative for history left to him, since the Kiowa stories have been either lost or repressed and Kiowa culture has been rewritten for two centuries by both well meaning and vicious cultural outsiders. Momaday, like so many other Native American writers, emphasizes that fragments are all he has left of his own heritage, but he will refuse to despair and instead will use those fragments as well as he can to form a personally and culturally meaningful sense of the past. There is no irony here, only a longing for identity and history combined with a realistic recognition of the unknowability of that past.

Momaday converts parataxis into simultaneity in this text: the three kinds of historical narratives in each numbered section of the book must exist simultaneously as vital elements of his own cultural past. He is not only Kiowa but also a scholar and citizen of the late-twentieth-century world; all three kinds of historical narration are useful to him, a post-traumatic healing and response to reconstructing a past in the face of History that has been lost or is ever receding from his grasp. To be truly meaningful, all three kinds of tales must be heard and accepted simultaneously. Only then can they flesh out a living past that speaks to him as a being in the world who struggles to come to terms with his own traumatic cultural history.[27]

To return to our question, then, what is the difference in metahistorical perspective between the simultaneous history constructed in *Chatterton* and that constructed in *House Made of Dawn?* Together, the novels illustrate two poles on a continuum of possibilities available to the First World, metahistorical imagination when working with simultaneous history. The continuum ranges from ironic, even nihilistic, deconstruction on the one hand to a reconstructed "secular-sacred" belief on the other. Significantly, as I posit in chapter 5, the former seems aligned with a postmodernist sensibility and novels written by authors who situate themselves within the arena of First World politics; the latter seems aligned with a postcolonialist sensibility and novels written by authors who situate themselves *outside* the First World cultural arena.

One way of understanding this difference is to turn once more to historiography itself. In *Figural Realism,* Hayden White argues that post-Enlightenment, Western written history is informed by Christian paradigms of historical process, specifically, by the notion of historical prefiguration. In White's view, Christian theologians worked out a notion of retroactive causation by which an event was to be historicized (distanced, placed in perspective, and assigned a positive or negative value) to the extent that it could be interpreted as an anticipation (a figure) of a later event or a fulfillment (*eine Erfüllung*) of an earlier event. This he calls the "figure-fulfillment model" of history: "The figure-fulfillment model (which is not linear, not cyclical, not dualistic, nor fractal . . . is a way of construing historical processes as a development in which an entity coming later in the order of time simultaneously exalts an entity preceding it as its own precursor *and* derogates it as an imperfect or partial or incomplete protomorph of the later and more fully actualized type to which both, though differentially, belong. The two entities do not have to be construed as genetically related, in the manner of an ancestor and descendent" (White, "Cosmos, Chaos" 13). Following its paradigm in St. Paul's Epistle to the Romans, the figure-fulfillment model of history is the process whereby a later event retroactively identifies an earlier entity as a precursor to itself *based on the knowledge gained by historical distance and perspective.* The importance of this Western way of understanding history is threefold. First, it constructs an implicit progressivism in Western history. Second, it differentiates that which is *historical* from that which is not (which is defined as that which is merely *anthropological*). Third, it elevates narrative as the discursive form in which this relationship of figure to fulfillment in history can be revealed.[28]

White articulates a model for history that nicely complicates simple claims of postmodernism's rejection of "linear history," a model implied and resisted by metahistorical romance for some time. The refusal of a narrativist mode for history, for example, answers the call for an alternative to a mechanical model for history in Pynchon's *Gravity's Rainbow.* At one point in the novel, the behavioral scientist Pointsman engages in a short debate with Roger Mexico about the value of scientism; whereas Pointsman advocates mechanical explanation, science, cause-and-effect logic, and "a clear train of linkages," Mexico advocates an alternative:

> "there's a feeling about that cause-and-effect may have been taken as far as it will go. That for science to carry on at all, it must look for a less narrow, a less . . . sterile set of assumptions. The next great breakthrough may come when we have the courage to junk cause-and-effect entirely, and strike off at some other angle."
>
> "No [replies Pointsman]—not 'strike off.' Regress. You're 30 years old, man. There are no 'other angles.' There is only forward—*into it*—or backward." (*Gravity's Rainbow* 89)

What are clearly opposed here are two models for history, both articulated in terms of space and mapping and both implying a metaphysics as well as a social ideology: a "linear," figure-fulfillment model propping up Western scientific institutions, and a desired Other to this that is a yearning for "another angle" that junks cause-and-effect logic for associative, even secular/sacred approaches. Simultaneous history in metahistorical romance may be understood as an attempt to escape Pointsman's figure-fulfillment model of history by replacing sequence with simultaneity. By flattening different historical times onto one plane of reality, simultaneous history denies the possibility of a figure-fulfillment model of history. In these novels, the whole notion of "before" and "after" is either complicated and turned into a chicken-and-the-egg conundrum or overtly represented as a political (rather than natural) construction. "I have read *Finnegans Wake* and am conversant with post-modernist critiques of the West," says Mimi in Salman Rushdie's *The Satanic Verses,* "e.g. that we have here a society capable only of pastiche: a 'flattened' world. When I become the voice of a bottle of bubble bath, I am entering Flatland knowingly, understanding what I'm doing and why" (261). In the post-Enlightenment, postmodern metahistorical romance—especially those that construct paratactic or simultaneous models for history—a metanarrativistic or global model for history such as the figure-fulfillment model is aligned with either a pre-Enlightenment religiosity or a disciplinary, positivist progressivism. It is not difficult to produce example after example of metahistorical romance written after 1960 that expose, resist, or try to escape from a figure-fulfillment model of history formally or thematically.

What results from this escape attempt, however, is a continuum of success. On the one hand, exemplified in novels such as *Chatterton,* is an attempt to escape that ends in irony because of a failure to reject the figure-fulfillment trope's viability and correspondence to reality. Finally, after all the cards are on the table, *Chatterton* resists but cannot escape from figure-fulfillment as a model of history. To paraphrase Linda Hutcheon's insight on postmodernism, the novel is finally complicitous with the paradigm it attempts to critique. On the other side of the continuum, exemplified by *House Made of Dawn,* are attempts to escape that complicity through a recognition of the trope *as trope* (rather than as reality) and therefore a recognition that subtends irony and posits the possibility of other, "real" ways of understanding history.[29] This may be the difference between a metahistorical imagination that stops at irony and a metahistorical imagination that conceives of alternatives to the Western way of understanding history.

The idea of spatial history allows us to analyze further exactly with *what* some postmodernist metahistory is complicitous. While it resists historical metanarrative, it often cannot escape the figure-fulfillment paradigm for history. As a result, like a debater who has run out of rhetorical options, it resorts to irony, the last resort of the desperate, as critique.

Recognizing that historical models are highly conventionalized, the metahistorical romance forms them anew in an evolutionary development of the classic historical romance. One experimental or avantgarde form of the metahistorical romance redefines linear models of history through the lens of a post-traumatic consciousness as paratactic or simultaneous history in an attempt to approach History and create a meaningful sense of the past. The metahistorical romance, in the manner of postmodern historiography, reveals its desire to "imagine a conception of history that would signal its resistance to the bourgeois ideology of realism by its refusal to attempt a narrativist mode for the representation of its truth" (*Content* 81). Conflating a listing by Ihab Hassan of the characteristics of postmodernism, a listing by Hayden White of characteristics of avant-garde parataxis, and a list incorporating my own claims in this chapter yields useful characteristics of spatialized history in avant-gardist metahistorical romance:

Historical Romance	*Metahistorical Romance*
Distance	Participation
Stratification	Juxtaposition
Social Hierarchies	Lateral Coexistence
Domination and Subordination	Democracy
Empiricism	Desire
Perspective	Deperspectivized Space
Closure	Openness
Metonymy	Metaphor
Linear	Planar
Structures	Fragments
Presence	Absence
Centering	Deferral
Interpretation	Action on behalf of belief
Narrative/*Grande Histoire*	Anti-narrative/*Petite Histoire*
Diachrony	Synchrony.[30]

Refusing, and re-fusing, narrative history through its construction of alternative historical models, the metahistorical romance continues to desire, to strive toward the historical sublime.

The notion of simultaneous metahistoricity is a common narrative strategy for novels by writers who situate themselves somehow outside the Anglo-European or Anglo-American literary tradition. Both paratactic and simultaneous history release images from the repressed (the culturally repressed as well as the libidinal and mythic unconscious) into the world, to walk among real people, creating a mythical world where different kinds of reality and time interact with one another or exist simultaneously on the same plane, the same historical moment.[31] Metahistorical romance refigures the spatial model of history most common to the post-Enlightenment, Anglo-European West in order to defamiliarize it and to make a point about the possibilities for other, and perhaps richer, kinds of historical knowledge. In a sense, History in these novels that spatialize history is the multidimensional space of the *pasts,* the site of desire, the multidimensional counter to the Lineland of disciplinary history.

4 | *Metamodernity*

The Postmodern Turn on
the Enlightenment

*There can be no great disappointment where there is
not great love.*
　　　　　　—The Rev. Dr. Martin Luther King, Jr.,
　　　　　　　　　　　　　　　　Why We Can't Wait

Walter Scott was deeply influenced by the stadialist thinking of the
Scottish philosophers (who in turn were indebted to circulating Enlightenment theories of history), but his historical romances also
championed a romantic and mythologized Scottish past. His novels
were thus a precursor form, or literary ancestor, for the metahistorical romance of today. If the metahistorical romance is understood to
be a chiasmatic genre predicated upon resistance to and questioning
of Enlightenment historiographical assumptions, then the proliferation since 1970 of historical novels set in eighteenth-century Europe
and the Americas is especially provocative.

In the postmodernism debates, the Enlightenment is generally understood as the birth time of late modernity, the "Age of Reason" her-
alded by the 1687 publication of Newton's *Principia* and consolidat-
ing a Newtonian science of nature as mathematical and mechanical.
The Enlightenment has become a looming presence in theories of
postmodernity, foregrounding the anxiety about postmodernism's
heritage and difference. Anxiety about differentiating the postmodern from the modern has led theory to three contemporary angles of
vision concerning Enlightenment modernity: (1) a position, either
radical or nostalgic, that critiques modernity from the position of a

desired premodernity; (2) a position that attempts to vindicate modernity against its detractors; and (3) a position that attempts an internal (postmodern) critique of key features of modernity (see Dallmayr 18–19). In view of this anxious construction of the postmodern boundary in current theoretical circles, one might ask what can it mean when this historical period becomes the focal point of contemporary fiction. Is it significant that a growing number of contemporary "eighteenth-century historical novels" are published at precisely the time when debates about postmodernity's relation to modernity are at their height?

Of course, Hollywood historical romance films as different as *Dangerous Liaisons, Orlando, Pride and Prejudice, The Last of the Mohicans,* and *Rob Roy* have splashed about in an eighteenth-century setting, but Hollywood's attempts to uncover the "sins of modernity" are usually informed precisely by its desire to remember (re-member) the Enlightenment, to reconstruct it in order to revel in its crimes, sins, and errors. If modernity is defined as detection—by the desire to seek out, reconstruct, and name the hidden or the repressed—then these films in a historical genre that purport to interrogate the eighteenth-century Enlightenment instead easily duplicate it. They attempt historical detection and are thus participants in the very modernity they supposedly critique. Like them, the classic historical romance is unembarrassed by its participation in and championing of modernity. Implicitly or explicitly, it searches for the *gründe,* an originary principle, within historical process; the genre is predicated upon historical detection and reconstruction (see Shaw 19 ff.). We see this in Scott's historical romances as well as Tolstoy's and Fenimore Cooper's, to very different purposes and effects.

But what about contemporary novels such as John Steffler's *The Afterlife of George Cartwright,* Francis Sherwood's *Vindication,* Allen Kurzweil's *A Case of Curiosities,* Lawrence Norfolk's *Lemprière's Dictionary,* J. M. Coetzee's *Foe,* Peter Ackroyd's *Hawksmoor* and *Chatterton,* Steve Erickson's *Arc d'X,* Patrick Süskind's *Perfume: The Story of a Murderer,* Brian O'Doherty's *The Strange Case of Mademoiselle P.,* John Fowles's *A Maggot,* Susan Sontag's *The Volcano Lover: A Ro-*

mance, and Barry Unsworth's *Sacred Hunger*? These are only a hand-
ful of some of the most provocative contemporary novels that take
the eighteenth century as their setting. They seem to ask what Callinicos argues is the central question of postmodern theory: "Was the
Enlightenment a Good Thing?" ("Reactionary Postmodernism?" 97).

The historical novels named above construct the same continuum
of attitudes toward the Enlightenment as does the fractured debate
within theory. However, in a number of these novels, the eighteenth
century is constructed by neither the simulated liberalism of Hollywood nor the conservative nostalgia of Walter Scott, but rather it is
confronted by a politics of the postmodern that attempts a Nietzschean redefinition of *gründe* (ground) as *weltanschauung* (perspective). I would argue, however, that in all of these novels, the Enlightenment becomes redefined as performative space or, perhaps it is
more accurate to say, performative history. The "real" Enlightenment
is always already before us: history as recreation and reenactment becomes history as a re-creation and enactment, a continual restaging
and re-presentation of eighteenth-century Europe and the United
States. The question is, why do so many metahistorical romances engage in this kind of recreative activity?

Two aspects of eighteenth-century Enlightenment science, or the
"heroic model of science," are particularly important to these novels
and to answering this question. First is the idea that scientific method
in the Age of Reason saw itself as motivated solely by the search for
truth and that this truth lay in the articulation of universally applicable, general laws. Second is the idea that heroic science offered a new
kind of secularized transcendence (Appleby et al. 15–16, 28–29).
Habermas writes that "Enlightenment thinkers . . . still had the extravagant expectation that the arts and sciences would promote not
only the control of natural forces but also the understanding of the
world and of the self, moral progress, the justice of institutions and
even the happiness of human beings" ("Modernity: An Incomplete
Project" 9). In other words, rational man could escape time and history by discovering and articulating universal secular truths. (Thus,
both modernity and postmodernity, by denying the possibility of

metaphysical or religious truth, throw us back into time and history—postmodernism more so, because its denial of *any* universals, religious *or* secular, is more . . . universal.)

Novels about the eighteenth century may be surfacing now and seem to rehearse theoretical debates about modernity because they grow out postmodern anxieties about these two optimistic premises of Enlightenment heroic science. These novels demonstrate that a need to differentiate the modern from the postmodern doesn't stem merely (as some cynics would have it) from academics' needs to publish new articles in a publish-or-perish gristmill. The postmodern psyche in all arenas seems compelled to rewrite the Enlightenment past as Other in order to construct, and perhaps vindicate, itself and to confront the promise of Enlightenment epistemology. The Enlightenment returns again and again in postmodern fiction, like the uncanny return of the repressed. Indeed, that might be the best definition of postmodernism, its key feature rooted in a number of cultural sources. As Fredric Jameson, Umberto Eco, Linda Hutcheon, Charles Jencks, and others have maintained, postmodernism is obsessed with the past; the aesthetics of experimentalism and metafiction, market capitalism, postcolonial and race and gender discourses, and fin-de-siècle anxieties all contribute to this obsession. Particularly in the historical novel genre, this anxiety can create both a skewed historical lens *and* a new, experimental novel form. The postmodern historical novels listed above galvanize these anxieties into symbolic spaces: eighteenth-century Europe and North America are constructed as postlapsarian/preapocalypse landscapes where colonialism, Enlightenment aesthetics, patriarchy, and the optimism of heroic science all grow on the Western tree of knowledge. Once bitten, these apples change the world in contradictory and ambiguous ways. Confronted with the emptiness of everyday life, the dehumanizing ideology of technocracy, economic inequalities in massively wealthy nations, political corruption and the transformation of statesmanship into media performance, gated communities and Hollywood history, the postmodern sensibility turns back to the Enlightenment and questions the sanctity of its proffered gifts. While these novels construct the Age of Reason in different ways akin to theory's three constructions of Enlightenment modernity, all also rewrite the eighteenth century in a way that asks whether the Enlightenment was a good thing and that makes room for a "new" postmodern space, one that is somewhat defensive, somewhat self-righteous about its ties to Enlightenment modernity. We therefore must understand these novels as the postmodern confronting the Law of the Father, its own originating symbolic moment and legacy.

Although some of these novels, such as Erikson's *Arc d'X* or Ackroyd's *Hawksmoor,* are formally experimental or metafictional, for the most part the metahistorical romances discussed here are more conventional in form than the more experimental paratactic or simultaneous metahistorical romances discussed in chapter 3. Whereas the latter novels use formalist strategies to critique Enlightenment historiography and Anglo-European history, the novels I analyze below embed this critique in theme or plot itself while generally conforming to more conventional modes of storytelling. It is perhaps best to understand this distinction in terms of the three kinds of postmodernism defined in the preface to this book. That is, in this chapter the novels discussed enter into the debate about epistemological postmodernism, a slightly different debate than one centering on sociocultural or aesthetic postmodernism.

These novels seem to construct the eighteenth century as a metonymy of modernity to support diverse positions concerning the value of the Enlightenment tradition and modernity itself—positions that have direct corollaries in postmodern theoretical debates. Some of these novels nostalgically attempt to identify the aporias of Enlightenment rationalism, the places where it breaks down, contradicts itself, or encounters static from the boundaries of "civilized" discourse; implicit in this position is a vindication of the more "enlightened" postmodern stance and a desire to distance the postmodern from the modern or underscore a postmodern sympathy with the premodern past. Others of these novels imply a Habermasian support for an unfinished modern project. A third group includes themselves within the critique of modernity they imply. As self-reflexive heirs to the historical romance tradition, these metahistorical romances acknowledge their own relation to the modern project of historical detection and reconstruction, and they confront their own participation in modernity as they remember it. The most ambiguous and experimental of these "eighteenth-century" novels support the Lyotardian contention that the modern and the postmodern are always intertwined.

Longing for Premodernity and Modernity

In *The Illusion of the End,* Jean Baudrillard seems almost nostalgic for an Enlightenment conception of history that had ontological meaning and was not pure simulation (7). Baudrillard's sympathy with a ritual time that opposes linear, modern time, however, is more indicative of a pre-Enlightenment (or even anti-Enlightenment) sentiment than an Enlightenment one. The eighteenth-century philosophes battled precisely this pre-Newtonian conception of ritual time in the form of Christian calendars and cosmologies. Baudrillard's postmodern longing for historical meaning embeds a nostalgia for a pre-Western past conceived as prelapsarian, and this implicit historical perspective is echoed in contemporary fiction.

John Steffler's *The Afterlife of George Cartwright,* for example, is likewise nostalgic for a premodern, pastoral, and knowable aboriginal past. In this novel, aboriginal peoples become the symbolic Other, familiar to Western readers as the stereotype of the "vanishing Indian" that nuanced accounts of nineteenth-century European explorers. Steffler's is a contemporary historical novel that accords with traditional generic definitions dating from Scott: the book is based on actual eighteenth-century events (it contains excerpts from the journal of the historical George Cartwright) and fictionalizes those events so that major social forces are seen in conflict from the point of view of a minor historical figure. Cartwright is an entrepreneur from a bourgeois family of declining fortunes. His financial schemes lead him to form a trading company that will eventually plunder Labrador, contribute to the spread of disease among the Inuit peoples, and economically enslave the remaining population. The postmodern "twist" in this novel is that Cartwright writes his first-person account of his life to us (presumably readers of his journal) after his death; we see him caught in a limbo/purgatory that physically resembles life on his family estate. Cartwright ends his journal and purgatorial stay by being eaten by a bear symbolizing, one supposes, the Inuit people's revenge for his plundering of their land and culture.

This novel attacks eighteenth-century exploitation of the New World and constructs the Inuit as innocent Other in a pastoral (if cold and potentially hostile) northern Garden. As such it embeds a nostalgia for a premodern past, one that offers at least imaginary solace and ontological stability to a frazzled contemporary Western consciousness. Thus this novel is much like Hollywood revisionings of the eighteenth century: Cartwright is writing a history of the present in his journal, and like him, we as readers are placed as historical detectives, reconstructing history to unravel the mystery of Cartwright's dilemma, which become indicative of the "sins" of the age. Finally, however, all we can deduce is a culpability based on purely Western ethical standards and Christian paradigms: Cartwright is in purgatory until he pays for his sins, and the agent of justice takes the form of those whom in life he had wronged. Even though Steffler attempts to attack the paradigm of modernity and elevate premodern values, the premodern remains a predictable and romanticized Other within an intact Western metaphysics; the novel seems to long for premodernity figured in the Other, but it also remains caught within the very modern paradigm it attempts to refute.

In contrast to Steffler's novel, others of these "eighteenth-century" historical novels recuperate the notion of Enlightenment science as a player in an eighteenth-century culture war that from the 1690s onward included battles between the philosophes and the clergy or peasant beliefs—battles pitting reason against Christian absolutisms and institutionalized superstition. In the seventeenth century, Francis Bacon and René Descartes had appealed for the new science of Galileo; in 1751, Diderot could describe the Enlightenment man "as an eclectic, a skeptic and investigator" who thought for himself and supported the new "Republic of Letters"; by the end of the eighteenth century, the heroic model of science was itself under attack from some quarters (Appleby et al. 17, 20–21, 27–28, 39). Thus today's defenders of Enlightenment rationalism argue that theorists promulgating postmodernism tend to ignore how the Enlightenment itself was a revolutionary and post-structuralist enterprise. Attacking the theories of Jean-François Lyotard, Alex Callinicos writes, "'Incredulity towards metanarratives' seems . . . to be at least as old as the Enlightenment which was so productive of grand narratives in the first place" (*Against Postmodernism* 10).[1] Likewise, Jürgen Habermas posits that there are aspects of the Enlightenment that are worth preserving. In "Modernity—An Incomplete Project," Habermas writes, "I think that instead of giving up modernity and its project as a lost cause, we should learn from the mistakes of those extravagant programs which have tried to negate modernity. . . . In sum, the project of modernity has not yet been fulfilled" (12–13). Indeed, much of the battle in theory has been waged between Habermasians and marxists defending Enlightenment rationalism and Lyotardians attacking or outmoding it.[2] A Habermasian perspective is implicit in three recent historical novels: *Vindication, A Case of Curiosities,* and *Lemprière's Dictionary.*

At first glance, it might seem odd to place Sherwood's novel in this kind of category. A novel that upon its publication provoked heated discussion among Wollstonecraft scholars, *Vindication* presents Wollstonecraft as a protagonist who experiences an unconsummated lesbian attachment in her childhood and a series of sexual and psychological abuses in adulthood that together form her adult feminist sensibility.[3] As an adult, she is a thwarted philosopher; a jilted and abused lover; a stifled revolutionary. During the course of the novel (and her life therein), Wollstonecraft's reason does not save her or allow her to rise above this scarring sexual battle. Publicly, she attempts to participate in the discourse of the philosophes but is only exoticized in that arena; privately, she turns to male lovers who destroy her sense of self. The two children she bears are burdens: the first she throws against a wall in a fury born of intellectual frustration, and the second kills her in childbirth. She is a woman who abuses and denies her own body and yearns to participate in the world of the mind, and as such she is completely defined by an Enlightenment gender politics that wants her either to be a man or to quietly disappear. Her only escape is suicide, and even at that she fails. It seems that Sherwood's point is a glum one: that the Age of Reason was or is a successfully hegemonic epistemology from which there was or is no escape, no alternative possible—a system that even the brightest women could not outthink, undermine, or join. This is hardly Habermasian in spirit.

Certainly the lives of intellectual eighteenth-century women were stifled by a hegemonic patriarchy. What is disturbing about this novel, however, is not only that Sherwood takes liberties with Wollstonecraft's documented biography,[4] but also that she presents (in the manner of a Hollywood remembering) a historical view congenial to the very episteme she seems to criticize. In fact, her novel justifies and vindicates the project of modernity again and again. This novel might give readers insight into the bleak realities of eighteenth-century intellectual women, but it also reinforces the idea that patriarchy is inescapable and that modernity is paradigmatic and seamless, without "postmodern" fissures or sites of real contention. If that is Sherwood's point, then for feminists this a very bleak book indeed, and it would be difficult to see the novel as sympathetic to anything but a politics of victimization.

However, even while presenting this horror of a life story, Sherwood's novel calls only for an enlightened Enlightenment, an Age of Reason that might include and respect women's bodies and intellects. The novel juxtaposes Enlightenment ideals professed by the philosophes to the actualities of eighteenth-century women's lives to show that the latter were excluded from the former. In consequence, what is questioned in this novel are not the basic tenets underlying Enlightenment rationalism but rather their real-world applications. In other words, the novel maintains that the project of modernity has not yet been fulfilled. According to the novel's narrating voice, Wollstonecraft's most famous political writing, *A Vindication of the Rights of Woman* (1792), "was a logical extension of the Enlightenment belief in the rights of man to the rights of woman. She suggested that women must be educated to be reasonable, and become reasonable to be virtuous, and virtuous so that all of society might be happier. If men were not reasonable, they would be sensualists and women slaves" (236). With this kind of logic, the narrating voice upholds the oppositional and hierarchical epistemology of discourse and its dependence on (gender) difference. Moreover, with a causal logic that should make feminists wince, Sherwood implies that Wollstonecraft's feminist sensibility results from her childhood abuse—thereby aligning this sensibility with emotional trauma and unreason, and vindicating the paradigm of causality underlying (a gendered) heroic science itself.

More playful and self-reflexive than Sherwood's novel, Norfolk's *Lemprière's Dictionary* investigates the eighteenth century as the seedbed of nineteenth-century capitalist economies and the will to power that inherently occupies them. The protagonist of the novel, John Lemprière, lives in rural Jersey in 1780 and is a classical scholar. Throughout the book Lemprière engages in two activities in London: to finish his "dictionary" of classical allusions, and to unravel the mystery of his family's association with the East India Company. As Lemprière digs deeper into the mysteries of his father's papers, he uncovers a centuries-old "Cabbala," comprising the nine original investors in the East India Company. Lemprière uncovers baroque plots, treachery, and mass murder in the East India Company's history, for he uncovers the original Cabbala's betrayal of the people of Rochelle in 1627 that resulted in mass death. Moreover, the East India Company hatches a plot to eradicate his family's claim to company shareholdings by driving young Lemprière insane: they recreate scenes of death from his dictionary in progress, and implicate him in the murders.

But though the plots of this novel are byzantine, they do finally sort themselves out in the end; even the structure of this book upholds Enlightenment values of causality and logic, with Lemprière finally "solving" the mystery of the Cabbala and his father's will. In addition, readers should find the protagonist John Lemprière a sympathetic character: he is written as a good and innocent man, and his scholarship, his dictionary project, and his personal values align him with the neoclassical ethics and aesthetics of the Age of Reason. The novel consistently implies that a warping of modernity—most importantly, in the rise of monopoly capitalism—is responsible for the chaos and tragedy in Lemprière's world. (The novel does not investigate whether capitalism and modernity are entwined.) A belief in progress has become perverted into a ruthless will to power on the part of a few; experimentation with democratic ideals has hardened into an antihumanist drive for profit; the empirical logic of heroic science has been corrupted to dehumanizing cyborg immachination. In this novel, what causes social entropy is the *perversion* of values promulgated by the eighteenth-century philosophes.

Likewise, in Kurzweil's brilliant novel *A Case of Curiosities,* it is the French Terror (Revolution) that ruins the possibilities of grace offered by heroic science. In his youth, in the village of Tournay, Claude Page had become the apprentice of the Abbé, a lapsed cleric and a philosophe of great and eclectic learning whose embitterment embodies the eighteenth-century conflicts between the church and practitioners of the new heroic science. When Claude leaves the Abbé's tutelage, he enters the chaotic world of Parisian pornographers, adulterers, and intellectual dabblers but remains true to his project: to design the most magnificent mechanical novelty ever produced. His creation, the Talking Turkish Gentleman, is an automaton that embodies the most skillful application of scientific learning to artistry yet to be seen in eighteenth-century France. The machine, in the form of a gentleman's talking head, also symbolically represents the acknowledged and unacknowledged values of the Age of Reason: subjectivity, Cartesian mind/body dualism, empirical science, and universalizing (and colonialist) hierarchies of stable value. (On the eve of the French Revolution, the "Turkish" automaton is made to speak the words, "Vive le Roi.") But this novel implies that, indeed, "instead of giving up modernity and its project as a lost cause, we should learn from the mistakes of those extravagant programs which have tried to negate modernity" (Habermas 12–13), for both reactionary church fundamentalism and the mindless revolutionary fanaticism of the Terror destroy hope of social, intellectual, and moral progress in this world. Interestingly, this novel separates the two characteristic impulses of the Enlightenment—democratic and revolutionary political philosophy, and the rationalism of deist philosophy and heroic science—into competing impulses of the age. The French Terror *grew out of* Enlightenment political philosophy, a fact that is ignored here; such leftist sentiment is instead shown to run counter to the pure goals of heroic science, embodied most dramatically in the deistic Abbé's ideal search for knowledge for its own sake. Like a secular godhead, Claude Page attempts to create, and eventually does create, a perfect machine symbolically in the image of man. This creation is destroyed, as is Claude, because of the hysteria and unreason of the Terror.

Curiously, all three novels—*Vindication, Lemprière's Dictionary,* and *A Case of Curiosities*—imply this position. In all three novels, an Enlightenment artist/scholar suffers (and her/his creation is threatened) at least to some degree because of the French Revolution and the mindless violence of the upsurging masses. Mary Wollstonecraft lives in Paris during the great insurrection but has no sympathy with the revolution around her; she hides out in a mansion of an aristocratic friend, who has fled the city. The revolution interrupts her writing and chances of gaining access to the philosophes' inner circles. John Lemprière is a classics scholar who seeks to rise socially through the production of a Johnsonian scholarly dictionary; in Paris and London his scholarship is interrupted by periods of unrest, when redcaps swarm the streets. (His other quest—one involving the sorting-out of his own family history—is likewise interrupted by the present-day Cabbala thugs, whose ancestors also gained their power in a time of social revolution.) And the Abbé in *A Case of Curiosities* is a secularized French cleric born of the aristocratic class and committed to esoteric learning; after Claude Page's apprenticeship to him is complete, Claude attempts to produce the most beautiful and sophisticated automaton ever created but is thwarted by the totalitarian repression of the new political regime.

Are these similarities significant? What is produced or naturalized in this presentation of modernity? Is there a rightist undertone in these novels, a reaction against socialist participatory democracy somehow born out of a need to vindicate the project of modernity? Or do these novels instead illustrate White's contention that the creation of disciplinary history (modern history) put the extreme Left and the Right ironically on the same side, since both defend modernity against utopianism or the historical sublime?[5] The three protagonists of these novels are intellectuals and artists; ultimately, they define their roles similarly as within the arena of aesthetics. (Even Wollstonecraft considers herself more a creative writer than a political theorist in Sherwood's novel.) The opposition in these novels of a sullied real-world politics (figured at least partially in the French Revolution) to a pristine aesthetic realm (the worlds of philosophy and literature where the faculties of judgment and taste are prized) implies an investment, in these novels, of the political in an aesthetic of the beautiful. In tension with this position is the dirty little secret of historicity itself, the fact that if one takes sides here (the fictional world of eighteenth-century Western Europe) in order to defend the project of modernity, one cannot defend aesthetic elitism or life in the abstract—because Enlightenment heroic science and political theory worked historically in the service of real world politics and social improvement, though they may have been used to different ends. What is particularly interesting in these novels is that they differ from expected positionings in their seeming defense of modernity: while defenders of modernity in contemporary theory often argue that modernity's obsolescence will engender fatuous relativism and nihilism in society, these novels imply that modernity's forced obsolescence threatens the possibility of aesthetic production or innovation. Finally, these novels raise questions about what political investment in the aesthetic of the beautiful is necessary in order to defend the project of modernity. I would argue that what we see here is a full investment in the Burkean division of the beautiful and the sublime. The first is aligned with artistic production (disciplinized art and history); the second is aligned with terror and chaos (realized in the Terror, the Revolution). As it was for Edmund Burke, the beautiful here promotes the values of civilized modernity and leads to true democratic freedom, while the sublime is anarchic, destabilizing, and ruinous to civil society.

The Immanent Critique

In a now-famous formulation, Lyotard has claimed that postmodernism imposes a "severe reexamination . . . on the thought of the Enlightenment, on the idea of a unitary end of history and of a subject," and has defined as modern "any science that legitimates itself . . . [by] making an explicit appeal to some grand narrative, such as the dialectics of Spirit, the hermeneutics of meaning, the emancipation of the rational or working subject, or the creation of wealth" (*The Postmodern Condition* 73, xxiii). While Lyotard argues that modernity has been superseded by postmodernity, his aesthetics of earlier and later books locates the postmodern within modernity itself: "Modernity is constitutionally and ceaselessly pregnant with its postmodernity" (*The Inhuman* 25).[6] As I noted earlier, this fetal postmodernism is directly related to Lyotard's theorization of the postmodern sublime. To Lyotard, representation can only oppose or be complicitous with the hierarchicalizing will to power that defines modernity. To oppose this (de)limiting activity of modern representation requires a thinking beyond, within, between representation. It requires a "drifting" (*The Inhuman* 74). One of Lyotard's examples of a postmodern "event" is the French Revolution, which he claims is outside discursive laws of its time.

This location of the postmodern *within* the modern has particular relevance to what I see as a third group of contemporary "eighteenth-century" novels and illustrates another way in which fiction can address the problem of the modern. That is, in contrast to Steffler's, Sherwood's, and Norfolk's novels, other metahistorical romances describe those elements out of the control of Cartesian reason and present the Enlightenment as a historical referential frame that contains within itself the Lyotardian postmodern—the unimaginable, the unrepresentable, the unsaid. They reconstruct the Enlightenment as the time when the historical sublime, as an apprehensible concept, is born; they examine how the postmodern intertwines with the modern at the historical site of eighteenth-century Europe. These metahistorical romances, informed by a Lyotardian distancing from but simultaneous incorporation of themselves within the modern, are often left with deferral of meaning, deferral of history, and provisional subject location as their only options for being in the world.

While Sherwood's and Norfolk's novels try to *represent* Enlightenment epistemology, and may be thus vulnerable to representation's self-contradictions, other metahistorical romances contain and foreground the postmodern Enlightenment event, that which is unrepresentable and is enmeshed with the modern. It is possible to identify common ways that these metahistorical romances construct the Enlightenment as a metonym of modernity in the sense discussed above: (1) they foreground a "postmodern" historical event, an unrepresentable space or limit event within the Enlightenment moment; and (2) they symptomatically locate this event within the figural rather than the discursive and thus locate it within the territory of the historical sublime.

The foregrounding of the event within these metahistorical novels takes a number of forms. Each of them is centered on an occurrence that jars its Enlightenment context, that exceeds the parameters of Western logic and reason that heroic science would construct as cognitive boundaries for apprehending the real. In *Arc d'X* and *Foe*, this event is manifested in the appearance of the Other. In *Hawksmoor, Perfume, Chatterton, The Strange Case of Mademoiselle P.*, and *A Maggot*, this event takes the form of the occult or the criminal that remains unrecognized, unspoken, or unexplainable within the framework of heroic science. In *The Volcano Lover* and *Sacred Hunger*, the event is a limit event—revolution.

These events are located within the Lyotardian figure, which complicates and to some extent inhabits discourse. The figural does not simply oppose discourse, because then it would *be* discursive, operating according to principles of opposition that are the foundation of discourse itself. According to Readings, "The figural opens discourse to a radical heterogeneity, a singularity, a difference which cannot be rationalized or subsumed within the rule of representation" (4).[7] This figuration constitutes the critique of the modern in these novels and signals their location of the postmodern within the modern.[8]

In two of these metahistorical novels, it is the figure of the black body in a colonialist space that lies outside the scope of Cartesian Reason and out of Reason's control. In his novel *Foe*, Coetzee retells the Daniel Defoe story *Robinson Crusoe;* interjects plot lines from Defoe's *Roxanna* and centralizes a woman character while backgrounding the Cruso/oe character; and makes Defoe himself (in the abbreviated patronymic "Foe") one of the central characters of the book. Critics have recently focused on Friday, the black servant of Cruso, who in Coetzee's retelling is a mute who accompanies the castaway Susan Barton back to England after her rescue from the island. However, Macaskill and Colleran have suggested most admirably what I would argue is the crucial interpretation of this character: Friday is the figure of the unrepresentable, the unspeakable, and the unsaid within Enlightenment colonialism and the will to power that drives modern Western epistemology. Unlike *The Afterlife of George Cartwright* (or, as I discuss in chapter 5, Vollmann's *The Rifles,* also about the Inuit), which unproblematically situates a knowable Other outside the hegemonic discourse of modernity, Coetzee's Friday is that which is, in Spivak's words, "wholly Other" and resistant to modern understanding. The famous author Foe, pondering the puzzle of Friday, says to Susan, "In every story there is a silence, some sight concealed, some word unspoken, I believe. Till we have spoken the unspoken we have not come to the heart of the story" (Coetzee 141).

Foe's perspective is that of heroic science, which assumes a knowable, logocentric universe; "speaking the unspoken" is the modern project. But Foe reveals a will to power at the heart of this agenda:

"We must *make* Friday's silence speak, as well as the silence surrounding Friday" (142; italics mine). However, Friday refuses to be spoken and is outside of language, symbolically mute to everyone in the novel, even Susan Barton, whose attempts to teach him language must be understood as attempts to fathom Friday and contain his signification. Even she realizes this: "If he [Friday] was not a slave, was he nevertheless not the helpless captive of my desire to have our story told? How did he differ from one of the wild Indians whom explorers bring back with them, in a cargo of parakeets and golden idols and indigo and skins of panthers, to show they have truly been to the Americas?" (150–51). Lyotard insists that within and against a text is always a figural other; according to Readings, "the discursive is always necessarily interwoven with the figural and vice versa, despite the fact that the discursive claim to accurate representation of full understanding rests upon the repression of figurality" (*Introducing Lyotard* 4–5). In *Foe,* Foe and Susan participate in the discursive, while Friday—whose communication consists only of drawings of marching eyes—inhabits the figural dimension repressed in Western discourse. Susan herself struggles to tell her own tale, which will always be incomplete as long as Friday remains unknowable, for he is the unspoken and unspeakable part of her story. Her story also never gets completely told without contamination from Foe's authorial vision. Within this complex of relations, Friday stands alone, a dark figure unable to be imagined by Western consciousness or contained within Western colonialist discourse. Friday is the postmodern haunting, drifting, within modern imperialist discourse.

Erikson's dazzling novel *Arc d'X* begins with a figure that resonates throughout the rest of the text and—since the novel takes place in a number of different time dimensions—all of history: a black slave woman named Evelyn burning on a pyre because she killed the white Virginian Jacob Pollroot who owned and repeatedly debased her. Her ashes, figuratively, smudge young Thomas Jefferson's fingers and choke his breathing and imagination. Evelyn's image is reborn in Sally Hemings, mistress to the older, widower Jefferson. Sally is thrice colonized: first as a colonial within former British territories, second as a black slave, third as a black woman who is raped and then kept as mistress by her slave-master. The Enlightenment scholar who ironically campaigns against slaveholding and is the darling of revolutionary French freedom fighters, Jefferson is haunted by an unspoken that mocks his reason and rhetorical triumphs:

> I've invented something. As the germ of conception in my head it was the best and wildest and most elusive of my inventions. It's a contraption halfcrazed by a love of justice. . . . But I know it's a flawed thing, and I know the flaw is of me. Just as the white ink of my loins has fired the inspiration that made it, so the same ink is scrawled across the order of its extinction. The signature is my own. I've written its name. I've called it America. (Erickson 46)

Here, "Jefferson" posits that America is born of a sexualized will to power, logocentric epistemology, and aesthetic idealism. But Erikson the author seems intent upon showing how America is flawed because it is built on a lie of human independence, defined by a man who cannot free his own slaves. America is, to some extent, Sally herself *as she is created and configured by theory* in a manner similar to how the nation itself is configured in or as theory. (Importantly, *America* is a word so antithetical to the being of the actual, human Sally, that, reincarnated in different futures, she cannot verbalize it.) The tragic knowledge that Jefferson intuits is that like the Saussurian sign, Sally and America are two sides of a sheet of paper; one goes with the other, not only because America is predicated on slave labor, but because both are part of the same system of representation, equally theoretical, equally unreal. While the real Sally, like Friday in Coetzee's *Foe,* remains unspoken within this discourse of power, the theoretical Sally is made into the transgressive other, the "unspeakable." Thus to Jefferson, Sally's "unspeakable" womanhood and blackness are essential to her dehumanization and her attraction: "It thrilled him, the possession of her. He only wished she were so black as not to have a face at all. He only wished she was so black that his ejaculation might be the only white squiggle across the void of his heart. When he opened her, the smoke [of Evelyn's burning] rushed out of her in a cloud and filled the room. It thrilled him, not to be a saint for once, not to be a champion. Not to bear, for once, the responsibility of something novel or good" (Erickson 25). Thus to Jefferson, Sally is not only "unspeakable" in the sense that she can only be imagined as a theoretical construct; she is also (as a result) both the "unspeakable" (i.e., horrifying and sinful) side of himself and the unspeakable Sadean thrill of transgression.

But from her side of the equation, Sally is also "unspoken" in the sense that she owns her own voice and will not be spoken by others, like Friday in Coetzee's novel. Her places of liberation in different historical times (the Rue d'X in revolutionary Paris, the apocalyptic X-Day which marks the end of linear time) are marked by X as outside the realm of signification, marked as chiasmata, places of reversals but also denials of representation. The letter X—an open signifier Malcolm X took on in history to deny his represented self in white discourse—appears in all of the time frames of this novel. America in all times and all dimensions is marked by Sally's unspoken blackness, and the X places where she is free are Pynchonesque Zones (called such in the novel) that oppose the flawed, broken dream of America. Quite literally, X marks the spot of graphite blackness that cannot be erased; Sally's black body is the palimpsest of theoretical America, and coexisting with this theoretical construct, her body becomes the postmodern figure at the heart of American history.

While in *Hawksmoor, Chatterton, The Strange Case of Mademoiselle P.,* and *Perfume* the event takes the form of the occult or the criminal that remains outside the organizing discourse of heroic science, each novel constructs its own figuration for this event.

In *Hawksmoor,* the architect Nicholas Dyer constructs a pentangle of churches, each consecrated by a murder, as monuments to his occult religion. Like Sally Hemings in Erickson's novel, these churches transcend historical time and spatialize history; they appear as the site of murders in the twentieth century that Nicholas Hawksmoor, a Scotland Yard detective, must solve.[9] Just as in the eighteenth-century setting these churches become figures of Dyer's rebellion against the Enlightenment positivism of his superior, Christopher Wren, just so in the twentieth-century setting the churches become the site where Hawksmoor's detection fails. He cannot solve the murders. The principles of heroic science are undermined by the churches' call to a premodern occultism, and Cartesian subjectivity blurs as characters in the novel begin to blend and merge into one another. Says Dyer, "I am not a slave of Geometricall Beauty, I must build what is most Sollemn and Awefull" (6). And yet Dyer's churches would not exist if it were not for the Enlightenment social optimism which prompts their commission. An eighteenth-century postmodernist, Dyer insists that at the heart of any interpretation is absence and that Western literature (and culture) has privileged closure and will to power over the flux of experience.[10] Moreover, Dyer is suspicious of systems and foregrounds "postcognitive" (or precognitive) questions, and his philosophy grows out of mass culture in its most brutal aspects (see McHale 10).

Moreover, in scenes illustrating how plague sweeps London at this time, the novel implies that the disease and ill health that breeds it and class poverty are the underbelly of the upper-class Royal Academy and the heroic science that supports it. Describing London as "Moloch," Dyer condemns the entire project of heroic science:

> And so when the Cartesians and the New Philosophers speak of their Experiments, saying that they are serviceable to the Quiet and Peace of Man's life, it is a great Lie: there has been no Quiet and there will be no Peace. The streets they walk in are ones in which Children die daily or are hang'd for stealing Sixpence; they wish to lay a solid Groundwork (or so they call it) for their vast Pile of Experiments, but the Ground is filled with Corses, rotten and rotting others. (*Hawksmoor* 123)

Dyer's occultism reverses heroic science's attempt at transcendence into an occult descent into the underworld; the trips are but mirror images of one another. *Hawksmoor* finally does not vindicate or deny the modern, but rather through the figure of Dyer's churches implies that Dyer's occultism is outside the control of Cartesian reason because it is the subconscious libidinal impulse beneath it.

Patrick Süskind's *Perfume: The Story of a Murderer* also implies that Enlightenment rationalism and the Sadean or occult impulse are close relatives. The central character, Jean-Baptiste Grenouille, like Dyer was a orphan of the lower classes, and like Dyer he is associated throughout his life with the supernatural (for instance, he has no body scent). And like Dyer, Grenouille is a kind of Enlightenment antihero. Using his olfactory gifts and the deductive processes of scientific method, he will strive to become the greatest perfumer of all time by isolating the scent of virgin girls, whom he kills to possess. His quest is the pursuit of the Kantian sublime, which he reduces to the beautiful because of his linking of sublimity with heroic science: "This one scent was the higher principle, the pattern by which the others must be ordered. It was pure beauty" (49). After killing his first victim, he erects a system, a "catalog of odors ever more comprehensive and differentiated, the hierarchy ever clearer. And soon he could begin to erect the first carefully planned structures of odor" (51). His nose is "analytical and visionary" (111), and as an apprentice at Giuseppe Baldini's perfumery he learns the chemistry of perfumes to complement his own natural gifts of perception.

Like Jefferson in *Arc d'X,* Grenouille is also a Sadean esthete, motivated only by his own pleasure. Moreover, as they were for Erikson's Jefferson, Grenouille's Sadean and rational sides are complementary. Unfortunately, his strongest desire is to have scent himself, and this is not ever to be: "And though his perfume might allow him to appear before the world as a god—if he could not smell himself and thus never know who he was, to hell with it, with the world, with himself, with his perfume" (306). This statement seems a bit ludicrous, but one might compare it to the sentiment expressed in James Baldwin's short story "Sonny's Blues," when the title character says, "Something kept telling me that maybe it was good to smell your own stink."[11] This idea of being able to "smell your own stink" seems an injunction to forego dangerous dreams of purity or false transcendence through the products of modern science (drugs, perfume, theory) and recognize one's animalistic humanity. The implication is that this recognition will lead one to humility and a communion with others, as well as to the ability to distinguish sublimity (that which is outside of or beyond the self and self-control) and mundanity (the territory of the political, the empirical, and the merely beautiful). In "Sonny's Blues," being able to smell his own stink allows Sonny paradoxically to connect with the sublime realm of Art precisely because it frees him from egotism. In *Perfume,* to have smell is to know oneself and control subjectivity. However, Grenouille is unable to do this, and so in an egotistical act of Nietzschean proportions, he kills himself by sprinkling himself with the scent of virgins and—in a scene echoing the myth of Acteon and also the ritual eating of the god—is ripped apart and eaten by a crowd maddened by the perfume's smell. In the absence of self-knowledge, Grenouille existentially asserts an identity that confers upon him mythic stature, oddly congruent with (because theoretical and constructed through intellect alone) Cartesian reason. His death is an attempt at ultimate control, an utter rejection of any commitment outside the self; the suicide is the ultimate human appropriation of the "I am" in the form of "I am not." At the end of *Perfume,* Grenouille seems at first to enter the realm of the postmodern sublime: his criminality and death seem unspeakable within modernity's historical membrane. Yet in actuality they are the products of a modern mind gone mad with a lust for control.

Chatterton and *The Strange Case of Mademoiselle P.* deal with a less sinister occultism and criminality. In *Chatterton,* a portrait becomes the figure within and outside of history—perhaps a forgery, perhaps an icon bearing the spirit of the poet Thomas Chatterton. Enlightenment rationalism is opposed in the novel by the occultism of the portrait and the romanticism of three time frames: that of Chatterton's own eighteenth century, that of 1856 when the poet George Meredith posed as Chatterton for the painter Henry Wallis, and that of the twentieth century in the dreams of the aspiring poet Edward Wychwood. In *The Strange Case of Mademoiselle P.,* a young, blind and hysterical girl named Marie Thérèse Paradies becomes the figure for that which eludes heroic science, and "occultism" takes the form of the science of hypnosis practiced by the protagonist Dr. Franz Anton Mesmer in eighteenth-century Vienna. "I have abandoned the logic of science," writes Mesmer in his journal, "which can only reflect its own assumptions and confirm its own methods. I am convinced (though I am a scientist) that we can learn from oracles and sybils and mountebanks, who live in a twilight that extends beyond the present into past and future. I do not mock seers and fortune-tellers. But these researches have their darker side. . . . I have gone beyond science in these later years" (171). To say that one has "gone beyond science" is to imply a recognition of the sublime in some form. Mesmer is on the way to curing Marie Parodies of her hysterical blindness when the girl is removed from his care by her brutal father and returned to her dysfunctional family. However, her memory haunts Mesmer for the rest of his life, for he can only intuit, not comprehend, her affliction. Parodies's malady is the singularity that cannot be rationalized; like the Chatterton portrait in Ackroyd's novel, she embodies the mystery that stands outside of discourse (even representation, for the Chatterton portrait finally self-destructs). Also like the Chatterton portrait, Marie can be observed but (literally and figuratively) cannot articulate her own vision. To rephrase J. Hillis Miller, she and the portrait become figures in time's carpet: like Friday in Coetzee's novel, they are silent signifiers repudiating the hegemonic control of reasonable discourse.

It is important to emphasize, however, that she and Friday can be understood as "silent signifiers" only if viewed from the perspective of the Western patriarchal gaze—or, perhaps, heard with a Western patriarchal ear. Friday would not be silent in his own culture; Parodies is allowed no language of her own to speak. These metahistorical novels may point to, or even lament, the silence of these representative characters, but the novels also cannot construct a discourse that would allow these voices to be heard. The paradox of this situation is figured in Mesmer, a rational man of science who goes beyond science to find a solution to the mystery of the human spirit.

In John Fowles's *A Maggot* there is an attempt to remedy this situation by allowing the other a voice. However, as a result, this novel illustrates even more clearly the difficulties faced by metahistorical romances when they confront the discourse of the Other. Fowles's novel is set in England in 1736; like Ackroyd's *Hawksmoor* and other metahistorical romances in this last grouping, it centers on a crime that must be investigated and a mystery that must be unraveled. The crime is the disappearance, perhaps because of foul play, of a nobleman's son and the death by hanging of his mute servant, Dick. The novel's narrator frequently interrupts the story action to comment on the cultural mores and political hierarchies of the eighteenth-century ruling and lower classes, and sometimes compares them to those in his own time. In addition to this narrating third-person voice, a series of textual forms swells the body of the narrative and includes reprinted pages from eighteenth-century historical chronicles, transcripts of witnesses' statements, and more traditional third-person prose narrative description. This allows a plurality of voices to enter the text and frequently undermine each other's claims.

The mystery at the core of the criminal investigation is why the nobleman's son hired a notorious whore and a mediocre actor and traveled with them and Dick to a countryside cavern, immediately preceding his own disappearance and the death of his servant. The nobleman's son, who is only revealed by his pseudonym "Mr. Bartholomew," is known to have rebelled against his father, and the son's former mentor at Christ's College writes that Bartholomew was taken with theories that seemed linked to the "black arts" and the occult, particularly in relation to the "science" of numerology. Like Dyer in *Hawksmoor* and Grenouille in *Perfume,* Mr. Bartholomew is intrigued by the unnatural superfetate in the natural, the science of prophecy and escape from the limitations of natural law. However, also like these two characters, he pursues the supernatural through the scientific, seeking the mystery of creation and otherworldly knowledge through numerology. Like Ackroyd and Süskind (and Lyotard), Fowles seems nominally to enfold the postmodern (the unnameable, the unrepresentable) within the belly of the scientific modern. And as do Erikson, Süskind and O'Doherty, Fowles links the postmodern to the figure of Woman as Other.

In *A Maggot,* the Other (a character named Rebecca Hockwell) is given a voice because she is interrogated as a suspect in the murder of Dick and the disappearance (presumed murder) of Mr. Bartholomew. Rebecca foils both scientific investigative method and the demands of Power, for she ultimately turns Ayscough's investigation into a farce. Comprising mainly transcripts that illustrate Ayscough's relentless interrogation, the novel stands as a testament to the failure of deductive logic and the patriarchal and aristocratic class premises upon which it is based. Ayscough cannot get to the bottom of the story, and we never find out what really happened to the menage à trois that ended up in the countryside cave. Rebecca provides two accounts of what happened that day. In her first account, told to the lower-class ne'er-do-well David Jones and repeated in his testimony to Ayscough, she tells of being forced by Bartholomew to copulate with Satan in the presence of three witches; in her own testimony to Ayscough, she tells of meeting "Mother Wisdom" (a Virgin Mary–like figure) and being taken to "June Eternal," a countryside where she meets Jesus Christ himself. Significantly, the two accounts position her within existing patriarchal narratives of Whore or redeemed Magdalene (for her, the option of Virgin would be too ridiculous)—the only two options for subjectivity allowed her.

The most likely explanation of what really happened to Dick and Mr. Bartholomew out in that countryside cavern is that they were murdered by Rebecca herself. Her testimony and encounter with Ayscough reveals Rebecca to be an intelligent, strong-willed woman with a clear understanding of her own oppression by male power; she is insolent to Ayscough, her class superior, and is obviously his equal in intelligence. It is possible that Rebecca's final testimony to Ayscough is an allegory of her own claims to female power. Did she finally rebel in that countryside cave, violently claiming her own identity and grasping at freedom by setting Mr. Bartholomew ablaze and, later, managing (with the aid of drugs or perhaps her friend David Jones) to hang Dick with violets in his mouth? Did she do this under the influence of drugs that made her see the whole activity as a scene of redemption? Ultimately, this novel (like *Hawksmoor* or *Chatterton*) does not answer these questions and shows only the foiling of power and the failure of deductive science in the face of this woman's unfathomable indeterminacy. Deduction is all wrapped up with desire here, and both are thwarted by the unknowability of the past.

Unlike these metahistorical novels in which the figured postmodern event takes the form of the occult or criminal, revolution becomes the unspeakable in Barry Unsworth's *Sacred Hunger,* set between 1752–53 and 1765: the mutiny aboard the *Liverpool Merchant* (see chapter 2) that establishes the polyandrous, multicultural Florida commune is absent from the novel and appears only as a set of recollections and legendary retellings, all of which are partisan and imply the distance between the actions that happen in real time and the way those actions are emplotted as history. In Susan Sontag's complex novel *The Volcano Lover,* the event also is figured as revolution. The novel specifically figures this event in the physical environment, correlating sexual climax, the eruption of Vesuvius, and the eruption of violence during the French Terror: "The lava of the revolution was flowing, the Terror was just reaching its climax—and in June 1794, nature rhyming with history, Vesuvius erupted" (185). The figure of Vesuvius becomes throughout this novel everything that stands outside Enlightenment logic and representation: the elemental and primitive, spectacle, passion, natural catastrophe. Most important, it becomes a figure for the blurring of definitional (including gender) boundaries: "It's the mouth of a volcano. Yes, mouth; and lava tongue. A body, a monstrous living body, both male and female. It emits, ejects. It is also an interior, an abyss. Something alive, that can die. Something inert that becomes agitated, now and then. Existing only intermittently. A constant menace. If predicable, usually not predicted. Capricious, untamable, malodorous. Is that what's meant by the primitive?" (5–6). The equation here of "the primitive" with these characteristics is provocative, and can only be understood from the perspective of the gaze of Western modernity. The volcano and the Revolution both erupt according to their own logic and explosive power; both are linked to passionate emotion in the novel; and both cause physical and social spaces to overturn, transmute, and self-destruct. To the Western imagination, the volcano becomes the perfect figuration of the French Revolution, which Lyotard has specifically cited as an example of an historical event that evades discourse and historical representation. Describing both the volcano and revolution in sexual metaphors emphasizes the distance of both from the empirical (Mind) and associates them with the libidinal (Body, Desire).

Of particular significance in *The Volcano Lover* is the reproduced photograph of a painting that Sontag has selected for the frontispiece to the novel. The picture illustrates how the rationalist mind, the scientific mind, comes to terms with this monstrous, sublime figure of the volcano: through dissection and reverse construction. The picture comprises really seven pictures or panels, each displaying the volcano in different stages. The first panel shows the volcano as it would appear after an eruption; the last picture shows the volcano intact, as it would appear *before* the eruption. The panels thus tell a story, a story that works from the present to the past, from post-explosion back to an hypothesized original, pre-explosion state. Moreover, in the last panel, parts of the volcano cone are alphabetically labeled to identify specific sections that blow off in succession; it is clear, in other words, that this series of panels is a visual representation of someone's theory of volcano eruption processes. The panel is a doubled ekphrasis, a story told within a picture within a story, and it is also a perfect representation for disciplinary history, which starts from the present and works backward in an attempt to reconstruct the absent original through deductive logic. Importantly, however, the epistemology underlying the painting is directly countered by the "romance" of the story that follows it, a story where logic is not at all the organizing principle of knowledge nor the means by which human beings come to terms with themselves and others in the world. The story is about passion, about will, and about sublimated libidinal desire; all of them trump the painting. The last voice in the novel is that of Elenora de Fonseca Pimentel, and what she emphasizes (after the spectacle of Napoleon's regime) is that the learning and revolutionary ideals of those in the ruling classes are ultimately false, and that what holds sway over the world is ambition and raw power.

In all eight of these metahistorical romances, the postmodern is defined as the event that erupts unspeakably from the modern, and it is figured significantly as Other, criminality, and revolution. On the one hand, it would be easy to conclude that through these figurations the postmodernist sensibility implicitly constructs itself as transgressor or outsider to the symbolic Western father. In that context, the postmodernist appropriation of these figures—for instance, the Kerouacian appropriation of the black body as self-identified symbol—becomes suspect as yet another act of Western colonial domination. From a different perspective, however, this postmodernist figuration signals something very different. What all eight books have in common is a negative investment in the aesthetic, a portrayal of *both* scientific rationalism and worldly aestheticism as ineffectual and impotent. In contrast to *Vindication, Lemprière's Dictionary,* and *A Case of Curiosities,* which validated the rationalized aesthetic (i.e., the aesthetic of the beautiful) against a negativized historio-political arena, in these eight novels the real-world, cognitive discursive mode is elevated above the speculative discursive mode. All of the books present artist/thinker figures that are ineffectual, lost, colonizing, or transgressively evil; effectual power is located in cultural forces, social institutions, and historical moments, as it was in the earlier three books, but this power is sublime. It is unspeakable, terrible, animalistic, chaotic, powerful. True force, true knowledge, lies beyond the domain of empiricist science.

This idea is particularly forceful in *Sacred Hunger.* One of the main characters in the novel, the physician Matthew Paris, is an ineffectual intellectual who is psychologically self-tortured because he cannot decide whether his need to stand against imperial power and champion insights of the New Science results from personal integrity or sheer hubris. Ironically, Paris's compulsion to act spurs the mutiny aboard *The Liverpool Merchant,* leaving this act of rebellion rooted in questionable motives.

Another figure, Delblanc, actually provides the rhetoric that founds the new classless society in Florida. Delblanc is a revolutionary aesthete, a utopian poet: at one point in the story, Paris realizes that the mutiny afforded him "the marvellous opportunity . . . to test his theories, vindicate man's natural goodness in this dream of a community living without constraint of government or corruption of money. A ship blown off course, a scuffle of sick and desperate men, the blood of a madman clumsily and almost casually spilt, he had seen in these a truth of politics, a revolution, the founding of a new order" (*Sacred Hunger* 536–37). The implication here is that Delblanc's revolutionary theory and his aesthetic practice are nurtured by the same principles and motivations. Delblanc the painter/poet is also a revolutionary theorist who intimately understands human psychology and its awe of power and has used the principles of deductive logic to formulate his philosophy. But Delblanc dies early in the life of the community he helped to found; moreover, by the end of the novel the commune, too, has died. It is clear that this beautiful utopian community, the product of a poet/rationalist's dreams, could never last long in the world because it crumples under the pressures of human needs for competition, power, and revenge.

Likewise, in *The Strange Case of Mademoiselle P.*, where Mesmer is portrayed as a cognitive philosopher who opposes the mindless violence within the bourgeois family, the scientific as well as the aesthetic is undermined as a value. Strongly implied throughout the book is the idea that his cure for Marie's blindness worked not because it was based on a radically new and correct theory of mind, but rather because Mesmer and Marie form a sexual and spiritual bond that begins to compensate the girl for the scarring psychological horror of her home life. Passion beyond theory (i.e., sublimity) is what is redemptive.

Also important is how social revolution against power in any form is presented in many of these texts. While in the earlier three books the French Revolution is presented as chaotic Terror that destroys order and undermines the production of beautiful Art (in the form of theory, in the form of the plastic arts), in these eight novels, revolution becomes a terrifying but liberatory force that combats aristocratic decadence. In Fowles's *A Maggot,* the French Revolution is absent as an immediate phenomenon (since the book takes place in 1736), but the climate of revolution permeates the book. Ayscough fixates on social change and how it threatens all he holds dear—class, order, hierarchies of power. The main figure in the book, Rebecca Hocknell, in fact is the mother of a religious insurrection, for she is the mother of Ann Lee, the founder of the Shakers. Likewise, in *Sacred Hunger,* revolution in the form of mutiny and the establishment of a classless, polyandrous, multiracial society dismantles virtually every value of Western patriarchal capitalist cultures emerging at the time of the action. Throughout the novel, Delblanc's Florida society is figured as the New Eden (remembered as paradise by the "Paradise Nigger," who is actually Paris's biracial son and spent his childhood in this utopian community). Like the biblical Eden, this place will be destroyed by humankind's weakness. Likewise, the French Revolution, presented as the triumph of passion/desire over rationalism, figures prominently in *The Volcano Lover.* The revolution and Napoleon disrupt but also breath life into a deadened aestheticism associated with the aristocratic class (represented in the Cavaliere and his obsession with art collections). The book's title doubly references this idea: on the one hand, in this novel Napoleon is a volcanic, passionate lover; but at the same time, the true "lover of volcanoes" is the Cavaliere, who is drawn to the unleashed power of the volcano even beyond his appreciation of it as an aesthetic symbol. At one point in *Arc d'X,* Sally Hemings escapes Jefferson and runs to the streets of Paris at precisely the moment when the Bastille is under siege; she seemingly must choose between the passionate, chaotic and perhaps dangerous freedom offered by the streets and the domestic slavery of her position as Jefferson's common-law wife.

In all of these novels, on the side of Reason and the representatives of Enlightenment are slavery, drudgery, and freedom only of the mind; on the side of the Sublime is terror, chaos and mad liberation of both mind and body. What is valorized, even implicitly, is passion over reason, disruption over order, life over theories that allow one to "develop" or "appreciate" life. What is valued in these novels, in other words, is the sublime as it was defined by Edmund Burke, John Dennis, Hugh Blair, and others in the early eighteenth century. Thurber writes that by 1783, the sublime was associated with "dramatic moun-

tain imagery, political rebellion, madness, witchcraft and de-
monology, to use Scott's terms, and above all with the anti-social,
even inhuman, voices of mayhem, rebellion, and political as well as
rhetorical insurrection" (94). *All* of these material registers of the sublime appear in these metahistorical romances.

What political consciousness, then, is rendered legible by the representation of the Enlightenment in these seven metahistorical romances? These novels seem to reverse violent hierarchies but seem
unable to reject those hierarchies wholesale; a transgressive but not
revolutionary consciousness can be the only result. What is evidenced
in these metahistorical novels is a suspicion of aestheticism attributed
to Enlightenment hierarchies of value, a suspicion in keeping with a
Lyotardian definition of the postmodern as nonrepresentation, un-
speakability, and eruption. Ironically, the very aestheticism that Lyotard is accused of in theoretical debates (but himself denies) becomes in these novels aligned with Enlightenment epistemology.
These texts support Langford's contention that "rather than being a
challenge to the Enlightenment . . . postmodernism is necessitated by
it and exists not as an external critique but as a product of the ongoing dialectic that Enlightenment thought maintains with itself"
(26). In these metahistorical romances, history is recuperated and retold, but only to problematize the interrelation between postmodernism and modernity. As a group, these contemporary novels face
down their Enlightenment heritage and contextualize it as a battle
between empiricism and sublimity, the scientific and the historical
sublime, thinking and being, and they should be understood as the
latest phase of modernity's self-questioning. These novels can validate
or challenge Enlightenment epistemological and social values, but
their significance lies not just in this activity but also in their implicit
self-interrogation, inherent in their position concerning the aesthetic
and the sublime.

Five points may be asserted in relation to the metahistorical romances in this group, specifically designated above as eighteenth-
century metahistorical romances: (1) their plots enact philosophical debates about the relation of modernity to postmodernity; (2) they are

concerned with origins; (3) they are linked through this concern for origins to the Enlightenment itself, which was characterized by and instantiated the search for origins as the Western metanarrative; (4) their obsessive focus on the Enlightenment may be seen as an interrogation of the Father, the originating Word, by a postmodernist sensibility; and, finally, (5) they share with other metahistorical romances an obsession with the "aesthetic" of the historical sublime, contrasting that to a debased and decadent aesthetic of the beautiful.

These metahistorical romances also raise the issue of postmodernist history's relation to feminism and the postcolonial. Jane Flax, Barbara Creed, Meaghan Morris, Linda Hutcheon, Linda Nicholson, and many other critics have discussed the uneasy relation between feminism and postmodernism, and distinguishing the postcolonial from the postmodern has become an important critical conversation in recent years. Certainly, understanding eighteenth-century metahistorical romances as, perhaps, unwitting champions of the Enlightenment they wish to dismantle may help readers to distinguish between postmodernism and postcolonialism—the first as a child of Western Enlightenment epistemologies and politics, the second lying outside the Western frame.

5

Western Modernity versus Postcolonial Metahistory

At the very time when it most often mouths the word,
the West has never been further from being able to live
a true humanism—a humanism made to the measure
of the world.

—Aimé Césaire, *Discourse on Colonialism*

The English hate each other and they hate England,
and the reason they are so miserable now is that
they have no place else to go and nobody else to
feel better than.

—Jamaica Kincaid, *A Small Place*

Leslie Marmon Silko's novel *Ceremony* (1977) is set in the 1940s, just after the end of World War II. Tayo, a Native American youth who has fought in the war, has returned home to the Laguna Indian reservation. He is in bad shape. As a mixed-blood child abandoned by his unwed, alcoholic mother, he was reared by his resentful aunt, who reminded him constantly of his shameful birth, his indebtedness to her kindness, and his inferiority to her own son, Rocky, whom she raises as an enlightened Christian scornful of traditional Laguna ways. He and Rocky have gone to war together, but only Tayo has returned. Unable to fulfill his role as Rocky's protector, he sees Rocky brutally murdered in the Philippines by the Japanese. He returns home to his aunt's anger and to find his father surrogate and loving mentor, Josiah, dead, the reservation suffering from years of drought, and his friends emotionally emasculated and vicious from the poverty, racism, and alcoholism that plagues all on the reservation. Wracked with guilt, sickened with post-traumatic stress disorder, disoriented and alone, Tayo struggles to recover a sense of wholeness and being in the world. He participates in a ritual ceremony with the medicine man Betonie, a renegade mixed-blood healer who practices a new kind of medicine combining ancient and newly created ceremonies. With the help of Betonie and the mixed-blood medicine woman T'seh, Tayo goes through a healing ceremony and takes a journey, and at the end of the novel he finally makes peace with his personal and cultural past and also gains insight about how to live in this world.

Silko's story is as much about history as it is about Tayo, for in this novel, the personal and the cultural, or subjectivity and history, reflect and shape one another. A metahistorical romance in many respects, *Ceremony* is about what history is. Rather than represent Native American history in terms familiar to Western readers (in the forms of the classic historical novel à la Fenimore Cooper or the ethnographic account of anthropology), this novel revisions Native history in its own narrative, cultural, and structural terms. Silko repeatedly disrupts the formation of a linear history predicated on ethnographic models and instead constructs a respatialized, multilayered history, most prominently in the way that the novel crosscuts stories of Tayo and his family history with narratives from the mythic past (tales of Spiderwoman/Thought Woman, Reed Woman and Corn Woman, Green-Bottle Fly, The Gambler, and witchery) that seem to echo the action in Tayo's present. As Old Grandma says at the end of the novel, "It seems like I already heard these stories before . . . only thing is, the names sound different" (*Ceremony* 260).

Through its interweaving of these different kinds of stories (myth, political fiction, history, and *bildungsroman*), this novel portrays history as the aggregate not only of simultaneously existing narratives but also of simultaneously existing times. History is not a line, it is *strata,* like a natural rock formation. As in Medicine Rock or the Black Hills themselves, in this novel time is a stratified formation where the present coexists with layers of the mythic and human past to form a strong and unified whole out of a diversity of smaller pieces.[1] As radical as this may seem to Western historiography—a way of seeing history that, for example, revolutionized historical study when Michel Foucault formulated it as "archeological" method transforming historical documents into monuments—this is actually a very traditional way for Native American people to understand history. From an American Indian perspective, it is, in fact, literary realism, mimicking the way that nature embeds history in geological and other material environments.

Ceremony presents history as an interweaving of vital lines that form meaningful patterns for individuals and communities and incorporate the body itself. History is a spiderweb, the web woven by Thought Woman out of her own body as she spins the world into being. In this respatialized model of history, History is a gift spun by a grandmother and a god; the entire world community (rather than merely its political leaders) is a child of history worthy of record. Thought Woman's is a three-dimensional history, a history that encompasses time (the first web lines threaded from one point to another, all intersecting at one center point that is the present) but also that encompasses the actions of both living and mythic beings (the web strands woven in concentric circles upon these intersecting threads of time). This spatial model for history weds the personal with the collective as well as human experience with mythic and religious experience. Understanding history is understanding oneself, for the past has things to teach now, and interacts with the present in vital, crucial ways.[2] For Silko, to rely solely on academic history as a way of understanding the world is paradoxically to alienate oneself from the world, from others, and from any connection to other realms of understanding and being. To deny Grandmother Spider's history is to live isolated, without a sense of connection to the universe of one's birth. In *Ceremony,* to deny this history is to be Western, secular, alienated, lost, and alone.

Another metahistorical romance, one written by a white man unaffiliated culturally or racially with Native Americans, seems at first to concern very similar ideas. William T. Vollmann's *The Rifles* (1994) is the third published in a series of seven projected novels about the indigenous people of Wineland the Good (i.e., North America) and their colonizers, narrated by a character named "William the Blind" who "dreams" these visions. *The Rifles,* the "Sixth Dream" of the sequence, is set in the late 1980s in the Arctic Circle, where a young man (presumably Vollmann) and his friend travel from the United States to acquaint themselves for journalistic and personal reasons with the life of the Inuit in northern Canada. While he is visiting, the protagonist—named "Bill" in the text and going by the moniker "Subzero"—has a relationship with an Inuit woman named Reepah. He lives with her in the town of Resolute for a time. There he sees firsthand the poverty and hopelessness of the relocated Inuit community. Young men and women sniff gasoline to get high; the town is ugly and poor; the traditional Inuit ways are fast becoming forgotten as the people become increasingly dependent on and formed by television, market economies, and rifles. Subzero takes Reepah to New York City for a visit, where she is exotic to the locals but also cannot communicate (her English is very bad), gets wild on alcohol, demands presents, and is completely dependent on his support. Later, pregnant with Subzero's unwanted child and faced with the (potential) reality of Subzero's Anglo-European wife, she returns to the Arctic Circle, bears his child, and then commits suicide by blowing her head off with a rifle.

For his part, during his stay up North, Subzero obsessively records what he sees in the form of dialogues, drawings, interviews, and scenic observations, all limned with historical background details he has accumulated from library research. He presents himself as a sometimes perplexed, sometimes disquieted outsider to the region and to the people, who seem to have lost all of their traditional Native ways and values in the face of two hundred years of European colonial interference and the introduction of the rifle as a new technology. Outraged by the colonial brutality he researches and of which he sees the effects, mourning the loss of traditional ways, Subzero nonetheless is mostly ironical about the state of things in Inukjuak, the destination of 1950s relocation for the Inuit. After Reepah is dead, in a last section of the book that shifts perceptibly in tone, Vollmann-as-Subzero charters a flight to the magnetic pole, where he will spend twelve days alone in an abandoned research station, testing his mettle against the frigid and brutal Arctic winter. He nearly dies but survives to call the charter and fly back to populated territories. His stay there is compared (in a long narrative section following the tale of his adventure) to the ultimately fatal trek by a nineteenth-century scientific explorer in Sir John Franklin's Arctic expedition along the frozen shores of Starvation Cove.

For as Vollmann (ever the self-reflexive postmodernist) himself notes, the "gimmick" in this book is that Subzero's experiences in a Pynchonesque manner "map onto" those of Franklin, who commanded three nineteenth-century expeditions to the Arctic. The third, an expedition to complete the Northwest Passage in 1845, cost him his life and the lives of his crew, when his ship became stuck fast in polar ice; Franklin and his men starved to death or died of lead poisoning from the tinned meat they ate for more than three years. Subzero finds out that Franklin is his "twin," and Reepah his "triplet"; he is joined to them in time somehow, but particularly he is tied to Franklin as a kind of reincarnation. Franklin is Subzero and is shown to have visions of Reepah and Subzero's life together; Subzero is Franklin, aware that he is living out in another and degraded context the explorations of the dead explorer. "He would find the Northwest Passage between Reepah's legs," Subzero notes to himself. Both he and Franklin are Anglo-European scientific observers in a hostile Arctic world; they are ill adapted to the unforgiving environment and dependent on the natives for survival, though both their presences are ironically ruinous to traditional Inuit lifestyles and values. The narrative precociously slides in and out of time and history zones, sometimes within one sentence sliding from a description of Franklin's expedition to a description of Subzero's life. The two historical events are "twins," to be understood as simultaneous. The message ostensibly is a political one: that Anglo-European (and Anglo-American) interference with the Inuit—most significantly, in their introduction of rifles to the People—has brought nothing but degradation and death, both to the Arctic environment (which is polluted and empty through commercial overhunting and waste of the native animal populations) and to the Inuit people, who no longer know, or care to know, how to live in their world without Western technology, media, or supermarket goods, none of which is well adapted to their culture, collective psyche, or physical environment.

There are many similarities between Silko's and Vollmann's novels. For example, both thematically concern how indigenous North American people are disastrously estranged from their cultural traditions because of the colonial interference of Anglo-Western, Christian culture. To make this point, both novels rework the classic historical romance genre by foregrounding not history but fabulation (romance). As I noted in chapter 1, according to Robert Scholes, postmodern fabulation is characterized by an extraordinary delight in design that asserts the authority and control of the designer, an implicit didacticism shaped into ethically controlled fantasy, a propensity to allegorize, and a rejection of realism (Scholes *Fabulation* 8–20). Both of these novels, albeit in different ways, return to fabulation via metahistorical investigation. For instance, both novels overtly level myth and documented history onto the same hermeneutic plane: Silko's novel weaves Laguna myth with the facts of G.I. experience in World War II and reservation life, while Vollmann weaves the facts of his own and Franklin's expeditions with Inuit myths, such as that of Sedna and the Fulmar. The results are a fantasizing or mythologization of reality, and a realization of myth, an equation of two kinds of reality operating on human consciousness and, perhaps, in the world.

Moreover, mixing myth, secular history, and personal experience in fabulatory narrative leads both novels to offer alternatives to linear models of history in order to make a metahistorical point. Both novels construct a "simultaneous history" of the kind discussed in chapter 3: time present and time past not only intersect but also overlap, existing simultaneously on one plane of historical reality. Both *Ceremony* and *The Rifles* disrupt the linear model of progressive, disciplinary history, but in doing so they make a point about empiricist historiography. These novels assert that whatever disciplinizes, rationalizes, and records the world also destroys it. The implications of this view are serious for a theory of history such as the "total his-

tory" of the *Annales* school, predicated on the idea that scientific pro-
cedures could and should govern the study and reconstruction of history. In both *Ceremony* and *The Rifles,* scientific observation is shown
to be false knowledge aligned with destructive evil: in *Ceremony,* science is thanatos, the psychic death wish and the divorcing of human
understanding from the earth that leads to the ultimate destructive
witchery of the atomic bomb; in *The Rifles,* the quest for scientific
knowledge is linked to eros, an imperialist and libidinal desire to exploit new territory that leads to the death of all living things that
stand in the path of colonial expansion.

However, something important differentiates these novels and
radically separates their metahistorical politics. Both novels confront
rather than repress the historical sublime (where "history that hurts"
meets the chaos and terrifying unknowability of abstract History or
the place of the past) in their search for history's meaning, for both
are willing to consider (for very different reasons) the possibility that
what really happened in the past is unknowable. Yet that confrontation with History leads these novels finally to different assertions
about the moral or ethical import and consequence of this "ahistorical" historical knowledge. This difference may be the difference between the postmodernist and the postcolonialist metahistorical imagination.

To clarify: I have posited that the metahistorical consciousness, as
a post-traumatic consciousness, redefines positivist or stadialist history and presents history as sublime, a territory that can never be
reached but only approached in attempts to understand human origins and the meaning of lived existence. That statement is true for
both the postmodernist and the postcolonialist metahistorical consciousness in the late twentieth century. As I have emphasized, for the
post-traumatic metahistorical imagination, history is desire, the desire for the unceasingly deferred, sublime space of History. The fabulatory impulses of metahistorical romance, in both its postmodernist
and postcolonialist incarnations, are one expression of this desire.[3]
This desire for History, for the "secular sacred" sublime in the absence of the gods—for certainty, hope, and awe-inspiring illumina-

tion—leads to metahistorical representations of the past, narratives that end up being at least as much about what history *is* as about the characters and plots that appear in those narratives.

The term *metahistorical romance* thus encompasses both postmodernist and postcolonialist fiction. Postmodernist historical fiction and some late-twentieth-century postcolonial fiction may share a metahistorical imagination, an imagination that returns to history and questions the grounds on which it has been epistemologically and politically established. Both react to the forces of modernization. Both kinds of fiction are a reaction-formation to the trauma of history itself. Both kinds of fiction question the relation between narrative and historical documentation, particularly as that relation has been defined in the political and aesthetic context of the secular-humanist First World. Both forms of metahistorical romance raise thorny and politically volatile questions about authorial imagination and intentionality and about the politics of historical critique. However, while postcolonial metahistory clearly announces itself as a critique of the West from outside its political, epistemological, economic, or cultural borders, postmodernist metahistory is an inquiry from within the First World frame, an insider's reevaluation of Western historiographical politics.[4] One might say that while postcolonialist metahistory frequently raises the question of the Self (as Other in history produced by a not-Self), postmodernist metahistory frequently raises the question of the Other (in relation to Self-as-producer-of-history). Yet even this is too glib a description of the complicated relation between postmodernism and postcolonialism, for the boundaries between these types of fiction are fluid.[5]

How much difference does a gaze make? As twentieth-century scientists, political theorists, and writers have taught us, where we stand when we view an atom, a landscape, a person, or a text significantly affects our perspective as well as the entity being observed. Where we stand ideologically, subjectively, and economically when we ask questions about history similarly affects and limits our abilities to come to terms with it. To say this of course opens the culture debates of the late twentieth century; it also raises the debate between essentialism

and antifoundationalism in all of its forms. Just as it rehearses theoretical positions about modernity and history circulating inside and
outside the academy after 1960, the *postmodernist* metahistorical romance contends with the late-twentieth-century hermeneutical question of the relationships between Self, Other, culture, and history. It
does so from a position of political advantage in many cases, but that
doesn't mean that this is fiction of lesser value or lesser moral virtue
than that written by authors outside the Western tradition. The postmodern metahistorical romance contends with these issues because
they are part of the "crisis of history" of the First World, and it often
clearly aligns itself with the liberatory politics of the postcolonial
novel, though its gaze is projected from a different point of origin.
How successful this alignment is in individual texts, however, is a
question that is raised by novels such as Vollmann's or by Günter
Grass's *The Flounder. The Flounder,* for example, self-consciously
highlights the cultural specificity of Anglo-Western feminism, for
which the linkages between women and earth, nurturing, and birth
may be patriarchal constructions. (Silko's *Ceremony,* or Toni Morrison's *Beloved,* would take a very different view of women's earth ties.)
It deftly complicates the metahistorical issue of what constitutes
"women's history": the narrator, drawing distinctions between patriarchal time relying on dates and history and matriarchal time based
on the rhythms of the body, notes that this female attitude toward
history is changing: "She wants to take her distance from herself as
she sits inside me," he writes, "or as, expressed by me, she becomes
history" (*The Flounder* 410). At the beginning of the novel, the
Flounder notes that perhaps "history can teach us what role women
played in historical events, in the triumph of the potato, for instance"
(28). Both statements are sharp attacks on microhistory, illustrating
how it may voice egalitarianism in the tradition of Enlightenment rationalism while still being mired in colonialist—or, in this instance,
sexist—politics. The ultimate irony in this novel is that women finally represent the male principle more effectively than do men.

Juxtaposing *The Flounder* or *The Rifles* to *Ceremony* illustrates that
a continuum of possibilities is available to the First World, androcen-

tric, metahistorical imagination when working with gender and post-colonial issues. The continuum ranges from ironic, even nihilistic, deconstruction on the one hand to a reconstructed "secular-sacred" belief on the other, as in the narrative technique of simultaneous history. The former seems aligned with a postmodernist sensibility and novels written by authors who situate themselves within the arena of First World politics; the latter seems aligned with a postcolonialist sensibility and novels written by authors who situate themselves *outside* the First World cultural arena (even if those writers are, technically, citizens of the First World).[6]

All three novels, for example, construct different kinds of simultaneous history—history as planar. All assert that progressivist history on the figure-fulfillment model serves colonial or imperialist male power, and all attempt to escape from this paradigm by flattening history into one plane that accommodates neither a "before" nor an "after" but, instead, presents all of history as simultaneous. However, *Ceremony* overtly constructs the figure-fulfillment model *as a trope* (rather than as reality) during the course of the novel's action through the characterization of Rocky and Auntie (as proponents of this false model) and the thematic symbol of uranium and atomic war. The novel is quite explicit in its identification and rejection of this paradigmatic Western historical model. In opposition to it, the novel posits the possibility of other ways of understanding history in the form of indigenous tribal mythologies and environmental knowledge. As Susan Scarberry has noted, memory is medicine in this novel, the key to Tayo's healing. One might say that in the face of both literal post-traumatic stress disorder and a post-traumatic cultural imaginary, Tayo recuperates memory rather than history to find a new sacred relation to the world.

One might note the similarities between such an approach and that toward history in postcolonial fiction. In Salman Rushdie's *The Satanic Verses,* for example, various historical epochs likewise converge; an Islamic historical past, religious past, and secular present exist simultaneously in time and in the consciousness of Gibreel Farishata. As a metahistorical romance, *The Satanic Verses* critiques the postmodernization of the East, particularly its secularization of time, but also the pre-Enlightenment time of myth. The result is blasphemy, a heresy against two very different "religious" beliefs.

The Imam, for example, is a representative of pre-modern, antihistorical religious fundamentalism, a "conjurer" who revolts against history: "History is the blood-wine that must no longer be drunk. History the intoxicant, the creation and possession of the Devil, of the great Shaitan, the greatest of the lies—progress, science, rights—against which the Imam has set his face. History is a deviation from the Path, knowledge is a delusion, because the sum of knowledge was complete on the day Al-Lah finished his revelation to Mahound. 'We will unmake the veil of history,' Bilal declaims into the listening night" (*Satanic Verses* 210). The Imam's time is static, deathlike: he claims the people love him "for my habit of smashing clocks"; that "after the revolution there will be no clocks"; that God's time is "timeless time, that has no need to move" and "encompasses past, present, and future" (214).[7] In contrast, Saladin Chamcha's postmodern time requires him also to destroy history, but in the service of assimilation. To be part of the postmodern world, he must reject his national and personal history and attempt to become a simulacrum of Englishness. He "is a creature of *selected* discontinuities, a *willing* re-invention; his *preferred* revolt against history being what makes him . . . 'false' " (427).

In this novel in both the secular and the sacred domains, history is hermetically sealed, teleological and single-voiced. When Chamcha attempts to internalize a simulated projection of Englishness, he finds only estrangement from family, self, wife, lover, and heritage; he initially believes that "a being going through life can become so other to himself as to *be another,* discrete, severed from history" (*Satanic Verses* 288). However, in *The Satanic Verses,* true history lies between these two poles, between the Imam's negation of history as something evil to be annihilated by atemporal orthodoxy, and the West's negation of history through its promotion of relativistic and empty secularism. It lies in the zone of the uncanny, the return of the repressed: by the end of the novel Chamcha is learning the regenerative potential of this "zone," the meaning behind Hal Valence's unconsidered sendoff, "Don't you get it? You're history" (270). This is what is shown when the dead/alive, young/old Rosa Diamond meets the dead/alive Martin de la Cruz/Gibreel Farishata (*Satanic Verses* 156–57). Past and present converge, and improvisation, becoming, unending metamorphosis and change—significantly, the operation of history at the border of the historical sublime—are celebrated.

As White and Lyotard also argue of the historical sublime, negotiating this zone requires an awareness and acceptance of responsibility for individual action and cultural history. The narrator says of Rosa Diamond when she is dying: "It was not possible to distinguish memory from wishes, or guilty reconstructions from confessional truths—because even on her deathbed Rosa Diamond did not know how to look her history in the eye" (*Satanic Verses* 153). Rosa Diamond will face and enact everything she has dreamed and subconsciously hidden away, just as Chamcha and Farishata will act out a repressed cultural history until they work out what history should be. Just as characters overlap, exchange identities, and switch roles, and binaries of all sorts break down or are made irrelevant, History is revealed to be a sublime zone comprising simultaneously existing pasts, all of which impinge on the present.[8]

Surprisingly similar to Rushdie's novel in this respect, Grass's *The Flounder* and Vollmann's *The Rifles* are able to diagnose and decry the state of Western cultural imperialism, but unlike Silko in *Ceremony,* they ultimately are unable to find a workable solution or a system of belief to combat it. Neither Grass's nor Vollmann's protagonists can escape belief in the figure-fulfillment model of history or are capable of seeing that model *as a trope* (rather than as a natural state of historical movement).

Vollmann's novel provides the best example. First, the "Dream cycle" of which it is a part implicitly supports a belief in the progressivism of Western history, though this progress is seen as negative, a logic of devolution; moreover, the novel repeatedly implies that this logic is *natural* rather than culturally constructed, a process akin to biological evolution: "Each Age was worse than the one before, because we thought we must amend whatever we found, nothing of what *was* being reflected in the ice-mirrors of our ideas. Yet we were scarcely blameworthy, any more than the bacilli which attack and overcome a living body; for if history has a purpose (if not, then there is nothing wrong with inventing one), then our undermining of trees and tribes must have been good for something."[9] The parenthetical comment here reveals Vollmann's distance from a postcolonial perspective; from the latter's point of view, there may indeed be something very wrong with inventing a "purpose" for history, particularly since that "purpose" has often been understood, for the First World, as the economic, religious, and cultural domination of the globe and the eradication of difference. In addition, the quote explicitly equates First World history with biological determinism; it seems that white people, like "bacilli which attack and overcome a living body," simply can't help attacking and overcoming colonial territories and peoples. It's their nature to do so. Even if Vollmann is being sly and ironic here, this kind of metaphorical logic is deeply disturbing, largely because it constructs history not only within a figure-fulfillment model but also within a deterministic one; there can be no accountability or need to feel responsibility for one's historical (or present) actions if in fact we are all like bacteria, acting out our biologically derived, innate racial drives and desires.

Second, the novel continues a distinction between the "historical" (which is part of devolutionary history and represented by the story of Sir John Franklin's expedition, notably aligned with Vollmann's own story) and the "anthropological" (the story of the Inuit, left out of history like the silent signification of Reepah's own broken speech). The Inuit are not really historical beings in this text; as anthropological "color" on the stage of history, they eventually drop out of the grand narrative of Western expansion. Accordingly, the novel does not allow the possibility of real indigenous resistance to colonialism. The defeat of the Inuit (and of the environment they inhabit) in this book is total.[10] The triumph of Western market capitalism is shown as a later event that retroactively identifies an earlier event—the state of nature—as a precursor to itself based on the knowledge gained by historical distance and perspective. Thus this novel not only fails to challenge the figure-fulfillment model of history; it actually quite strongly supports that model.

And third, the novel's last section, which is a Hemingwayesque adventure tale of a white man's (Vollmann's) existential battle alone with a hostile and exotic environment (an abandoned Arctic communications station in the dead of winter), undermines much of the social critique that went before. Here a familiar Western genre reemerges in an ironic context: readers can see (indeed, are told to see by the narrator) the absurdity and hubris of Subzero's desire to test his survival skills against the Arctic winter. Yet the androcentric, politically conservative adventure tale genre (from Homer's *Ulysses* to Defoe's *Robinson Crusoe* to Gene Roddenberry's *Star Trek*) is imprinted on the Western collective unconscious to the degree that Subzero cannot help but emerge as a triumphant individualist explorer at the end of the tale, in a Man-Against-Nature sort of heroic struggle. The West may have conquered and polluted the Arctic and killed its populations, the coda implies, but after all, these colonialist guys *were* mighty brave, manly sort of men, even if absurd in their heroic struggles. A book that is at times brilliantly beautiful and at other times arrogant, self-contradictory and desperate, *The Rifles* tries hard to be a political outcry against (specifically designated) white, androcentric, First World imperialism and scientific rationality. Yet it also lets a white male citizen of the First World who is also a writer and obsessive recorder have the last word. The final sections of the book glorify Vollmann's/Subzero's absurd, individualist struggle for knowledge and paint as heroic his attempt to unify his split subjectivities through the act of environmental (and sexual) mastery. Moreover, in an appendix to the novel, this last word stunningly takes the form of a *catalog and quality-control evaluation of store-bought camping goods,* written by Vollmann himself to help future Arctic adventurers get the best equipment for their money. In the only section of the book that's "straight" and not ironic (and that is explicitly situated as "outside" the fictional narration, in the real world of the reader), rather than protest Western capitalist domination, Vollmann here becomes its sales representative.[11]

The difference between *Ceremony* and *The Rifles,* and the metahistorical consciousnesses that inform them, may be understood as that between an integrated and a self-contradictory artistic vision. But it also may be understood in terms of what Fredric Jameson calls "situational consciousness." Recalling Hegel's analysis of the master-slave relationship as a cultural logic, Jameson writes that while the slave is forced to labor for the Master and therefore knows what reality and the resistance of matter really are, the Master

> is condemned to idealism—to the luxury of a placeless freedom in which any consciousness of his own concrete situation flees like a dream, like . . . a nagging doubt which the puzzled mind is unable to formulate.
>
> It strikes me that we Americans, we masters of the world, are in something of that very same position. The view from the top is epistemologically crippling, and reduces its subjects to the illusions of a host of fragmented subjectivities, to the poverty of the individual experience of isolated monads, to dying individual bodies without collective pasts or futures bereft of any possibility of grasping the social totality. This placeless individuality, this structural idealism . . . offers a welcome escape from the "nightmare of history," but at the same time it condemns our culture to psychologism and the "projections" of private subjectivity. All of this is denied to third-world culture, which must be situational and materialist despite itself. ("Third-World Literature" 85)

In *Flight to Canada,* Ishmael Reed states this idea more polemically: railing against the White Aestheticists, the slave Raven Quickskill tells the mixed-blood Native American Princess Quaw Quaw Tralaralara, "They're as Feudalist and Arthurian as Davis, but whereas he sees it as a political movement, they see it as a poetry movement" (96). At the end of Sontag's novel *The Volcano Lover,* an intellectual woman, summarizing her life choices, notes precisely this relation:

> How naturally human beings adapt to abjection, to lies, and to unearned prerogatives. Those whom birth or appropriate forms of

ambition have placed inside the circle of privilege would have to be dedicated misfits . . . *not* to enjoy themselves. But those whom birth or revolt have cast outside, where most beings on this earth live, would have to be obtuse or slavish in temperament not to see how disgraceful it is that so few monopolize both wealth and refinement, and inflict such suffering on others. . . . They [the privileged] were despicable. Damn them all. (417–18, 419)

Sontag's novel attests to the links between the disenfranchised—be they indigenous peoples in a colonial state or women in a patriarchal culture or the poor everywhere, anywhere. What we see in her novel, as well as in other novels such as Charles Johnson's *Middle Passage,* is an illustration of how the metahistorical consciousness can align itself with the consciousness of either the master or the slave. Vollmann's novel in fact embeds the idealism and "nagging doubt" of the American "masters of the world," and for his character Subzero, the view from the top is indeed epistemologically crippling. Subzero beautifully illustrates how the First World subject, the inheritor of the master, is fragmented into "the poverty of the individual experience of isolated monads," without collective pasts or futures and unable to grasp a sense of the social totality except in a negative, debased vision of social devolution. Subzero is confronted with the nightmare of history. His abstraction offers him some solace, but as the last section of the novel makes clear, this same abstraction also condemns him to an alienated and blinkered individualism.

History makes the Difference. It seems that for the Western imagination, the marginalized Other can *become* the uncanny at the border (of the imagination, of History, of society). Approaching the border of History armed with colonial mythology and colonial power, projecting one's private subjectivity onto the subjugated Other (who in turn defines the colonial self) can only result, concurrently, in denials of History's final sublimity and assertions of history's knowability and rationalist course. That is, the ideological operations of colonialism deny the traumatic recognition that sublime History eludes us—a denial of history's multidimensionality, openness to otherness, and infinite potential for narrativization that has implications for how we understand the present and future as well as the past. Instead, colonialism attempts to fix history (as well as the Others placed there) at its uncanny border in a reassuring, unwavering, and panoptic colonial gaze. The colonialist might establish the imperial ego, but the result is that approaching the Other, located at the border of history and the margin of society, results in a continual feeling of the uncanny, of returning to that which has been repressed (e.g., the Other, or Sublime History). Vidler in fact says that the uncanny "might be characterized as the quintessential bourgeois kind of fear: one carefully bounded by the limits of real material security and the pleasure principle afforded by a terror that was, artistically at least, kept well under control." At the same time, however, every time it is performed, this imperialist one-way approach toward the Other reinscribes the ideological claim that history is knowable, secular, linear, and aligned with the Western narrative of individualism.[12]

The only way out of the view of the Master for the Western, First World (particularly U.S.) consciousness may be a return to a premodern/postmodern recognition of the historical sublime. In trying to explain what I mean by this, I am going to reference and rewrite Ernst Van Alphen's insightful discussion of Holocaust history, the uncanny, and the sublime in his book *Caught by History.* In the last section of the book, "Giving Memory a Place," Van Alphen talks about the uncanny presence he feels in his new home, once owned by the Jewish architect Harry Elte, who with his family was killed by the Nazis in Theresienstadt. Van Alphen wonders if there is a way to overcome the uncanny feeling in the house, any way to synthesize the presence of the traumatic past with his own psychological and physical existence. Referencing work by Freud, F.W.J. Schelling, Anthony Vidler, and Edmund Burke,[13] Van Alphen illustrates that only by recuperating knowledge of the uncanny and the sublime will he find this reconciliation. According to Freud, the uncanny is the return of something that is familiar and repressed; its repression leads to defined ego boundaries, because the subject constructs these boundaries as a defense. The uncanny is thus directly related to "individualism" as that is understood in popular terms. The boundaries, however, may be threatened when the uncanny reappears. When a subject depends on his own memories and sense of individualism for an experience of wholeness, he makes himself vulnerable to a return of the repressed, vulnerable to the uncanny. The sublime, on the other hand, is a repression of this repression; it is the subject's openness to selflessness. In this second-level repression, there is "an inclination to lose the self in the extensions of the ungraspable and unattainable, and thus to engage with it."

Using Burke's formulation of the sublime, by extension, Van Alphen reasons that

> in order to overcome the uncanny, to overcome our inclination to strengthen ego boundaries or the self by means of the boundaries of the private home, the second phase in the process can reverse that individualist repression. By turning the tables on individualism, we can use sublime experience to break out of individualism. The subject's orientation is now directed outward. . . . Precisely because the content of the Holocaust, its meaning, is ungraspable, its sublime ungraspability can become the significance of the moment in which our individualism crumbles away. . . . My house does not delimit only my own boundaries anymore; it is invested not only with the memories of *my* past, but also with the memories of his [Harry Elte's] past. (204–5)

What Van Alphen learns is that *if he wants to be a moral being,* he can come to terms with living in his house not by attempting to fill it with his own presence and thereby eliminating the memory of Elte's family (which would make him vulnerable to the uncanny return of the repressed), nor by giving the house over to the past and moving out (the ultimately useless, sentimental solution). What he has to learn to do is embrace the house as a sublime monument that encompasses the ungraspable meaning of the past. Doing so would unravel the individualism that alienates him from others. The house can be both his house and Elte's house if it is understood as a memorial to the Holocaust experience, something that can't be understood rationally but which forms a bridge of continuity between the present and the past. His house becomes not his Self, but the world. It becomes History, of which he and everything else is a part (201–5). As such, he must take responsibility for it and place himself within it— not as a transcendental signified, but contextually, in relation to others, especially the others whom he has displaced.

If we replace "nation" for "house" in the above quote, Van Alphen's statement can be seen to offer one ethical (though not economic) alternative to Jameson's "situational consciousness," for it articulates a rejection of "placeless individuality" and "the poverty of the individual experience of isolated monads, to dying individual bodies without collective pasts or futures bereft of any possibility of grasping the social totality." The fact that this is an ethical as well as a social decision is crucially important. Van Alpen is talking about how, *as an ethical being,* he can live in a house inhabited, in his mind, by the ghosts of killed Jews; his experience, however, can easily be correlated to the question of how to live in a nation inhabited by the ghosts of (killed or expelled or disenfranchised) indigenous peoples. His dilemma is essentially an ethical dilemma, a social dilemma posed for a moral human being. What we have in Van Alphen's analysis is an evocation of the historical sublime as a potential solution to the problem of how to live in the world honestly without egotism. A similar need to recognize the historical sublime as an alternative to individualist, colonial history may exist for the First World writer coming to terms with the present crisis of history. The alternative addresses not material issues such as repatriation but attitudinal, epistemological, and ethical issues. Of course, this idea of *anamnesis,* or "unforgetting," has a long history in philosophical discourse about history, from Plato to Nietzsche to Adorno.[14] Holocaust studies and postcolonial critiques of modernity have brought this ongoing conversation to the foreground of postmodern critique.

For some time in feminist theory as well as in postcolonial culture theory, the dialectic of self/Other prevailed. Suffused with the just anger borne of political oppression, culture theorists identified the Other that had been mythologized, marginalized, repressed, or simply killed off under patriarchy or colonialism. A dialectical model that posited an ongoing negotiation between insider and outsider,

Self and Other had the potential to expand discussions of cultural difference—to make both cultural and gender difference, which was often denied existence, visible in the first place. Such a model also forced consideration of historical contexts upon what had been considered primarily aesthetic domains. At every turn, history exploded into the conversation about narrative art; there was no way to discuss difference without historicizing it, returning to historical and material conditions of real people in a real past. This first generation model, however, has been gradually overspoken by a second generation that focusses on hybridity as an unsettling and dislocating operation concurrent with the construction and exercise of colonial power. Rather than taking as its aim the revelation of power relations between colonizer and colonized (or patriarchy and woman, or Self and Other) and the theorization of values inherent in that political and ideological relation, much recent postcolonial culture theory and feminist theory identifies the hybrid character of the national state or the androcentric or heterosexist standard that wants to position and imagine itself as coherent, whole, or pure. The importance of the margin to the center, of the colonized to the colonizer's own world or identity construction (or of the female Other to the male Self, or of the homosexual Other to the straight Self) is underscored, as empire is shown to be ineluctably shot through with difference and crucially dependent on the Other it renders silent in both its own cultural unconscious and in its public mythology. Theorists in postcolonial studies, however, are now questioning the model of hybridity itself. Robert Young, for example, has lucidly illustrated how culture theorists in the academy have embraced the idea of hybridity without proper investigation, unaware that it was precisely this concept that informed and even birthed the racist colonial theories of the nineteenth century.[15]

Understanding the relation between colonizer and colonized in different terms, in terms of the historical sublime, seems posited by a number of late-twentieth-century fiction and nonfiction texts as an alternative to both of these models. Metahistorical romance seems to offer an alternative way of looking at history that potentially avoids (or at least, defers) a model of "linear history" while it defers objecti-

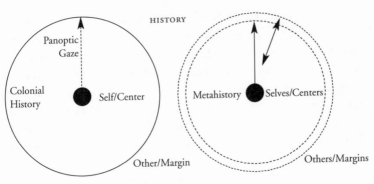

Figure 1: The Operation of History in Colonial and Metahistorical Narratives

fication of the Other and deconstructs the relation between center and margin. Writers of metahistorical romance seem to reject the notion of border and replace it with the action of deferral. A nondialectical relation is established in the metahistorical romance's movement toward History, toward the boundary between a static and unspeakable historical past (History) and a dynamic historical present.[16] This boundary embodies *différance,* for it is unremittingly different and ceaselessly deferred from the present.[17] Through its operation of deferral, the metahistorical romance can invert the notion of margin and center: the margin of history, the border, is what defines the center, History itself. In the context of metahistorical postmodernism, History is the marginalized center, the place where we think we set out from, but really the place that is never reached, that is always before us and always deferred in the operation at the hermeneutical border. It is the city of the Shining Rocks that is ever out of reach.

This model of metahistory (Figure 1) posits the possibility of a deferred border to history. If colonialism requires the construction of a boundary and the location of the Other *at* the ex-centric border, the operations of metahistory instead require a constantly deferred border. As chapter 3 illustrated, what this model offers is a perspective of history other than that seen from the Point of the King; it dislocates the panoptic gaze. Moreover, this constantly deferred border necessarily offers a constantly deferred location of the Other.[18] I don't mean to imply, of course, that the First World imagination doesn't seek, or construct, Others. This representation of metahistorical history merely illustrates how metahistorical romance moves in pendulum motion not only from the "realism" of Scott's historical novel form, through the abstraction of modernist spatial form and postmodern fabulation, back toward the "realism" of postcolonial politics but also in a pendulum motion between its own history and that of the Unspoken Other at its borders. In relation to the colonial history of the West, the First World, postmodern metahistorical romance is again unable to break free to a real access to History. Not only caught within two literary genres no longer associated with the Real (realism and romance), it also is confined between two angles of vision on Progress: one perspective it no longer trusts, and the other (Other) perspective it cannot really know. If colonialism necessarily closes political as well as hermeneutical borders and constructs a "linear" history dependent upon a figure-fulfillment paradigm and the narrative of individualism, metahistory constructs history as (a weirdly healthy) repetition compulsion, a loss of the self and a journey from the center to the margins that is repeated endlessly because the borders of knowable history it seeks are themselves constantly receding (Figure 2). This, then, is the postmodern crisis of history. This endlessly repeated movement toward the historical sublime/History repeatedly voices and inverts the relation between subject and object, center and border, Self and Other: the Self searching for History finds nothing and loses itself, and is instead set on a never-ending, spiraling quest toward the meaning of the social, the self, and the other. And in reality, all this is no more abstract a model for historical "progression" than is the dialectical model, which also can be plotted geometrically.

I am not claiming that history *is* spiral, or circular, or fractal. Instead, I am articulating a model for history that seems congenial to, if not constructed by, the postmodern metahistorical imagination, a model that by definition resists closure and, by analogy, "linearity" of the type implied by progressivist and colonialist models. The post-

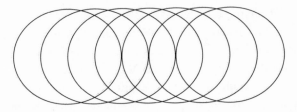

Figure 2: The Inversion and Replay of the Metahistorical Movement toward History

modernist metahistorical imagination seems to approach traumatic colonial history as if it needed to make moral sense of it but also as if it realized that history was incomprehensible and forever out of cognitive reach. As a result, the metahistorical romance reaches out its hand to History but seems terrified that it might actually grasp it. Longing for the surety of historical knowledge but painfully aware that all previous human attempts to grasp History have led only to narcissism, war, bloodshed, imperialism, inequality, and the rape of the natural world—that is, the cosmopolitan culture of theoretical modernity—the metahistorical consciousness can only ceaselessly approach and withdraw from History, from Truth, from Certainty. The model of history it constructs, as a result, effectively interrupts the panoptic gaze, but such repetitions inevitably also decenter the center as well as dislocate the boundary. Every repeated journey outward from the Self and approach toward (but not grasp of) the Other will rebound to a Self that has changed. In this model, the Self is not a hybrid but a process growing out of traumatic history, something Other *and* the Self that was left on the journey toward the border.[19]

The "compromised politics" of postmodernism may in fact be a necessary first move for a First World consciousness wanting to break out of the solipsism of the master. It redefines "linear," colonial time, infusing a "scientific" process with a moral process of attempted integration with History, with the Other, and with the Self-as-process.[20] In Fanon's words, Anglo-European, First World peoples must "decide to wake up and see themselves, use their brains, and stop playing the stupid game of the Sleeping Beauty" (*The Wretched of the Earth* 106).

The novel form was born out of modernity and the doctrine of individualism; if the metahistorical romance contests modern individualism, the isolated monad of the self, then it contests its own origin and grounding. As a result, by definition the novel that questions the validity of Western individualism is a split, self-contradictory form. If as Ortega suggested, the novel is the new modern form that directs itself against and demystifies the older form of the romance, then the metahistorical romance reverses this critique, turning romance (fabulation) against the modern novel (which is itself).[21] The movement from realism to romance that characterized metahistorical fiction from the 1960s to the 1990s is a tentative movement, as metahistorical fiction—informed by post-Holocaust, feminist and postcolonial *reality*—uses postmodern romance against classical *realism*.

In the late twentieth century, fiction informed by the traumatic historical events of its time seems willing to recognize that the "unreal" Zone of romance is displaced by reality itself as the fabulous: when reality becomes nightmare, and real actions begin to take on allegorical significance even as they are enacted, the traumatized human consciousness blurs the boundaries between realism and romance, fabulation and the world. What should be real is indefinable, inexact, hallucinatory; what should be fiction (or at the least, the narrative of memory) becomes the vehicle to organize this disorder of reality. One wonders whether this statement might apply to a cultural consciousness as well. The call for an Enlightenment belief in empiricism (of the kind underlying the value of mimesis) seems utopian in the face of repeated scholarly, media, and political exposure of colonial and postcolonial violence, which can only be opposite to the rational. Yet the metahistorical consciousness fights to "make sense" or come to terms with the moral and political realities of historical violence. To mime an unreal reality may be the project of avant-garde metahistorical romances such as Pynchon's *Gravity's Rainbow* or Reed's *Flight to Canada,* yet this tactic is increasingly rejected by fiction of the 1980s and 1990s in the wake of the postmodernists' inability to move out of abstraction—the abstraction of fabulation—into the arena of political or ethical action. Instead, at the end of the twentieth century, there is an increasing tendency to return to "realism," but a realism of a very different sort, one constantly attacked by fabulatory or romance elements.

Madison Smartt Bell's *All Souls' Rising*, for example, is a reworking of the classical historical romance that makes real the nightmarish unreality of Haiti's late-eighteenth-century slave economy. The action of *All Souls' Rising* takes place primarily between 1791 and 1793, when slave uprisings began on Haiti's sugar and coffee plantations and eventually moved into Le Cap and the other major port towns held by France. The Enlightenment setting is important to all thematic and political aspects of the novel; Bell connects the political and social upheaval of the French Revolution to the uprisings in France's Caribbean colony. The novel presents a relatively large cast of characters but focuses primarily on the French physician Antoine Hébert and the family he creates with the mulatto woman Nanon; Michel Arnaud, a cruel Creole plantation master, and his crazed wife, Claudine; the white Creole aristocrat Isabelle Cigny, who presides over her salon in Le Cap; Toussaint-Louverture, a black Creole slave who participates in the uprisings and eventually becomes a general under Spanish colors; Riau, an African brought over on the middle passage who is Toussaint's protégé for a time; Choffleur, a mulatto Creole who is the bastard son of one of the most vicious of the royalist *grand blancs,* the white landed gentry; and Captain Maillart, a "philosophe" in the French army attempting to keep order in Haiti.

In *All Souls' Rising* (dedicated to Bob Marley), Bell complicates the master/slave relation because he is aware of it and quite clearly ethically opposed to its historical manifestation in the Caribbean. Like Barry Unsworth in *Sacred Hunger,* in this (post–World War II, post-Holocaust) novel Bell shows how Enlightenment ideals of emancipation (and rationalism) can be cruelly warped into actually justifying the most monstrous of human relations. Like Unsworth, Bell is intent on examining the effects of colonialism upon human psychology and material bodies. A naturalistic novel and one that illustrates vividly how reality is nightmare, *All Souls' Rising* shows how colonialism sets in motion a logic of events and a trajectory of violence. The novel is a brutal read, showing not only the cruelty of race relations in plantation economies (we are shown, for example, slave owners raping their female slaves while their white wives are forced to listen in adjoining rooms, and scenes showing how mulatto women are prostituted) but also the horrors engendered by absolute power, the kind of power held by plantation overseerers and slave owners but also by petty dictators and revolution leaders.

The cinematic novel begins with a scene of horror. As Dr. Hébert, recently arrived from France, rides onto the main grounds of a sugar plantation, he is confronted with a crucifixion: a black slave woman has been literally crucified on a wooden cross for killing her child to keep it from slavery (we hear echoes of Morrison's *Beloved* here). The woman is dying a slow and excruciating death, the afterbirth from her delivery still attached to her body. The doctor, who is finally a sympathetic white character in the novel, is horrified by the scene but rides on, leaving the "property" to be disposed of by its rightful male owner. Later in the novel, this scene is repeated between women themselves, as the insane and alcoholic wife of one of the cruelest Creole masters (the one who crucified the slave woman at the beginning of the novel) ties up in a crucifixion pose a slave woman pregnant with the master's child and proceeds in a drunken fury to cut the unborn child from the woman's womb. Brutally and precisely, the author illustrates Aimé Césaire's claim that colonization

> dehumanizes even the most civilized man; that colonial activity, colonial enterprise, colonial conquest, which is based on contempt for the native and justified by that contempt, inevitably tends to change him who undertakes it; that the colonizer, who in order to ease his conscience gets into the habit of seeing the other man as *an animal,* accustoms himself to treating him like an animal, and tends objectively to transform *himself* into an animal. It is this result, this boomerang effect of colonization (*Discourse on Colonialism* 20).[22]

The violence in *All Souls' Rising* is not, however, limited to white-on-black violence. Later in the novel, in the slave uprisings, we see frenzied black slaves viciously killing their white masters (speared white babies are carried as standards in the riots as the violence escalates into burnings, rapes, and horrific murder, mimicking the tactics of punishment formerly used by Creole landowners). After the most powerful series of uprisings, bloodthirsty "generals" emerge among the black "army," and these militaristic leaders create torture camps and their own despotic military states. The upended moral universe of the colonial slave state is embodied in the relation between Sieur Maltrot (one of the cruelest and absolutely hateful of all of the landowners) and his publicly disowned bastard mulatto son, the sadistic Choufleur: off by themselves at one of the torture camps following the first wave of uprisings, the son slowly skins his father alive, eventually emasculating him and putting his dried testicles in a snuff box as a gift to a mulatto ex-mistress (Nanon) in town.

The overdetermined violence of *All Souls' Rising* is unremitting but not gratuitous. Bell, as a white U.S. southerner, projects his national heritage of violence, colonialism, and slavery into a context that signifies for him safely and meaningfully precisely because it is indisputably colonial and, from the perspective of the First World, newly voiced: historical study has finally caught up with colonialism and exposed it both materially and theoretically in and outside the academy. The more cynical might argue that the cinematic violence of Bell's novel exists to limn the book with sales potential (it's easy to see which scenes would be cut into the stunning movie trailer). However, the violence of the book is necessary to its political and ethical perspective. For the violence of Bell's text enacts what Frantz Fanon argued years ago:

> The violence which has ruled over the ordering of the colonial world . . . that same violence will be claimed and taken over by the native at the moment when, deciding to embody history in his own person, he surges into the forbidden quarters. . . . colonialism is not a thinking machine, nor a body endowed with reasoning faculties. It is violence in its natural state, and it will only yield when confronted with greater violence. (40, 61)

History is the Burkean sublime in *All Souls' Rising;* it is a terrifying space that is both in the past and in the present but also out of time, out of control.

Bell underscores the idea that there is no "making sense" of the reality of Haiti; no economic, or historical, or sociological study can encompass the truth of the violent history there. The novel implies that the truth of Haiti may be an unspeakable truth, something linked to the truth about humanity itself. *All Souls' Rising* implies that this truth is able to be presented as a figure only. In the last pages of the novel, Bell compares the inhuman violence engendered by slavery to fire that burns throughout history, a fire that is still smoldering and that "is burning still, still striving to find its way into the future, wanting to burn through to you who believe yourself inured to atrocity, to murder in the streets" (504).

Significantly, however, though the novel is almost naturalistic in its depiction of colonial and revolutionary violence, this novel repeatedly recalls the motifs of romance to construct its political and ethical themes. The most explicit of these romance elements (in addition to the love between Hébert and Nanon and the unreality of the wartime setting and action) is the movement toward the end of the novel by Doctor Hébert and his family, as well as by other refugees, from city to country as an allegorical movement from experience to innocence, modernity to premodernity, decadent urbanity to holistic primitivism. As the Doctor and the others flee the burning coastline cities, they move deep into the island's interior, where sugar plantations eventually give way to tropical jungle and the only path is the one left by the Carib Indians who were themselves exterminated by the first European colonists. This set of characters, like the Carib Indians whose footsteps they literally follow, represents a utopian solution to the problem of colonial modernity: a multicultural and familial group, Hébert's company flees literally into the space of the past. In one of the last scenes of the book, in fact, we see an allegorical representation of the Christian Holy Family as the Doctor walks toward the jungle, his woman Nanon riding atop a mule with their son. They are described as "pilgrims" (Bell 497). The new world that they will start, however, is ambiguous, for at the end of the novel, the end of their journey is another plantation, *on the other side of the jungle,* where the doctor meets his long-lost sister, and his mulatto child and her white child hold out hands to one another in greeting. This ending is ambiguous not only because of the troubling signification of its setting (we are back, as it were, where we started), but also because it seems to construct a utopian hope that the colonial rift can be reversed and revised, that we can start over and make the world anew.

Countering this utopian romance, however, is another ending in *All Souls' Rising,* occurring before the conclusion of Hebert's story and very different in tone and import. It is Riau's ending. Riau is not a Creole, born on Haiti; he is brought directly from Africa to the island and has first-hand knowledge of the Middle Passage and all aspects of slavery. Riau escapes during the uprisings, participates fully, and guiltlessly, in their violence, eventually joins the "army" of one of the uprising's leaders. Finally, when he sees a black revolutionary leader create a *zombi* out of another black man, he ends his ordeal by leaving everything—the whites, the blacks, and the entire social system—behind, and in his speech he too figures himself as a Christ figure:

> In Guinée I was alive, but they brought me out a dead thing. I was not three days but three months in my tomb. Each day they brought us on the deck and made us eat and made us dance, still nothing moved but the *corps-cadavre* [the body]. As a dead thing I was sold to Bréda [a plantation owner]. There Toussaint was my *parrain* [instructor], and there could be none better. Toussaint taught me how to be a slave, how to bear my death. It was the *hûngan* Achille [leader of an uprising], when he came down from the mountain with his band, who touched my lips and eyes and made me live again.
>
> So I was running behind Jean-Pic, quick and sure-footed in the dark below the trees. No one was chasing us, but we ran because we liked to. The air of the night was sweet on my whole skin, and they were both the good black color. I could not see Jean-Pic or see myself in all this dark, but I knew I was Riau again, only Riau, and I was glad to be running away to Bahoruco. (475–76)

Riau here rejects not only the slave system, but also the revolutionary state that replaced it. In both, he claims, he is made into a dead thing, a body without free will. The ex-slave leaders of the revolution create more and more ties to the French military: "At the end of the day when Captain Riau took off his uniform, I had to look at myself all over very carefully to be sure that my skin was not fading into white" (469). Only by returning to his blackness, running in the island jungles toward an all-black forest community, does he return at least partially to his African self. Unfortunately, his flight is limited, stranded as he is on the island. Riau's is the only first-person narration in the novel, as if Bell were emphasizing the importance of his having his own voice in relation to colonial history. This voice wholly rejects the Enlightenment project of universal freedom and suffrage as a utopian lie, thereby also rejecting the romantic "ending" experienced by the white Hébert.

Both Smartt's and Unsworth's novels, in fact, insist that what the world is about is not justice but power, and that the thirst and struggle for power is the only universal, race-transcending value known by humankind. The figure of universal and ever-present human violence, the fire that ends the book, mocks Enlightenment rhetoric about the Rights of Man, for it implies that the truth about humanity is that it is animalistic, driven by innate desires for power and supremacy. The vision at the core of both books is Nietzschean: the truth about Western civilization is not that it is a taming of the will to power but that it is a manifestation of it, the most organized, efficient, and powerful expression of it in the human animal. Setting the novel at the time of the revolutions of the eighteenth century allows Bell (as it does Steve Erikson in *Arc d'X*) to underscore the contradictions inherent in colonialism, birthed precisely at the historical moment when the West was formulating its complex theories of the universality of man.

In *All Souls' Rising*, the complicitous relation between Enlightenment emancipatory rhetoric and colonial power is made explicit in the relation between Napoleon Bonaparte, supposedly the great liberator of the proletariat, and Toussaint-Louverture, who is imprisoned by Bonaparte for sedition against the colonial state. Similarly, near the end of *Sacred Hunger*, the ex-slave Kireku confronts Matthew Paris directly and angrily asserts his difference in relation to humanist universalism. At one point in this confrontation, Kireku specifically mocks what Edward Said has called "traveling theory" in the form of the European Enlightenment's theories of universal suffrage:

> You allus try make adder people belong you idea. Like you play game wit dem, move here, move dere, like *amati* game, you sabee? You try make people here dis place do like you want, so you feel good, make man free. Den Paree [Matthew Paris] feel good, oh-hoh! No feel bad no more, make man free, win de game. But Kireku not piece *amati* game pick up, put down. I no stay in place you want. I strong pas' you. You a fool. You tink dis speshul place but it altageddar same adder place. Iboti, Callee, Libbee, dese men slave, you no change dat never. . . . Paree, where you been? Dis de real worl', you no sabee dat? (579)

Kireku accuses the Enlightenment scholar of theorizing his own drive for control; he accuses theory of being a disguise for the machinations of power and the operations of surveillance. But he also voices the Nietzschean idea that some men are born to be leaders, others slaves, and that Enlightenment democratic universalism is a lie, a utopian dream. In *All Souls' Rising*, Bell (like Unsworth) opposes the master/slave relation yet also posits that it may be the central defining dynamic of human relations. In the face of this truth, one must act, alone.

Is this the First World working through its own history in relation to colonialism, or excusing it?

The Link to Historical Romance

The metahistorical movement toward History has direct links to the construction and identity of oral literatures and oral traditions; this link may explain the enormous interest in orality in late-twentieth-century literary criticism as well as provide another link between the metahistorical romance and its forebear, the classic historical romance of Scott. Walter Ong wrote in his central study of oral literatures, *Orality and Literacy*, that anxiety about the alienating effects of writing are particularly strong for cultures transitioning from oral to written modes.[23] Postmodernism seems a reversal of this process, a return or attempted return to the primacy of the oral and the mythic (what Elam would term *romance*) after the triumph of written technologies and disciplinary history. In historiography, authenticity is often associated with the oral account, and oral narrative or testimony has played an increasingly important role in the writing and theorization of late-twentieth-century histories: in the recording of Holocaust survivors' narratives, in the circulation and theorization of Native American and African American oral traditions in opposition to anthropological reconstructions of them, in descriptions of women's oral history, in the movement toward "microhistories" in social history; in post-*Annales* historiography's focus on narrative in or as history. It is probable that this desire for authentic and unmediated history, embodied in the oral, is directly related to the Anglo-Western reappraisal of its own (past and present) colonial history, for the oral is almost always invoked as the tradition of the Other that has been suppressed, repressed, or eliminated by Western technologies of writing and the secularity, commodification, and abstractions that they construct and uphold.

Walter Scott himself was concerned about the loss of mythic import that occurred in the transition from oral to written forms and linked this to colonial politics. Building from Ong's work in her discussion of Scott and orality, Penny Fielding writes that oral storytelling moves "from the metaphysics of presence" first because of its repetition and alterity (which replace authorial control and static form with repetitions of telling by various voices) and because of its blurring of the boundaries between fiction and reality (99–152). Fielding notes that Scott was ambivalent toward oral storytelling: while on the one hand he saw oral memory (e.g., that found in ballads) as limiting, on the other hand—particularly in his novel *Redgauntlet*—he considered the idea that oral history might be an acceptable alternative to written historical accounts. Oral narrative embodied in memory can be a means to reclaim history but also to bind together different elements of society (103 ff.).[24] It also, however, can be labeled unauthenticated, or inauthentic, hearsay.

According to his critics, Scott seems to have recognized the problems inherent in an opposition between "real" history (documented and canonized by disciplinary history and anthropology) and "inauthentic" folk history that was associated with the Highland oral tradition (i.e., that which was the focus of analysis by anthropology but still in the hands of the "natives"): the problem is that the former relies heavily upon the latter but tries to erase this debt. Scott's ambivalent attitude toward oral narrative seems to have formed his attitude toward romance and the telling of history, resulting in a hybrid narrative genre, his "historical romance." Elam correlates this problematic relation of oral to written history in Scott to that faced by historians themselves, citing, for example, Ranke's comparison of Scott's romantic Highland Middle Ages to that described in 'historical' material: "To be a realist historian is to forget the past by claiming that it is unauthentic" (60).[25] Elam illustrates how the romance of Scott's historical fiction opposes but also necessarily supplements the documented historical information upon which he relies.

The uneasy relation between (unauthorized) oral history and ("author-ized") written history has direct implications for the problem of postcolonial historical revisionism. First, it alludes to a connection between postmodernist metahistory and the recuperation of lost voices in history (voices associated with cultural memory repressed by the operations of colonial power). In *Midnight's Children,* Saleem Sinai notes, "Morality, judgment, character . . . it all starts with memory . . . and I am keeping carbons" (253). Saleem's words illustrate the uneasy relation between written and oral, memory and history, in the metahistorical world. As noted in chapter 1, postmodernist metahistory is a tropological swerving from the priorities of classic historical romance. In this case, we see an inversion not just of the priority of history over romance (the metahistorical romance privileging the latter), but also of orality over writing and of memory over documented history. Particularly in works such as Maxine Hong Kingston's *The Woman Warrior: Memories of a Girlhood among Ghosts* or Christa Wolf's *Cassandra,* readers are confronted with metahistory as an admixture of the oral and the written, the personal and the public.

Scott considered the value of oral history, but ultimately sided with the Western, written, and authenticated forms. For example, by many critics' accounts one of the most provocative of Scott's novels, *Redgauntlet,* forces the reader to consider questions about the meaning of history, about what constitutes a "real" historical event, about the role of the editor of historical narratives, about the difference between personal and historical truth, about the value of oral history and legend in relation to written historical accounts. The metahistorical romance tends to challenge Scott's final answer to these questions. It attempts to recuperate oral traditions and question the binary opposition "unauthorized/authorized" on which the decision to exclude orality was based. What was left out of documented history becomes the obsession of the metahistorical romance, and this often means the recuperation of the repressed *voice* of the Other in the First World literary house.

The second question raised by my metahistorical model for history concerns the relation between the historical novel genre and colonialism itself. The historical romance was birthed in a time when the value of romance was a hotly debated issue. The novel form was seen as either instructive or decadent, depending on how one used the knowledge it contained—for social instruction and improvement or merely for entertainment and as a means to withdraw narcissistically from life. Even if Scott was also careful to recontextualize his fictions as stories of times upon which the modern was founded, he did consciously craft prefaces to his novels that emphasize the distinction between the real/history/useful and the imaginary/romance/decadent. As Dryden notes, "The movement from South to North, from England to Scotland, from the Lowlands to the Highlands . . . represents the dualisms of law and nature, civilized and primitive, reason and passion, history and romance" (7). These are by now familiar dualisms (and we see them again in *All Souls' Rising*). They oppose Western civilization with its ethic of use value to its primitive Other (implicitly assigned to primitivism and uselessness).

Paradoxically, however, Scott was writing at a time when political history was first being challenged by newer definitions of *the histori-*

cal that included the domain of culture, a change in perspective to which apparently the Waverley novels themselves significantly contributed.[26] As Ina Ferris notes, Scott's historical fictions "participated in the emerging conviction that forces outside those conventionally featured in the discourses of history (whether it be political, legal, military, or ecclesiastical) had historical import" (199). Ferris writes that Scott's work apparently influenced historians such as Augustin Thierry, whose *History of the Conquest of England by the Normans* turns to the particular and to the oral to fill in the gaps of official recorded history, and Thomas Babington Macaulay, who called for a redefinition of history that would include the specific and particular. However, while Scott's historical novels opened up the gaps of history and filled them with the stuff of oral legend, his focus on narration and imagination—on romance—does not displace official history or its practice but instead acts as a supplement to or an enrichment of it. Scott negotiates the difficult line between official and unofficial history. He offers his stories as possible historical events, not as true alternative accounts of activities in the historical past.

It is important as well to remember that Scott was a Scotsman as well as a self-proclaimed Jacobite. Suspicious for his entire career of uniformity, official history, modernity, and the melting-pot mythologies of colonial empires, yet completely resigned to all, Scott is the focus of a new academic interest not only as the creator of the historical romance novel and a transitional figure in the move to modern approaches to history but also as a postcolonial voice.[27] Part of Scott's interest in Scottish history—an interest shared by politicians, historians, philosophers, and novelists of his time—was engendered when the effects of the Union of 1707 were felt economically, such as in the opening up of the English colonies to Scottish merchants and the growth of Glasgow into an important port for West Indian sugar and U.S. tobacco, both products of slave economies. True, it is Scott who greeted George IV in Scotland in 1822 and portrayed him as the legitimate leader of the Scottish clans, Scott who became the first chairman of the Oil Gas Company and who had railway interests.[28] But it was also Scott who lamented the loss of the Scottish clan sys-

tem and national past. David Daiches notes that Scott looked with
nostalgia, excitement, and fondness on Scotland's violent clan past
but simultaneously welcomed Scotland's merger with England as a
guarantee of peaceful future progress for his country. He portrays
Scott as a writer who combines the two major cultural responses to
the Union of 1707: a nostalgic, antiquarian, and folkloristic response
that recuperated folk traditions, and a progressive response that attempted to elevate Scottish philosophy, arts, and politics to the "enlightened" standard of Europe of the time.[29] Whereas the Scottish
philosophes such as Adam Smith, Adam Ferguson, and John Millar
may have given Scott a model for history in the stadialist view they
theorized, they also were interested in purging English of the "primitive" Gaelic voice as part of their Enlightenment project of improvement—an interest with which Scott had mixed sympathy.[30]

According to some critics, part of Scott's "postcolonial" vision is
evident in his portrayal of the Scots Highland people: Scott's novels
present some social populations as unknowable and alien to the modern imagination, namely, outcasts and the mad, and the speakers of
Gaelic in the clan world. Kathryn Sutherland has called this the "unreadable core" of the Waverley novels (121), while Ferris argues that
Scott directs readers explicitly to this unreadable core in the retelling
of family tales, myths, and oral stories but never makes it available for
interpretation. This "unreadable core" is what becomes the gesture
toward the historical sublime in the metahistorical romance. (In the
context of colonial issues, the metahistorical romance often figures
this unreadable core as the uncanny Other—Friday in Coetzee's *Foe,*
or Raiu in *All Souls' Rising,* or Kireku in *Sacred Hunger.*) James Kerr
contends that Scott's work finally denies as well as asserts the possibility of grasping history in fiction; in the Waverley novels, historical
romance "is a zone of freedom" and a "fictive reconstruction of a historical subtext of which English colonialism is a central pattern."[31]
Liz Bellamy has shown how Scott explored local and regional Scots
culture in the interest of themes and ideas about the process of cultural imperialism and the relation between local and national character. And P. H. Scott makes a related case that Scott's *Letters of*

Malachi Malagrowther is "the first manifesto of modern Scottish nationalism" presenting ideas that seem very contemporary in their
general formulation for example, that diversity is preferable to cen-
tralization, Scottishness is valuable for its own sake, government
should be local, etc. (216).[32] Countering these views, however, is
Manfred Malzahn's analysis of *Waverley* as an example of Scott's Con-
radian point of view of his Highland subject. Malzahn points out
that Scott himself wrote in 1826 that his novels imitated the fiction of
Washington Irving: according to Malzahn, the same frontier imagery
found in nineteenth-century U.S. fiction appears in *Waverley* and
other Scott novels. In particular, in certain metaphoric descriptive
passages in the novels, Scott's Highlanders are explicitly linked to the
rebellious "dark Others" of other continents and colonial locations—
that is, Native Americans on the U.S. western frontier, the Irish
Catholics who began to arrive in Scotland after 1798, and people of
color in the West Indies. (Scott's own brother had gone to Jamaica
and had been pulled into the environment of slave rebellion). In this
reading, Scott is firmly aligned with a colonial sensibility and, moreover, is one of a coterie of nineteenth-century writers whose artistic
and historical vision depends on a conjunctive series of binary oppositions: colonizer/colonized, white/dark, Self/Other, progressive/
primitive, knowledge/feeling, historical/anthropological, speaking/
silent, continuing/extinct. As Malzahn notes, "Classical, Oriental,
African and [Native] American images to a certain extent reflect, but
also intensify, the perception [in *Waverley*] of the Gaels as essentially
alien in an enlightened Anglo-Scotland" (7).

Walter Scott clearly recognized that industrialization and capital
brought about inequality; however, his answer to this problem was
neither to advocate a return to a pre- industrial state or to formulate
an early version of Marxism. According to P. H. Scott, his response
was a belief that community could be restored if society continued to
be divided into classes determined by property. P. H. Scott argues
that Walter Scott's position was influenced by Ferguson, Adam
Smith, and other thinkers of his time, and he notes that John Millar's
Observations Concerning the Distinction of Ranks in Society (1771) con-

tains sentiments duplicating what Scott himself believed—namely, that whatever were the institutions of a country, they are "suited to the state of the people by whom they have been embraced" and therefore any improvements to that state must be made cautiously and gently, from "a gradual reformation of the manners" that affect social conditions.[33] Congruent with this stadialist belief in gradual change from within a society was Scott's and others' distrust of democracy, a distrust that grew out of the example of the French Revolution.

Going back to the historical romances of Walter Scott as a generic precursor to the metahistorical romance illustrates that Scott's novels are concerned with many of preoccupations of the twentieth-century form: a politicized regionalism; a nostalgia for and revaluation of community and of native culture; a reappraisal of the value of orality as a way of telling history and preserving culture; and shared concerns with the historiography of the time, particularly the ethical dilemma of colonial history. The problem of colonial history was a central concern of Scott's historical romance. David Daiches writes, "It was almost predicable that the historical novel should have been invented in eighteenth-century Scotland," for "the Scots in the eighteenth century were engaged in a prolonged contemplation of their own history to a unique degree, and history itself was responsible for this" ("Scott and Scotland" 38). Much could be said for the metahistorical romance of our time. Kerr's analysis of Scott is particularly interesting in light of a discussion of metahistory, for he (like Diane Elam) sees Scott's work as "metafictional" as well as postcolonial and participating in many of the narrative games that postmodernism will bring to the fore two centuries later. As Mary Cullinan notes, Scott's *Redgauntlet* even goes so far as to reverse the priorities of his previous historical romance. That is, the novel doesn't just center on a historical event and romanticize it; it concerns a political event that looks historical but that actually is "hypothetically historical" because it has no counterpart in Scottish history or legend. Alexander Welsh notes that Scott's "reality" is in fact a projection of manners, a reality not of things but of relations (137). Postmodernism apparently didn't invent metahistoricity, or fabulation, or even metafiction. What the fiction of the late twentieth century *did* invent was its relation to its own historical context and to these experimental narrative modes.

The metahistorical consciousness seems caught between its First World, post-traumatic turn toward the historical sublime (the silent and unknowable past) and its obsessions with experiential history (the history that hurts), and this dilemma leads the genre to a compulsive, repetitive turning toward the past that is a ceaselessly deferred resolution to the questions of historical agency that it poses. While chapter 3 illustrated how metahistorical desire can appear in postmodernist fiction as a formal technique (the spatialization of history), chapter 4 illustrated how this desire can appear as a thematic subject (the questioning of modern history's disciplinary origins in Enlightenment philosophies). The latter is present in novels that interrogate the assumptions of Enlightenment historiography and ask the question, "What kind of history have we inherited, and how does it constrain us?" And asking this question makes these novels appear self-critical, because their impulse is deconstructive, their gaze fixed on their own origin. In this chapter I posit yet another way that postmodernist metahistorical desire is revealed: through narratives that attempt to come to terms with both the West's own colonial history and with social philosophies that oppose Anglo- European capitalism, empiricism, and cultural assumptions about race and gender.

In other words, what has emerged forcefully since 1960, particularly in the 1980s and 1990s, are novels written by First World authors that attempt to look at their own Western history from the perspective of its Others. These metahistorical romances seem very much influenced by late-twentieth-century discussions of feminist and civil rights social theories, multiculturalism, and postcolonialist politics. Not unproblematically feminist or postcolonial novels as those terms are strictly understood today, these novels by British, European, Canadian, and U.S. authors seem to turn away from a preoccupation about their own Enlightenment origins and turn instead to the contemplation of *alternatives* to the West's paradigmatic model for thinking about, and through, history. Novels such as Madison Smartt Bell's *All Souls' Rising,* Barry Unsworth's *Sacred Hunger,* William T.

Vollmann's Wineland the Good books, Günter Grass's *The Flounder,* or Jane Smiley's *The All-True Travels and Adventures of Lidie Newton* concern the resistance to Western history by minority or non-Western cultures, gynocentric social theories, or anticapitalist economies. Novels and mixed-genre texts such as William Kennedy's *Legs,* Valerie Miner's *All Good Women,* Christa Wolf's *Cassandra,* Ishmael Reed's *Flight to Canada,* Toni Morrison's *Beloved,* or Charles Johnson's *Dreamer* frankly consider civil rights, multiculturalist, feminist, and postcolonial issues within First World societies. As an evolutionary form of the historical romance, the postmodernist metahistorical romance inherits a generic tradition in relation to these subjects; as a postmodernist aesthetic form, it is socially and historically situated itself in relation to them.

Extrapolating from Freud's definition of the uncanny as the unfamiliarity of that which is assumed to be familiar, Julia Kristeva noted in *Strangers to Ourselves* that on the basis of the other, one becomes reconciled with one's own otherness-foreignness. While this does not seem to describe *The Rifles,* it is applicable to *Ceremony,* where the narrative derives it force from its integration of otherness into and with the self. The space of the deferred border of History is not only *not* threatening nor alienating in *Ceremony;* it is also only slightly anthropomorphized into the Other (in Silko's text, the whites that are used by witchery) from which one can derive a personal (even if negative) sense of identity and control. Silko makes it clear in the novel that the uncanny Other that must be fought, and against which one must define oneself, is not the whites at all but the witchery that moves through the whites and ultimately also destroys them. The novel, infused with a postcolonialist sensibility, contests the codes of colonialism—individualism and psychologism, bounded territory, Otherization, disciplined and mono-narrativized history—and reasserts the openness of mixed-blood possibility as well as the value of communal history. This assertion of alternatives is something toward which the postmodern metahistorical romance seems headed, the sublime desire at the core of its metahistorical imagination.

6 Coda

The Sot-Weed Factor and
Mason & Dixon

All talk of cause and effect is secular history, and
secular history is a diversionary tactic.
— Thomas Pynchon, *Gravity's Rainbow*

Comparing a metahistorical romance such as Jeanette Winterson's
The Passion to Walter Scott's historical romance *Redgauntlet* seems absurd until one recognizes that they actually have much in common: a
focus on times of revolution, a preoccupation with class and gender
relations and the role of imposture, a complication of the naïve assumptions of mimesis, a melding of the fantastic with the historical,
a prioritization of orality and voice. *The Passion* (or *Mumbo Jumbo,* or
The Name of the Rose) can be seen as the latest, postmodern incarnation of a genre that from its inception was inscribed with contradiction and worried the lines between the written and the oral, the aboriginal and the modern, the progressive and the regressive, insider
and outsider. The metahistorical romance, like its literary precursor,
is defined by its internal conflicts, conflicts inherent in Enlightenment-birthed progressivism and Enlightenment-birthed universal
democratic ideals. (Both philosophies, ironically, supported the economic privilege of the landed bourgeoisie, as one sees in Scott's own
letters and in the philosophies of the eighteenth-century Founding
Fathers of the United States). Contradictory anxieties and desires
structure the metahistorical romance as surely as they did the historical romance: desire for and anxiety about the racialized colonial

Other, the security of privilege, capitalism and accumulation, global economies, nationhood and indigenous cultures, and exocentric nature versus the progressive urban center.

Situating late-twentieth-century First World historical fiction in relation to its own literary and generic history reveals how metahistorical romance moves in pendulum motion from the "realism" of Scott's historical novel form, through the abstraction of modernist spatial form and postmodern fabulation, back toward the "realism" of postcolonial politics. Because they inherit the dialectic between realism and romance structuring Scott's novels, writers of metahistorical novels seem to hang suspended between these poles and captive to pendulum motion, acutely self-reflexive about their inability to break free to a real access to History and confined within two literary genres they tend no longer to associate with the Real. Through metahistorical romance, these novelists often problematically attempt to voice the Other that their own national histories have demonized and rendered historically silent; they always pose an ethical dilemma for themselves and for their readers in relation to the founding ideology of historical romance and to their own First World location. They pose this dilemma by evoking the historical sublime as part of the aesthetic and political project of metahistorical romance. This is not fiction comfortable with nationalist mythologies or optimistic predictions about the triumph of global capitalism. Faced with the dilemma of its own identity, and new revelations concerning the West's relation to androcentrism, colonialism, imperialism, and genocide, the metahistorical romance spins in the realm of the historical sublime, searching for an impossible solution to the problem of how to atone and live in the world other than as an isolated, monadic subject.

Comparing John Barth's *The Sot-Weed Factor* and Thomas Pynchon's *Mason & Dixon* illustrates how the four characteristics of metahistorical romance (see chapter 2) remain constant in this narrative form throughout the second half of the twentieth century but also illustrates how this search for a new approach to Western history grows in force as the millennium approaches. Generally, Barth's and Pynchon's various novels have been linked in literary criticism since the 1970s. Numerous studies remark the metafictionality of the two authors' writings, debate over the postmodernity of their narrative stylistics, comment on their resuscitation of the encyclopedic novel, and identify in their fiction the "black humor" characteristic of 1960s fiction.[1] Huge baggy monsters of novels, *The Sot-Weed Factor* and *Mason & Dixon* are separated in time by thirty years. Yet, like the novels discussed in chapter 4, both recuperate an eighteenth-century context that metafictionally rebounds to the cultural politics of the present, and like the novels discussed in chapter 5, both are self-reflexive about the First World colonial gaze. And like almost all of the novels discussed in this study, both reenergize the historical romance genre by inverting its dominant, melding fantasy, anachronism, metafictionality, and other fabulatory techniques with the facts of history.

Though set mainly in the late seventeenth century, *The Sot-Weed Factor* mimics the eighteenth-century bildungsroman and künstlerroman of Fielding, Richardson, and Sterne, and attempts to recuperate those novel forms. The novel concerns the journey from innocence to experience of the English poet Ebenezer Cooke, an actual poet who wrote an actual poem entitled "The Sot-Weed Factor" (published in 1708) but who is transformed in Barth's novel into a bildungsroman hero. The novel is set in Barth's home state of Maryland at the end of the seventeenth century, well after John Rolfe had introduced Trinidadian tobacco in 1612 to Virginia and Maryland, transforming the economies of the Chesapeake colonies. Yet while much has been made of *The Sot-Weed Factor* as a historical novel basing its action on recorded history, Barth's novel is almost pure fabulation, blurring the links between history and romance. *The Sot-Weed Factor* relies heavily upon value oppositions common to traditional romance (innocence vs. experience, secular vs. sacred, natural freedom vs. civilization's control, self vs. Other, the city vs. the country). Such oppositions occur on numerous levels of the story and can be seen best in the book's ironic leitmotif, the physical as well as the moral "innocence" of the Virgin Poet, Ebenezer. Contrasting to Ebenezer's vow to preserve his innocence is Barth's ribald rewriting of the tale of John Smith and Pocahontas, an antiromance that, like all blasphemy, pays homage to doxa by inverting and insulting its structure and values. Another link to romance in *The Sot-Weed Factor* is its presentation of the modern condition as the *human* condition, even though it seems to go back to the historical past and deconstruct the idea of universal humanism. "I don't know what my view of history is," Barth has stated, "but insofar as it involves some allowance for repetition and recurrence, reorchestration, and reprise. . . . I would always want it to be more in the form of a thing circling out and out and becoming more inclusive each time—springing out . . . from a heart" (Lampkin 489–90). Barth clearly means "heart" here to signal a comedic, value-defined center, reconstructing history as romance.

If that reconstruction is not recognized, this parody of the *künstlerroman* set in the late seventeenth century may seem an odd choice of narrative subject and style by a U.S. novelist writing at this particular point in U.S. history. In 1960, at the time of this novel's publication, the United States was experiencing the beginnings of what would become the most vehement internal political turmoil since the Civil War. In 1959 and 1960, the civil rights movement was in full swing after Rosa Park's refusal to move to the back of a bus and the initiation of lunch-counter sit-ins throughout the Deep South; the Cold War was at its height; tensions were escalating in Vietnam through continued U.S. support of the South Vietnamese government led by President Ngo Dinh Diem (and the entanglement of French colonialist goals with U.S. anticommunist politics that this situation created) and the creation in 1960 of the National Liberation Front; the Roman Catholic John F. Kennedy was elected to the U.S. presidency and subsequently created both a pro–civil rights government and, in "Camelot," a mock aristocracy modeled on the British gentry; the Students for a Democratic Society (SDS) officially formed their organization; college campuses were becoming increasingly politicized; and the 1960s counterculture—including all of its pop culture manifestations in sex, drugs, and folk rock as well as its political incarnations in what would later be the New Left—was gaining momentum. One might understand why a novel like Joseph

Heller's *Catch 22* (1961) or John Updike's *Rabbit Run* (1960) would appear in this cultural climate—but a mock eighteenth-century *künstlerroman?*

In some ways, Barth's novel is very much of its time. *Sot-Weed* predicates itself on the assumption of similarity, rather than difference, between the Old World and the New, and by indirection points to how the United States' history of racism, colonialism, and misogyny conflicts mightily with its own sanitized national mythology and its founding principles of democratic liberalism. There are few, if any, tears shed in this novel for the Lost Garden that was the precolonial United States. Not only is the Old like the New, but the Then is like Now: Barth's novel rewrites the past in terms of the anxieties of his present. The vehicle for this rewriting is the idea of history as "plot" or conspiracy. The novel at first seems to be a farcical tour de force of American history, presenting the colonial period as one characterized by political conspiracies and struggles for dominance of the North American continent by all manner of political factions. The intricate conspiracies, many based on the real history of the Maryland territory, lead Ebenezer from England to the colonies onboard passenger ships and pirate ships and into the Maryland marshes and countryside. The novel weaves intrigues and, through the machinations of Henry Burlingame and the bumbling adventures of Ebenezer himself, reveals Machiavellian struggles for control of the American courts and control of the colonial territory.[2]

Barth creates two central conspiracies that Burlingame and Ebenezer must finally confront and thwart. The first concerns religion: there is some kind of plot afoot to turn the colonies Roman Catholic, and there is a counter-movement to prevent this papist faction from claiming victory. The plan to implant Roman Catholicism on American soil involves discrediting the current Protestant government by corrupting the colonials and weakening their resistance: the conspirators plan to do this by importing opium and whores in huge quantities to the colonies and attempting to make the nation into a swiving, drug-addicted, corrupt, and politically impotent populace. Another brewing conspiracy that must be countered involves displaced Native Americans and African slaves who have escaped from slavery. These two forces have merged in an odd multicultural community in the Maryland marshes and, led by kings from both factions, plan a coup on the British colonial government that will drive the whites from America and put control of the territory into the hands of Indians, former Africans, and ex-slaves. By the end of the novel, both conspiracies have been thwarted by Burlingame, Ebenezer, and their various and sundry cohorts.

What we see here, then, is the grafting of the subjects of 1960s social turmoil onto a parodied setting of their historical origin. Conflicts about religion (specifically, fears about the ascendency of Roman Catholic political leaders), about race (and the potential for revolt among black and brown peoples against a white majority populace), about politics (particularly the entanglement of colonialism with the idea of national security), about drugs (opium is a hallucinogenic), and about the disintegration of morals (everybody's doing it, baby)—these are the intersection points between the time of the novel's writing and the time of the novel's setting. John F. Kennedy's presidency becomes the Roman papist conspiracy; the civil rights movement becomes parodied as the multicultural community in the marshes; student activists are parodied as coffeehouse poets; the hippie scene becomes the drug conspiracy threatening the new colony's stability. On a first reading, Barth's novel may look "radical"; its over-the-top history may seem at first a deconstructive move, even a subversive slap at a nationalist history that glosses over the absurdity, greed, and viscousness of its founders in order to create a pristine mythology concerning its genesis and growth as a nation. And even though Barth's book seems apolitical, it clearly embeds the sociopolitical issues of its time and links these to their origin in Western Enlightenment thought and colonial practice.[3] However, if one looks at the outcome of Barth's various plots here and correlates them to what seem clear analogues in the people and events of 1958–60, one sees a deeply reactionary core to this novel. If there is a politics in this novel, it must be linked to the facts that the Africans and Indians lose, the whores get the pox and die, the advocates of drugs and conspiracy against the landed aristocracy get bested, and the hero Ebenezer finally and happily lives the life of a gentleman on his family's estate in Maryland until he is an old man. Seen this way, this novel seems reactionary, unless it is being ironic even about is own attempt at political commentary.

It is disturbing also that what is emphatically foregrounded in the novel is not really history, or even politics, but romance, and that for all its historical self-reflexivity, the novel seems to have no ethical or political center. By 1696, when Barth's Ebenezer Cooke begins his adventures, indentured servants had long become an important part of the Chesapeake labor force, which was in fact being supplemented with imported convicts and slaves. The slave trade blossomed in the Chesapeake colonies at the end of the seventeenth century, and, by 1850, would be the predominant labor source in the region. A plantocracy based on a single cash crop economy, Maryland would eventually enter the Civil War on the side of the Confederacy. All of these historical facts are turned to use in the novel, fueling Ebenezer's travel from England to Maryland and his picaresque adventures on colonial soil. Yet they form no ethical or political core in the novel, ultimately remaining stage setting only.

"There is a temper wont to twist the past into a theater piece," notes Burlingame, "mistak[ing] the reasonable for the historical" (Barth 145). This is an apt description for Barth's own temper in *The Sot-Weed Factor*. The book is a masterpiece of mythopoesis; it pays tribute to the romance of history and illustrates the vastness of Barth's storytelling abilities. But finally, the book also is content to twist the past into a theater piece and to stop short of asserting the kind of ethical valuation of the First World history called for by White, Jameson, LaCapra, Ankersmit, and others today.[4] When Barth tries to define history in interviews, he tends not only to emphasize its narrative nature and links to romance, but also the links between history and memory: "History is a kind of dream. . . . History in an almost literal way, is a dream that we keep re-dreaming. . . . We keep on redreaming the dream generation by generation. And the changing perception does not concern even the subjects of the dream" (Bezner 8).

This idea of history as a "redreaming" is a mighty abstraction and not only alienates history from scientific method; it constructs history as a memory linked to the return of the repressed (it keeps coming back) *and* as an incessant, never-ending movement. In this sense, Barth's conception of history is close to that of the later writers of metahistorical romance. Schultz has called this the metaphysical universe of "black humor" fiction, a non-hierarchical universe of uncertainty where cause-and-effect logic is discarded, reality is merely a mental construct, and the present is a parodic reconstruction of the past (17–25). In contrast, Zamora contends that this desire for return (what Barth calls "redreaming") is a mark of the apocalyptic structure of history in Barth's fiction. Yet I would counter that this is the romance element on its way to being redefined within what will emerge later in the century as metahistorical romance, the preoccupation with and incessant return to history by writers who, because they operate within a cultural imaginary traumatized by its own self-awareness, return to romance—with difference, as *différance*. But in *The Sot-Weed Factor,* this process stops short.

Tellingly, Barth actually coined a term in his novel *The End of the Road* for the state of paralysis induced in modern man through an epiphany that reveals the "state of universal comprehension, universal weariness, universal futility"—*cosmopsis*.[5] Many of the artist figures in Barth's fiction—Jacob Horner in *The End of the Road,* but also Ebenezer Cooke in *The Sot-Weed Factor*—experience cosmopsis as a traumatic revelation of existential truth, as a glimpse of the nihilistic, or existential, life condition of "Man." In *The Sot-Weed Factor,* cosmopsis is linked to existentialism in one of the most famous scenes of the novel, when Ebenezer is given an existence lesson by his tutor Henry Burlingame (373 ff.). Burlingame makes Ebenezer look at the star-studded night sky in order to demolish the comforting seventeenth-century hypothesis of a Heavenly Dome that implied a living God watching over and ordering existence:

> The stars were no longer points on a black hemisphere that hung like a sheltering roof above his head; the relationship between them he saw now in three dimensions, of which the one most

deeply felt was depth. The length and breadth of space between the stars seemed trifling by comparison: what struck him now was that some were nearer, others farther out, and others unimaginably remote. Viewed in this manner, the constellations lost their sense entirely; their spurious character revealed itself, as did the false presupposition of the celestial navigator, and Ebenezer felt bereft of orientation. He could no longer think of up and down: the stars were simply *out there,* as well below him as above, and the wind appeared to howl not from the Bay but from the firmament itself, the endless corridors of space.

"Madness!" Henry whispered. (374)

Confronting the sublime in nature in his first real vision of the night sky, Ebenezer is thrown into a state of disequilibrium that challenges his assumptions about the reality of identity, social structures, and moral value. The remedy for this revealed state of existential nothingness, Burlingame later tells him, is existential action, the definition of the ego against the limitless, unbounded Void. To not construct ego boundaries is, literally, to go mad, to dissolve into the infinite multiplicity of schizophrenic otherness. Sanity is making that otherness part of the Self and subordinating it to the Self, through the sheer act of will.

This injunction toward existential will has implications for what *history* is in this novel. First, history becomes a narrative about self-construction; second, since controlling one's world is the only alternative to madness, constructing a controlled or disciplined history would not necessarily be a bad thing. Moreover, Alan Holder has noted that *The Sot-Weed Factor* refuses to commit itself to one particular version of the past, wanting the freedom to assert and embrace simultaneously existing possibilities, much as Henry Burlingame the "Cosmic Lover" in the novel embraces all of the world (Holder 130). Such a claim emphasizes how Barth's novel decenters history and disrupts its authority and value as a disciplinary social mechanism. However, precisely the opposite may be true in this novel. History, as well as the self, becomes an act of will in *Sot-Weed,* an ordering of the meaningless chaos of time and space. Manfred Puetz has suggested convincingly that Barth's use of historical materials and in particular the constraints of form (e.g., in his choice of an eighteenth-century style) actually puts a check on the postmodern impulse to discard all established truths and "exit from a world of self-generated fictions, to engineer an escape from the pitfalls of mythopoesis" (144). Likewise, McConnell suggests that cosmopsis for Barth is the inversion of the romantic idea of sublime vision.[6]

Because Barth's novels focus on conditions of being in the world for privileged white men, "cosmopsis" is really the state induced by an epiphanic glimpse of the historical sublime by a First World consciousness. The "universality" of the paralysis as Barth defines it is not universal. It is a pathology of the West, and it is centered in philosophy internal to Western metaphysics. It is a state of existential paralysis that is linked to privilege—the privilege inherent in having time to view the horizon through the gaze of the master. It is no accident in *The Sot-Weed Factor* that the character who falls prey to cosmopsis, Ebenezer, is also a member of the landed gentry. Quilted into the concept of cosmopsis is the assumption that a First World consciousness, solipsistically considering its own place in time and space, will be immobilized by the absurd contradiction that its own self-absorption leads to a realization of its own absence (i.e., its own lack of significance and meaning in relation to the indecipherable cosmos). In Fredric Jameson's formulation, the epistemologically crippling view from the top reduces subjects to dying individual bodies without collective pasts or futures bereft of any possibility of grasping the social totality. In Gertrude Stein's phrase (appropriate for Barth's Gentleman Poet, born on American soil), there is no *there* there. If Barth's text gestured toward this implication, or seemed at all self-reflexive about the post-traumatic, distinctly Western politics of history it was constructing, that would be one thing. Its presentation of cosmopsis as a universal human condition would be, then, ironic. But I believe the novel never does this.

There is a distinct shift in sensibility on this point between *The Sot-Weed Factor* and *Mason & Dixon*. Pynchon's novel is a frame tale: the Rev. Wicks Cherrycoke in Philadelphia, some twenty years after their adventure, tells the story of Charles Mason's and Jeremiah

Dixon's two journeys. The first journey was to plot the Transit of Venus at the Cape of Good Hope, the second to survey the boundary between Maryland and Pennsylvania that would become the iconic Mason/Dixon Line. The first journey takes them into the heart of a slave economy. The second allows them to watch and participate in the second Fall, the despoiling of the New World by Europe's colonial powers.

The difference in politics and narrative thematics between Barth's and Pynchon's novels can be illustrated by comparing Ebenezer Cooke's star-gazing scene in *The Sot-Weed Factor* to a startlingly similar star-gazing scene in *Mason & Dixon*. Near the end of Pynchon's novel, Charles Mason looks at the Heavenly Dome of the night sky and, like Ebenezer, has an epiphany. But his leads to very different conclusions:

> Yet at last arrives a clear night of seeing, so clear in fact that sometime after Midnight, supine in the Star-light, rigid with fear, Mason experiences a curious optical re-adjustment. The Stars no longer spread as upon a Dom'd Surface,—he now beholds them in the *Third Dimension* as well,—the Eye creating its own Zed-Axis, along which the star- chok'd depths near and far rush both inward and away, and soon, quite soon, billowing out of control. He collects that the Heavenly Dome has been put there as *Protection,* in an agreement among Observers to report only what it is safe to see. Fifteen years in the Business, and here is his Initiation. (725)

Like Ebenezer Cooke, Charles Mason has looked up at the sky and seen how culture has imposed on nature. Moreover, once he realizes that the sky is not contained by the astronomical theory of his day and is something more vast, something indicative of the sublime, he is unmoored. Yet while Ebenezer's revelation in the face of the material sublime was about his own existential nothingness, Mason's revelation in the face of exactly the same phenomenon is about the social construction of history. What he intuits is that disciplinary science constructs explanations of the world in order to provide comfort to the citizenry and to exercise social control, and his own work as an astronomer will be used by writers of history this way as well.

In *The Sot-Weed Factor,* Henry Burlingame's solution to Ebenezer's epiphanic disorientation is simple: in the face of meaninglessness and nature's unspeakable and awful sublimity, "One must needs make and seize his soul, and then cleave fast to't, or go babbling in the corner. . . . One must *assert, assert, assert,* or go screaming mad" (373). This existential task is at the core of the metahistorical romance and also postmodern historiography. Yet the difference between the assertion necessitated by Mason's intuitions of the *historical* sublime and the assertion advocated by Burlingame in the face of merely the *material* sublime is that Burlingame (and Barth) seems fairly confident that any kind of assertion is a good assertion, as long as it serves to define the provisional self. In contrast, in Pynchon's *Mason & Dixon* (or in theories about postmodern history from Jameson to White), the West's need to assert the self is actually part of the whole problem of violence in the world. Barth's vision is very much aligned with that of the existentialist modernists, while Pynchon's is closer to that of the postmodern metahistorians: for the latter, what is needed is a social response to sublimity, not an individualistic one. Furthermore, for writers such as Pynchon, a social response will necessarily call for a vision of the historical sublime, not merely the material sublime, for a social vision must be predicated on shared history.[7]

What is particularly revealing is that *The Sot-Weed Factor* and *Mason & Dixon* cover roughly the same historical territory. Barth's novel in fact concerns the state of affairs that *lead to* the conflict necessitating Mason and Dixon's line survey: Charles I's 1632 grant of unsettled land from the Potomac River, north to the fortieth parallel and west on a meridian through the Potomac's origin, to the second Lord Baltimore, Cecil Calvert. This grant later conflicted with Charles II's 1681 grant to William Penn of adjoining territory bounded on the south by the fortieth parallel. According to Monmonier, controversy arose when surveyors discovered that early seventeenth-century maps had placed the fortieth parallel too far south, leaving a nineteen-mile strip of territory in dispute. At the root of the controversy was a 1608 map by Captain John Smith (Monmonier 109). The border between Maryland and Delaware was also part of the disagreement between the Calverts and the Penns. While Barth cites Smith, Calvert, and proto-capitalist conspiracies as the targets for satire, Pynchon focuses on the consequences of these actions and the implications of multinational capitalist conspiracies that attack not individual political players, but individual and social freedom itself.

One example of these novels' differing treatments of historical injustice occurs in a scene toward the end of *Mason & Dixon,* when the Quaker Jeremiah Dixon confronts a slave-driver on the streets of Baltimore, Maryland. While Charles Mason's response to the scene is to keep out of it or, at best, to go get help from the authorities (not understanding, apparently, that the slave system is promoted by the same), Dixon's response is immediate civil action: he attacks the slave merchant (threatening to beat and even kill him), unchains and frees the slaves, and forcibly takes the whip from the merchant. Slavery does not form part of the "local color" in this novel, as it tends to do in Barth's tale; rather, slavery, colonialism, Indian massacre, and the rape of North America by colonial interests are its central thematic concerns.

For instance, in Pynchon's novel, Charles Mason starts his journeys with Jeremiah Dixon by charting the Transit of Venus, by observing and measuring distance from the stars.[8] Terribly important to the novel's thematics is the fact that the men are to observe the Transit at the Cape of Good Hope, in a colonial province whose economy depends upon slavery. Funded by the Royal Society, the two men start their journeys by looking at the heavens, literally and figuratively, through the lens provided by colonial power; as the novel progresses, however, they begin to suspect that more is going on than a simple astronomical observation, and that they are somehow pawns in a political power play of a global scale. As this revelation hits home and as they experience life in the African and North American colonies, the men more and more distance themselves from their "originating world."

Through the experiences of Mason and Dixon, the novel repeatedly explores the idea of cooption and control, as did Pynchon's *V.,* *The Crying of Lot 49,* and *Gravity's Rainbow.* Resistance to both in

Mason & Dixon lies not in "drawing the line" (as in Barth's novel Henry Burlingame repeatedly does, drawing artificial boundaries around his own ego in order to "assert" it against the Void); rather, salvation lies in refusing to draw lines or in complicating the lines one has already drawn, keeping oneself open to the flux and infinite freedom of possibilities.[9] When Mason sees the night sky *as it really is* for the first time (in the passage quoted above), he is led to a messianic revelation: "The place where it [the comet] pointed was the place I knew I must journey to, for beneath the Sky-borne Index lay, as once beneath a Star, an Infant that must, again, re-make the World,—and this time 'twas a Sign from Earth, not only from Heaven, showing the way" (726). The vision of infinitude that Mason sees in the night sky—free of tangent lines and boundaries—leads him to a vision of the sacred, to the possibility of redemption through the remaking of the world. Significantly, this is directly contrasted to the "Vector of Desire" that is the Line. The two kinds of desire—desire for the sacred, and desire for political power—are antithetical, the first causing one to look up to the sky in an everexpanding field of vision, the other causing one to look at the earth in ever smaller, diminishing parcels.

Significantly also, Mason's institutional sponsor (the man who has gotten him his research grants) has Mason strike this passage about the night sky from his official report. The authorities are not interested in revelation, but in the production of fact that can lead to territorial conquest. Mason's encounter with his employers opposes two ways to see the sky: as the raw material of power, which busies itself with drawing ownership lines and territorial boundaries around the world; or as the sublime, the power of space and time manifesting secularsacred meaninglessness that spurs the mortal on to ethical action.[10]

This opposition between lines and space, boundaries and possibilities is embodied in the Mason/Dixon Line, the central thematic motif of the novel that becomes a metonymy of power but also, paradoxically, an image of possibility. Mason's and Dixon's revelation about the Line comes after drawing the Visto between Pennsylvania and Maryland, then Maryland and [West] Virginia, out to the Warrior Path, a main highway artery for the Native American tribes throughout the Territory: "Having acknowledg'd at the Warpath the Justice of the Indians' Desires, after the two deaths [of their axmen], Mason and Dixon understand as well that the Line is exactly what Capt. Zhang and a number of others have been styling it all along— a conduit for Evil. So the year in Delaware with the Degree of Latitude is an Atonement, an immersion in 'real' Science, a Baptism . . . and even a Rebirth" (701). Along the Visto will grow towns; Pynchon slyly calls these "promenades" and "malls" to conflate the Line with highways in the late twentieth century that spawn suburban strip malls; also these highways are lines from the city to the country that will destroy the latter by using it for profit and also lines that are often associated with race partitioning and class power. The Mason/ Dixon Line will also, of course, be the line between the Union and Confederate States in the Civil War, closely associated in history with race and colonial power. In *Mason & Dixon,* mapping becomes the central metaphor for modernization, and modernization is the curbing of desire for the infinite (or even community in the here-and-now) and the promotion of desire for power and control, aligned with empiricism and, to Pynchon, the death drive.

Serendipitously, Pynchon has found a brilliant corollary to the arc of *Gravity's Rainbow*'s V-2 rocket in the arc of the territorial divide between the proprietorships of Delaware and Pennsylvania. Pynchon (through his narrator Cherrycoke) explains the weird machinations of James II, then Duke of York, to "preserve from encroachment his seat of Government" in New Castle by drawing a twelve-mile circle around the city and (contrary to the laws of geometry) attempting to link the radius of this circle with the southern and western boundaries of Delaware—the arc, the tangent, and the meridian somehow miraculously coming together to form the boundaries of the Delaware proprietary. The history here is accurate; one can see a portion of the arc today at Delaware's northwest boundary. The point of the story, however, is not only that this dream was of multiple intersections (of power lines, of territorial lines, of dynastic lines) doomed to failure— the lines are geometrically impossible and were proven to be politically impossible to maintain as well—but also that it confused the "lines" between dreaming and reality, science and mythos. The brokers of power *dreamed* the territorial arc into being, yet the colonialist dreamers of the New World became subject to the consequent line, a scalpel cut on the belly of the New World that birthed its own progeny of colonialism and civil war.

For Pynchon, power arcs—the arc of electricity that Ben Franklin will harness, the dynastic arc, the arc of the rocket, the arc of narrative plot—are connected as manifestations and trajectories of power. In this novel, the "bomb" arcing its way to earth, the "sphere of power" that will wreak destruction upon the New World and its inhabitants, is a line (as all arcs are); this one is a line drawn by virtue of the mapping sciences. Surveyor's lines, most notably the line between Pennsylvania and Maryland which came to be known as the Mason-Dixon Line, will be the conduits of power that transform the land into what will be "circuit board cities" like San Narciso in Pynchon's *The Crying of Lot 49*. (Oedipa Maas in that novel must learn the forgotten lesson of the land underneath this circuit board, the pre-America where all connections were possible, all dreams equally likely, a place where power could flow outside, between, beneath and around official circuits before the rationalist gridding of the world. Oedipa digs through the circuit-board city toward a buried world, the one that Mason and Dixon started with and then helped to blanket with power lines.)

In Delaware, the imaginary circumscribed circle at the center of which is the King of England's power (the Point of the King) becomes a Zone in this novel, a weird, dangerous place where two worlds (the Old and the New) meet. And we see it growing outward, like the blast wave from an atomic bomb, as surveyors' lines radiate from it into new territories. This Zone is the place marked forever by apocalyptic, technocratic death culture, linear thought literally projected upon the earth as a territorial marker in the service of political power, but also conceptually projected upon the New World as the logic of science and the millennial trajectory of Western history. Like science in *Gravity's Rainbow,* science in *Mason & Dixon* is neutral but can easily be coopted by emissaries of thanatos. In *Gravity's Rainbow*, Pointsman was one such character. In *Mason & Dixon*, it is Dr. Benjamin Franklin, who at one point in the novel appears dressed up as the Grim Reaper, conducting electrical experiments on his tavern fellows during a lightening storm (293–95). Opposed to the thanatonic culture of the Old World is Eros, the world of spirit (where live ghosts, spirits, and poetic inspiration) and the uncolonized New World, also a Zone, a place of (archetypal) freedom, romance, and life. In one of the book's most beautiful passages, this relation is made clear:

> Does Britannia, when she sleeps, dream? Is America her dream?—in which all that cannot pass in the metropolitan Wakefulness is allow'd Expression away in the restless Slumber of these Provinces, and on West-ward, wherever 'tis not yet mapp'd, nor written down, nor ever, by the majority of Mankind, seen,—serving as a very Rubbish-Tip for subjunctive Hopes, for all that *may yet be true*,—Earthly Paradise, Fountain of Youth, Realms of Prester John, Christ's Kingdom, ever behind the sunset, safe till the next Territory to the West be seen and recorded, measur'd and tied in, back into the Net-Work of Points already known, that slowly triangulates its Way into the Continent, changing all from subjunctive to declarative, reducing Possibilities to Simplicities that serve the ends of Governments,—winning away from the realm of the Sacred, its Borderlands one by one, and assuming them unto the bare mortal World that is our home, and our Despair. (345)

This—"the winning away from the realm of the Sacred its borderlands one by one"—is a perfect image of the development of history out of History. The Sacred is infinite possibility; while terrifying, it is also liberating. It is defiled by boundaries, chained by empiricism, and for Pynchon, the loss of sacred potential leads to "our Despair." For Pynchon, a debilitating condition like Barth's cosmopsis results not from a glimpse of the Infinite, but from its demise at the hands of science allied with power.

The American West in this novel, as it is in the U.S. national mythology, is the projection of Desire—the desire of the Old World, worn out and trashed by its own modern project, dreaming of innocence, youth, and possibility. A late chapter (chapter 73) in *Mason &*

Dixon actually takes place in this American West of Desire, out of historical time. Written as alternate history, the chapter shows Mason and Dixon moving westward after having measured the boundary between Pennsylvania and Maryland: we see the "Linemen" continue their journey like proto-Huckleberry Finns, lighting out for the Territory. In this alternate history, Mason and Dixon continue their line westward, through the Great Plains and into the Rocky Mountains; they experience the American West as a wild garden, a place of utter beauty, diverse cultures, limitlessness. This is utopian America, the America of freedom and potential, a multicultural and unbounded Territory of dreams. Appropriately in this dream landscape, Mason and Dixon become characters in an allegorical romance. The Linemen discover a new planet and try to return East to fame and institutional rewards, yet as they retrace their steps they find all of the discord they have sown as they moved from East to West. The line that they have continued has not only divided the Territory but divided lives, values, communities; their presence and their science have destroyed the peace of every relation with which they have had contact, and the people they have affected are enraged. The point of the chapter, then, is not to give a historical account of the men's actions (they never went West in actuality), or even to deconstruct the real historical account; rather, the point seems to be to infuse history with the ethical content of romance, to present a "moral" about modernity itself.

Yet true to the complex vision that characterizes all of Pynchon's work, the line as a central image in this novel resists easy binary oppositions. Lines, by definition, have no height, width, or depth; they are nowhere, places that are real only in a Platonic sense. If the Line is a metonymy of the modern, the quest to limit, demarcate, constrain, and control the natural world, in *Mason & Dixon* the Line is also the space of the excluded middle, between One and Zero, North and South, East and West. Toward the end of *Mason & Dixon,* weird things begin happening precisely on the space of the line. It is, for example, where the mechanical Invisible Duck, now free, chooses to live. Implied is the idea that the line is all we have left of freedom and possibility to live on after the destruction of Paradise. And the pun is intentional: to put one's life on the line is also a moral imperative to ethical action.

Recent work in cartographic studies can help readers deal with this complex and paradoxical construction of the Line. As noted earlier, postmodernism is characterized by a shift from (modernist) tropes of time to tropes of space. This shift corresponds to a rise in discussions of the politics of mapping and specifically of the relation between the ascendance of cartographic vision with the discovery and conquest of America. William Boelhower, for example, asserts that so interwoven is this relationship that America *is* the European cartographic revolution (477). The culture of the map and the conquest of Euro-American territory are entwined; Boelhower goes as far as to argue that America actually derives its cultural form *from the map itself:* "Without boundaries there could be no *patria*" (478). But as Boelhower, quoting Voltaire, also notes, what maps reveal that is most important about territory is that the discovery of territory itself is not as important as how that territory is seen (479).[11] A map conceals its own founding ideology so that to interrogate the map "is to open up a cartographic *mise en abyme* in which there are maps within maps." In addition, a genealogical interrogation of maps leads one to "think the removed and the unwritten" (494). Boelhower articulates the possibilities and ideological power of the cartographic line, and his claims merit extended quoting here:

> The system of the line is more than a descriptive metaphor for the linear intensity of "America" as biblical/political allegory: both line and nation-building are merciless with geography in the historical process of ordering it into built space. . . . The way the line goes about its mapping business, particularly on the national map, is a sure guide to one side of American cultural formation. As a system, the line projects topography onto a single geometric grid, an invisible network of abstract structural ties and infinite possibilities of calculation. Lacking the image-system's *physis,* it defies gravity and thus escapes Icarian catastrophe. . . . The scale map as panopticon is the result of the line's achievement of an absolute and closed system no longer dependent on the local perspectivism of the image. With map in hand, the physical subject is theoreti-

cally everywhere and nowhere, truly a global operator. Since the line is a non-place—indeed, it seeks to overcome the pitfalls of local discontinuity by representing a logic of permanent circulation—it follows that the person who relies on its technics also seeks to be free of empirical obstacles.

Cartographically, we might then say that the epos of Euro-American expansion is progressively structured by the line's mathematical constructions; while its narrative climax, nationhood, is based on absolute circulation: a strategy of cultural closure aiming at a seeing clearly of all boundaries. (494–96)

Boelhower's analysis is eerily Pynchonesque. Throughout all of his novels, Pynchon has been developing the idea of the line—or the Line—as a system, a whole network involving politics, ideology, economics, mythology, social control, power, and desire. Linearity in all of Pynchon's work is double-edged, both the death-culture thought projection of the Elect/Them *and* the vehicle for exposing alternative models and realities. Like the act of metaphor, which in *The Crying of Lot 49* is "a thrust at truth and a lie, depending where you were: inside, safe, or outside, lost" (129), the Line creates the possibility for the panopticon as well as the modern utopia, the closed system as well as the revelation of space.

In other words, if the cartographic line is indeed a "non-place" that allows "a logic of permanent circulation" free of "empirical obstacles," then it is the space between One and Zero, the space of the ever-moving, never captured possibility *as well as* the basis for the calculated, controlled space of the grid. The idea of the line as an arc of velocity, Dt, "defying gravity" in *Gravity's Rainbow* is given a different context in *Mason & Dixon,* where (like Boelhower's map lines) the Line also defies gravity through its very perspective, the aerial perspective of the map. In *Mason & Dixon,* William Emerson, Dixon's mentor, tells Dixon that the goal of the mapmaker is to soar in the unbounded territory of the historical sublime, in his terms a territory that both is dependent upon maps and exceeds them:

"Earthbound," Emerson continued, "we are limited to our Horizon, which sometimes is to be measur'd but in inches.—We are bound withal to Time, and the amounts of it spent getting from one end of a journey to another. Yet aloft, in Map-space, origins, destinations, any Termini, hardly seem to matter,—one can apprehend all at once the entire plexity of possible journeys, set as one is above Distance, above Time itself." (505)

When Dixon finally completes his map of the Line and its surrounding territories, Mason tells him, "This is beauteous Work. Emerson was right, Jeremiah. You were flying, all the time" (689). Boelhower expresses this as the ability of the line to defy gravity and thus escape "Icarian catastrophe"—that is, to remain in the realm of possibility, the territory of the romantic dreamer and overreacher. And yet it is Dixon who connects his and Mason's work to the most heinous aspects of colonialism. "Ev'rywhere they've sent us,—the Cape, St. Helena, America,—what's the Element common to all?" he asks Mason, and then answers, "Slaves . . . and now here we are again, in another Colony, this time having drawn them a Line between their Slave-Keepers, and their Wage-Payers, as if doom'd to re-encounter thro' the World this public Secret, this shameful Core. . . . Where does it end? No matter where in it we go, shall we find all the World Tyrants and Slaves?" (692–93).

The Sot-Weed Factor, finally, has many more ties to the romance tradition than to the historical novel tradition, as odd as that might seem at first; in some ways, Barth's novel exemplifies the modernist turn away from historical realism. *The Sot-Weed Factor* illustrates how the late-modernist historical romance, pure fabulation, morphs into the postmodern form by reversing the dominant of the classic historical novel from history to romance, yet it also illustrates how difficult it is to unveil the situational consciousness of the First World Master or to offer an alternative logic to it. *The Sot-Weed Factor* spoofs U.S. nationalist history as just another stage of the modern project and a continuation of, rather than break with, the Old World. America, Henry Burlingame notes, is "just a piece o' the great world like England" (180). Yet the novel fails to find an ethical center and may be, as Earl Rovit maintains, finally just a prolonged academic joke (116).

Analysis

In contrast, in *Mason & Dixon* Thomas Pynchon returns to what he implies is the historical consolidation of the multinational military-industrial complex and European imperialism and colonialism. The origin is the late eighteenth century, and the catalyst is the political need to map colonial territory. As a definitive metahistorical romance, *Mason & Dixon* goes beyond the joke and asks serious questions about what history is, what a sublime apprehension of time and space might lead us to do, and what really counts in the final reckoning of History. As the main narrator of the whole story, the Reverend Wicks Cherrycoke, notes, "Rather, part of the common Duty of Remembering,—surely our Sentiments,—how we dream'd of, and were mistaken in, each other,—count for at least as much as our poor cold Chronologies" (696).

Appendix

A Listing of Some
Metahistorical Romances

The following is a list of books that might be called *metahistorical romances,* as this study defines that term. The list is not meant to be exhaustive but rather is a starting point for readers and a catalyst for critical debate.

Ackroyd, Peter. *Chatterton: A Novel.* New York: Ballantine, 1987.
———. *Hawksmoor: A Novel.* New York: Harper, 1985.
———. *Milton in America.* New York: Doubleday, 1997.
Apple, Max. *The Propheteers.* New York: Harper and Row, 1987.
Barnes, Julian. *Flaubert's Parrot.* New York: Vintage Books, 1990.
Banville, John. *Doctor Copernicus.* Boston: David R. Godine, 1976.
Barker, Pat. *The Ghost Road.* New York: Plume, 1996.
Barth, John. *The Sot-Weed Factor.* 1960. Reprint, New York: Bantam/
    Doubleday, 1967.
Bell, Madison Smartt. *All Souls' Rising.* New York: Penguin, 1996.
Berger, Thomas. *Little Big Man.* New York: Delacorte, 1989.
Boyle, T. Coraghessan. *World's End: A Novel.* New York: Penguin Books,
    1987.
———. *The Road to Wellville.* New York: Viking, 1993.
Burgess, Anthony. *A Dead Man in Deptford.* New York: Carroll and
    Graf, 1996.
Coetzee, J. M. *Foe.* New York: Penguin, 1986.
Coover, Robert. *The Public Burning.* New York: Bantam/Viking, 1976.
Crace, Jim. *The Gift of Stones.* New York: Ecco, 1996.
———. *Quarantine.* New York: Farrar, Straus and Giroux, 1998.
DeLillo, Don. *Libra.* New York: Penguin, 1991.
Dexter, Pete. *Deadwood.* New York: Penguin, 1976.
Doctorow, E. L. *Ragtime.* New York: Random House, 1974.
Eco, Umberto. *The Name of the Rose.* New York: Harvester Books, 1994.
Erickson, Steve. *Arc d'X.* New York: Poseidon, 1993.

————. *Leap Year.* New York: Poseidon, 1989.

Findley, Timothy. *Famous Last Words.* 1981. Reprint, London: Arena, 1987.

Fowles, John. *The French Lieutenant's Woman.* New York: New American Library, 1969.

————. *A Maggot.* New York: New American Library, 1985.

Fuentes, Carlos. *Terra Nostra.* Trans. Margaret Sayers Peden. New York: Farrar, Straus and Giroux, 1976.

Frazier, Charles. *Cold Mountain.* New York: Atlantic Monthly, 1997.

Glancy, Diane. *Pushing the Bear: A Novel of the Trail of Tears.* New York: Harcourt Brace and Company, 1996.

Grass, Günter. *The Flounder.* New York: Fawcett Crest, 1977.

Johnson, Charles. *Dreamer.* New York: Scribner, 1999.

————. *Middle Passage.* New York: Penguin, 1990.

Kennedy, William. *Legs.* New York: Penguin, 1975.

Kurzweil, Allen. *A Case of Curiosities.* New York: Ballantine, 1992.

Malouf, David. *Remembering Babylon.* New York: Pantheon, 1993.

Millhauser, Steven. *Martin Dressler.* New York: Vintage Books, 1997.

Miner, Valerie. *All Good Women.* Freedom, CA: Crossing Press, 1987.

Momaday, N. Scott. *The Way to Rainy Mountain.* Albuquerque: U of New Mexico P, 1969.

Morante, Elsa. *History: A Novel.* Trans. William Weaver. New York: Vintage, 1984.

Morrison, Toni. *Beloved.* New York: Penguin, 1987.

Norfolk, Lawrence. *Lemprière's Dictionary.* New York: Ballantine, 1991.

Phillips, Caryl. *Cambridge.* New York: Alfred A. Knopf, 1992.

————. *Crossing the River.* New York: Knopf, 1994.

Powers, Richard. *Gain.* New York: Picador, 1999.

Pynchon, Thomas. *Gravity's Rainbow.* New York: Penguin, 1995.

————. *Mason & Dixon.* New York: Henry Holt, 1997.

Reed, Ishmael. *Flight to Canada.* New York: Atheneum, 1989.

————. *Mumbo Jumbo.* New York: Simon and Schuster, 1972.

Schama, Simon. *Dead Certainties (Unwarranted Speculations).* New York: Knopf, 1991.

Sherwood, Frances. *Vindication.* New York: Penguin, 1993.

Silko, Leslie Marmon. *Almanac of the Dead.* New York: Penguin, 1992.

————. *Ceremony.* New York: Penguin, 1988.

Smiley, Jane. *The All-True Travels and Adventures of Lidie Newton.* New York: Alfred A. Knopf, 1998.

Sontag, Susan. *The Volcano Lover: A Romance*. New York: Farrar, 1992.

Spiegelman, Art. *Maus: A Survivor's Tale: My Father Bleeds History.* New York: Pantheon, 1993.

Süskind, Patrick. *Perfume: The Story of a Murderer*. Trans. John E. Woods. New York: Pocket Books/Simon and Schuster, 1986.

Swift, Graham. *Waterland*. New York: Pocket Books/Washington Square P, 1983.

Thomas, D. M. *The White Hotel*. New York: Penguin, 1993.

Thorpe, Adam. *Ulverton*. New York: The Noonday Press/Farrar, Straus and Giroux, 1992.

Unsworth, Barry. *Sacred Hunger*. New York: W. W. Norton, 1992.

Vollmann, William T. *Fathers and Crows*. New York: Penguin, 1992.

———. *The Ice Shirt: A Book of North American Landscapes.* vol. 1. New York: Penguin, 1993.

———. *The Rifles: A Book of North American Landscapes.* vol. 2. New York: Penguin, 1995.

Vonnegut, Kurt. *Slaughterhouse Five or the Children's Crusade: A Duty Dance with Death.* New York: Dell Publishing, 1991.

Walker, Alice. *The Temple of My Familiar.* Washington Square P, 1997.

Williams, Nigel. *Star Turn*. London: Faber and Faber, 1985.

Winterson, Jeanette. *The Passion*. New York: Vintage/Random House, 1989.

———. *Sexing the Cherry*. New York: Vintage International, 1989.

Wolf, Christa. *Cassandra: A Novel and Four Essays*. Trans. Jan Van Heurck. New York: Farrar, Straus and Giroux, 1984.

Zencey, Eric. *Panama*. New York: Farrar, Straus and Giroux, 1995.

Notes

Introduction

1. The many fine discussions of postmodernism that attempt broad, inclusive definitions include Hutcheon, *The Politics of Postmodernism;* Bertens, *The Idea of the Postmodern;* Boyne and Rattansi, "The Theory and Politics of Postmodernism"; Anderson, *The Truth about the Truth;* Jencks, *Post-modernism.* Alex Callinicos defines three types of "postmodernism" as three kinds of intellectual trends: a philosophical trend, characterized by poststructuralism, especially in the work of Foucault, Derrida, and Deleuze; a social theories trend, especially theories of postindustrial capitalism, such as by Daniel Bell (e.g., *The Coming of Post-Industrial Society* 1973); and a cultural trend, originating in reactions against modernist abstraction in painting and architecture (especially in the International Style) ("Reactionary Postmodernism?" 100–101). In an excellent discussion about postmodernism, Johnston categorizes three areas as well: literary/aesthetic postmodernism, historical (or sociocultural) postmodernism, and theoretical postmodernism. See also Lyotard, "Note on the Meaning of 'Post-,'" in *The Postmodern Explained* 75–80. Jameson's powerful marxist analysis of postmodernism constructs the triad modernism, modernity, and modernization; see *Postmodernism, or, The Cultural Logic of Late Capitalism.*

2. This chapter assumes a definition of modernism as a cultural product of the Western Enlightenment that has undergone the Weberian process of "rationalization" and differentiation. See Habermas, "Modernity;" Dallmayr 17; Lash, *Sociology of Postmodernism.*

3. Discussions in this category of "epistemological postmodernism" might include primary works by Jürgen Habermas, Jean-François Lyotard, Gilles Deleuze and Félix Guattari, Michel Foucault, Jacques Derrida, and other poststructuralists as well as all of the secondary literature about them. Useful general studies would include Best and Kellner's excellent *Postmodern Theory.* Essay collections focusing mainly on this kind

of postmodernism would include *Postmodernism,* ed. Appignanesi; sec. 1 of *Feminism/Postmodernism,* ed. Nicholson; *Modernity and Identity,* ed. Lash and Friedman; *Postmodern Conditions,* ed. Milner et al.; *Theory, Culture & Society* (Special issue: Postmodernism) 5.2–3 (1988). Pertinent monographs include McGowan's *Postmodernism and Its Critics* and Norris's *The Truth about Postmodernism;* also, Madison's *The Hermeneutics of Postmodernity* and Ermath's *Sequel to History.*

4. This is the definition of postmodernism underlying the essays within *Postmodernism Across the Ages,* ed. Readings and Schaber.

5. See Baudrillard, "The Precession of Simulacra," as the classic formulation of this term.

6. See Bauman, *Intimations of Postmodernity;* Lash, *Sociology of Postmodernism;* Haraway, *Simians, Cyborgs, and Women;* Harvey, *The Condition of Postmodernity;* Kroker and Cook, *The Postmodern Scene;* Rose, *The Postmodern and the Postindustrial;* and Rosenau, *Post-Modernism and the Social Sciences.* One might note as valuable introductions to sociocultural postmodernism the essays in *Social Postmodernism,* ed. Nicholson and Seidman; secs. 2 and 3 of Nicholson's *Feminism/Postmodernism; Postmodernism & Social Inquiry,* ed. Dickens and Fontana; *The Anti-Aesthetic,* ed. Foster; *Postmodernism and Politics,* ed. Arac; *Universal Abandon?,* ed. Ross; *Postmodernism and Society,* ed. Boyne and Rattansi; *The Lesbian Postmodern,* ed. Doan. Important essays in this debate are those by Howe ("Mass Society and Post-Modern Fiction"), Fiedler ("The New Mutants"), Wasson ("Notes on a New Sensibility"), Hassan ("Pluralism in Postmodern Perspective"), and Bertens ("Postmodern Culture"). Other central articles include Jameson's "Postmodernism and Consumer Society," and "Postmodernism, or, The Cultural Logic of Late Capitalism"; Rorty's "Postmodernist Bourgeois Liberalism"; West's "Black Culture and Postmodernism"; and Appiah's "Is the Post- in Postmodernism the Post- in Postcolonial?"

7. This linking of late-twentieth-century philosophies of art with concurrent social movements occurs, for instance, in Marcus's *Lipstick Traces,* or in *Discourses,* ed. Ferguson, Olander, Tucker, and Fiss.

8. For a discussion of new realism in painting in relation to British postmodernist fiction, see Jameson, *Postmodernism;* also, Hutcheon's *Politics of Postmodernism,* which usefully discusses this kind of sociocultural postmodernism.

9. See Haraway, "A Manifesto for Cyborgs."

One: Sorting Out Connections

1. MacHardy, for instance, distinguishes two forms of the *crisis in history:* a *disciplinary crisis* (concerning the relation of history to the social sciences), and a *cognitive crisis* (affecting philosophers of language concerned with the relationship between history and literature).

2. Definitions of the historical novel abound in Scott criticism, where they tend to derive from the prefaces of Scott's novels. See Elam for citations of these sources. Iser distinguishes the historical romance from the gothic romance and bourgeois novel in *The Implied Reader,* 81–100. Frye's *The Secular Scripture* is central and contains a section on Walter Scott's Waverley novels. Other studies I found central included those by Levin, Henderson, Pearce, and Leisey. Thematic, marxist, and formalist approaches to the historical novel yield different kinds of definitions. Cowart illustrates a thematic approach, constructing four categories of historical presentation in fiction dating between 1951 and 1986: fictions whose authors aspire purely or largely to historical verisimilitude; fictions whose authors reverse history to contemplate the future; fictions whose authors seek to pinpoint the precise historical moment when the modern age or some prominent feature of it came into existence; and fictions whose authors project the present into the past (Cowart 8–9). Lukács's *The Historical Novel* is the starting point for marxist analyses of the genre; later studies, such as Foley's excellent *Telling the Truth,* tend to follow the marxist orientation if not the thesis of Lukács' study. Lukács argues that the task of the historical novel on Scott's model, through its portrayals of minor or fictional historical figures, is to bring the historical extremes in the novel into contact with one another. In contrast is Fleishman's formalist definition listing seven criteria defining a historical novel.

3. The reference here is to Isaiah Berlin, "The Hedgehog and the Fox," in *Russian Thinkers* (New York, 1978), as quoted in Mossman, 250.

4. See Mossman for a useful discussion of Tolstoy's mechanistic view of history.

5. Critical discussions of Pynchon's writings are a rich source for discussions about postmodernism and quantum science; the emerging discourse about literature and chaos, for instance, that of Hayles's *Chaos Bound,* is important to my assumptions here.

6. My account here is indebted to Ferris (199–237), who notes that

the Waverley novels both cooperate with and disorient the official discourse about history in their time.

7. Discussions of Scott's schooling and admiration for the historical philosophy of the Scottish School abound in critical discussions of historical fiction and Scott's writing. Most illuminating are those by Dekker in *The American Historical Romance;* McMaster in *Scott and Society,* esp. chap. 2; Forbes; Daiches, "Sir Walter Scott and History" and "Scott and Scotland"; Brown; Garside.

8. See Natoli's discussion of *classic* or *naive* realism in *A Primer to Postmodernity.*

9. Some scholars claim that Scott actually anticipated Romantic historiography and its belief (evident in the work of Carlyle, Macaulay, and Marx) in a dialectically progressive character of history (Richter, "From Medievalism to Historicism" 96; Walsh). There are, of course, contradictions between this portrait of Scott and one sketching him as supporter of Enlightenment historiography. The philosophers of the Scottish school were deeply skeptical of Rousseau, whose ideas were central to nineteenth-century American romanticism.

10. Walter Scott himself made distinctions between simple use of the fantastic/supernatural and the construction of romance or fable. See his essay "On the Supernatural in Fictitious Composition" for such comparative distinctions.

11. See Swann for a discussion of Scott's contemporaries' reactions to his work. See Harkin's "Romance and Real History" for an overview of this duality in Scott. Budick's *Fiction and the Historical Consciousness* and Dekker's *The American Historical Romance* discuss the historical romance in U.S. literary history.

12. I recommend Kerr's study of Scott's fiction, *Fiction against History,* in relation to this point, for Kerr emphasizes how Scott turned history into fable, fantasy, and romance in the face of political history. His study has direct relevance to my claims about postmodern metahistorical romance.

13. See Onega's argument that postmodernist historical fiction attempts to reveal truth "without losing its condition of human construct" and attempts to represent the identity of a hero residing on the cultural fringe ("A Knack for Yarns" 17).

14. "Criticism, History, Foucault" 369. My discussion of Foucault and the historicized Subject here and in chap. 2 is indebted to Docherty's lucid analysis. In "Nietzsche, Genealogy, History" (153), Foucault ad-

dresses the point here. For other discussions of poststructuralism and the difference between modern and postmodern apprehensions of history, see Cascardi; also Stempel. For a provocative discussion of postmodern identity, see Dunn.

15. One would need to cite all of the studies on Foucault for a complete listing of sources discussing his theory of epistemes. See as brief examples of this point Docherty, "Criticism, History, Foucault" 370; Lemert and Gillan; White, *Tropics of Discourse* 239–60; Dews "Foucault"; Poster 134–41; LeGoff 177–79.

16. See Bürger 73–93. As Engström notes, "The sublime encourages the recognition not so much that we can't grasp things in their totality (for we don't need to, and I don't know of any philosopher proposing that we can) but that we can grasp difference and be stunned by it. The sublime is not, then, with Kant's assistance, a (now-politicized) prohibition against presenting; it is more a mixture of narrative frustration, respect for difference, and a developed sense of stylistic craft and tradition that one hopes to catch by surprise" (196). My discussion of the Lyotardian sublime in this section and elsewhere is indebted to Engström's own and the following: Best and Kellner; Crowther; Ingram; Lacoue-Labarthe; Norris, "Kant Disfigured," in *The Truth about Postmodernism;* Readings; Veerman.

17. I recommend here Readings's extremely lucid and informative analysis of Lyotard's "event" and history as anachronism and the immemorial. See *Introducing Lyotard* 57–62.

18. Hirsch has admirably examined these responses to Holocaust photography and counter-responses to them in "survivor art." See *Family Frames.*

19. Social history has itself split into various branches and subdisciplines such as historical demography, labor history, urban and rural history. It is now considered distinct from economic history, which itself increasingly has focused on consumption, management, and communications/media history. Vying with social and economic history is political history, now increasingly divided between grass-roots and government history. The "new history" within the social sciences should not be confused with the New Historicism or other historical approaches in literary and cultural studies, though it is fascinating to observe how literary scholars have traced almost precisely the same characteristics in the 1970s "new history" approach in literary studies. See, for example, Lindenberger, chap. 9, for an example of this overlap.

20. Le Goff puts this date at 1919 in *History and Memory*. My discussion of the *Annales* school is deeply indebted to Le Goff's discussion of its various characters and history in *History and Memory;* Appleby, Hunt, and Jacob's definition in *Telling the Truth about History;* Peter Burke's *New Perspectives on Historical Writing;* Iggers's *Historiography in the Twentieth Century;* Ricoeur's *Contribution of French Historiography to the Theory of History;* Stoianovich's *French Historical Method;* and articles by Olábarri and by Carrard.

21. One of the best illustrations of this conflict between an old guard of historians intent on preserving the boundaries and authority of their profession and a new wave of historiographers intent on asking questions about what historians do is the interchange, in 1995, between Marwick and White in *Journal of Contemporary History* and the flurry of responses by other historians in subsequent issues of the journal. Appleby, Hunt, and Jacob, in chap. 6 of *Telling the Truth about History,* summarize this disciplinary problem, and McRae discusses how science paradigms affect historical knowledge. In her discussions of the interconnections between chaos theory and literary analysis, Hayles also posits a synchronicity in late twentieth-century theoretical discourses such as science, astrophysics, literary and cultural studies, and music. What she argues is that all these postmodern disciplines converge on certain ideas: the substitution of nonlinear for linear models; the necessity of paradox to new logic paradigms; the acceptance of uncertainty, multidimensionality, and complexity; the rejection of Newtonian mechanism and causality in both physical and metaphysical systems; the concomitant revaluation, and interactive synthesis, of intuition and observation of actual behavior and recursive symmetries; an analytical turn from discrete units to informational systems; the construction of new relationalities between margin and center.

22. See Burguière for a discussion of poststructuralist historiography in relation to at least two previous historiographical approaches and historical perspectives, a narrative history concerned with political power dating from the chroniclers of the Middle Ages through seventeenth-century scholarship to positivist, event-oriented, late nineteenth-century history; and "historical anthropology," dominating romantic historiography and later developed by the *Annalistes.*

23. For discussions of New Historicism and cultural materialism as two kinds of historical inquiry akin to post-*Annales* historiography see Francis Barker, Peter Hulme, and Margaret Iversen, eds., *Uses of History:*

Marxism, Postmodernism and the Renaissance (Manchester: Manchester UP; New York: St. Martin's, 1991), particularly essays by Howard Felperin and Jean Howard.

24. One could also count Foucault as one of the most prominent of the post-*Annales* historians, though it is likely that he would have vehemently objected to this label. While Furet and Le Goff have written trenchant analyses of history's changing disciplinary practices and research philosophies, they are more aligned with the *Annales* school of philosophy in many ways than with postmodern or poststructuralist approaches to history. See Furet, *In the Workshop of History,* or Le Goff, *History and Memory.* For some discussion and definitions of postmodernism and history and/or postmodernist historiography, see essays by Topolski, Carr, and Wrzosek in *Historiography between Modernism and Postmodernism,* ed. Topolski; Ankersmit, "The Dilemma of Contemporary Anglo-Saxon Philosophy of History"; Goodman; D'Hondt; Stone, "History and Postmodernism"; Gossman; Lindenberger.

25. As Partner notes, "Narrative theory . . . continues to be . . . of far less interest for cutting edge study of fiction (perhaps because narrative merely defines the novel, doesn't challenge its definition). But for history, essentially narrativist questions like: Whose history?—itself a conflation of: The history of whom? and Who gets to write it?—are contentious matters, matters of power with real repercussions in the political world" (171). My definition of post-*Annales* historiography here and below is greatly indebted to the superb article by Olábarri and to these other sources: Lang, "Nostalgia for the Future"; Howard; Ankersmit, "Historiography and Postmodernism"; Cascardi; Weinstein; Orr; Poster; LaCapra, *History & Criticism;* Burke, ed., *New Perspectives on Historical Writing.* My discussion of historians' definitions of this "crisis in history" depends on the following: MacHardy; Olábarri; Bailyn; Rabb and Rotberg, eds.; Stone, "History and Postmodernism"; Baron; Burke, ed.; Holton; White, *The Content of the Form;* Poster; LaCapra, *History, Politics, and the Novel.*

26. One could explore in addition the work of de Certeau, which has been extremely influential. Paul Ricoeur's *Time and Narrative* (trans. Kathleen McLaughlin Blarney and David Pellauer, 3 vols. [Chicago: Chicago UP, 1984–88]) and *The Rule of Metaphor: Multi-disciplinary Studies of the Creation of Meaning in Language* (trans. Robert Czerny with Kathleen McLaughlin and John Costello [London: Routledge and Kegan Paul, 1978]) explore a nonmarxist terrain also important to

White's work (notably the role of tropes and narrative to the writing of history), albeit to different ends. J. Rüsen's "historics" also emphasizes how history is disciplined and is reminiscent of Habermas in terms of its social vision; see Allan Megill's "Jörn Rüsen's Theory of Historiography between Modernism and Rhetoric of Inquiry" (*History and Theory* 33.1 [1994]: 39–60). My focus on White's work to the exclusion of that of de Certeau, Ricoeur, and Rüsen—and Benjamin and Nietszche—is a necessary but unfortunate constraint of time and subject.

27. The far-reaching influence of White's work is apparent when one examines how his work is categorized by various disciplines and who claims him as their own. In Richter's anthology of literary criticism, *The Critical Tradition,* White appears with Michel Foucault, Pierre Bourdieu, Clifford Geertz, Edward Said, Stephen Greenblatt, Nancy Armstrong, and Homi K. Bhabha under the heading "New Historicism and Cultural Studies." In *The Johns Hopkins Guide to Literary Theory and Criticism* (Baltimore, 1994), White is described by Hans Kellner as an American scholar influenced by existentialism and structuralism whose work on narrative "serves as a warning to any criticism or would-be New Historicism that would ground readings of texts in given historical contexts" (729). In *Encyclopedia of Contemporary Literary Theory* (Toronto: U of Toronto P, 1993), David Carr describes White as a historian and philosopher of history "best known for applying concepts derived from literary theory to the analysis of historical writings" (486).

28. At the 1997 annual meeting of the American Historical Association in New York a special session was held on the influence of Hayden White's work, and the papers were published in *History and Theory* 37, no. 2 (1998). See Domanska ("Hayden White") and Partner for a discussion of *Metahistory* in this context. Jenkins, in chap. 5 of *On "What Is History?,"* provides an analysis of White's work that is particularly germane here. Other useful accounts of White's work, especially his metahistory, include those by Domanska, *Encounters;* Iggers, chap. 10 of *Historiography in the Twentieth Century;* Kellner, "Twenty Years After" and "A Bedrock of Order"; and Roth, chap. 7 of *The Ironist's Cage.*

29. Hayden White, "The Politics of Historical Interpretation: Discipline and De-Sublimation," *The Content of the Form,* 58–82, rpt. from *Critical Inquiry* 9, no. 1 (1982), hereafter cited as *Content.*

30. The essays here referenced by White are reprinted in *Two Essays by Friedrich von Schiller: "Native and Sentimental Poetry" and "On the Sublime: Two Essays,"* trans. Julius A. Elias (New York: 1966).

31. Significantly, though marxists as well as positivists both claim a scientific approach to history that seems to transcend this opposition, both also advance the utopian aims (radical in the case of marxists, progressive liberalism in the case of positivists) that a properly disciplined historical consciousness rejects. Both are thus tinged with the utopianism ruled out by a disciplined history. White's first claim is, therefore, that in the discipline of history, where realism has become synonymous with antiutopianism, there is an active yet unseen politics of interpretation always at work, and this puts marxists and liberal positivists surprisingly on the same side. Paradoxically, however, while this disciplined history labels marxism utopian and often counters it for this reason, marxism surprisingly emerges as *antiutopian—on the same side as disciplined history*—if positioned within the discourse of the sublime. Marxism, like its bourgeois counterparts, is antiutopian in terms of its conviction that history is not a sublime spectacle but a comprehensible process. As such, it is deluded by its own totalizing narrative.

32. One should note that White's approach to the association of aesthetics with fascism is very different from that of Lyotard, who not only understands the project of the avant-garde as antithetical to that of totalitarian regimes but differentiates totalitarianisms from one another. The totalitarianism of capitalism, for example, is very different for Lyotard than the totalitarianism of Nazism, and different avant-gardes may oppose each. What is finally resistant to totalitarianism is something akin to Adorno's "politics of micrologies": "I've emphasized the importance of the moment of dissent in the process of constructing knowledge, lying at the heart of the community of thought," he writes to Augustin Nancy in 1985 ("Postscript to Terror and the Sublime," in *The Postmodern Explained* 73).

33. This may be the "linguistic humanism" that Hans Kellner also identifies in White's work (see "A Bedrock of Order"). Kellner notes that two themes are predominant in White's work: cultural politics or how a tradition elicits assent and censors the debate it makes possible, and the important role of human choice in the construction of possibility of mastery, particularly the opposition between a dead scholasticism and a vital rhetoric that makes opposition and choice possible. Wary of "explanation" as a Western prejudice, White consistently asserts rhetoric as figures of thought (109). I recommend Kellner's article as a most thoughtful appraisal of White's work.

34. The contempt of the Right to the discourse of the sublime reveals

a weird double-think, an investment in precisely the politics of the real that it frequently condemns or rhetorically situates itself above. While the rhetoric of the Right often depends on the construction of a new age, a better world where humankind can be free because we are striving toward a "sublime" social goal—as, again, White notes, is often the case of the rhetoric of the extreme fascist Right—the final solution (if that phrase can used discursively) almost always depends on an evacuation of the sublime, a resituation of the concept in a worldly social context and a consequent dissection of it in the formulation of a social program based on ultrarationalist reasoning or in the identification of pleasure (versus the experience of ethical freedom). State or market mechanisms and scientism merge in application and empty the sublime of its meaning—or, more appropriately, fill the "empty," unrepresentable category of the sublime with ideological content, such as "scientific" programs for social improvement.

The contempt of the extreme Left is in some ways more understandable, because it at least is not self-contradictory. Christopher Norris argues that the aesthetic has been a domain notoriously colonized by right-wing ideologues and has often served surrogate discourse where political interests were obliquely or covertly in play (Norris, *What's Wrong with Postmodernism?*, 16). What is enacted when the Left recalls the sublime as a conceptual category is the conflict between a system that believes reason has found the workable pattern within human history and a belief that such a system is by definition impossible. At base, for example, there is a fundamental incompatibility between marxist positions and the Neoplatonism of the discourse surrounding the sublime. The marxist position conceptualizes freedom as the end point of material history, product of a social system that has been diagnosed by human reason and is situated squarely within—indeed, which is the culmination of—the social processes set in motion after feudalism and the rise of capitalism. The discourse of the sublime, in contrast, posits an absolute break with such systems, an attempt to think and act outside the paradigms set in place by rationalism itself. Marxism posits the attainability of freedom by revolution from within; the discourse of the sublime posits the possibility of freedom by rejection of the "within" and constant reevaluation of constructed systems of value from without.

35. See, for example, McClure, "Postmodern/Post-Secular," as well as Berry and Wernick, eds., *Shadow of Spirit,* for a good introduction to this topic of "postsecularism."

Two: The Metahistorical Romance and the Historical Sublime

1. See Jane Bellamy, *Affective Genealogies; Psychoanalysis, Postmodernism, and the "Jewish Question" after Auschwitz* (Lincoln: U of Nebraska P, 1997); Michael André Bernstein, *Foregone Conclusions: Against Apocalyptic History* (Berkeley: U of California P, 1994); Cathy Caruth, *Unclaimed Experience: Trauma, Narrative, and History* (Baltimore: The Johns Hopkins UP, 1996) and the essays in her edited collection *Trauma: Explorations in Memory* (Baltimore: The Johns Hopkins UP, 1996); Saul Friedlander, *Reflections of Nazism: An Essay on Kitsch and Death,* trans. Thomas Weyr (New York: Harper & Row, 1982); Hirsch, *Family Frames;* LaCapra, *History and Memory after Auschwitz;* Efraim Sicher, ed., *Breaking Crystal: Writing and Memory after Auschwitz* (Urbana: U of Illinois P, 1998); and the essays in *Is the Holocaust Unique?: Perspectives on Comparative Genocide,* ed. Alan S. Rosenbaum (Boulder, Colo.: Westview P, 1996). My claim that the postmodern historical imagination participates in a post-traumatic imaginary should be distinguished from discussions of how the Holocaust should be represented in history. Braun, Kellner (" 'Never Again' Is Now"), LaCapra (*Representing the Holocaust*), Lang ("Is It Possible to Misrepresent the Holocaust?"), White ("Historical Emplotment and the Problem of Truth"), and Young have linked the question of how to represent the Holocaust to the more general question of how to represent limit events in history and the ethical as well as historical implications of various kinds of representation.

2. It is perhaps inevitable that this lens will imply that "the West" has a "mind" in an almost Hegelian sense, and that implication is unfortunate. I mean to use the phrase *post-traumatic imaginary* here in a less anthropomorphizing sense. The phrase should imply an ideological shift, or a cultural imaginary, or, if one will, a zeitgeist.

3. For a clear discussion of the distinction between metaphor associated with transcendence and metonymy associated with materialism (formal analysis) from the political position of the latter, see Singer's insightful article "Desire's Desire."

4. In relation to Lyotard's conception of politics that emphasizes local struggle, Schatzki comments, "This emphasis probably also reflects a disillusionment with large-scale, systematic politics born of a series of events during and after World War II. For example, as disproof of all the great 'metanarratives' which motivated political action in the nineteenth and twentieth centuries, Lyotard cites singular occurrences: Auschwitz,

Budapest 1956, May 1968, the economic crisis of 1929, the 1974–79 crisis of overcapitalization" (43). I heartily recommend Dainotto's "The Excremental Sublime" as an innovative discussion of postmodern sublimity in terms of psychic blockage and release. Dainotto builds her argument not only from Longinus's and Edmund Burke's theories of the sublime but also from the intriguing arguments of Hertz; Pease; and Hebidge. Dainotto notes that this postmodern sublime probably has exhausted itself and is an untenable strategy for the survival of real subjects.

5. LaCapra also grapples with the difference between what he calls a "sublime" experience felt by Nazi soldiers in the midst of killing sprees of Jewish citizens and the experience of the sublime discussed by Kant and Lyotard; he asks whether what the Nazis experienced was a "negative sublime," a version of the "secular-sacred" requiring the sacrificial slaughter of victims. As I have defined it in chap. 1, Lyotard's postmodern sublime, combined with Hayden White's notion of the historical sublime, results in a conception of the *postmodern historical sublime* that disallows the possibility of a 'negative sublime'—not only because a negative sublime would actually locate the sublime in the realm of judgments and thus equate it with the aesthetics of the beautiful (the Kantian response) but also because the postmodern historical sublime by definition rejects the binary logic of opposition itself. The elation felt by murderers in a killing frenzy of sacrificial victims is not sublime in a Kantian or a Lyotardian sense (it is the product of will, and it is only the hidden Dionysian psychic reverse of logic, of ultra-rationality). More importantly, this genocidal frenzy is not the *historical* sublime. The historical sublime is a concept that links a very general definition of the sublime to history itself, an understanding of *the far past* and how that receded past is formed, understood, and lived in the present. This is a very different territory than the emotional one experienced psychically by killers in the Serbian death camps or their Nazi and Stalinist precursors.

6. Heehs argues that myth and history have traditionally been understood as "antithetical modes of explanation"; however, historians are becoming increasingly aware of the mythic nature of historical writing and are recognizing that the two interpenetrate.

7. Ankersmit notes that "one might discover in postmodernist historical writing a wish to return to a prehistorist historical consciousness" (*History and Tropology* 225, note 6), while Rosenau concludes that the postmodernist attitude toward history manifests "a deep respect for the primitive and an attraction to tradition" (65). One also thinks of the dis-

tinction McHale has made between the epistemological dominant of modernism and the contrasting ontological dominant of postmodernism as another way of approaching the postmodern return to premodernist modes.

Postmodernism as a "post-secular philosophy" is broached in the collection *Post-Secular Philosophy*, ed. Blond. All of the essays explore how secular society (not exclusively post–1945 societies) have recuperated, embedded, or explored the sublime or the power of the gods after their supposed death. In "The Sublime in Kierkegaard," for example, Milbank claims that poststructuralist writing "might well be characterized as a discourse 'on the sublime'. For it is a discourse 'about' the indeterminable, and seeks, in its very mode of utterance, to pay tribute to this ineluctable margin" (131). Wernick, in his essay "Jean Baudrillard," remarks that Baudrillard's mysticism is that of a "disillusioned revolutionary" (359).

8. An illuminating study correlating the sublime to technology and concepts of time in postmodern fiction is Tabbi's *Postmodern Sublime*. Ermath discusses postmodern time and narrative in *Sequel to History*, particularly in relation to pendulum motion. Mossman claims that science provides metaphors for modernist history in *War and Peace* and *Doctor Zhivago* and that while Newtonian physics provided literature with mechanical metaphors and Darwin provided literature with biological metaphors, one must understand scientific language as metaphoric and part of a larger poetics of history (262). See also Docherty, "Authority, History and the Question of Postmodernism" (67) for a discussion of postmodernism as a "slippage" from concepts of mass to concepts of energy.

9. Many theorists of the postmodern have recently begun to recognize the ties between postmodernist historical paradigms and premodern historical understanding. For example, discussing the work of Kojève, Blanchot, Bataille, and Klossowski, Jean-Philippe Mathy has illustrated how postmodern interpretations of American culture often imply that the United States is the paradigmatic model for postmodernity and a Hegelian end of history. In the work of these writers, he argues, the United States is a mythic and ideological space as well. Mathy argues that right-wing continental critics of U.S. democracy have always understood its decadence as the normal consequence of bourgeois utilitarian values over aristocratic ideals, promoting civilization over culture (274). This positivistic materialism has direct consequences for the postmodern concept of time in the United States: "The American concept of time is closer to the cyclical recurrence of primitive cultures than to the linear unfolding of historical time" (276–77). Other writers, such as

Alexandre Kojève, arrive at similar conclusions about but different valuations of U.S. culture. Kojève refers to the United States as a posthistorical society; man, no longer needing to battle an extinguished nature as Other, is useless and returns to "animality," a state of nature at the end of history that is an ambiguous eternity of play and desire (278). Kojève thus equates postmodern America with premodern states of being. Mathy also notes that in *Amerique,* Baudrillard (for similar reasons) characterizes the United States as "the only great primitive society of modern times" (277). All of these theorists imply a dystopian character of this postmodern end to history.

10. This is a slightly different framing of Hutcheon's insightful claim that postmodernism is "border discourse" (see *Politics of Postmodernism*). Nancy also understands the sublime as a process of deferral: "[Kant's use of the term *Bestreben*] is not to be understood here in the sense of a project, an envisioned undertaking that one could evaluate either in terms of its intention or in terms of its result. This striving cannot be conceived in terms of either a logic of desire and potentiality or a logic of the transition to action and the work or a logic of the will. . . . [Rather, striving or transport toward the sublime] consists in a relation to the limit: a continuous effort is the continuous displacement of a limit. . . . it is less a question of the tendency toward something, of the direction or project of a struggling subject, than of the tension of the limit itself" (Nancy, "The Sublime Offering" 45).

11. The degree to which this is peculiar to literature of the United States and hence is being "exported" to other national literatures is an interesting question. Budick comments that "the burden of historical responsibility under the pressure of skepticism is . . . the distinguishing feature of American historical romance" (x). Henderson, in *Versions of the Past,* writes that much postmodernist fiction of the United States is a direct descendant of the American historical romance tradition of the eighteenth and nineteenth centuries, represented by the work of Cooper and Hawthorne—historical romances that bore similarities to those of Scott but arguably had a different philosophical and national base.

12. Van Alphen is here combining definitions of the uncanny and the sublime by Freud, Edmund Burke, and Anthony Vidler in *The Architectural Uncanny: Essays in the Modern Unhomely* (Cambridge: MIT P, 1992), and by Friedrich Wilhelm Joseph Schelling in *Philosophie der Mythologie* (1835).

13. For discussions of the sublime as or in terror, see Monk; Clery; Weiskel.

14. De Certeau works with this idea that history is located in the "between space" of reality and textuality, or reality and the past. See Poster's discussion in *Cultural History + Postmodernism* of how de Certeau defines history itself as an uncanny reality maker that produces *reality effects* (Roland Barthes's term).

15. Kant, *The Critique of Judgment,* trans. J. H. Bernard (New York: Hafnere, 1951), sec. 26, 174; 91, as quoted in Nancy, "The Sublime Offering" 40.

16. Analysts of Thomas's book who underscore its attack on positivistic science include Cowart, who notes Thomas's simultaneous use and subversion of Freudian theory; Hutcheon (*A Poetics of Postmodernism*), who calls the book "sadistic and plagiaristic (or parodic)" and discusses its presentation of female subject formation. McHale argues that Thomas stays within the bounds of traditional historical fiction in this novel but implies that realistic norms may be fantastic, ironically coopting historical figures (e.g., Freud) and historical events (e.g., the massacre at Babi Yar) (89). Olsen notes that the text is concerned with multiple perspectives and relative truths, while Lee focuses on subjectivity and its construction in a postmodern context (94–98).

17. It is ironic, then, that Thomas has been accused of plagiarism because of his use of Dina Pronicheva's account of Babi Yar in Anatoli Kuznetsov's *Babi Yar;* see Lynn Felder, "D. M. Thomas: The Plagiarism Controversy," *Dictionary of Literary Biography Yearbook 1982* (Detroit: Gale Research, 1982), 79–82, for details of this controversy. See also Cowart, 223 n. 22, where he discusses this controversy.

18. I am grateful to Ryan S. Trimm sharing with me his useful written discussion and ideas about *Sacred Hunger.*

19. Central to the narrative operations of metahistorical romance are questions such as those posed by Gossman about the historiographical context for literature itself: "But how does one establish a relation between a rhetoric or an ideology and historical reality (not an account or representation of class conflict, for instance, but actual class conflict)?" (286). Gossman's reading recontextualizes historiography within the bounds of literary history and raises important questions about historicist referentiality.

20. See Holton's *Jarring Witnesses,* chap. 1, for a useful discussion of

the Covering Law Model and of the issues related to narrative and point of view in the historical profession.

21. For a sampling of this debate about history and/as narrative and discussions of the logical contradictions in each of these extreme positions, see White, "Historical Emplotment and the Problem of Truth," "The Narrativization of Real Events," and the essays in *The Content of the Form;* Anchor, "Narrativity and the Transformation of Historical Consciousness"; Anderson, "On Emplotment"; Ankersmit, *History and Tropology;* Dray, "On the Nature and Role of Narrative in Historiography"; Funkenstein, "History, Counterhistory, and Narrative"; Hughes, "Narrative, Scene, and the Fictions of History"; Jacques, "The Primacy of Narrative in Historical Understanding"; McCullagh, "Metaphor and Truth in History"; Mink, "History and Fiction as Modes of Comprehension"; Orr, "The Revenge of Literature"; Stambovsky, "Metaphor and Historical Understanding"; Stone, "The Revival of Narrative"; Topolski, "A Non-postmodernist Analysis of Historical Narratives." In "The Origins of Postmodernist Historiography" and in *History and Tropology,* Ankersmit claims that historism, developing in the late eighteenth century, is an older critique of metanarrative akin to Lyotard's later critique and bears importantly on the debate on history and narrative. Ankersmit, in fact, claims that postmodernism can "best be seen as a radicalized form of historism" (93).

22. See previous citations of White's work; also, Kellner, *Language and Historical Representation;* Ankersmit, *Narrative Logic* and *History and Tropology.*

23. Osland has discussed Doctorow's novel *Ragtime* in relation to reading patterns that through metaphorical understanding are able to lend coherence to seemingly fragmented texts. For other discussions of metaphor, history, and contemporary fiction related to this idea, see Elias, "Oscar Hijuelos's *The Mambo Kings Play Songs of Love . . .*"; Lodge, *The Modes of Modern Writing.*

24. I recommend Vann's essay, "Turning Linguistic."

25. Doctorow notes, "I could claim that history is a kind of fiction in which we live and hope to survive, and fiction is a kind of speculative history, perhaps a superhistory, by which the available data for the composition is seen to be greater and more various in its sources than the historian supposes" ("False Documents," *American Review* 26 [1977], 217).

26. As the book jacket notes, Schama is a Cambridge University–trained historian, who at the time of this writing was Mellon Professor in

the Social Sciences and Senior Associate at the Center for European Studies at Harvard University. He is the author of numerous historical studies, such as the prizewinning *Citizens: A Chronicle of the French Revolution* (New York: Random House, 1990).

27. Strout castigates Schama for waffling between traditional historicism and historical skepticism in a commentary on *Dead Certainties* for *History and Theory:* "The current prestige of radical skepticism seems to have more to do with academic literary fashion and the belief by political radicals in the advantages of asserting it than with the empirical problems of working historians, who are not in general intellectually paralyzed by doubt or driven to write fiction instead" (159). This is a common argument by traditionalist historians. Strout's conclusion is, however, at one with my own: "These comic games with history suggest the genre of an antihistorical novel whose purpose is political and whose effect is to breed distrust of both the process of history and the writing of history" (160–61).

28. Fine studies that derive a lineage of historical fiction from Scott to the present include Wesseling's *Writing History as a Prophet,* which contextualizes post-1945 historical fiction in terms of Scott and the "uchronian" novel predicated on a model of utopian science fiction; Elam's *Romancing the Postmodern,* which discusses the romance elements in Scott's fiction and traces a lineage from Scott to postmodernist romance; and Budick's *Fiction and the Historical Consciousness,* which links the historical romance in the United States to a male tradition of skepticism whose terms are self and other, mind and world, imagination and history and which sets up a dialectical relationship between the world of historical reality and the world of the mind.

29. McHale's study on postmodernist fiction is broad ranging, and in his chapter on postmodernist historical novels he notes three rules for the construction of classic historical novels: (1) real characters could not be introduced if their presence contradicted the official historical record; (2) anachronism had to be avoided in a faithful representation of the past material culture; and (3) the world of the novel had to be a realistic one. These are the three criteria that postmodernist fiction sometimes blatantly violates.

30. Critics who argue that *Gravity's Rainbow* opposes characters espousing classical attitudes about determinism and characters who tread the middle ground include Schwartz (169) and Wilde (89–90). It is not possible to cite here all of the critical discussions that have noted numerous ways in which *Gravity's Rainbow* promotes simultaneous, "and/and"

thinking over binary, "either/or" thinking— for example, in the way characters "map on" to one another, thereby destroying identity and plot boundaries. One might see Slade, Levine and Leverenz (see note 31, below), and Tanner as beginnings to this discussion.

31. For discussions of theology, history, or mythology in Pynchon's *Gravity's Rainbow*, see essays in Harold Bloom, ed., *Thomas Pynchon's "Gravity's Rainbow": Modern Critical Views* (New York: Chelsea House, 1986); George Lewis Levine and David Leverenz, eds., *Mindful Pleasures: Essays on Thomas Pynchon* (Boston: Little, Brown, 1976); Edward Mendelson, ed., *Pynchon: A Collection of Critical Essays* (Englewood Cliffs, N. J.: Prentice Hall, 1978); and Richard Pearce, ed., *Critical Essays on Thomas Pynchon* (Boston: G. K. Hall, 1981). Monographs include Kathryn Hume's *Pynchon's Mythography: An Approach to Gravity's Rainbow* (Carbondale: Southern Illinois UP, 1987); articles include those by Chaffee; Eddins; Hite; McHoul. Anticipating my claim about the postmodern historical sublime, Wolfley notes Norman O. Brown's assertion that "the link between the theory of neurosis and the theory of history is the theory of religion" (Wolfley 880).

Three: Cracking the Mirror

1. The sources for this conversation about postmodernism are too numerous to cite here. For good general overviews and discussions of postmodernism in architecture, city planning, and the plastic arts, see Jencks; Bertens 53–81; Harvey 66–98 and Connor 66–102 (two especially good summary discussions); Zukin; Caygill; Rose 101–49; Watson.

2. Soja goes on to define *postfordism* as a second kind of spatialization linked to the fourth modernization of capitalism characterized by Harvey's criteria and "postmodernism" as a third kind of spatialization (overlapping with the other two categories) in which geography increasingly matters as a vantage point of culture ("Postmodern Geographies and the Critique of Historicism" 61–62). The main thrust of Soja's call for a "trialectic" of spatiality, historicity, and sociality as a model for "contextualizing fields of expression" is a call for a critique of historicism. Focusing on public spaces and geography and elaborating upon Foucault's observation that the twentieth century substitutes an epoch of space for a nineteenth-century epic of historicity, Soja argues that our notions of the spatial must evolve from notions of static space and geography to notions of space as a cognitive process (*Postmodern Geographies* 133).

I recommend the discussion by Jones, Natter, and Schatzki, on Karl Mannheim's "Conservative Thought" (1927) as a precursor to postmodernist spatial understanding of history.

3. 225, n. 90. The brackets in the quote are Ankersmit's. Ankersmit's cited source for Stocking is *Victorian Anthropology* (New York: Free Press, 1987); 6.

4. As a marxist, Jameson takes exception to spatial theories of history such as Foucault's, "with its empty rhetoric of cutting, sorting, and modifying, a kind of spatial language in which you organize data like a great block to be chopped up in various ways" (Stephanson 6). Postmodern spatiality is identified by Jameson as an attack upon historicism, not a Foucaultian refocusing of its sights. Discussions of Foucault's work constitute a distinct area of philosophical inquiry and are too numerous to cite here. See White, *Tropics of Discourse* 230–60, for a good overview of Foucault's theories, and D'Hondt for a discussion of "rupture" and history. For discussions of Foucault and history pertinent to my thesis, see Hutton, "Michel Foucault," in *History as an Art of Memory* 107–23; Dews; Docherty, "Criticism, History, Foucault"; and Sax.

5. As Lemert and Gillan note, Foucault "does not replace temporal with spatial analysis. . . . He allows all the many layers of social formation to have their own times. Hence, there can be repetition, return, and discontinuity, just as much as continuity. He, therefore, speaks not of social change, but of transformation. History is not a question of progress, but rearrangements in the relations among the multiple forces—material, economic, social—that comprise a social formation" (12).

6. For excellent discussions of this new inquiry, see Harley, "Deconstructing the Map," "Maps, Knowledge, Power," and "Cartography, Ethics and Social Theory"; Edney; Boelhower; Zukin.

7. For discussions and examples of some of these alternate historical spatial models, see Ermath.

8. See Arnheim, Zoran, Davis for this discussion of spatiality.

9. Among these scholars one might include Charles Altieri, Majorie Perloff, and Jerome Mazzaro. See Connor, 117–31, for a discussion of this type of spatiality in relation to these scholars' works.

10. For a discussion of a different kind of spatialization of narrative, see Friedman's article "Spatialization," on Julia Kristeva's theory of spatialization.

11. *The Widening Gyre* 8–9. See also Frank, "Spatial Form: Some Fur-

ther Reflections," and "Spatial Form: An Answer to Critics," where Frank refines his thesis somewhat.

12. Foust provides a clear discussion of this term (196).

13. For summaries of both positions in this debate, see Smitten; Mickelsen; and Michael Spencer. Smitten and Daghistany, eds. give the most comprehensive bibliography to date of works concerning spatialization.

14. For a sampling of critics who assert the viability of spatial form theory and apply it to new contexts, see Malmgren; Meeter; Du Plessis; Zamora. Smitten and Daghistany's *Spatial Form in Narrative* is an excellent starting point. Zoran has written a fascinating dissection of narrative space as well. Kenshur argues that Frank's spatial form is diametrically opposed to Umberto Eco's notion of the open work (*opera aperta*), challenging my claim that metahistorical romance retains both a spatialized sense of history and a willingness to see history as infinitely open. Most notably, Sharon Spencer has identified what she terms "architectonic novelists" who simulate plastic structures in the reader's imagination by abandoning a controlling authorial voice. The architectonic novel subsumes character development to a focus on narrative structure. In the place of authorial voice, architectonic novelists adopt juxtaposition as an organizing principle. While narration necessarily assumes a linear shape, this juxtaposition abolishes the ideas of a beginning and end, the need for overt transitions, and causality and frees readers to form new relationships between these narrative components (xxi). In "Time Sequence in Spatial Fiction," Vidan investigated whether plot itself could be considered a factor of spatiality (132). Noting that reflexive reference cannot alone create a spatial form, Vidan maintains that spatiality can be achieved in a narrative only if chronology is abandoned. For example, in novels such as *The Sound and the Fury*, the repetition of image patterns or structural parallels is secondary to the suspension of plot development, which significantly contributes to readers' feelings of spatiality and lack of linear progression in the novel. Vidan then presents four kinds of novels which exhibit spatial form; the fourth category overlaps with Sharon Spencer's definition of the *architectonic novel*. Critics who have written against spatial form theory include Frank Kermode ("A Reply to Joseph Frank," *Critical Inquiry* 4, no. 3 [1978]: 579–88); Spanos ("The Detective and the Boundary"); Walter Sutton ("The Literary Image and the Reader: A Consideration of the Theory of Spatial Form," *Journal of Aesthetics and Art Criticism* 16 [1957]: 112–23); and Michael E. Danahy

("A Critique of Recent Spatial Approaches to Flaubert and Related Theory of Fiction," *Nineteenth-Century French Studies* 10, nos. 3–4 [1982]: 301–16).

15. Malmgrem (131–42) specifically links formal parataxis to Dos Passos's work, which he calls *paraspatial*. Malmgrem's astute analysis notes how historical facts in this text increase its intertextuality and make it a "multimodal system."

16. See McHale's characterization of postmodernist fiction as fiction that posits ontological questions (versus modernism, which posited epistemological questions).

17. In relation to this point, see Elias, "Oscar Hijuelos' *The Mambo Kings Play Songs of Love . . .*" for a discussion of White's contention that postmodernist parataxis is 'deconstructionist' and politically threatening to Western metanarratives and his differentiation of a syntactical from a paratactical consciousness. See also Partner for a discussion of White's definition of parataxis.

18. In *Mimesis*, Auerbach discusses parataxis as a rhetorical device in the service of a metaphysical system in narrative from Augustine's writing to the *Chanson de Roland*. He argues that early Christian cultures depended upon parataxis to construct a figure-fulfillment model of history of the kind defined by Hayden White and discussed below in this study. The Christians linked parataxis to a conception of history that was by definition "sublime": history was unknowable to the human mind, outside of time because controlled and overseen by God, who alone was able to "make the connections" (i.e., create a hypotactic, linear narrative of historical progression). Humans were left only with glimpses of the Creator's grand plan; those glimpses were the paratactic fragments of history, that could only be seen *in retrospect* to fit together meaningfully in terms of Christian life.

19. McHale has noted that Fowles foregrounds the temporal distance between the act of narration and the object narrated and that the minimal structure of non-ending destabilizes the ontology of the projected world (94, 110); Waugh contends that Fowles's novel uses the device of authorial intimacy ultimately to *destroy* the illusion of reality (32).

20. See Hutcheon (*Politics* 78–80) for a discussion of postmodernism and historical emplotment. Combining spatial discourse with theories of postmodern subjectivity, Peter Currie argues that a 'non-linear' conception of character has emerged in postmodernism (64). Contrasting *Flaubert's Parrot* to examples of British literary realism, Lee maintains

that while Braithwaite is obsessed about "reading" history through the realist mode, he can't do this because in this narrative world there is no direct correspondence between the written word and 'reality' (38–39). But text and historical record (reality) *do* correspond in their mutual lack of connectives, and there is a realism imbedded in this text's paratactic presentation of history—be it personal or literary history.

21. As noted above, McHale argues that ontological inquiry is the central defining feature of postmodernist narrative. Like other postmodernist texts such as Pynchon's *The Crying of Lot 49* or Calvino's *If on a Winter's Night a Traveler,* Winterson's novel challenges the world at an ontological level, implicitly posing the question, which world is real—the fantastic world of the imagination or the fantastically constructed world of empirical fact?

22. Contrary to what Wesseling asserts in her study of postmodern historical fiction, metahistorical romances may thus rely upon readers' acquaintance with the detective story to defamiliarize the process of historical emplotment. One of the best discussions of postmodernist views of detection can be found in Holquist. He argues that modernist intellectuals attacking rationalism turned both to myth and to the popular genre of the detective story, which reassuringly upheld all that modernist high culture understood as lost and was seeking to reinstate: positivism, scientism, historicism. However, antagonistic to the cultural reassurance earlier provided by the lowbrow detective story model, postmodernist literature reverses modernist strategies and use the detective story to shock readers and interrogate cultural codes (147–48, 155). For other cogent discussions of postmodernism and the detective story, see also Tani; Hutcheon (*A Poetics of Postmodernism*); and Lee, especially her discussion of *Hawksmoor.*

23. Comparing this novel to Lyotard's *The Différend* (1988), Hutcheon writes that the sequentially ordered sections [of both] are equally disrupted by a particularly dense network of interconnections and intertexts, and each enacts, performs, and theorizes "the paradoxes of continuity and disconnection, of totalizing interpretation and the impossibility of final meaning" (*Poetics* 15).

24. See Lee (67–71) for an excellent analysis of this novel.

25. Thus Ackroyd has created what Spanos might call "existence-Art," which "by refusing to resolve discords into the satisfying concordances of a *telos,* constitutes an assault against an *art*-ificialized Nature in behalf of the recovery of its primordial terrors." Writing early in the post-

modernism debates and espousing an existentialist postmodern theory, Spanos claimed that the contemporary writer's most immediate task was "undermining the detective-like expectations of the positivistic mind . . . by evoking rather than purging pity and terror—anxiety" ("The Detective and the Boundary" 167–68).

26. For other discussions of postmodernism and gothicism, see *Modern Gothic,* ed. Sage and Smith, in particular Smith's essay "Postmodernism/Gothicism." He identifies commonalities between the postmodern and the gothic: a quality of indeterminacy; an evocation of epistemological crisis that foregrounds questions of ontology; an aesthetics of the surface; nostalgia/archaism and a focus on history as a "museum of pastness"; pastiche and self-reflexivity; comic effects produced through epistemological uncertainty, that is, "black humor"; attention to the unspeakable, criminal, and excessive; and paranoia as an informing motif.

27. This is a position taken by many Native American writers. As the Cherokee character Maritole notes in Glancy's *Pushing the Bear,* "Bushyhead [the Cherokee preacher] and the white minister who walked with us preached Christ as the corn god, the giver of life, along with Selu. I thought that if any of us made it to the new land, then it must be true. Both Christ and myth. It would take both" (112). Similarly, the medicine man Betonie explains to Tayo in Silko's *Ceremony,* "At one time, the ceremonies as they had been performed were enough for the way the world was then. But after the white people came, elements in the world began to shift; and it became necessary to create new ceremonies. . . . She taught me this above all else: things which don't shift and grow are dead things" (126). See also Vizenor, *Manifest Manners,* for another discussion of the need to combine traditional Native knowledge with the modern.

28. White's figure-fulfillment model of history is a restatement, in another disciplinary context, of Thomas Kuhn's theory of scientific revolution. In *The Structure of Scientific Revolutions,* Kuhn writes that science as progressive, cumulative knowledge with a teleological end never existed and in fact was constructed by science textbooks and other disciplinary mechanisms (138). Kuhn contends that the history of science constructs what is basically a figure-fulfillment model of history, where a later event is recontextualized *in light of consequent historical knowledge* to seem the fulfillment of an earlier historical event. To Kuhn, "progress" is an obvious attribute of science and technology; however, he defines this term carefully within the bounds of scientific inquiry so that progress ex-

cludes *telos*. The implicit or explicit notion which must be discarded is that scientific progress carries society closer to Truth.

29. Significantly, another writer of simultaneous history, Ishmael Reed, noted in an 1978 interview, "I've always been a history buff, yes. Always been fascinated by it—especially the stuff that established historians left out of their work. . . . according to *vodoun,* the past is contemporary. This is an element that many African religions had in common. . . . In *Flight to Canada* I tried to make novelistic use of the concept, though everybody called *anachronism,* after digging back into their literary glossaries. I was trying to work with the old *vodoun* theory of time" (Reed quoted in Domini 35). Reed is correct in his assertion that critics read his works as traditional literary anachronism; for a recent example, see Jacobs, 88–104.

30. See White's "The Culture of Criticism" and Hassan's *The Postmodern Turn* (91–92) for the lists noted here. Another complication of my thesis that must remain unexplored here is Engelberg's distinction (20) between modernist notions of time versus space, as in the following list:

Modernist Space	*Modernist Time*
Contemplative stasis	Action-*durée*
Finite (Schiller's "naive")	Infinite (Schiller's "sentimental")
Objective	Subjective
Conscious	Unconscious
Rational	Irrational
Concrete (Worringer's "Abstraction")	Abstract (Worringer's "Empathy")
Realist	Idealist.

31. Simultaneous histories constructed by metahistorical romance often recall the techniques of surrealism to make this point: dream narrative, collage and frottage, *cadavres-exquis,* a foregrounding of the marvelous or the absurd, and predication on "objective chance" or coincidence. See Roger Shattuck, introduction to Maurice Nadeau, *The History of Surrealism* (Cambridge: Belknap P of Harvard UP, 1989), 9–34.

McHale (90–94) understands the collision of historical worlds that I am calling "simultaneous history" as "creative anachronism": multiple worlds disrupt laws of nature, and mingle natural and supernatural elements. McHale writes that there are specific strategies for constructing/deconstructing space in the Pynchonesque zone of the postmodern historical novel—juxtaposition, interpolation, superimposition, and misattribution; in the paradigmatic zone of *Gravity's Rainbow,* "a large number of fragmentary possible worlds exist in an impossible space" (45). If geographical sites and levels of the Real collide in the postmodernist zone, historical worlds collide in the realm of simultaneous history.

Four: Metamodernity

1. See also Arac xv–xx; Honneth; Best and Kellner, 246–55, 234–36.

2. See, as examples, Habermas, "Neoconservative Culture Criticism in the United States"; Rorty "Cosmopolitanism" and "Habermas and Lyotard"; Cascardi; Bürger; Callinicos, *Against Postmodernism;* Dallmayr; Langford; Nagl; Jay.

3. Ironically, a novel such as Sherwood's—which blatantly falsifies history—was cited by *Publishers Weekly* as one of the twenty best novels of 1993, while Coetzee's *Foe* has been censured by critics because it deviates from social realism. Chapman, for instance, writes, "In a crisis-ridden South Africa . . . it might be necessary to 'shut down' difference and affirm, even dogmatically, certain grand narratives of history" (327). Implied by Sherwood and Chapman is the idea that the project of modernity must be salvaged at all costs—at the cost of historical veracity, at the cost of literary innovation.

4. In an author's note, Sherwood writes: "*Vindication* is a work of fiction. It is based on the life of Mary Wollstonecraft (1759–1797) but there are many deviations in the novel from the actual history of Mary Wollstonecraft and her contemporaries. They were the inspiration thanks to which an imaginative world of its own came into being."

5. For example, as an associate of the Frankfurt School, Habermas takes a position that is almost always congenial, with qualifications, to the marxist positions of Norris and Callinicos and has opposed his own view to that of Derrida, Lyotard, and Foucault.

6. Lyotard continues: "Neither modernity nor so-called postmodernity can be identified and defined as clearly circumscribed historical entities, of which the latter would always come 'after' the former. Rather we have to say that the postmodern is always implied in the modern" (*The Inhuman* 25).

7. For Lash ("Discourse or Figure?" 1988), "the discursive 1) gives priority to words over images; 2) valuates the formal qualities of cultural objects; 3) promulgates a rationalist view of culture; 4) attributes crucial importance to the *meanings* of cultural texts; 5) is a sensibility of the ego

rather that of the id; 6) operates through a distancing of the spectator from the cultural object. The 'figural' in contradistinction: 1) is a visual rather than a literary sensibility; 2) it devalues formalisms and juxtaposes signifiers taken from the banalities of everyday life; 3) it contests rationalist and/or 'didactic' views of culture; 4) it asks not what a cultural text 'means,' but what it 'does'; 5) in Freudian terms it advocates the extension of the primary process into the cultural realm; 6) it operates through the spectator's immersion, the relatively unmediated investment of his/her desire in the cultural object" (313–14).

8. My remark somewhat distorts Lyotard's philosophy for the sake of literary application by accounting for an event's "meaning" by relocating it within discourse. As Readings notes, "Once the postmodern is formally recognizable, it is no longer opening up a hole in representation; rather than testifying to the unpresentable, it will have presented it" (56).

9. For discussions of this novel, see Lee 66–74; Finney 246–49.

10. See Spanos, "De-Struction and the Question of Postmodern Literature," for an early treatment of this link between postmodernism and existential destruction. Early in the postmodernism debates, Palmer argued that postmodernism "means calling into question the Enlightenment's faith in endless progress through scientific rationality," ultimately calling the "will to power" at the heart of technology into question (365).

11. James Baldwin, "Sonny's Blues," *The Heath Anthology of American Literature,* Paul Lauter, gen. ed., 3rd ed. (Boston: Houghton Mifflin, 1998), 2221–243.

Five: Western Modernity versus Postcolonial Metahistory

1. This was actually a central insight of structuralist anthropology, which studied aboriginal cultures and their conceptions of time. Louis Owens, in *Other Destinies,* has noted that *Ceremony* constructs ceremonial, nonlinear time and a "web of meaning" (372), while Jahner argued as early as 1979 that Tayo's personal journey is an "event experience" in which linear, narrative time and mythic, "timeless" time intersect to form a new level of consciousness about the world that gives priority to event structure over temporal sequence (37–39). Arnold has argued that space/time in *Ceremony* is best understood in terms of fractal geometry. Certainly, the spatial history that *Ceremony* constructs is in keeping with a postmodernist spatialization of history and creation of microhistories to replace macrohistory or the belief in "total history." In a different con-

text altogether, but again updating and humanizing Lévi-Strauss's claim, Feldman has noted alternate, non-Western conceptions of time in Anton Shammas's *Arabesques;* she notes that simultaneously with Judeo-Christian, linear time and memory, Shammas constructs circular, arabesque memories that are folkloric in origin but identified with what postmodernism has called *fragments, impressions, mémoires, alternative scripts,* and *petits récits* (378).

2. For discussions of this spatial web of narrative and history in *Ceremony,* see Cousineau, "Leslie Silko's *Ceremony,*" and Fleck's introduction to *Critical Perspectives to Native American Fiction.*

3. As Elam notes, "Rather than simply being opposed to realism (which is, after all, still fiction), romance writes a reality that is *invested by desire*—desire that cannot itself be given 'realist' expression, that remains alien to realism" (155–56).

4. This is the important distinction made by postcolonial critics themselves; see, for example, Appiah's important article that distinguishes between postcolonial and postmodernist literature in this way. Postmodernism to these critics is an insider's game—which, one might add, it is in Lyotard's theory of postmodernity as well. For an insightful discussion of this distinction, see Hutcheon, "Circling the Downspout of Empire."

5. The list of sources pertaining to this distinction or overlap between postmodernism and postcolonialism—or the cultural theories associated with each—is too long to rehearse here. For an introduction to the problem, one might consult Adam and Tiffin, eds., *Past the Last Post;* Jameson and Myoshi, eds., *The Cultures of Globalization;* Ashcroft, Griffiths, and Tiffin, eds., *The Postcolonial Studies Reader,* particularly the essays in pt. 4; Tiffin and Lawson, *De-Scribing Empire;* Ashcroft and Tiffin, *The Empire Writes Back.*

6. The fly in the ointment here is that Silko is a member of a population problematically related to U.S. culture; the Laguna Pueblo Indians, like other Native American populations in the United States, have been under a state of colonial siege since the sixteenth century. Calling the reservation state "postcolonial" is extremely problematic, not only because it forces Native populations into a Western theoretical paradigm they sometimes resist but also because the Bureau of Indian Affairs still oversees U.S. reservations and Indian life, and many Native people feel themselves to be subalterns in a continuing colonial state. Including Silko and other Native American writers as part of the First World is also

problematical; many late twentieth-century Native American writers are U.S. or Canadian citizens, live off reservations, practice Christian or other religions, have gone to major U.S. colleges, and hold teaching positions in U.S. universities, but they often might still personally and culturally identify with traditional (and colonized) tribal communities and values and still are subject to racism in many forms. Many North American Native people consider themselves still to be living in separate nations within the geographical boundaries of the United States, thus making their situation truly a colonial one. This problem of definition shows up in critical analyses of Silko's novel. While Moore, for example, argues that Tayo in *Ceremony* is able to move beyond colonial subjugation, Ruppert has written that *Ceremony* should in fact be understood as a mediational text, one that situates Western and Native American discourses in a dialogical relation to create a "new structures of meaning" (75). Wald contends that the novel, as does all minority literature in the U.S., represents "internal colonialization," a concept derived from vol. 1 of Marx's *Capital.*

One could claim that *Ceremony* is difficult to identify either as a postcolonial or a postmodernist novel. I identify it as a text participating in a postcolonial imaginary and written by an author operating under a colonial state, and I accept the terms about the debate set by Native authors themselves. *Ceremony* resists hegemonic Western historical models and values; it represents one pole on a continuum available to the metahistorical imagination dealing with postcolonial history and politics.

For other discussions of *Ceremony* as a postcolonial text, see Bird's "Towards a Decolonization of the Mind and Text" and Moore's "Myth, History, and Identity in Silko and Young Bear." For good general discussions and examples of Native American literature in the different contexts of postcolonialism, see Emberley's *Thresholds of Difference;* Goldie's *Fear and Temptation;* Tongson-McCall's "The Nether World of Neither World"; Whitt's "Cultural Imperialism and the Marketing of Native America"; and Dirlik's "The Past as Legacy and Project."

7. If the narrator of *The Satanic Verses* is meant to be God, then this is true, for the story does indeed encompass past, present, and future in the timeless time of simultaneous history. Indications that the narrator is God appears on 4, 256, 408. However, equally likely is the narrator as Satan (see 133, 234), the angel Gibreel (112), or Rushdie himself (424, 464).

8. This reading of Rushdie's novel ignores consideration of it as a postcolonial text embodying other sets of resistances and tensions to

Western European post-Enlightenment historical assumptions. As noted in my preface, the scope of the discussion is necessarily limited to "First World" postmodernist historical perspectives. For other perspectives on Rushdie's novel, see Spivak, "Reading *The Satanic Verses*"; Appignanesi and Maitland, eds., *The Rushdie File*.

9. Preface to *The Ice Shirt*. The parenthetical clause here is actually stated as a footnote to the preface.

10. One might compare my evaluation of Vollmann here to that of Conrad by Said in *Culture and Imperialism*: "All Conrad can see is a world totally dominated by the Atlantic West, in which every opposition to the West only confirms the West's wicked power. What Conrad cannot see is an alternative to this cruel tautology" (xviii). This rewriting of the Other's history—so that this history is shown to be irrelevant or irrecoverable to the present—also illustrates Frantz Fanon's major point in *The Wretched of the Earth*: namely, that one of the most effective operations of colonialism is the estrangement of the Other's history and the redefinition of it as important only as it contributes to and illustrates the development of the colonizer's narrative history.

11. When the Canadian government granted territory status to Inuit country—the 730,000 square miles of land renamed Nunavut—on April 1, 1999, Vollmann wrote an article for *Outside* magazine in which he baldly told whites to stay home and not contribute to the spoilage of this territory or its people. Though the article is a moving one and clearly shows Vollmann's love of the region and the Inuit, he sends a weirdly contradictory message: a white man who has won grants for and made much of his career from visiting and writing about the Inuit for a (largely white) U.S. audience, telling that audience to stay away from the territory because they will, essentially, ruin it. Moreover, he writes this message in a magazine devoted to precisely the kind of cultural tourism he denounces. For example, in a sidebar to Vollmann's article, Eric Hansen gives *Outside*'s camp-happy (largely white) readership the skinny on camping, hunting, and travel in the newly created Nunavut, using Vollmann's article as an advertisement for the region (see "Out on the Land: Adventures in Culture for the Icebound," *Outside* 24, no. 7 (1999): 59). After quoting Vollmann on the need for travelers to respect Inuit elders and to be patient with discomfort and high prices, Hansen proceeds to list the region's best outfitters (complete with phone numbers and price-per-person rates) and websites for prospective vacationers. Vollmann may see himself as a sympathetic outsider and protector to the Inuit, but

he has clearly made a pact with the "devil" he attempts to thwart, contributing to the exploitation of Nunavut through the exposure he has given it in his romantic denunciations of its exploitation.

12. Anthony Vindler, *The Architectural Uncanny: Essays in the Modern Unhomely* (Cambridge: MIT P, 1992): 4, as quoted inVan Alphen (199). One might also note, in relation to the Lyotardian figure, Derrida's deconstruction of the relation between center and the margin in *Of Grammatology* (1974) and and *Writing and Difference* (Chicago: U of Chicago P, 1978).

13. Sigmund Freud, "The Uncanny," in *The Standard Edition,* ed. James Strachey (London: Hogarth P, 1974 [1919]); Friedrich Wilhelm Joseph Schelling, *Philosophie der Mythologie* (Darmstadt: Wissenschaftliche Buchgesellschaft, 1966 [1835]); Anthony Vidler, *The Architectural Uncanny: Essays in the Modern Unhomely* (Cambridge: MIT P, 1992); Edmund Burke. Burke's definition of the sublime is important to Van Alphen; while Kant subjectivizes the sublime, Burke externalizes it by placing it in the realm of objects. This externalization is central to Van Alphen's thesis.

As justification for using Van Alphen's work in this much different context, I would cite LaCapra: "Much recent debate in critical theory and historiography is recast if the Holocaust is perceived as at least one more or less repressed divider or traumatic point of rupture between modernism and post-modernism. In this light, the postmodern and the post-Holocaust become mutually intertwined issues that are best addressed in relation to each other. The question to be posed to the postmodern critique of certain presumed modern projects such as totalization and liberation then becomes whether or to what extent various postmodern initiatives constitute symptomatic intensifications of generalized disarray—at most the acting-out of posttraumatic stress—or, serving to some extent as an antidote, . . . further the possibility of counteracting a fatalistic repetition compulsion and thus of responsibly working through problems" (*Representing the Holocaust* 188).

14. For an illuminating account of *anamnesis* in relation to the work of Benjamin, Adorno, and Lyotard and a discussion relevant to my argument here, see the article by Newman.

15. See Young's brilliant analysis of the historical etymology of "hybridity" in *Colonial Desire* 1–28.

16. Beyerman has enunciated a related notion of historical represen-

tation in relation to Ralph Ellison's work and African American modernism. See *Fingering the Jagged Grain,* esp. chap. 1.

17. Much has been published on the relation between deconstruction and postmodernism, which I see as intimately related but also separate inquiries. See Dews, "Writing in the Lifeworld."

18. Of course, the model I am articulating would allow the West to "save itself." I can only say with Jean-Paul Sartre, "You see, I, too, am incapable of ridding myself of subjective illusions; I too, say to you: 'All is lost, unless . . .' As a [American] European, I steal the enemy's book, and out if it I fashion a remedy for Europe" (preface to Fanon, *The Wretched of the Earth* 14).

19. The kind of movement I ascribe here to postmodern history has been mentioned in a different context by Küchler in *Postmodern Gaming,* particularly 89–91. In a third context, Acland writes, "Further, given that so many, worldwide, have lived in circumstances that have ultimately obliged them to leave places of origin (as immigrants, as refugees, etc.), the very idea of 'home' needs to be revised to include the simultaneous making and unmaking of nations and identities. Instead of privileging homelessness, I submit that postcolonial criticism in part must offer some explanation of how places are constructed as homes, however provisional it may be. As [Amin] Maalouf puts it, there is always a question of *appartenance,* of belonging" (123). This applies to the consciousness of the First World as well as for others; moreover, the historical sublime offers precisely this home that is not a home.

20. One might recall here Walter Benjamin's call for a formulation of "the meaning of time in the economy of the moral universe," a conceptual form of time that would articulate an alternative to millennial, bounded, and retributive time and that would take the form of forgiveness ("The Meaning of Time in the Moral Universe," in *Selected Writings,* 286). Benjamin further asserted, "Only that historian will have the gift of fanning the spark of hope in the past who is firmly convinced that *even the dead* will not be safe from the enemy if he wins" ("Theses on the Philosophy of History," sec. 6, p. 255).

21. For a discussion of this idea, see Dryden's illuminating study, *The Form of American Romance.*

22. As a marxist, Césaire railed against capitalism as the catalyst for colonialization and thus the progenitor of colonial abuse. But he also linked the trauma of postcolonial history to the trauma of the Holo-

caust. In 1955, he noted the direct link between the "civilizing" project of Enlightenment modernity, U.S. capitalism, and the atrocities committed by Nazis during World War II. The first contains the seeds of the second, which flourishes through a continuation of colonial economies and hence colonial brutality. This colonial brutality is finally turned back on the colonizer in the form of Nazi terror. To Césaire, it turns the terror it had reserved for the dark peoples of the world back on its own First World agents of destruction and leads them to destroy their own—the other white peoples of Eastern and Western Europe.

23. See Ong 30 ff.

24. Scott's *Redgauntlet* has been particularly provocative for critics interested in history, orality, and romance. See Criscuola; Cullinan; Elam 108–15; and Kerr.

25. My discussion of Scott and orality is indebted to Elam's *Romancing the Postmodern* 54–79.

26. On Scott's contribution to newer foci of historiography, see Phillips; Ferris, esp. 195–236, where she cites Scott's influence on Thierry, Ranke, and Macaulay.

27. On Scott as a transitional figure between "romance" (predicated on orality) and modern realism, see Wilt.

28. See Trela for a discussion of Scott and the English monarchy. Bellamy makes the cogent point that it is precisely when the old Highland culture is no longer seen as a threat to British hegemony that the revival of regionalism takes hold among the Scottish and Irish bourgeoisie, and, ironically, that Scott's regional novels were vital to reconstructing this regionalism *by making the point* that it had disappeared as a real social and political threat (76). See also Trumpener's study of national character in the age of *Waverley.*

29. My comments here are deeply indebted to "Scott and Scotland," Daiches's outstanding essay on Scott and postcolonialism.

30. For a discussion of this tension, see Bellamy.

31. Kerr says that "we must bear in mind that the anglicization of Scotland is more than an issue in regional history, a minor disagreement between Britons. It is a version, writ small, of a larger pattern of exploitation, a movement central to England's relationship with Ireland and Wales, which would occur on a much greater geographical and economic scale in India and Africa. To borrow the phrasing of a recent social-historical account, the deeper historical subtext of the novel is the process of 'internal colonialism'" (3–4). He takes the phrase "internal

colonialism" from Michael Hectare's study of Scottish Highland history, *Internal Colonialism: The Celtic Fringe in British National Development* (Berkeley: U of California P, 1975).

32. One cannot call Scott's vision *postcolonial* without evacuating that term of much of its political import, for Scott clearly sided with colonial progressivism and, as Malzahn has illustrated, portrayed non-European or dark peoples as "unenlightened" and quintessentially Other. Perhaps a better term for Scott's approach would be *politicized regionalism*. Certainly, however, Scott's historical romances question the political and social relation between indigenous and colonizing cultures, a focus that becomes stronger yet, but reversed, in the First World metahistorical romance (reversed because now the colonizer is posing these questions).

33. John Millar, *Observations Concerning the Distinction of Ranks in Society* (1771), as quoted in P. H. Scott, 213.

Six: Coda

1. Critics who have treated Pynchon and Barth together include Karl (chap. 11); Schultz; McHale. Pynchon criticism has become such an industry in the past few decades that I can cite in this chapter but a portion of the articles relevant to Pynchon's work.

2. Virtually all reviews and articles about *The Sot-Weed Factor* comment at some point on how it constructs history as conspiracy. See, for example, Holder, 126–28.

3. *The Sot-Weed Factor* has always prompted critics to note its peculiar embedding of post-1960s attitudes but not necessarily its specific historical references. To McHale, for example, Henry Burlingame is "equipped with a full complement of late-twentieth-century intellectual attitudes and opinions—in cosmology, anthropology, sexuality, and even literary criticism" and writes that Barth "carefully avoids anachronisms of material culture, but seems positively to flaunt anachronisms of *Weltanschauung*" (88). Karl pins down the historical intertext as the 1950s (468); Stark comments on anachronism in the novel (161). Margolies notes Barth's use of alternative histories that depend upon present-day concerns.

4. Rovit notes that "Barth's conscious decision to organize his talents within the circumscribing form of a rigorous parody leads him inevitably to surrender his own moral opportunity to create values. The form which he arbitrarily selects denies him the chance to project his own unique metaphor of existence, and denies his novel the necessary illusion

of engagement in human affairs which it must have in order to live" (122). One might contrast this statement to that of Oedipa Maas in *The Crying of Lot 49*, who asks, "Shall I project a world?"

5. This quote is from McConnell 132. McConnell provides a useful discussion of cosmopsis on 132–37.

6. Commentators on Barth's novel have noted that Ebenezer's family estate in the novel is named Malden and is an inversion—philosophically and politically—of Thoreau's Walden, marked by an "upside-down" initial capital. While the palimpsest for Barth's narrative form here is clearly the eighteenth-century novel, the palimpsest for his philosophical disquisition on modern "Man" seems to be the nineteenth-century transcendentalists, the quintessential philosophers of the sublime, inward-turning vision (best illustrated by Emerson's exclamations about transparent eyeballs). See Malloy for discussion of this eighteenth-century context.

7. In "Is it O.K. To Be a Luddite?," Pynchon writes, "To insist on the miraculous is to deny to the machine at least some of its claims on us, to assert the limited wish that living things, earthly and otherwise, may on occasion become Bad and Big enough to take part in transcendent doings. . . . But if we do insist upon fictional violations of the laws of nature—of space, time, thermodynamics, and the big one, mortality itself—then we risk being judged by the literary mainstream as Insufficiently Serious" (5). Likewise, in "The Deadly Sins/Sloth," Pynchon correlates "sinning against the machine" to freedom.

8. For excellent background on the Transit, see Fernie, "Transits, Travels and Tribulations," pts. 1 and 2.

9. At the time of this writing, *Mason & Dixon* was still relatively new and had not yet generated the massive critical apparatus that it surely will in years to come. An essential starting point for criticism of this novel is the Pynchon-L listserve, particularly "Mass Discussion of *Mason & Dixon*," which provides chapter plot summaries and commentary. List owners are Oliver Xymoron and Murthy Yenamandra, whoever they may be, and the list is located at <http://www.waste.org/pynchon-l>. Of use also is Louis Menand's review, "Entropology" (*New York Review of Books* June 12, 1997, 22–25).

10. It is significant, as Mooney notes in his *Los Angeles Times* review, that the novel is retold by the Rev. Cherrycoke in a succession of afternoons from Advent to Epiphany. Also, Rosenbaum notes that the Line separates two religious states, the Quaker Pennsylvania and the Catholic

Maryland, "two radially different visions of the Incarnation" (2). This is an important point as well, differentiating the territoriality of the Line (and its relation to political power) to the boundary free sky observed by Mason. Boyle, in his *New York Times Book Review* review of Pynchon's novel, writes that "the method is sublime. It allows for the surveyors' story to become an investigation into the order of the universe . . . and yet at the same time to reflect the inadequacy of reason alone to explain the mystery that surrounds us. The haunted world, the suprareal, the ghostly and the impossible have the same valence as the facts of history as we receive them" (9).

11. The idea that maps need to be examined as ideological and cultural constructs rather than accepted as knowledge products of scientific or objective intellectual investigation is central to all of the studies of mapping and cartographic politics emerging since 1985. See, for example, ground-breaking studies by Harley ("Deconstructing the Map" and "Cartography, Ethics and Social Theory"); Monmonier; John B. Friedman; Reitan. For a discussion particularly relevant to the drawing territorial and longitudinal boundaries, see Edney.

Works Cited

Abbott, Edwin A. *Flatland: A Romance of Many Dimensions*. New York: Signet, 1984.

Ackroyd, Peter. *Hawksmoor: A Novel*. New York: Harper, 1985.

———. *Chatterton: A Novel*. New York: Ballantine, 1987.

Acland, Charles. "Hybridity and the Subversion of Frontiers." *The Raft of the Medusa: Five Voices on Colonies, Nations and Histories*. Ed. Jocelyne Doray and Julian Samuel. Montréal: Black Rose Books, 1993. 113–29.

Adam, Ian, and Helen Tiffin. *Past the Last Post: Theorizing Post-Colonialism and Post-Modernism*. Alberta: U of Calgary P, 1990.

Anchor, Robert. "Narrativity and the Transformation of Historical Consciousness." *Clio* 16.2 (1987): 121–37.

Anderson, Perry. "On Emplotment: Two Kinds of Ruin." *Probing the Limits of Representation: Nazism and the "Final Solution."* Ed. Saul Friedlander. Cambridge: Harvard UP, 1992. 54–65.

Ankersmit, F. R. "The Dilemma of Contemporary Anglo-Saxon Philosophy of History." *History and Theory, Beiheft* 25 (1986): 1–27.

———. "Historiography and Postmodernism." *History and Theory* 28, no. 2 (1989): 137–53.

———. *History and Tropology: The Rise and Fall of Metaphor*. Berkeley: U of California P, 1994.

———. *Narrative Logic: A Semantic Analysis of the Historian's Language*. The Hague: Martinus Nijhoff, 1983.

———. "The Origins of Postmodernist Historiography." *Historiography between Modernism and Postmodernism: Contributions to the Methodology of the Historical Research*. Poznań Studies in the Philosophy of the Sciences and the Humanities 41. Ed. Jerzy Topolski. Amsterdam: Rodopi, 1994. 87–119.

Appiah, Kwame Anthony. "Is the Post- in Postmodernism the Post- in Postcolonial?" *Critical Inquiry* 17 (Winter 1991): 336–57.

Appignanesi, Lisa, ed. *Postmodernism: ICA Documents.* London: Free Association Books, 1989.

Appignanesi, Lisa, and S. Maitland, eds. *The Rushdie File.* London: Fourth Estate, 1989.

Apple, Max. *The Propheteers.* New York: Perennial/Harper & Row, 1987.

Appleby, Joyce, Lynn Hunt, and Margaret Jacob. *Telling the Truth about History.* New York: Norton, 1994.

Arac, Jonathan, ed. *Postmodernism and Politics.* Minneapolis: U of Minnesota P, 1986.

Arnold, Ellen L. "An Ear for the Story, An Eye for the Pattern: Rereading *Ceremony.*" *Modern Fiction Studies* 45, no. 1 (1999): 69–92.

Arnheim, Rudolf. "A Stricture on Space and Time." *Critical Inquiry* 4 (1978): 645–55.

Ashcroft, Bill, Gareth Griffiths, and Helen Tiffin. *The Empire Writes Back: Theory and Practice in Post-Colonial Literatures.* London: Routledge, 1989.

———, eds. *The Post-Colonial Studies Reader.* London: Routledge, 1995.

Ashfield, Andrew, and Peter de Bolla, eds. *The Sublime: A Reader in British Eighteenth-century Aesthetic Theory.* Cambridge: Cambridge UP, 1996.

Attridge, Derek, Geoff Bennington, and Robert Young. *Post-Structuralism and the Question of History.* Cambridge: Cambridge UP, 1987.

Auerbach, Erich. *Mimesis: The Representation of Reality in Western Literature.* Trans. Willard R. Trask. Princeton: Princeton UP, 1953.

Bailyn, B. "The Challenge of Modern Historiography." *American Historical Review* 87 (1992): 1–24.

Barnes, Julian. *Flaubert's Parrot.* New York: McGraw-Hill, 1984.

———. *A History of the World in 10 1/2 Chapters.* New York: Vintage International, 1989.

Baron, Salo W. *The Contemporary Relevance of History.* New York: Columbia UP, 1986.

Barth, John. "The Literature of Exhaustion." *The Atlantic* (August 1967): 29–34.

———. *The Sot-Weed Factor.* 1960. Rpt. New York: Bantam/Doubleday, 1967.

Baudrillard, Jean. *The Illusion of the End.* Trans. Chris Turner. Stanford: Stanford UP, 1994.

———. "The Precession of Simulacra." *Art and Text* 11 (1983): 3–47. Rpt. *Art after Modernism: Rethinking Representation.* Ed. Brian Wallis.

New York: New Museum of Contemporary Art; Boston: David R. Godine, 1984. 253–81.

Bauman, Zygmunt. *Intimations of Postmodernity.* London: Routledge, 1992.

Bell, Daniel. *The Coming of Post-Industrial Society.* New York: Basic Books, 1973.

Bell, Madison Smartt. *All Souls' Rising.* New York: Penguin, 1995.

Bellamy, Liz. "Regionalism and Nationalism: Maria Edgeworth, Walter Scott and the Definition of Britishness." *The Regional Novel in Britain and Ireland, 1800–1990.* Ed. K.D.M. Snell. Cambridge: Cambridge UP, 1998. 54–77.

Benjamin, Walter. "The Meaning of Time in the Moral Universe." *Walter Benjamin: Selected Writings, Vol. 1, 1913–1926.* Ed. Marcus Bullock and Michael W. Jennings. Cambridge: Belknap P, Harvard UP, 1996. 286–87.

———. "Theses on the Philosophy of History." *Illuminations.* Ed. Hannah Arendt. Trans. Harry Zohn. New York: Schocken Books, 1968. 253–64.

Bennington, Geoff, and Robert Young. "Introduction: Posing the question." *Post-Structuralism and the Question of History.* Ed. Derek Attridge, Geoff Bennington, and Robert Young. Cambridge: Cambridge UP, 1987. 1–11.

Berger, Thomas. *Little Big Man.* New York: Delta/Seymour Lawrence, 1964.

Berry, Philippa, and Andrew Warnick, eds. *Shadow of Spirit: Postmodernism and Religion.* London: Routledge, 1992.

Bertens, Hans. *The Idea of the Postmodern: A History.* New York: Routledge, 1995.

———. "Postmodern Culture(s)." *Postmodernism and Contemporary Fiction.* Ed. Edmund J. Smyth. London: B. T. Batsford, 1991. 123-37.

Best, Steven, and Douglas Kellner. *Postmodern Theory: Critical Interrogations.* New York: Guilford Press, 1991.

Bezner, Kevin. "An Interview with John Barth." *San Francisco Review of Books* (April 1980): 7–8.

Bird, Gloria. "Towards a Decolonization of Mind and Text I: Leslie Marmon Silko's *Ceremony.*" *Wicazo sa review* 9, no. 2 (1993): 1–8.

Blond, Phillip, ed. *Post-Secular Philosophy: Between philosophy and theology.* London: Routledge, 1998.

Boelhower, William. "Inventing America: A Model of Cartographic Semiosis." *Word and Image* 4.2 (1988): 475–97.

Bogue, Ronald. *Deleuze and Guattari.* New York: Routledge, 1989.

Bosse, Malcolm. *The Vast Memory of Love.* New York: Ticknor and Fields, 1992.

Boyle, T. Coraghessan. "The Great Divide." *New York Times Book Review* (May 18, 1997): 9.

———. *The Road to Wellville.* New York: Viking, 1993.

———. *World's End: A Novel.* New York: Penguin Books, 1987.

Boyne, Roy, and Ali Rattansi. "The Theory and Politics of Postmodernism: By Way of an Introduction." *Postmodernism and Society.* Ed. Roy Boyne and Ali Rattansi. New York: St. Martin's, 1990. 1–45.

Braun, Robert. "The Holocaust and Problems of Historical Representation." *History and Theory* 33, no. 2 (1994): 172–97.

Brown, David. *Walter Scott and the Historical Imagination.* London: Routledge and Kegan Paul, 1979.

Budick, Emily Miller. *Fiction and Historical Consciousness: The American Romance Tradition.* New Haven: Yale UP, 1989.

Bürger, Christa. "Modernity as postmodernity: Jean-François Lyotard." *Modernity and Identity.* Ed. Scott Lash and Jonathan Friedman. Oxford: Blackwell, 1992. 73–93.

Burguière, André. "The Fate of the History of Mentalities in the *Annales.*" *Comparative Studies in Society and History* 24 (1982): 424–37.

Burke, Edmund. *A Philosophical Enquiry into the Origin of Our Ideas of the Sublime and Beautiful.* (1751) Ed. J. T. Boulton. London: Routledge and Kegan Paul, 1958.

———. *Reflections on the Revolution in France.* Ed. J. G. A. Pocock. Indianapolis: Hackett Publishing, 1987 [1790].

Burke, Peter, ed. *New Perspectives on Historical Writing.* University Park: Pennsylvania State UP, 1991.

Byerman, Keith E. *Fingering the Jagged Grain: Tradition and Form in Recent Black Fiction.* Athens: U of Georgia P, 1986.

Callinicos, Alex. *Against Postmodernism: A Marxist Critique.* New York: St. Martin's, 1990.

———. "Reactionary Postmodernism?" *Postmodernism and Society.* Ed. Roy Boyne and Ali Rattansi. New York: St. Martin's, 1990: 97–118.

Calvino, Italo. *Cosmicomics.* Trans. William Weaver. San Diego: Harvest/Harcourt Brace, 1965, 1968.

Carr, David. "Getting the Story Straight: Narrative and Historical Knowledge." *Historiography between Modernism and Postmodernism: Contributions to the Methodology of the Historical Research.* Poznań

Studies in the Philosophy of the Sciences and the Humanities 41. Ed. Jerzy Topolski. Amsterdam: Rodopi, 1994. 119–23.

Carrard, Philippe. "The New History and the Discourse of the Tentative: Le Roy Ladurie's Quotation Marks." *Clio* 15, no. 1 (1985): 1–14.

Carroll, David. "Diachrony and Synchrony in *Histoire*." *Modern Language Notes* 92, no. 4 (1977): 797–824.

Cascardi, Anthony J. "History, Theory, (Post)Modernity." *Ethics/Aesthetics: Post-Modern Positions.* Ed. Robert Merrill. Washington, D.C.: Maisonneuve Press, 1988. 27–45.

Caygill, Howard. "Architectural Postmodernism: The Retreat of an Avante-Garde?" *Postmodernism and Society.* Ed. Roy Boyne and Ali Rattansi. New York: St. Martin's, 1990. 260–89.

Césaire, Aimé. *Discourse on Colonialism.* New York: Monthly Review Press, 1972. Rpt. of *Discours sur le colonialisme.* Editions Presence Africaine, 1955.

Chabot, C. Barry. "The Problem of the Postmodern." *Zeitgeist in Babel: The Post-Modernist Controversy.* Ed. Ingeborg Hoesterev. Bloomington: Indiana UP, 1991. 22–39.

Chaffee, Patricia. "The Whale and the Rocket: Technology as Sacred Symbol." *Renascence* 32 (1980): 146–51.

Chapman, Michael. "The Writing of Politics and the Politics of Writing: On Reading Dovey on Reading Lacan on Reading Coetzee on Reading . . ." *Journal of Literary Studies* (Pretoria, South Africa) 4 (1988): 327–41.

Clery, E. J. "The Pleasure of Terror: Paradox in Edmund Burke's Theory of the Sublime." *Pleasure in the Eighteenth Century.* Ed. Roy Porter and Marie Mulvey Roberts. Washington Square: New York UP, 1996. 164–81, 250–51.

Coetzee, J. M. *Foe.* New York: Penguin, 1986.

Coover, Robert. *The Public Burning.* New York: Bantam/Viking, 1976.

Connor, Steve. *Postmodernist Culture: An Introduction to Theories of the Contemporary.* Oxford: Basil Blackwell, 1989.

Cooke, Philip. *Back to the Future: Modernity, Postmodernity and Locality.* London: Unwin Hyman, 1990.

Cousineau, Diane. "Leslie Silko's *Ceremony:* The Spiderweb as Text." *Revue Française d'Études Américaines* 15, no. 43 (1990): 19–31.

Cowart, David. *History and the Contemporary Novel.* Carbondale: Southern Illinois UP, 1989.

Crace, Jim. *Quarantine.* New York: Farrar, Straus and Giroux, 1998.

Criscuola, Margaret M. "Constancy and Change: The Process of History in Scott's *Redgauntlet.*" *Studies in Scottish Literature* 10 (1985): 123–36.

Crowther, Paul. *Critical Aesthetics and Postmodernism.* Oxford: Clarendon P, 1993.

Cullinan, Mary. "History and Language in Scott's *Redgauntlet.*" *Studies in English Literature* 18 (1978): 659–75.

Currie, Peter. "The Eccentric Self: Anti-Characterization and the Problem of the Subject in American Postmodernist Fiction." *Contemporary American Fiction.* Ed. Malcolm Bradbury and Sigmund Ro. London: Edward Arnold, 1987. 53–69.

Daiches, David. "Scott and Scotland." *Scott Bicentenary Essays: Selected Papers Read at the Sir Walter Scott Bicentenary Conference.* Ed. Alan Bell. New York: Harper and Row/Barnes and Noble Books, 1971. 38–60.

————. "Sir Walter Scott and History." *Etudes Anglais* 24 (1971): 458–71.

Dainotto, Roberta Maria. "The Excremental Sublime: The Postmodern Literature of Blockage and Release." *Essays in Postmodern Culture.* Ed. Eyal Amiran and John Unsworth. New York: Oxford UP, 1994. 133–72.

Dallmayr, Fred. "Modernity in the Crossfire: Comments on the Postmodern Turn." *Postmodern Contentions: Epochs, Politics, Space.* Ed. John Paul Jones III, Wolfgang Natter, and Theodore R. Schatzki. New York: Guilford Press, 1993. 17–38.

Davis, Nick. "Narrative Composition and the Spatial Memory." *Narrative: From Malory to Motion Pictures.* Ed. Jeremy Hawthorn. London: Arnold, 1985.

Deane, Seamus. *Strange Country: Modernity and Nationhood in Irish Writing since 1790.* Oxford: Clarendon P, 1997.

de Certeau, Michel. *The Writing of History.* Trans. Tom Conley. New York: Columbia UP, 1988.

De Kretser, Michelle. *The Rose Grower.* New York: Carroll and Graf, 2000.

Dekker, George. *The American Historical Romance.* Cambridge: Cambridge UP, 1987.

Dews, Peter. "Foucault and the French Tradition of Historical Epistemology." *History of European Ideas* 14, no. 3 (1992): 347–63.

————. "Writing in the Lifeworld: Deconstruction as Paradigm of a Transition to Postmodernity." *Postmodernism and the Re-reading of Modernity.* Ed. Francis Barker, Peter Hulme and Margaret Iversen. Manchester: Manchester UP; New York: St. Martin's, 1992. 274–300.

D'Hondt, Jacques. "On Rupture and Destruction in History." *Clio* 15.4 (1986): 345–58.

Dickens, David R., and Andrea Fontana, eds. *Postmodernism & Social Inquiry.* New York: Guilford Press, 1994.

di Lampedusa, Giuseppe. *The Leopard* (Il Gattopardo). Trans. Archibald Colquhoun. New York: Signet Books, 1961.

Dirlik, Arif. "The Past as Legacy and Project: Postcolonial Criticism in the Perspective of Indigenous Historicism." *American Indian Culture and Research Journal* 20, no. 2 (1996): 1–31.

Doan, Laura. *The Lesbian Postmodern.* New York: Columbia UP, 1994.

Docherty, Thomas. "Authority, History and the Question of Postmodernism." *What Is an Author?* Ed. Maurice Biriotti and Nicola Miller. Manchester: Manchester UP, 1993. 53–71.

Doctorow, E. L. "Criticism, History, Foucault." *History of European Ideas* 14.3 (1992): 365–78.

———. *Ragtime.* New York: Random House, 1974.

Domanska, Ewa. *Encounters: Philosophy of History After Postmodernism.* Charlottesville: UP of Virginia, 1998.

———. "Hayden White: Beyond Irony." *History and Theory* 37, no. 2 (1998): 173–81.

Domini, John. "Ishmael Reed: A Conversation with John Domini." *American Poetry Review* 7 (1978): 32–36.

Dos Passos, John. *The 42nd Parallel.* New York: Modern Library, 1930 [1937].

Dray, W. H. "On the Nature and Role of Narrative in Historiography." *History and Theory* 10, no. 2 (1971): 153–71.

Dryden, Edgar A. *The Form of American Romance.* Baltimore: The Johns Hopkins UP, 1988.

Dunn, Robert G. *Identity Crisis: A Social Critique of Postmodernity.* Minneapolis: U of Minnesota P, 1998.

Du Plessis, Michael. "Space, Story and History: Reading Gold Reef City." *English Studies in Africa* 30, no. 2 (1987): 105–12.

Eddins, Dwight. "Orphic contra Gnostic: Religious Conflict in *Gravity's Rainbow.*" *Modern Language Quarterly* 45 (1984): 163–90.

Edney, Matthew H. "Cartographic Culture and Nationalism in the Early United States: Benjamin Vaughan and the Choice for a Prime Meridian, 1811." *Journal of Historical Geography* 20, no. 4 (1994): 384–95.

Elam, Diane. *Romancing the Postmodern.* London: Routledge, 1992.

Elias, Amy J. "Oscar Hijuelos' *The Mambo Kings Play Songs of Love,* Ishmael Reed's *Mumbo Jumbo,* and Robert Coover's *The Public Burning." Critique* 41.2 (2000): 115–28.

Ellison, Ralph. *Invisible Man.* New York: Vintage Books, 1972 (1947).

Emberley, Julia. *Thresholds of Difference: Feminist Critique, Native Women's Writings, Postcolonial Theory.* Toronto: U of Toronto P, 1993.

Engelberg, Edward. "Space, Time, and History: Towards the Discrimination of Modernisms." *Modernist Studies: Literature & Culture 1920–1940* 1, no. 1 (1974): 7–26.

Engström, Timothy H. "The Postmodern Sublime?: Philosophical Rehabilitations and Pragmatic Evasions." *boundary 2* 20, no. 2 (1993): 190–204.

Erickson, Steve. *Arc d'X.* New York: Poseidon, 1993.

Ermath, Elizabeth Deeds. *Sequel to History: Postmodernism and the Crisis of Representational Time.* New Jersey: Princeton UP, 1992.

Fanon, Frantz. *The Wretched of the Earth.* Trans. Constance Farrington. Harmondsworth, Middlesex: Penguin, 1961.

Featherstone, Mike. *Consumer Culture and Postmodernism.* London: Sage, 1991.

Felder, Lynn. "D. M. Thomas: The Plagiarism Controversy." *Dictionary of Literary Biography Yearbook 1982.* 79–82.

Feldman, Yael S. "Postcolonial Memory, Postmodern Intertextuality: Anton Shammas's *Arabesques* Revisited." *PMLA* 114, no. 3 (1999): 373–89.

Fell, Alison. *The Pillow Boy of the Lady Onogoro.* New York: Harcourt Brace, 1996.

Felperin, Howard. "'Cultural Poetics' versus 'Cultural Materialism': The Two New Historicisms in Renaissance Studies." *Uses of History: Marxism, Postmodernism and the Renaissance.* Ed. Francis Barker, Peter Hulme and Margaret Iversen. Manchester: Manchester UP; New York: St. Martin's, 1991. 76–100.

Ferguson, Frances. "The Sublime of Edmund Burke, or the Bathos of Experience." *Glyph* 8 (1981): 62–78.

Ferguson, Russell, William Olander, Marcia Tucker, and Karen Fiss, eds. *Discourses: Conversations in Postmodern Art and Culture.* New York: New Museum of Contemporary Art; Cambridge: MIT P, 1990.

Fernie, J. Donald. "Transits, Travels and Tribulations I." *American Scientist* 85 (1997): 120–22.

———. "Transits, Travels and Tribulations II." *American Scientist* 85 (1997): 418–21.

Ferris, Ina. *The Achievement of Literary Authority: Gender, History, and the Waverley Novels*. Ithaca: Cornell UP, 1991.

Fiedler, Leslie A. "The New Mutants." *Partisan Review* 32, no. 4 (1965): 505–25.

Fielding, Penny. *Writing and Orality: Nationality, Culture, and Nineteenth-Century Scottish Fiction*. Oxford: Clarendon P, 1996.

Findley, Timothy. *Famous Last Words*. London: Arena, 1981, 1987.

Finney, Brian. "Peter Ackroyd, Postmodernist Play and *Chatterton*." *Twentieth Century Literature* 38, no. 2 (1992): 240–61.

Finney, Jack. *Time and Again*. New York: Simon and Schuster, 1970.

Fleck, Richard F., ed. *Critical Perspectives on Native American Fiction*. Washington, D.C.: Three Continents Press, 1993.

Fleishman, Avrom. *The English Historical Novel: Walter Scott to Virginia Woolf*. Baltimore: The Johns Hopkins UP, 1971.

Foley, Barbara. *Telling the Truth: The Theory and Practice of Documentary Fiction*. Ithaca: Cornell UP, 1986.

———. "From *U.S.A.* to *Ragtime*: Notes on the Forms of Historical Consciousness in Modern Fiction." *E. L. Doctorow: Essays and Conversations*. Ed. Richard Trenner. Princeton: Ontario Review P, 1983. 158–78.

Forbes, Duncan. "The Rationalism of Sir Walter Scott." *Cambridge Journal* 7 (1953): 20–35.

Foster, Hal, ed. *The Anti-Aesthetic: Essays on Postmodern Culture*. Port Townsend, Wash.: Bay P, 1983.

Foucault, Michel. "Nietzsche, Genealogy, History." *Language, Counter-Memory, Practice*. Ed. Donald F. Bouchard. Trans. Donald F. Bouchard and Sherry Simon. Ithaca: Cornell UP, 1977. 139–64.

———. *The Archeology of Knowledge and the Discourse on Language*. Trans. A. M. Sheridan Smith. New York: Pantheon Books, 1972.

Foust, Ronald. "The Aporia of Recent Criticism and the Contemporary Significance of Spatial Form." *Spatial Form in Narrative*. Ed. Jeffrey R. Smitten and Ann Daghistany. Ithaca: Cornell UP, 1981. 179–201.

Fowles, John. *The French Lieutenant's Woman*. New York: New American Library, 1969.

———. *A Maggot*. New York: New American Library, 1985.

Frampton, Kenneth. "Towards a Critical Regionalism: Six Points for an Architecture of Resistance." *The Anti-Aesthetic: Essays on Postmodern Culture*. Ed. Hal Foster. Port Townsend, Wash.: Bay P, 1983. 16–30.

Frank, Joseph. "Spatial Form in Modern Literature." *Sewanee Review* (1945): 221–40, 433–56, 643–53. Expanded and reprinted in *The*

Widening Gyre: Crisis and Mastery in Modern Literature. Bloomington: Indiana UP, 1963.

———. "Spatial Form: An Answer to Critics." *Critical Inquiry* 4, no. 2 (1977): 231–52.

———. "Spatial Form: Some Further Reflections." *Critical Inquiry* 5, no. 2 (1978): 275–90.

Frazier, Charles. *Cold Mountain.* New York: Atlantic Monthly P, 1997.

Friedman, John B. "Cultural Conflicts in Medieval World Maps." *Implicit Understandings: Observing, Reporting, and Reflecting on the Encounters between Europeans and Other Peoples in the Early Modern Era.* Ed. Stuart B. Schwartz. New York: Cambridge UP, 1994. 64–95.

Friedman, Susan Stanford. "Spatialization: A Strategy for Reading Narrative." *Narrative* 1, no. 1 (1993): 12–23.

Fukuyama, Francis. *The End of History and the Last Man.* New York: Avon Books, 1992.

Funkenstein, Amos. "History, Counterhistory, and Narrative." *Probing the Limits of Representation: Nazism and the "Final Solution."* Ed. Saul Friedlander. Cambridge: Harvard UP, 1992. 66–81.

Furet, François. *In the Workshop of History.* Trans. Jonathan Mandelbaum. Chicago: U of Chicago P, 1984.

Furniss, Tom. *Edmund Burke's Aesthetic Ideology: Language, Gender, and Political Economy in Revolution.* Cambridge: Cambridge UP, 1993.

Frye, Northrop. *The Secular Scripture: A Study of the Structure of Romance.* Cambridge: Harvard UP, 1976.

Garside, P. D. "Scott and the 'Philosophical' Historians." *Journal of the History of Ideas* 30 (1975): 497–512.

Gates, Henry Louis. *The Signifying Monkey: A Theory of African-American Literary Criticism.* New York: Oxford UP, 1988.

Glancy, Diane. *Pushing the Bear: A Novel of the Trail of Tears.* New York: Harcourt Brace and Company, 1996.

Goldie, Terry. *Fear and Temptation: The Image of the Indigene in Canadian, Australian, and New Zealand Literatures.* Kingston: McGill-Queen's UP, 1989.

Goodman, David. "Postmodernism and History." *Australasian Journal of American Studies* 10, no. 1 (1991): 11–15.

Gossman, Lionel. *Between History and Literature.* Cambridge: Harvard UP, 1990.

Graff, Gerald. "The Myth of the Postmodernist Breakthrough." *TriQuarterly* 26 (1973): 383–417.

Grass, Günter. *The Flounder.* Trans. R. M. Hermann Luchterhand Verlag, 1977. New York: Harcourt Brace Jovanovich, 1978.

Groden, Michael, and Martin Kreiswirth, eds. *The Johns Hopkins Guide to Literary Theory and Criticism.* Baltimore: Johns Hopkins UP, 1994.

Habermas, Jürgen. "Neoconservative Culture Criticism in the United States and West Germany: An Intellectual Movement in Two Political Cultures." *Habermas and Modernity.* Ed. Richard J. Bernstein. Cambridge: MIT P, 1985. 78–94.

———. "Modernity—An Incomplete Project." *New German Critique* 22 (Winter 1981). Rpt. *The Anti-Aesthetic: Essays on Postmodern Culture.* Ed. Hal Foster. Port Townsend, Wash.: Bay P, 1983. 3–15.

Hansen, Eric. "Out on the Land: Adventures in Culture for the Icebound." *Outside* 24, no. 7 (1999): 59.

Haraway, Donna. "A Manifesto for Cyborgs: Science, Technology, and Socialist Feminism in the 1980s." *Socialist Review* 80 (1985). Rpt. *Feminism/Postmodernism.* Ed. Linda J. Nicholson. New York: Routledge, 1990. 190–233.

———. *Simians, Cyborgs, and Women: The Reinvention of Nature.* New York: Routledge, 1991.

Harkin, Patricia. "Romance and Real History: The Historical Novel as Literary Innovation." *Scott and His Influence: The Papers of the Aberdeen Scott Conference, 1982.* Aberdeen: Association for Scottish Literary Studies, 1983. 157–68.

Harley, J. B. "Cartography, Ethics and Social Theory." *Cartographica* 27, no. 2 (Summer 1990): 1–23.

———. "Deconstructing the Map." *Cartographica* 26, no. 2 (Summer 1989): 1–20.

———. "Maps, Knowledge, and Power." *The Iconography of Landscape: Essays on the Symbolic Representation, Design and Use of Past Environments.* Ed. Denis Cosgrove and Stephen Daniels. Cambridge: Cambridge UP, 1988. 277–312.

Harvey, David. *The Condition of Postmodernity: An Enquiry into the Origins of Cultural Change.* Oxford: Basil Blackwell, 1989.

Hassan, Ihab. *The Postmodern Turn: Essays in Postmodern Theory and Culture.* Columbus, OH: Ohio State UP, 1987.

———. "Pluralism in Postmodern Perspective." *Critical Inquiry* 12, no. 3 (1986). Rpt. in *Exploring Postmodernism: Selected Papers Presented at a Workshop on Postmodernism at the XIth International Comparative*

Literature Congress, Paris, 20–24 August 1985. Ed. Matei Calinescu and Douwe Fokkema. Amsterdam: John Benjamins, 1987.

Hayles, N. Katherine. *Chaos Bound: Orderly Disorder in Contemporary Literature and Science.* Ithaca: Cornell UP, 1990.

Hebdige, Dick. "The Impossible Object: Towards a Sociology of the Sublime." *New Formations* 1 (1987): 47–76.

Heehs, Peter. "Myth, History, and Theory." *History and Theory* 33, no. 1 (1994): 1–19.

Henderson, Harry. *Versions of the Past: The Historical Imagination in American Fiction.* New York: Oxford UP, 1974.

Hertz, Neil. "The Notion of Blockage in the Literature of the Sublime." *Psychoanalysis and the Question of the Text.* Ed. Geoffrey H. Hartman. Baltimore: Johns Hopkins UP, 1978.

Hirsch, Marianne. *Family Frames: Photography, Narrative, Postmemory.* Cambridge: Harvard UP, 1997.

Hite, Molly. "Holy-Center-Approaching in the Novels of Thomas Pynchon." *Journal of Narrative Technique* 12, no. 2 (1982): 121–29.

Holder, Alan. " 'What Marvelous Plot . . . Was Afoot?': John Barth's *The Sot-Weed Factor.*" *Critical Essays on John Barth.* Ed. Joseph J. Waldmeir. Boston: G. K. Hall, 1980. 123–33.

Holquist, Michael. "Whodunit and Other Questions: Metaphysical Detective Stories in Post-War Fiction." *New Literary History* 3, no. 1 (1971): 135–56.

Holton, Robert. *Jarring Witnessees: Modern Fiction and the Representation of History.* New York: Harvester Wheatsheaf, 1994.

Honneth, Axel. "An Aversion Against the Universal." *Theory, Culture, and Society* 2, no. 3 (1985): 147–57.

Howard, Jean E. "Towards a Postmodern, Politically Committed, Historical Practice." *Uses of History: Marxism, Postmodernism and the Renaissance.* Ed. Francis Barker, Peter Hulme, and Margaret Iversen. Manchester: Manchester UP; New York: St. Martin's, 1991. 101–22.

Howe, Irving. "Mass Society and Post-Modern Fiction." *Partisan Review* 26, no. 3 (1959): 420–36.

Hughes, Peter. "Narrative, Scene, and the Fictions of History." *SPELL: Swiss Papers in English Language and Literature.* Germany: Gunter Narr Verlag Tübingen, 1984.

Hutcheon, Linda. "Circling the Downspout of Empire." *Past the Last Post: Theorizing Post-Colonialism and Post-Modernism.* Ed. Ian Adam and Helen Tiffin. Calgary: U of Calgary P, 1990. 167–89.

————. *A Poetics of Postmodernism: History, Theory, Fiction*. New York: Routledge, 1988.

————. *The Politics of Postmodernism*. London: Routledge, 1989.

Hutton, Patrick H. *History as an Art of Memory*. Hanover: UP of New England, 1993.

Huyssen, Andreas. *After the Great Divide: Modernism, Mass Culture, Postmodernism*. Bloomington: Indiana UP, 1986.

Ibsch, Elrud. "Historical Changes of the Function of Spatial Description in Literary Texts." *Poetics Today* 3, no. 4 (1982): 97–113.

Iggers, Georg. *Historiography in the Twentieth Century: From Scientific Objectivity to the Postmodern Challenge*. Hanover, N.H.: Wesleyan UP, 1997.

Ingram, David. "The Postmodern Kantianism of Arendt and Lyotard." *Review of Metaphysics* 42 (1988): 51–77.

Iser, Wolfgang. *The Implied Reader: Patterns of Communication in Prose Fiction from Bunyon to Beckett*. Baltimore: The Johns Hopkins UP, 1978.

Jacobs, Naomi. *The Character of Truth: Historical Figures in Contemporary Fiction*. Carbondale: Southern Illinois UP, 1990.

Jacques, T. Carlos. "The Primacy of Narrative in Historical Understanding." *Clio* 19, no. 3 (1990): 197–214.

Jahner, Elaine. "An Act of Attention: Event Structure in *Ceremony*." *American Indian Quarterly* 5, no. 1 (1979): 37–46.

Jameson, Fredric. "Third-World Literature in the Era of Multinational Capitalism." *Social Text* 15 (1986): 65–88.

————. *The Political Unconscious: Narrative as a Socially Symbolic Act*. Ithaca: Cornell UP, 1981.

————. *Postmodernism, or, The Cultural Logic of Late Capitalism*. Durham: Duke UP, 1991.

————. "Postmodernism, or, The Cultural Logic of Late Capitalism." *New Left Review* 146 (1984): 53–93.

————. "Postmodernism and Consumer Society." *The Anti-Aesthetic: Essays on Postmodern Culture*. Ed. Hal Foster. Port Townsend, Wash.: Bay P, 1983. 111–25.

Jameson, Fredric, and Masao Miyoshi, eds. *The Cultures of Globalization*. Durham: Duke UP, 1998.

Jay, Martin. "Habermas and Modernism." *Habermas and Modernity*. Ed. Richard J. Bernstein. Cambridge: MIT P, 1985. 125–39.

Jencks, Charles. *Post-modernism: The New Classicism in Art and Architecture*. London: Academy, 1987.

Jenkins, Keith. *On "What Is History?": From Carr and Elton to Rorty and White.* London: Routledge, 1995.

———. *Re-thinking History.* New York: Routledge, 1992.

Johnson, Charles. *Dreamer.* New York: Simon and Schuster, 1998.

———. *Middle Passage.* New York: Plume/Penguin, 1990.

Johnston, John. "Postmodern Theory/Postmodern Fiction." *Clio* 16, no. 2 (1987): 139–58.

Jones, John Paul III, Wolfgang Natter, and Theodore R. Schatzki. " 'Post'-ing Modernity." *Postmodern Contentions: Epochs, Politics, Space.* Ed. John Paul Jones III et al. New York: Guilford Press, 1993. 1–16.

Karl, Frederick R. *American Fictions, 1940/1980.* New York: Harper and Row, 1983.

Kellner, Hans. "Twenty Years After: A Note on Metahistories and Their Horizons." *Storia della Storiografia* 24 (1993): 109–17.

———. "A Bedrock of Order: Hayden White's Linguistic Humanism." *History and Theory, Beiheft* (1980): 1–29.

———. *Language and Historical Representation: Getting the Story Crooked.* Madison: U of Wisconsin P, 1989.

———. " 'Never Again' is Now." *History and Theory* 33, no. 2 (1994): 127–44.

Kenshur, Oscar S. "Fragments and Order: Two Modern Theories of Discontinuous Form." *Papers on Language and Literature* 17, no. 3 (1981): 227–44.

Kerr, James. *Fiction against History: Scott as Storyteller.* Cambridge: Cambridge UP, 1989.

Kroker, Arthur, and David Cook. *The Postmodern Scene: Excremental Culture and Hyper-Aesthetics.* New York: St. Martin's, 1988.

Küchler, Tilman. *Postmodern Gaming: Heidegger, Duchamp, Derrida.* New York: Peter Lang, 1994.

Kuhn, Thomas. *The Structure of Scientific Revolutions.* 2nd ed. Chicago: U of Chicago P, 1970.

Kurzweil, Allen. *A Case of Curiosities.* New York: Ballantine, 1992.

LaCapra, Dominick. *History, Politics, and the Novel.* Ithaca: Cornell UP, 1987.

———. *Representing the Holocaust: History, Theory, Trauma.* Ithaca: Cornell UP, 1994.

Lacoue-Labarthe, Philippe. "On the Sublime." *Postmodernism: ICA Documents.* Ed. Lisa Appignanesi. London: Free Association Books, 1986. 11–18.

Lampkin, Loretta M. "An Interview with John Barth." *Contemporary Literature* 29, no. 4 (1988): 485–97.

Lang, Berel. "Is It Possible to Misrepresent the Holocaust?" *History and Theory* 34, no. 1 (1995): 84–89.

———. "Nostalgia for the Future, Waiting for the Past: Postmodernism in Philosophy." *Studies in Historical Change*. Ed. Ralph Cohen. Charlottesville: UP of Virginia, 1992. 306–22.

Langford, Larry L. "Postmodernism and Enlightenment, Or, Why Not a Fascist Aesthetics?" *SubStance* 67 (1992): 24–43.

Lash, Scott. "Discourse or Figure? Postmodernism as a 'Regime of Signification.'" *Theory, Culture & Society* 5 (1988): 311–36.

———. *Sociology of Postmodernism*. New York: Routledge, 1990.

Lash, Scott, and Jonathan Friedman. "Introduction: Subjectivity and Modernity's Other." *Modernity & Identity*. Ed. Scott Lash and Jonathan Friedman. Oxford: Blackwell, 1992. 1–30.

———. *Modernity & Identity*. Oxford: Blackwell, 1992.

Le Goff, Jacques. *History and Memory*. Trans. Steven Rendall and Elizabeth Claman. New York: Columbia UP, 1992.

Lee, Alison. *Realism and Power: Postmodern British Fiction*. London: Routledge, 1990.

Leisey, Ernest. *The American Historical Novel*. Norman: U of Oklahoma P, 1950.

Lemert, Charles C., and Garth Gillan. *Michel Foucault: Social Theory and Transgression*. New York: Columbia UP, 1982.

Levin, David. *In Defense of Historical Literature: Essays on American History, Autobiography, Drama, and Fiction*. New York: Hill and Wang, 1967.

Lindenberger, Herbert. *The History in Literature: On Value, Genre, Institutions*. New York: Columbia UP, 1990.

Lloyd, David. "Arnold Ferguson, Schiller: Aesthetic Culture and the Politics of Aesthetics." *Cultural Critique* 2 (1985–1986): 139–52.

Lodge, David. *The Modes of Modern Writing: Metaphor, Metonymy, and The Topology of Literature*. London: Edward Arnold, 1977.

Lukács, Georg. *The Historical Novel*. Trans. Hannah and Stanley Mitchell. Lincoln: U of Nebraska P, 1962, 1983.

Lyotard, Jean-François. "Complexity and the Sublime." *Postmodernism: ICA Documents*. Ed. Lisa Appignanesi. London: Free Association Books, 1989. 19–26.

———. *The Differend: Phrases in Dispute*. Trans. G. Van den Abbeele. Minneapolis: U of Minnesota P, 1983, 1988.

————. *Discours, figure.* Paris: Klincksieck, 1971.

————. *The Inhuman: Reflections on Time.* Trans. Geoffrey Bennington and Rachel Bowlby. Stanford: Stanford UP, 1991.

————. *Lessons on the Analytic of the Sublime.* Trans. Elizabeth Rottenberg. Stanford: Stanford UP, 1994.

————. *The Postmodern Condition: A Report on Knowledge.* Trans. Geoff Bennington and Brian Massumi. Minneapolis: U of Minnesota P, 1984.

————. *The Postmodern Explained.* Trans. Don Barry et al. Minneapolis: U of Minnesota P, 1992.

————. "After the Sublime: The State of Aesthetics." *The States of 'Theory': History, Art, and Critical Discourse.* Ed. David Carroll. Stanford: Stanford UP, 1990. 297–304.

MacHardy, Karin J. "Crises in History, or Hermes Unbounded." *Storia della Storiografia* 187 (1990): 5–27.

Macaskill, Brian, and Jeanne Colleran. "Reading History, Writing Heresy: The Resistance of Representation and the Representation of Resistance in J. M. Coetzee's *Foe.*" *Contemporary Literature* 33, no. 3 (1992): 432–57.

Madison, G.B. *The Hermeneutics of Postmodernity: Figures and Themes.* Bloomington: Indiana UP, 1990.

Makaryk, Irena R., gen. ed. *Encyclopedia of Contemporary Literary Theory: Approaches, Scholars, Terms.* Toronto: U of Toronto P, 1993.

Malloy, Jeanne M. "William Byrd's Histories and John Barth's *The Sot-Weed Factor.*" *Mississippi Quarterly* 42, no. 2 (1989): 161–72.

Malmgren, Carl Darryl. *Fictional Space in the Modernist and Postmodernist American Novel.* Lewisburg, PA: Bucknell UP, 1985.

Malzahn, Manfred. "Exorcising the Past: Scottish Gentlemen and Gentleman Savages." *Scott Newsletter* 29–30 (1996-1997): 1–13.

Manzoni, Alessandro. *On the Historical Novel.* Trans. Sandra Bermann. Lincoln: U of Nebraska P, 1984.

Marcus, Greil. *Lipstick Traces: A Secret History of the Twentieth Century.* Cambridge: Harvard UP, 1989.

Margolies, Edward. "John Barth and the Barbarities of History." *American Literature in Belgium.* Ed. Gilbert Debusscher. Amsterdam: Rodopi, 1988. 205–11.

Marwick, Arthur. "Two Approaches to Historical Study: The Metaphysical (Including 'Postmodernism') and the Historical." *Journal of Contemporary History* 30 (1995): 5–35.

Mathy, Jean-Philippe. "Out of History: French Readings of Postmodern America." *American Literary History* 2, no. 2 (Summer 1990): 267–98.

McCaffery, Larry, ed. *Postmodern Fiction: A Bio-bibliographical Guide.* New York: Greenwood P, 1986.

McClure, John A. "Postmodern/Post-Secular: Contemporary Fiction and Spirituality." *Modern Fiction Studies* 41, no. 1 (1995): 141–63.

McCullagh, C. Behan. "Metaphor and Truth in History." *Clio* 23, no. 1 (1993): 23–49.

McGowan, John. *Postmodernism and Its Critics.* Ithaca: Cornell UP, 1991.

McHale, Brian. *Postmodernist Fiction.* New York: Methuen, 1987.

McHoul, Alec. "Labyrinths: Writing Radical Hermeneutics and the Post-ethical." *Philosophy Today* 31 (1987): 211–22.

McMaster, Graham. *Scott and Society.* Cambridge: Cambridge UP, 1981.

McRae, Murdo William. "Stephen Jay Gould and the Contingent Nature of History." *Clio* 22, no. 3 (1993): 239–50.

Meeter, Glen. "Rudy Wiebe: Spatial Form and Christianity in *The Blue Mountains of China* and *The Temptations of Big Bear.*" *Essays on Canadian Writing* 22 (1981): 42–61.

Megill, Allan. "Jörn Rüsen's Theory of Historiography between Modernism and Rhetoric of Inquiry." *History and Theory* 33, no. 1 (1994): 39–60.

Mews, Siegfried. "The 'Professorial' Flounder: Reflections on Grass's Use of Literary History." *The Fisherman and His Wife: Günter Grass's The Flounder in Critical Perspective.* Ed. Siegfried Mews. New York: AMS Press, 1983. 163–78.

Mikelsen, David. "*A rebours:* Spatial Form." *French Forum* 3 (1978): 48–55.

Milbank, John. "The Sublime in Kierkegaard." *Post-Secular Philosophy: Between Philosophy and Theology.* Ed. Phillip Blond. London: Routledge, 1998. 131–56.

Milner, Andrew, Philip Thomson, and Chris Worth, eds. *Postmodern Conditions.* Victoria, Australia: Centre for General and Comparative Literature, Monash University, 1988.

Mink, Louis O. "History and Fiction as Modes of Comprehension." *Historical Understanding.* Ed. Brian Fay, Eugene O. Golob, and Richard T. Vann. Ithaca: Cornell UP, 1987. 541–58.

Minter, David. "Family, Region, and Myth in Faulkner's Fiction." *Modern Critical Interpretations: William Faulkner's Absalom, Absalom!* Ed. Harold Bloom. New York: Chelsea House, 1987: 75–89.

Mitchell, W.J.T. "Spatial Form in Literature: Toward a General Theory." *Critical Inquiry* 6, no. 3 (1980): 539–67.

Momaday, N. Scott. *The Way to Rainy Mountain.* Albuquerque: U of New Mexico P, 1969.

Monk, Samuel H. *The Sublime: A Study of Critical Theories in XVIII-Century England.* 1935. Rpt. Ann Arbor: U of Michigan P, 1960.

Monmonier, Mark. *Drawing the Line: Tales of Maps and Cartocontroversy.* New York: Henry Holt, 1995.

Mooney, Ted. *"Mason & Dixon." Los Angeles Times.* <http://hyperarts.com/pynchon/mason-dixon/la-times.html>.

Moore, David L. "Myth, History, and Identity in Silko and Young Bear: Postcolonial Praxis." *New Voices in Native American Literary Criticism.* Ed. Arnold Krupat. Washington, D.C.: Smithsonian Institution P, 1993. 370–95.

Morrison, Toni. *Beloved.* New York: Penguin, 1987.

Mossman, Elliott. "Metaphors of History in *War and Peace* and *Doctor Zhivago.*" *Literature and History: Theoretical Problems and Russian Case Studies.* Ed. Gary Saul Morson. Stanford: Stanford UP, 1986. 247–62.

Nagl, Ludwig. "The Enlightenment—A Stranded Project? Habermas on Nietzsche as a 'Turning Point' to Postmodernity." *History of European Ideas* 11 (1989): 743–50.

Nancy, Jean-Luc. "Finite History." *The States of 'Theory': History, Art, and Critical Discourse.* Ed. David Caroll. Stanford, CA: Stanford UP, 1990. 149–72.

———. "The Sublime Offering." *Of the Sublime: Presence in Question.* Trans. Jeffrey S. Librett. Albany: SUNY P, 1993. 25–53.

Natoli, Joseph. *A Primer to Postmodernity.* Oxford: Blackwell, 1997.

Newman, Michael. "Suffering from reminiscences." *Postmodernism and the Re-reading of Modernity.* Ed. Francis Barker, Peter Hulme and Margaret Iversen. Manchester: Manchester UP; New York: St. Martin's, 1992. 84–114.

Nicholson, Linda, ed. *Feminism/Postmodernism.* New York: Routledge, 1990.

Nicholson, Linda, and Steven Seidman. *Social Postmodernism.* Cambridge: Cambridge UP, 1995.

Norfolk, Lawrence. *Lemprière's Dictionary.* New York: Ballantine, 1991.

Norris, Christopher. *The Truth about Postmodernism.* Oxford: Blackwell, 1993.

————. *What's Wrong with Postmodernism: Critical Theory and The Ends of Philosophy.* Baltimore: The Johns Hopkins UP, 1990.

O'Doherty, Brian. *The Strange Case of Mademoiselle P.* New York: Pantheon Books, 1992.

Olábarri, Ignacio. "'New' New History: A *Longue Durée* Structure." *History and Theory* 34, no. 1 (1995): 1–29.

Olsen, Lance. *Ellipse of Uncertainty: An Introduction to Postmodern Fantasy.* New York: Greenwood Press, 1987.

Onega, Susana. "'A Knack for Yarns': The Narrativization of History and the End of History." *Telling Histories: Narrativizing History, Historicizing Literature.* Ed. Susana Onega. Amsterdam: Rodopi, 1995. 7–18.

Ong, Walter. *Orality and Literacy: The Technologizing of the Word.* London: Routledge, 1988.

Orr, Leonard. "Varieties of Time in the Nonlinear, Nonteleological Novel." *Destructing the Novel: Essays in Applied Postmodern Hermeneutics.* Ed. Leonard Orr. Troy, N.Y.: Whitston, 1982. 155–83.

Orr, Linda. "The Revenge of Literature: A History of History." *Studies in Historical Change.* Ed. Ralph Cohen. Charlottesville: UP of Virginia, 1992. 84–108.

Osland, Dianne. "Trusting the Teller: Metaphor in Fiction, and the Case of *Ragtime.*" *Narrative* 5, no. 3 (1997): 252–73.

Owens, Craig. "The Allegorical Impulse: Toward a Theory of Postmodernism. Part I." *October* 12 (1980): 67–86.

Palmer, Richard E. "Postmodernity and Hermeneutics." *boundary 2* 5, no. 2 (1977): 363–93.

Partner, Nancy. "Hayden White: The Form of the Content." *History and Theory* 37, no. 2 (1998): 162–72.

Pearce, Roy Harvey. *Historicism Once More: Problems & Occasions for the American Scholar.* Princeton: Princeton UP, 1969.

Pease, Donald. "Sublime Politics." *The American Sublime.* Ed. Mary Arensberg. Albany: State U of New York P, 1986. 21–49.

Pefanis, Julian. *Heterology and the Postmodern: Bataille, Baudrillard, and Lyotard.* Durham: Duke UP, 1991.

Perloff, Majorie. Introduction to *Postmodern Genres.* Ed. Marjorie Perloff. Norman: U of Oklahoma P, 1988. 3–10.

Phillips, Mark. "Macaulay, Scott and the Literary Challenge to Historiography." *Journal of the History of Ideas* 50 (1989): 117–33.

Posse, Abel. *The Dogs of Paradise.* Trans. Margaret Sayers Peden. New York: Atheneum, 1989.

Poster, Mark. *Cultural History + Postmodernism: Disciplinary Readings and Challenges*. New York: Columbia UP, 1997.

Powers, Richard. *Gain*. New York: Picador, 1998.

Puetz, Manfred. "John Barth's *The Sot-Weed Factor:* The Pitfalls of Mythopoesis." *Critical Essays on John Barth*. Ed. Joseph J. Waldmeir. Boston: G. K. Hall, 1980. 134–45.

Pynchon, Thomas. *The Crying of Lot 49*. New York: Harper and Row, 1966.

———. "The Deadly Sins/Sloth; Nearer, My Couch, to Thee." *The New York Times on the Web* (June 6, 1993). 5 pp. <http://www.nytimes.com/books/97/05/18/reviews/pynchon-sloth.html>

———. "Is It O.K. To Be a Luddite?" *New York Times on the Web* (October 28, 1984). 8 pp. <http://www.nytimes.com/books/97/05/18/reviews/pynchon-luddite.html>

———. *Gravity's Rainbow*. New York: Viking, 1973.

———. *Mason & Dixon*. New York: Henry Holt, 1997.

Rabb, T. K. and R. I. Rotberg, eds. *The New History: The 1980s and Beyond*. Princeton: Princeton UP, 1982.

Readings, Bill. *Introducing Lyotard: Art and Politics*. London: Routledge, 1991.

Readings, Bill, and Bennet Schaber, eds. *Postmodernism across the Ages*. Syracuse, N.Y.: Syracuse UP, 1993.

Rabkin, Eric S. "Spatial Form and Plot." *Critical Inquiry* (Winter 1977) 4: 253–270. Rpt. *Spatial Form in Narrative*. Ed. Jeffrey R. Smitten and Ann Daghistany. Ithaca: Cornell UP, 1981. 79–99.

Reed, Ishmael. *Flight to Canada*. New York: Atheneum, 1989.

———. *Mumbo Jumbo*. New York: Simon and Schuster, 1972.

Reitan, E. A. "Popular Cartography and British Imperialism: *The Gentleman's Magazine*, 1739–1763." *Journal of Newspaper and Periodical History* (1986): 2–13.

Richter, David H., ed. *The Critical Tradition: Classic Texts and Contemporary Trends*. 2nd ed. Boston: Bedford Books, 1998.

Richter, David H. "From Medievalism to Historicism: Representations of History in the Gothic Novel and Historical Romance." *Studies in Medievalism* 4 (1992): 79–104.

Ricoeur, Paul. "Christianity and the Meaning of History" (Le Christianisme et le sens de l'histoire, in *Christianisme social* [1951]). Rpt. in *History and Truth*. Trans. Charles A. Kelbley. Evanston: Northwestern UP, 1965. 81–97.

————. *The Contribution of French Historiography to the Theory of History.* New York: Oxford UP, 1980.

————. "The History of Philosophy and Historicity" (Histoire de la philosophie et historicité). *L'Historie et ses interprétations* (conversations with Toynbee). Paris: Mouton, 1961. Rpt. *History and Truth.* Trans. Charles A. Kelbley. Evanston, Ill.: Northwestern UP, 1965. 63–77.

Rorty, Richard. "Cosmopolitanism without Emancipation: A Response to Lyotard." *Modernity and Identity.* Ed. Scott Lash and Jonathan Friedman. Oxford: Blackwell, 1992. 58–72.

————. "Habermas and Lyotard on Postmodernity." *Habermas and Modernity.* Ed. Richard J. Bernstein. Cambridge: MIT Press, 1985. 161–75.

Rosenbaum, Ron. "*Mason & Dixon.*" *New York Observer* (November 18, 1996). 4 pp. <http://www.hyperarts.com/pynchon/mason-dixon/rosenbaum.html>.

Ross, Andrew, ed. *Universal Abandon? The Politics of Postmodernism.* Minneapolis: U of Minnesota P, 1988.

Rose, Margaret A. *The Post-Modern and the Post-Industrial: A Critical Analysis.* Cambridge: Cambridge UP, 1991.

Rosenau, Pauline Marie. *Post-Modernism and the Social Sciences: Insights, Inroads, and Intrusions.* Princeton: Princeton UP, 1992.

Roth, Michael S. *The Ironist's Cage: Memory, Trauma, and the Construction of History.* New York: Columbia UP, 1995.

Rovit, Earl. "The Novel as Parody: John Barth." *Critical Essays on John Barth.* Ed. Joseph J. Waldmeir. Boston: G. K. Hall, 1980. 116–22.

Rowe, John Carlos. "Postmodern Art and the Invention of Postmodern Capital." *American Quarterly* 39, no. 1 (1987): 155–73.

Ruppert, James. *Mediation in Contemporary Native American Fiction.* Norman: U of Oklahoma P, 1997.

Rushdie, Salman. *Midnight's Children.* New York: Avon Books, 1980.

————. *The Satanic Verses.* New York: Viking, 1989.

Rushdy, Ashraf H. A. "Ishmael Reed's Neo-HooDoo Slave Narrative." *Narrative* 2, no. 2 (1994): 112–39.

Said, Edward W. *Culture and Imperialism.* New York: Vintage, 1993.

Sax, Benjamin C. "Foucault, Nietzsche, History: Two Modes of the Genealogical Method." *History of European Ideas* 11 (1989): 769–81.

Scarberry, Susan J. "Memory as Medicine: The Power of Recollection in *Ceremony.*" *American Indian Quarterly* 5, no. 1 (1979): 19–26.

Schama, Simon. *Dead Certainties (Unwarranted Speculations)*. New York: Knopf, 1991.

Schatzki, Theodore R. "Theory at Bay: Foucault, Lyotard, and Politics of the Local." *Postmodern Contentions: Epochs, Politics, Space*. Ed. John Paul Jones III, Wolfgang Natter, and Theodore R. Schatzki. New York: Guilford P, 1993. 39–64.

Scholes, Robert. *The Fabulators*. New York: Oxford UP, 1967.

———. *Fabulation and Metafiction*. Urbana: U of Illinois P, 1979.

Schultz, Max F. *Black Humor Fiction of the Sixties: A Pluralistic Definition of Man and His World*. Athens: Ohio UP, 1973.

Scott, P. H. "The Politics of Sir Walter Scott." *Scott and His Influence: The Papers of the Aberdeen Scott Conference, 1982*. Ed. J. H. Alexander and David Hewitt. Aberdeen: Association for Scottish Literary Studies, 1983. 208–17.

Scott, Walter. "Essay On Romance." *Essays on Chivalry, Romance, and the Drama*. London: Frederick Warne, 1887. 65–108.

———. *The Life of Napoleon Buonaparte*. 9 vols. Edinburgh, 1827.

———. *The Waverley Novels*. Dryburgh Edition. 25 vols. Edinburgh: Adam and Charles Black, 1893–94.

Shaw, Harry E. *The Forms of Historical Fiction: Sir Walter Scott and His Successors*. Ithaca: Cornell UP, 1983.

Sherwood, Frances. *Vindication*. New York: Penguin, 1993.

Sicher, Efraim. "The Holocaust in the Postmodernist Era." *Breaking Crystal: Writing and Memory after Auschwitz*. Ed. Efraim Sicher. Urbana: U of Illinois P, 1998. 297–328.

Silko, Leslie Marmon. *Ceremony*. New York: Penguin, 1977.

Singer, Alan. "Desire's Desire: Toward an Historical Formalism." *enclitic* 8, nos. 1–2 (1984): 57–67.

Slade, Joseph. *Thomas Pynchon*. New York: Viking, 1973.

Smith, Allan Lloyd. "Postmodernism/Gothicism." *Modern Gothic: A Reader*. Ed. Victor Sage and Allan Lloyd Smith. Manchester: Manchester UP, 1996: 6–19.

Smitten, Jeffrey R. "Approaches to the Spatiality of Narrative." *Papers on Language & Literature* 14, no. 3 (1978): 297–314.

Smitten, Jeffrey R., and Ann Daghistany, eds. *Spatial Form in Narrative*. Ithaca: Cornell UP, 1981.

Soja, Edward W. "Postmodern Geographies and the Critique of Historicism." *Postmodern Contentions: Epochs, Politics, Space*. Ed. John Paul Jones III et al. New York: Guilford Press, 1993. 113–36.

———. *Postmodern Geographies: The Reassertion of Space in Critical So-cial Theory.* London: Verso, 1989.

Sontag, Susan. *The Volcano Lover: A Romance.* New York: Farrar, Straus Giroux, 1992.

Spanos, William V. "Modern Literary Criticism and the Spatialization of Time: An Existentialist Critique." *Journal of Aesthetics and Art Criti-cism* 29, no. 1 (1970): 87–104.

———. "De-struction and the Question of Postmodern Literature: To-wards a Definition." *par rapport* 2 (1979): 107–22.

———. "The Detective and the Boundary: Some Notes on the Post-modern Literary Imagination." *boundary 2* 1, no. 1 (Fall 1972): 147–68. Rpt. *Early Postmodernism: Foundational Essays.* Ed. Paul A. Bové. Durham: Duke UP, 1995. 17–39.

Spencer, Michael. "Spatial Form and Postmodernism." *Poetics Today* 5, no. 1 (1984): 182–95.

Spencer, Sharon. *Space, Time and Structure in the Modern Novel.* New York: New York UP, 1971. Rpt. Chicago: Swallow, 1974.

Spinks, Lee. "Jefferson at the Millennial Gates: History and Apocalypse in the Fiction of Steve Erickson." *Contemporary Literature* 40, no. 2 (1999): 214–39.

Spivak, Gayatri Chakravorty. "Reading *The Satanic Verses." What Is an Author?* Ed. Maurice Biriotti and Nicola Miller. Manchester: Man-chester UP, 1993: 104–34.

———. "Theory in the Margin: Coetzee's *Foe* Reading Defoe's *Cru-soe/Roxana." Consequences of Theory.* Ed. Jonathan Arac and Barbara Johnson. Baltimore: The Johns Hopkins UP, 1991. 154–80.

Stambovsky, Phillip. "Metaphor and Historical Understanding." *History and Theory* 27, no. 2 (1988): 125–34.

Stark, John O. *The Literature of Exhaustion: Borges, Nabokov, Barth.* Durham: Duke UP, 1974.

Steffler, John. *The Afterlife of George Cartwright.* New York: Henry Holt, 1994.

Stempel, Daniel. "History and Postmodern Literary Theory." *Tracing Lit-erary Theory.* Ed. Joseph Natoli. Urbana: U of Illinois P, 1987. 80–104.

Stephanson, Anders. "Regarding Postmodernism: A Conversation with Fredric Jameson." *Universal Abandon? The Politics of Postmodernism.* Ed. Andrew Ross. Minneapolis: U of Minnesota P, 1988. 3–30.

Stoianovich, Traian. *French Historical Method: The Annales Paradigm.* Ithaca: Cornell UP, 1976.

Stone, Lawrence. "History and Post-Modernism." *Past and Present* 131 (May 1991): 217–18.

———. "The Revival of Narrative." *Past and Present* 85 (1979): 2–24.

Strout, Cushing. "Border Crossings: History, Fiction, and *Dead Certainties*." *History and Theory* 31, no. 2 (1992): 153–62.

Süskind, Patrick. *Perfume: The Story of a Murderer.* Trans. John E. Woods. New York: Pocket Books/Knopf, 1986.

Sutherland, Kathryn. "Fictional Economies: Adam Smith, Walter Scott and the Nineteenth-Century Novel." *English Literary History* 54 (1987): 97–127.

Swann, Charles. "Past Into Present: Scott, Galt and the Historical Novel." *Literature and History* 3 (1976): 65–82.

Swartz, Richard Allen. "Thomas Pynchon and the Evolution of Fiction." *Modern Fiction Studies* 8 (1981): 165–72.

Swift, Graham. *Waterland.* New York: Pocket Books/Washington Square P, 1983.

Tabbi, Joseph. *Postmodern Sublime: Technology and American Writing from Mailer to Cyberpunk.* Ithaca: Cornell UP, 1995.

Tanner, Tony. *Thomas Pynchon.* London: Methuen, 1982.

Tani, Stefano. *The Doomed Detective: The Contribution of the Detective Novel to Postmodern American and Italian Fiction.* Carbondale: Southern Illinois UP, 1984.

Theory, Culture & Society. (Special Issue: Postmodernism) 5, nos. 2–3 (June 1988).

Thomas, D. M. *The White Hotel.* New York: Pocket Books, 1981.

Thurber, Barton. "Scott and the Sublime." *Scott and His Influence: The Papers of the Aberdeen Scott Conference, 1982.* Ed. J. H. Alexander and David Hewitt. Aberdeen: Association for Scottish Literary Studies, 1983. 87–98.

Tiffin, Chris, and Alan Lawson. "Conclusion: Reading Difference." *De-scribing Empire: Post-colonialism and Textuality.* London: Routledge, 1994. 230–35.

———, eds. *De-scribing Empire: Post-colonialism and Textuality.* London: Routledge, 1994.

Tiffin, Helen. "Post-Colonialism, Post-Modernism and the Rehabilitation of Post-Colonial History." *Journal of Commonwealth Literature* 23, no. 1 (1989): 169–81.

Tolstoy, Leo. *War and Peace.* Trans. Rosemary Edmonds. New York: Penguin Books, 1978 [1869].

Tongson-McCall, Karen. "The Nether World of Neither World: Hybridization in the Literature of Wendy Rose." *American Indian Culture and Research Journal* 20, no. 4 (1996): 1–40.

Topolsky, Jerzy. "A Non-postmodernist Analysis of Historical Narratives." *Historiography between Modernism and Postmodernism: Contributions to the Methodology of the Historical Research.* Poznań Studies in the Philosophy of the Sciences and the Humanities 41. Amsterdam: Rodopi, 1994. 9–86.

———, ed. *Historiography between Modernism and Postmodernism: Contributions to the Methodology of the Historical Research.* Poznań Studies in the Philosophy of the Sciences and the Humanities 41. Amsterdam: Rodopi, 1994.

Trela, D. J. "Sir Walter Scott on Oliver Cromwell: An Evenhanded Royalist Evaluates a Usurper." *Clio* 27, no. 2 (1998): 195–220.

Trumpener, Kate. "National Character, Nationalist Plots: National Tale and the Historical Novel in the Age of *Waverley,* 1806–30." *English Literary History* 60, no. 3 (1993): 685–731.

Unsworth, Barry. *Sacred Hunger.* New York: W. W. Norton, 1992.

Van Alphen, Ernst. *Caught by History: Holocaust Effects in Contemporary Art, Literature, and Theory.* Stanford: Stanford UP, 1997.

Vann, Richard T. "Turning Linguistic: History and Theory and *History and Theory,* 1960–1975." *A New Philosophy of History.* Ed. Frank Ankersmit and Hans Kellner. Chicago: U of Chicago P, 1995. 40–69.

Veerman, Dick. "Introduction to Lyotard." *Theory, Culture & Society: Postmodernism.* 5, nos. 2–3 (1988): 271–76.

Venturi, Robert, Denise Scott Brown, and Steven Izenour. *Learning from Las Vegas: The Forgotten Symbolism of Architectural Form.* Cambridge: MIT Press, 1972.

Vidan, Ivo. "Time Sequence in Spatial Fiction." *Spatial Form in Narrative.* Ed. Jeffrey R. Smitten and Ann Daghistany. Ithaca: Cornell UP, 1981. 131–57.

Vizenor, Gerald. *Manifest Manners: Postindian Warriors of Survivance.* Hanover, N.H.: Wesleyan UP; Minneapolis: U of Minnesota P, 1994.

Vollmann, William T. *The Ice-Shirt.* New York: Penguin, 1990.

———. *The Rifles.* New York: Penguin, 1994.

———. "The Very Short History of Nunavut." *Outside* 24, no. 7 (July 1999): 54–62, 64, 128–29.

Wald, Allen. "The Cultural of 'Internal Colonialism': A Marxist Perspective." *MELUS* 8, no. 3 (1991): 18–27.

Works Cited

Walsh, Catherine Henry. "The Sublime in the Historical Novel: Scott and Gil y Carrasco." *Comparative Literature* 42, no. 2 (1990): 29–48.

Wasson, Richard. "Notes on a New Sensibility." *Partisan Review* 36, no. 3 (1969): 460–77.

Watson, Stephen H. "*In Situ:* Beyond the Architectonics of the Modern." *Postmodernism—Philosophy and the Arts.* Ed. Hugh J. Silverman. New York: Routledge, 1990. 83–100.

Waugh, Patricia. *Metafiction: The Theory and Practice of Self-Conscious Fiction.* London: Routledge, 1984.

Weiskel, Thomas. *The Romantic Sublime: Studies in the Structure and Psychology of Transcendence.* Baltimore: The Johns Hopkins UP, 1976.

Welsh, Alexander. *The Hero of the Waverley Novels.* New Haven: Yale UP, 1963.

Wernick, Andrew. "Jean Baudrillard: Seducing God." *Post-Secular Philosophy: Between Philosophy and History.* Ed. Phillip Blond. London: Routledge, 1998. 346–64.

Wesseling, Elisabeth. *Writing History as a Prophet: Postmodernist Innovations of the Historical Novel.* Philadelphia: John Benjamins, 1991.

West, Cornell. "Black Culture and Postmodernism." *Remaking History.* Ed. Barbara Kruger and Phil Mariani. Seattle: Bay Press, 1989. 87–96.

White, Hayden. "The Burden of History." *History and Theory* 5 (1966): 111–34.

———. *The Content of the Form: Narrative Discourse and Historical Representation.* Baltimore: The Johns Hopkins UP, 1987.

———. "Cosmos, Chaos, and Sequence in Historiological Representation." Unpublished paper. 1998. 1–18.

———. "The Culture of Criticism." *Liberations: New Essays on the Humanities in Revolution.* Ed. Ihab Hassan. Middletown, Conn.: Wesleyan UP, 1971.

———. *Figural Realism: Studies in the Mimesis Effect.* Baltimore: The Johns Hopkins UP, 1999.

———. "Historical Emplotment and the Problem of Truth." *Probing the Limits of Representation: Nazism and the "Final Solution."* Ed. Saul Friedlander. Cambridge: Harvard UP, 1992. 37–53.

———. *Metahistory: The Historical Imagination in Nineteenth-Century Europe.* Baltimore: The Johns Hopkins UP, 1973.

———. "Response to Arthur Marwick." *Journal of Contemporary History* 30 (1995): 233–46.

———. *Tropics of Discourse: Essays in Cultural Criticism.* Baltimore: The Johns Hopkins UP, 1978.

Whitt, Laurie Anne. "Cultural Imperialism and the Marketing of Native America." *American Indian Culture and Research Journal* 19, no. 3 (1995): 1–31.

Williams, Nigel. *Star Turn.* London: Faber and Faber, 1985.

Wilt, Judith. *Secret Leaves: The Novels of Sir Walter Scott.* Chicago: U of Chicago P, 1985.

Winterson, Jeanette. *The Passion.* New York: Vintage/Random House, 1989.

———. *Sexing the Cherry.* New York: Vintage International, 1989.

Wolfley, Lawrence C. "Repression's Rainbow: The Presence of Norman O. Brown in Pynchon's Big Novel." *PMLA* 92 (1977): 873–79.

Wood, Neal. "The Aesthetic Dimension of Burke's Political Thought." *Journal of British Studies* 4, no. 1 (1964): 41–64.

Young, James. *Writing and Rewriting the Holocaust: Narrative and the Consequences of Interpretation.* Bloomington: Indiana UP, 1990.

Young, Robert J. C. *Colonial Desire: Hybridity in Theory, Culture and Race.* London: Routledge, 1995.

Zagorin, Perez. "Historiography and Postmodernism: Reconsiderations." *History and Theory* 29, no. 3 (1990): 263–74.

Zamora, Lois. *Writing the Apocalypse: Historical Vision in Contemporary U.S. and Latin American Fiction.* Cambridge: Cambridge UP, 1989.

Zencey, Eric. *Panama.* New York: Farrar, Straus and Giroux, 1995.

———. *Virgin Forest: Meditations on History, Ecology, and Culture.* Athens: U of Georgia P, 1998.

Zoran, Gabriel. "Towards a Theory of Space in Narrative." *Poetics Today* 5, no. 2 (1984): 309–35.

Zukin, Sharon. "Postmodern Urban Landscapes: Mapping Culture and Power." *Modernity and Identity.* Ed. Scott Lash and Jonathan Friedman. Oxford: Blackwell, 1992. 221–47.

Index

Index